EVERYTHING's BIGGER in TEXAS

EVERYTHING's BIGGER in TEXAS

The Life and Times of Kinky Friedman

MARY LOU SULLIVAN

Backbeat
Books

Essex, Connecticut

Backbeat Books

An imprint of Globe Pequot, the trade division of
The Rowman & Littlefield Publishing Group, Inc.
4501 Forbes Blvd., Ste. 200
Lanham, MD 20706
www.rowman.com

Distributed by NATIONAL BOOK NETWORK

British Library Cataloguing in Publication Information available

Library of Congress Cataloging-in-Publication Data available

Names: Sullivan, Mary Lou author.
Title: Everything's bigger in Texas : the life and times of Kinky Friedman / Mary
    Lou Sullivan.
Description: Montclair, NJ : Backbeat Books, 2017. | Includes bibliographical
    references and index.
Identifiers: LCCN (print) 2017017303 | ISBN 9781495058967 (cloth) | ISBN
    9781493065196 (paper)
Subjects: LCSH: Friedman, Kinky. | Country musicians—United States—
    Biography.
Classification: LCC ML420.F845 S85 2017 | DDC 782.421642092 [B] —dc23
LC record available at https://lccn.loc.gov/2017017303

To Kinky Friedman for trusting and believing in me and for giving me a rare glimpse into the heart and soul of a sweet guy named Richard Friedman

Contents

Foreword

I'll be honest with you. I haven't read this book. Don't get me wrong. I hear great things about it. But I'm currently on page 907 of Winston Churchill's *A History of the English-Speaking Peoples* and I could go into a diabetic coma at any time. You see, all misunderstood geniuses read Churchill. Yet if God punished me by making me a misunderstood genius, He rewarded me by commanding that I write the foreword to my own biography. I must report, however, that I haven't been paid yet. God's check is still in the mail.

Nevertheless, the opportunity to write the foreword to a biography of yourself is probably something every self-absorbed asshole on the planet would indubitably jump at. I, of course, am no exception. For one thing, I want to demonstrate to people that I am not dead; I'm just not currently working on a project.

I am now seventy-two years old though I read at the seventy-four-year-old level. Soon enough I *will* be dead and then people may start to take me more seriously, even though most of my work has been ghost-written by J. K. Rowling. Actually, if I'd thought about it, I might have asked J. K. Rowling to write this foreword. The downside of that, I'm afraid, would be that about a trillion tri-polar twelve-year-olds would illegally download my story.

Therefore, I've decided to leave my life in the capable hands of my biographer, Mary Lou Sullivan. Mary Lou has in her possession the private notes of my shrink, Willie Nelson. She can corroborate the salient information that transpired in our conversation of a year ago. It was about three o'clock in the morning when Willie called me. Willie was in Hawaii. I was at the ranch in Texas.

"What're you doing?" said Willie.

"I'm watching *Matlock*," I said.

"That's a sure sign of depression," he said. "Turn it off and start writing, Kinky. Start writing."

Inspired by Willie, I wrote fourteen new songs which I sometimes refer to as "The Matlock Collection." A few months ago I called Willie and told him about the songs. He suggested I send them to him, which I did. Then he said, "By the way, Kinky, what channel *is Matlock* on?"

I have no regrets about what I told Mary Lou or what she may have written. Like I say, there's a fine line between fiction and nonfiction and I believe Jimmy Buffett and I snorted it in 1976.

Now all I have to do is finish this foreword before the attorneys for the hare serve papers on the tortoise at the finish line. What makes things worse is that the "e" key on my typewriter appears to be going out. When the "e" key goes out, you're basically fucked. It doesn't matter if you're writing a foreword to your own biography or a love letter to Anne Frank. When the "e" key goes out, the only thing you can be thankful for is that you're not e.e. cummings.

And, yes. I do plan to read this book. They tell me it's great. But they say the foreword could use a little work.

Kinky Friedman
April 7, 2017
Somewhere in Texas

Acknowledgments

To Kinky, who shared a heapin' helping of Texas hospitality, walks with the Friedmans (his dogs) to Wallace Creek, clippings from his night-blooming cereus, and his cowboy culinary talents during my overnight visits to his ranch. You allowed me to push you well beyond your comfort zone with my questions during our interviews and for that I'm grateful.

Warm thanks to Kinky's friends, family, fellow musicians, and Echo Hill Ranch campers who generously shared their time and memories: Hank Alrich, Dan Aykroyd, Ruth Buzzi, Brian "Skycap Adams" Clarke, Randy "Rainbow Colors" Cullers, Dylan Ferrero, Danny "Panama Red" Finley, George "Commander Cody" Frayne, Roger Friedman, Meyer Goldberg, Cleve Hattersley, Will Hoover, Ken "Snakebite" Jacobs, Kacey Jones, Corky Laing, Roger McGuinn, John McCall, Brian Molnar, Valerie Monson, Van Dyke Parks, Ron Rakoover, Joe Rude, Billy Joe Shaver, Jeff "Little Jewford" Shelby, Larry "Ratso" Sloman, Shawn Siegel, Michael Simmons, Nancy "Cousin Nancy" Simons, Bob "Daddy-O" Wade, and Chuck E. Weiss. And to Shakespeare, the rescue cat that rescued me.

To the photographers and artists who generously shared their work: Bruce Asato, Beverly Cusimano, Bob Daemmrich, Augusta Girard, Gary Glade, Cleve Hattersley, Ken Hoge, Brian Kanof, Kink Kume, Ron McKeown, Melinda Joy Moore, Ray Navage, Micael Priest, Bill Records, Marcia Resnick, Leslie Rouffe, Jeff "Little Jewford" Shelby, Cleveland Storrs, Lisa Wade, and Jay Willie. Special thanks to the William J. Clinton Presidential Library, the Mark Twain House & Museum, *Texas Monthly*, and Brian Kanof, who drove 500 miles to provide clear images of Kinky's photos that were encased in glass.

To the editors, agent, and Mark Twain scholar who shed light on Kinky's life as a writer: Chuck Adams, Esther Newberg, Jeff Nichols, and Brian Sweany.

To the filmmakers, music industry professionals, and political insiders who generously shared their insights: Bill Arhos, Steve Barri, Bill Brownstein, Simone DeVries, Chuck Glaser, Jim Glaser, Bill Hillsman, James Mazzeo, and Dave Wilkes.

For help with logistics: Dan Beck, Cathy Casey, Vinny Cervoni, Louis Glaser, Mallory Howard, Jacques Lamarre, Greg Lew, Gary Moore, Lincoln Myerson at McCabe's Guitar Shop, Gerald Peary, Kent Perkins, Herbert Ragan, Detlef Schmidt, Tony Simons, and Pete Souza. Special thanks to Jay Willie for taking me to see Kinky at the Turning Point Café in New York, a show that proved to be a turning point in my life.

To my agent, Lloyd Jassin, who played Kinky's records on WBCR at Brooklyn College and decades later sealed the deal (and established my credibility) smoking cigars and hanging out with Kinky after a show in New Jersey.

For their vision, passion, and enthusiasm for the project: John Cerullo, Bernadette Malavarca, and Steven Thompson, my dream team at Backbeat Books.

To my dear writer/musician friends—Tom Guerra and Tom Smith—who cleared their schedules to provide input on my final manuscript. I couldn't do it without you.

Special thanks to Tom Nielsen for his musical knowledge, and to Roger Wallace, whose insight into the Texas mystique helped me capture the essence of the Kinkster.

Very special thanks to the friends who offered moral support throughout the project: Timothy Britt (who is always my first reader), Dylan Ferrero, Travis Healy, Will Hoover, Nancy LeBeau, Little Jewford, Leea Mechling, Johnny Schex Jr., and Joshua Sullivan. Your sage advice and heartfelt encouragement sustained me more than you'll ever know.

1
Growing Up in the Lone Star State

"I was born in Chicago, lived there a year, and couldn't find
work. So I moved to Texas, where I haven't worked since."
— *Kinky Friedman*

When Richard "Kinky" Samet Friedman was born on November 1, 1944, in Chicago, Illinois, Adolf Hitler had been systematically murdering Jews for three years. President Franklin D. Roosevelt was on his way to an unprecedented fourth term, and World War II continued to rage. Anne Frank, the thirteen-year-old girl who put a face on the Jews annihilated in the Holocaust, had written the final entry to *The Diary of a Young Girl* and would die four months later in the Bergen-Belsen concentration camp.

It was a nerve-racking time for Kinky's parents, as well as other young couples torn apart by the war. His mother, Minnie Samet Friedman, was living with her family to wait out the war. Commissioned as an officer, Kinky's father, S. Thomas Friedman, was in the heat of battle, piloting a B-24 (Liberator) bomber with the Eighth Air Force based in England. Considered to be the greatest air armada in history, the Mighty Eighth had a history of turning young women into widows. Nearly one-half of the U.S. Army Air Force's World War II casualties, including more than 26,000 deaths, occurred to young men in that military unit.

Tom fought in the 565th squadron of the 389th Bomb Group of the Second Air Division. Well aware of his chances of returning to his pregnant wife and unborn child, Tom remembered the first words of his commanding officer. "The CO told them to look at the man on their left and look at the man on their right," Kinky wrote in an essay about his father. "When you return," he'd said, "they will not be here."

The couple met at the Jewish People's Institute, a local Jewish community center that offered community theater. Minnie, who later lectured on Shakespeare, was a creative spirit with dreams of being an actress. Although those dreams were discouraged by a teacher, who told her acting was not a proper profession for a "Jewess," her love for the stage was passed down to her firstborn son. The couple married on July 26, 1940, when Tom worked as a psychologist at the Vocational Guidance Agency of Chicago.

As first-generation Americans—the daughter of Russian immigrants and the son of Polish immigrants—the young couple listened to the news in horror as Nazi Germany continued its quest for world domination. The threat escalated with the invasions of Poland, where most of Tom's relatives lived, and the Soviet Union, where Minnie's father had been a target of Hitler's regime for helping fellow Russians immigrate to the U.S.

Unwilling to sit back while Hitler continued his rampage that eventually killed six million Jews (including ninety percent of Poland's Jewish population), Tom had enlisted for flight training in the United States Army Air Force. The couple lived at Lackland Airforce Base in San Antonio until he was deployed overseas.

It was a difficult time for the young wife, who also had two brothers serving overseas. She had been forced to leave her own home in military housing to live with her parents, and to go through her pregnancy with contact limited to an occasional letter. Her heartfelt emotional letter telling Tom he was the proud father of a son didn't reach him for nearly a week.

At twenty-three, Tom was the oldest member of his ten-man crew and the only one with a college degree. In a plane called *I've Had It*, he flew thirty-five successful missions over Germany, the last on November 9, 1944 (eight days after Kinky was born). He received eight decorations and awards, including the Distinguished Flying Cross and the Air Medal with three Oak Leaf clusters.

With a B.A. in psychology with high honors from the University of Illinois, and an M.A. in psychology from the University of Chicago, Tom was reassigned to the Psychological Research Project of the Army Air Force after returning to the States. When his service ended in 1945, he left the military at the rank of first lieutenant with an honorable discharge.

Raised in an educated, intellectual family that fostered achievement and social consciousness, Kinky had an intensity, focus, and intelligence well beyond his years. His maternal grandmother spoke Russian, English, Hebrew, Yiddish, and Hungarian; his maternal great-grandfather was a prominent rabbi in Russia. His parents' marriage was a true partnership of equals. After Tom returned from combat, Minnie enrolled in Northwestern University and earned a master's degree. The only Jew and one of very few women in graduate programs at Northwestern, she spent her summers working as a drama counselor at Lake of the Woods Camp in Decatur, Michigan.

Tom remembers Kinky beginning to talk at the age of seven months, and speaking in full sentences by the time he was a year old. Delighted by the precociousness of his first son, he taught him how to play chess. Kinky picked up the game so quickly that by 1952, at the age of seven, he was the youngest of fifty competitors to play grandmaster Samuel Reshevsky in a marathon match in a Houston hotel. The match gave Kinky his first taste of fame when the *Houston Chronicle* ran a front-page photo of him contemplating his next move against the grandmaster.

"I was a chess prodigy when I was about seven," says Kinky with a smile. "My dad took me to a match where we all sat around a table. Reshevsky would make a move, keep walking around the table, and played all fifty people simultaneously. He beat everybody in an hour even though some people were cheating. I was the only child and did better than a number of the adults."

With his father's support and encouragement, Kinky approached the match with his trademark cool. "I wasn't nervous because it was fun," he says. "After the match, he told my father he was really sorry he had to beat me but he has to be very careful whenever he's playing a young kid. With the number of matches he plays, he's always going to lose a few every couple of years. If he loses to a child, it's the end of his career. He beat me in thirty-six moves, and he beat a lot of the people faster than that. For me, being a child prodigy, it was downhill from there," he deadpans.

When the Friedmans moved from Chicago to Houston, Kinky's parents experienced culture shock. The Jewish population in Houston, the fourth most populous city in the U.S., was a mere 14,000, compared to 342,800 in Chicago. But the Friedmans quickly assimilated to living in Texas. Tom worked as executive director of the Southwestern Jewish Community Relations Council, where he oversaw community organization in Texas, Oklahoma, and northern Louisiana. Minnie enjoyed breaking new ground as one of the first speech therapists at the Houston Independent School District. She wrote a textbook about speech therapy in elementary schools that was published by the University of Texas

Press and foreshadowed Kinky's career as a writer. "Both my parents were very brilliant people and very supportive," he says.

The family lived in a ranch-style home at 2635 Nottingham in West University Place with Texas Sabal palm trees and a China cherry tree in the front yard. Kinky and his brother, Roger, born on September 13, 1948, grew up comfortably in that middle-class neighborhood. Their sister, Marcie, wouldn't be born until 1960.

The boys spent many carefree afternoons at Shakespeare's Pool, a swimming hole in Buffalo Bayou, a shady, slow-moving river that runs through Houston. A Saturday night treat was a trip to Prince's Drive-In for burgers, fries, and chocolate malteds. Kinky and Roger loved watching the pretty carhops in satin majorette costumes roller-skating to the cars with the orders.

With Tom on the road and Min working in the school system, the family hired a black woman named Lottie Cotton to help with cooking and childcare. From the time Kinky was three years old until he made his bar mitzvah at age thirteen, Lottie was a constant in his life. He still has fond memories of the popcorn balls and chocolate chip cookies she made for him and Roger, and of the fun-filled afternoons she spent playing with them and Rex, their cocker spaniel. Despite the charges of racism that still surface whenever he runs for office, Kinky thought of Cotton as a second mother and stayed in touch with her throughout his life. When she died at the age of 100 in 2003, he attended her funeral in Houston and eulogized her in a heartfelt essay in *Texas Monthly.*

"I don't know what else you can say about someone who has been in your life forever, someone who was always there for you, even when 'there' was far away," he wrote. "Yours is not the narrow immortality craved by authors, actors, and artists of this world. Yours is the immortality of a precious passenger on the train to glory, which has taken you from the cross ties on the railroad to the stars in the sky."

Whether influenced by his father's credo of "treating children like adults and adults like children" or perhaps by overhearing his parents' conversations, Kinky grew up with a serious and somber approach to life. A sensitive child deeply affected by events that would have never crossed the radar of most children, Kinky was upset when Stevenson lost the 1952 presidential election to Dwight D. Eisenhower, or, as he later wrote, "lost the potato-sack hop at the company picnic to good ol' Ike, the Garth Brooks of all presidents, who turned out to be the most significant leader we'd had since Millard Fillmore and remained as popular as the bottle of ketchup on the kitchen table of America."

Kinky cried when his musical hero Hank Williams died on New Year's Day 1953, and calls him "a twenty-nine-year-old American prophet and hillbilly Shakespeare, burning out of control like a country music comet exploding in the soul of every kid who ever wanted to be a country star." He wept that June when Julius and Ethel Rosenberg—who had been charged with spying for Russia ("many thought falsely," he says)—were executed at Sing Sing. Their death orphaned their ten- and six-year-old sons, a frightening thought for an eight-year-old with a four-year-old brother. The cruel persecution of innocent Jews during the Holocaust moved him to tears when he read *The Diary of a Young Girl* by Anne Frank, another one of his heroes.

Kinky has always felt a kinship with misunderstood geniuses, so it seems quite fitting he attended an elementary school named after Edgar Allan Poe. He would line up in the schoolyard with his class-mates—boys in collared shirts and cuffed jeans and girls in crisp cotton dresses—to filter into a classroom with slate chalkboards and rows of wooden tables carved with decades' worth of initials. But it wasn't the innocent classroom of the 1950s depicted in *Leave It to Beaver*. After the Soviets exploded their own atomic bomb, fears of an attack on the U.S. escalated throughout the nation. Kinky and his classmates regularly ducked under those tables during drills mandated by *Duck and Cover*, a 1952 film by the Federal Civil Defense Administration. A frightening (as well as ludicrous) film for young children, it dramatized the dangers of the atomic bomb and instructed viewers to watch for a flash that "would be brighter than the sun and could burn you worse than a terrible sunburn, especially if you're not covered."

The alienation of growing up as a Jew in Texas—where "kike" was a common slur, and "No Jews or Dogs" signs were not unusual—permeated Kinky's early years. That feeling was exacerbated by the school's devoutly religious principal, who led the children through a recitation of the Lord's Prayer and the Twenty-Third Psalm over the school loud-speaker every morning.

The only Jewish child in his class, Kinky was forced to take part in

the Christmas pageant in the third grade. When he refused to partici-
pate the following year, he was told to stay in the classroom by himself
during rehearsals. Rather than doing busywork during his time-out,
he amused himself by writing poems. One was about the pretty young
school librarian, who had told him she couldn't sleep at night because
she could hear every little sound.

The very best eyesight there ever was,
Was accomplished by eating carrots.
But the very best hearing on earth by far,
Is sure to be Miss Barrett's.

Principal Doty was not amused. "I'm sure she believed I was going
to hell," he says.

"There was still a lot of prejudice against Jews," says Meyer Goldberg, who also grew up in Houston in the 1950s. "I can remember neighbors saying, 'You killed Jesus; you'll never go to heaven. You'll go to
hell because you haven't been saved.' In junior high school somebody
would throw a penny at you or toss it down to see if anybody picked it
up. Whether it was a Jewish person or not, if you picked it up you were
called a Jew."

After attending Hebrew school in Houston, Kinky had his bar
mitzvah with Rabbi Robert I. Kahn at Temple Emanu El, a Reform
synagogue. But he never became very involved with Jewish dogma or
rituals. "Either I'm not a practicing Jew or else I've got to practice a little
bit more," he quips.

Kinky, who jokes he's forgotten half his life or purposely repressed
it, says he experienced "almost no anti-Semitism growing up in Texas"
and uses humor to deflect the question. "Texans were preoccupied with
picking on the Mexicans, so the Jews did pretty well—at least I think we
skated," he adds. "I didn't see a lot of that. If I had, I certainly wouldn't
have been a victim. I liked being an underdog, being in the minority,
being on the outside looking in."

Before he learned to cover up his sensitive nature with humor or
sarcasm, Kinky had a difficult time dealing with older kids in Houston
who enjoyed killing small creatures. There was Dale Haufrect, who
took Kinky's pet goldfish out of the fish bowl—one by one—slit their
sides with his fingernail, and dropped them on the floor. Kinky was so

devastated by the cruelty, he wrote about it more than three decades later. "The goldfish never came back to life like Dale Haufrect said they would," he wrote in *Musical Chairs*. "Instead little drops of cotton-candy-colored blood fell from the fish to the floor and my own eyes of ancient childhood filled up with tears."

Another neighborhood kid got a BB gun for Christmas and began shooting birds in Kinky's front yard. Kinky tried in vain to get him to stop, but Ken Ford was much bigger. The lawn was littered with dead birds when Tom got home from work. The elder Friedman asked Ford if the gun was his and if he could see it. When the kid proudly handed it over, Tom broke it over his knee into two pieces and handed them back to the boy without speaking. That wordless lesson stayed with Kinky throughout his life.

A man with a strong social conscience, Tom imparted many lessons to his young son. "He taught me a person can be characterized by the size of the enemies he fights," Kinky says. "Small battles are indicative of small minds; large battles are in keeping with being in a possession of a strong spirit."

An interest in civil rights and politics were also passed down from father to son.

"When I was twelve or thirteen, my dad took me to see Adlai Stevenson and Orval Faubus in Houston," says Kinky. "Adlai Stevenson lost the presidential race in 1952 and 1956 and Orval Faubus was an arch segregationist who was the governor of Arkansas. He fought integration and did everything he could to stop it." A national symbol of segregation for his 1957 stand against the desegregation of the Little Rock School District, Faubus defied a unanimous decision of the United States Supreme Court by ordering the Arkansas National Guard to stop black students from entering Little Rock Central High School.

To create a peaceful haven from life in Houston and a sense of community for Jews in Texas, Tom bought a 400-acre ranch in Medina, a sparsely populated rural area in Texas Hill Country northwest of San Antonio and south of Kerrville. Tucked away in a bucolic green valley surrounded by rugged hills as high as 2,000 feet, the ranch consisted of rocky land with native grasses, brush, junipers, mesquite, dense thickets of low shrubs, Southern live oaks, and Texas cedars. Wallace Creek, a clear, spring-fed tributary of the Guadalupe River, ran through the property.

Although they were the only Jewish family in Medina—with only one other Jewish family in Bandera County—the Friedmans embraced their rural neighbors as friends. When Minnie held the Passover seder in the living room of the rustic lodge, she invited their Hill Country friends: wrangler Earl Buckelew; Leon "Slim" Dodson, a World War II vet who washed dishes at Echo Hill Ranch; as well as Cabbie, a neighbor with an old coon dog.

Working as a team, Tom and Min founded and ran Echo Hill Ranch as a summer camp for Jewish boys and girls. Tom greeted the campers arriving in charter buses, raised the flag in the morning, sliced watermelons at picnic suppers, and had quiet conversations with campers who were feeling homesick or had problems with their bunkmates. He'd also tell them about the hummingbirds that nested in the juniper tree outside the lodge and drank from the feeders hanging from the porch. Fascinated that the jewel-colored iridescent birds migrated thousands of miles each year and could fly backwards, campers quietly listened for the buzzing sound made by tiny wings flapping seventy times a second.

Hummingbirds still migrate each year to Echo Hill from Mexico and Central America, arriving in mid-March and leaving in late summer. Kinky continues to welcome his seasonal guests with an array of feeders filled with yellow or blue sugar water. His mother filled the first feeder with the traditional red sugar water when the camp opened in 1953. An integral part of Echo Hill, she helped with the Navajo campfires, hoedowns, and friendship circles under the stars, and organized the camp rosters and menus at her desk with a sign that read, "Courtesy is owed, respect is earned, love is given." That motto still stands out in Kinky's memory.

Minnie was the first woman in Texas to be a certified American Camping Association (ACA) camp director. A founder of the Camp Association for Mutual Progress in Texas, Minnie was later recognized by the ACA for her regional and national role in professionalizing camp management with a posthumous "Camp Legends" award.

"Uncle Tom and Aunt Min had hundreds and hundreds of people going through and they knew everybody's name," says Goldberg, who attended the camp in the early 1960s. "They were very father- and mother-like—very warm and engaging, and very approachable. They made you feel important. They knew kids—especially the first time at camp and the younger ones—could be homesick and were very accommodating. If you had an issue you could go talk to them; if it was more of a dispute they would direct you back to your counselors at your bunk."

Although the camp was not exclusively Jewish, it became a haven for Jewish families and children. "Echo Hill was *the* Jewish camp for Reform Jews and Jews that weren't that observant, as opposed to the Young Judea Camp, which was more conservative, with Hebrew prayers," he says. "Echo Hill was a very prestigious Jewish camp and brought a lot of people together from Dallas, Houston, San Antonio, and the few Jewish families in little towns like San Saba. Going to one of those two camps was very important."

The thirty-minute drive from Kerrville to Echo Hill Ranch curves along a winding two-lane road with roller-coaster hills and hairpin and corkscrew turns as it passes through the verdant countryside of Texas Hill Country. The camp turn-off onto Wallace Creek Road is a rocky unpaved road flanked by gullies on both sides. The final 100 feet has visitors driving through an inch or two of Wallace Creek flowing over a small paved area. A right turn leads to the camp; a left to the rustic lodge built with weathered logs and a picturesque porch with wind chimes, hummingbird feeders, Adirondack chairs, and a magnificent view of the Texas hills.

Campers slept in bunk beds in wooden cabins set behind the lodge; two counselors were assigned to each cabin. "There were daddy long-legs everywhere and occasionally you'd see a scorpion," remembers Goldberg. "You didn't see them all the time, but you had to be careful when you went to the showers, because they like dark, dank, moist places."

The cabins circled a flat, grassy clearing with a flagpole with a loudspeaker that served as a hub for camp activities. Campers gathered under the wide open sky for hoedowns, friendship circles, and campfire singalongs. On Friday nights, they met by the flagpole dressed in white and facing west for the Shabbat candle lighting and prayers. "Happy Trails to You," by Roy Rogers and Dale Evans, and songs by Johnny Cash, Hank Williams, Jimmie Rodgers, and Bob Wills and the Texas Playboys serenaded campers from the loudspeaker during the day. Campers still smile when they talk about hearing Johnny Cash's

"Ring of Fire" while strolling through the grounds in the brutal heat of a Texas summer.

During his second summer in Texas Hill Country, an eight-year-old Kinky got his first and last taste of hunting on a night that lives on in his memory. He and five-year-old Roger were going coon hunting with Cabbie, a Hill Country neighbor, when Roger suggested he kiss Rip, the old coon dog, on the nose. Despite the blood and tears from the dog bite on his nose that he remembers as a "traumatic experience," Kinky discovered two things: a love of dogs and a dislike of hunting. He would later write, "What a wonderful sport, I thought, to send a tiny metal projectile through the skull of a peaceful, harmless animal."

Echo Hill Ranch has been a constant in Kinky's life. He spent his summers there, first as a camper, then as a camp counselor and Red Cross-certified swimming instructor throughout high school and college, and returned for a year after his Peace Corps assignment in Borneo. He rode his first horse and built his first campfire there—and played the accordion at age eight in a skit with fellow campers. While the other kids used the greasepaint to mimic Indian war paint, Kinky drew a Salvador Dali mustache on his face and a curl on his forehead.

Those early years in Texas Hill Country shaped Kinky in many ways. They inspired his fascination with cowboys and Texas history and provided a stage to put on skits, make people laugh, and sing and play guitar for attentive audiences. In fact, he met Jeff Shelby, a.k.a. Little Jewford, at the camp. Kinky and Jewford's early performances led to a lifelong friendship and the roots of what would become Kinky Friedman and the Texas Jewboys.

"I met Kinky at camp in 1958 when I was eight and he was thirteen," remembers Jewford. "I remember his smile was funny, but when you're eight years old you don't usually get into deep metaphysical observations. He probably did something humorous and I thought, 'I can relate to that.' Kinky was just a camper back then, but I figured out quickly he was the son of the owner. It was a delight because I loved the Hill Country from the second I saw it. There was a western and cowboy influence from the people on ranches and the farms. You could hear Jimmie Rodgers, Bob Wills, and lots of country music being played on AM radio. That part of the world wasn't the reality I knew in Houston. This was cowboy-fied."

Jewford attended both Echo Hill summer camp sessions for fifteen years, from the early summers when he and Kinky put on skits for the campers, until the summer of 1973, when they worked out songs that would eventually appear on *Sold American*.

"As I got a little older, we bonded in BS and musicality," he says. "The precursors of the Jewboys were definitely at Echo Hill—through the bits and repartee, the characterizations, and certainly the musicality. I remember performing when we were both kids in the dining hall, the tennis court, and by a campfire. I was always the class clown and I fed off of that energy. Kinky did, too, whether it was from a good response, the music, or just being in front of an audience."

Echo Hill also gave Kinky his first taste of attracting an entourage of fans.

"I met Kinky my first year," says Goldberg. "I remember him as very tall and thin, with a propriety of the place since it was his family's business. Not quite as warm and open as Uncle Tom and Aunt Min, but warm enough and easy to approach. He was charismatic and people followed him around in little groups. Even then he had groupies; people loved to ask him to sing. He'd sing songs like 'Fraulein' [a country song recorded by Bobby Helms in 1957 that hit #1 on the country charts, stayed on those charts for year, and crossed over to the *Billboard* charts] and 'Good Ole Mountain Dew' [an old Appalachian folk song recorded by Grandpa Jones in 1947].

"Sometimes he would sit on a porch in the evening and strum his guitar and sing. Other times it would be an activity where people could go in and listen. In the heat of the day, everybody had to go back to their cabins and write letters to their parents. Right before or after that, he'd be playing on the porch of the cabin where he was a counselor. He was not larger than life like he is now, but he was charismatic. People enjoyed being around him."

During the two years Goldberg attended the camp, Kinky was a student at the University of Texas and talking about joining the Peace Corps.

"I had a different counselor and was just a little kid looking up to him, so he wouldn't remember me," says Goldberg. "But he was one of five or six people that inspired me to join the Peace Corps."

During those carefree summers the Peace Corps was a distant dream. Campers focused on fun activities that included archery, swimming, horseback riding, arts and crafts, hiking along the creek, exploring the hills, climbing Mount Baldy, and earning marksmanship awards shooting BB guns and pellet guns.

"We'd ride horses around the camp acreage," remembers Jewford. "Kinky was on a horse at some point, but I can't say either one of us is a horseman. We're Jewish and you kind of back away from the horse thing pretty quickly. We swam in an area of the creek designated for teaching swimming. The shallow end, where Kinky lives now, is where they taught little kids."

"It was a beautiful creek and very refreshing, even as hot as it gets in Texas in the 100-degree summers," adds Goldberg. "We had nature studies with a guy named Uncle Floyd Potter who I just adored. He would take us out to the canyons finding fossils and learning about the flora and fauna around the creek and on the flat."

Evening activities at Echo Hill included overnight camping trips, movie nights, sing-along nights, and theme nights, where each bunk of twenty campers and two counselors created the evening's entertainment based on a theme.

"We did a few overnight camping trips—made a campfire and slept in sleeping bags," says Jewford. "It was never far from the camp, but enough to give the impression you're sleeping out. Theme nights could be counselors' night, music night, or backwards night where we did everything backwards. Each bunk would do a skit or dress backwards or create a scenario."

"Theme nights were great," adds Goldberg. "We were given a burlap sack with six odd items and had to make a story out of it. They might include a buckle, a wrench, and a woman's scarf. There was no TV. You could bring a little transistor, but there wasn't much reception. Once in a while you could pick up a Houston Astros game."

Music nights and sing-alongs inspired Kinky's first foray into comical songwriting at the age of eleven, when he penned and sang "Ol' Ben Lucas" to the delight of his fellow campers.

"I was writing poems and making them into songs when I was here at camp as a child," Kinky says from the porch of the lodge where he now lives. "Like 'My Jocks in Hock,' 'Ol' Ben Lucas,' and 'Make My Coffee Blue'—those were three early childhood songs. I never quite finished 'Make My Coffee Blue,'" he says before singing with a country twang, "Well, I may drink a red, red wine, but make my coffee blue."

"'Ol' Ben Lucas' was a big one of that era—'Ol' Ben Lucas had a lot of mucus, coming right out of his nose.' It's a song that's not played on the radio much but is very well known. Even when I'm touring places like Australia, everybody knows the song. I vaguely remember writing a song called 'The Jewish Christmas Song.'"

Decades before the media dubbed Kinky the "Jewish Cowboy," he became enamored of cowboys and Texas legends. He loved swimming in Wallace Creek, but it was William A. "Bigfoot" Wallace, the creek's namesake, who captured his imagination. Kinky considers Wallace, a Texas folk hero whose exploits as a soldier, Texas Ranger, and back-woodsman made him a legend, one of the three greatest frontiersmen—along with Sam Houston and Davy Crockett—who ever set foot in Texas.

Passionate about Texas history, Kinky made frequent visits to the remains of the Alamo mission in San Antonio, where Crockett fought and died for the spirit of Texas. Kinky's fascination with the frontiersman who fought Indians, was elected to Congress, and later left politics with the declaration "You may all go to hell and I will go to Texas" planted the seeds for his own larger-than-life persona and political ambitions.

You didn't have to live in Texas to become enthralled by the cowboy mystique in the 1950s and '60s. You could turn on your TV and watch *The Roy Rogers Show*, *Have Gun—Will Travel*, and *Bonanza*. But the TV cow-boys couldn't hold a candle to Earl Buckelew, the camp wrangler who handled, groomed, and trained the horses; taught campers how to ride; maintained the corrals, and took care of the saddles, stirrups, bridles, halters, reins, bits, and harnesses. Buckelew was an authentic cowboy who had driven a horse and wagon, broken wild horses, sheared sheep, built houses with his own hands, and had a grandfather captured by the Comanche Indians.

Annoyed by actors and even politicians being recognized as cowboys, Kinky set the record straight when Chuck Connors from *The Rifleman*, James Drury from *The Virginian*, and Barry Goldwater were inducted into the National Cowboy Hall of Fame. "One of the few real cowboys I know is a man named Earl Buckelew, who has lived all his life in the heart of the hill country near Medina, Texas," he wrote in a *New York Times* opinion piece. "For more than seventy-six years, Earl has lived on the land, ridden the range, and loved and understood horses. And, what is even rarer, he loves and understands himself."

"Earl Buckelew was a true cowboy wrangler," says Jewford. "One of those guys you just had an affinity for. He had a raw, raw personality that's real. Earl was fascinating to me because he was part of the earth and part of the horse culture."

Kinky's childhood love of cowboys and Indians led to countless visits to the Frontier Times Museum in nearby Bandera, which is called the "Cowboy Capital of the World" and known for its National Rodeo Champions. Originally inhabited by Apache and Comanche Indians, Bandera had been a staging area for cattle drives after the Civil War, with cowboys herding longhorn cattle along the Great Western Trail to Fort Robinson, Nebraska.

Housed in a primitive limestone building, the Frontier Times Museum celebrates the legacy of the American cowboy, cattle ranching, and the Old West. Western saddles perch on a rail fence; cowboy hats, heads of cattle and longhorn steer, and vintage photographs of cowboys adorn the walls.

Kinky loved the antique firearms, a collection of knives that included a saber, the rattlesnake carcass, the mummified squirrel, the two-headed goat, and the shrunken head of a Jivaro Indian killed by a poisonous dart shot through a blowgun. When he stared at it in awe, he had no idea that fifteen years later he'd be in the jungles of Borneo eating monkey brains with pygmies who hunted with blowguns, and visiting Kayan natives in longhouses with baskets of Japanese heads hanging on the porch.

Then there were the arrowheads set in the limestone walls that inspired Kinky to start digging at the ranch to amass his own collection. "I've got arrowheads in the walls of the lodge that were found here on the ranch," he says. "And I've got arrowheads in my back. That's how you can recognize a pioneer; he's got arrowheads in his back."

Kinky pauses to think about what may have been a throwaway remark. "I suppose I am a pioneer of sorts," he says. "Billy Joe [Shaver] just reminded me how proud everybody was when I played the Grand Ole Opry for the first time. That was a big deal in Nashville because Nashville was a close-knit, good ole Southern Christian boy society of musicians that didn't even like Hank Williams."

When he played the Grand Ole Gospel Show, Kinky was the first performer to bring a black artist (Dobie Gray) onto center stage. Reverend Jimmie Snow introduced him as "the first full-blooded Jew to ever appear on the Grand Ole Opry," and his band as the "Texas Jews." But his remark to Kinky backstage reflected the true Nashville mindset:

"This is the first time we're having a real live Jew and a nigger play at the Grand Ole Opry."

Even before the self-proclaimed Texas Jewboy confused the Bible-thumping audiences in Nashville, he followed the inner compass that made him a pioneer. When Kinky attended the University of Texas (UT), Jim Crow laws were in full force, and campus drugstores, restaurants, and dormitories were still segregated. He tried to integrate his fraternity, but his Tau Delta Phi frat brothers reneged on their promise and planted sheriffs at the door to keep his black friends out. Disgusted, Kinky quit the fraternity, joined the Students for a Democratic Society (SDS), and picketed two businesses on the UT campus that discriminated against black patrons.

In the early 1970s, when Jewish entertainers changed their names to hide their ethnicity, he proudly defied the status quo by calling his band Kinky Friedman and the Texas Jewboys.

During his early music career, he wrote and recorded the first pro-choice country and western song ("Rapid City, South Dakota"), and the only country and western song about the Holocaust ("Ride 'Em Jewboy"). He also became the first (and only) artist whose performance was taped and then deemed to be too offensive to air on *Austin City Limits*.

When his cocaine habit derailed his music career and almost killed him, he quit drugs cold turkey and became the first country and western artist to reinvent himself as an author. To date he has written eighteen detective novels and thirteen nonfiction books.

When he entered the Texas gubernatorial race in 2005, he became the first candidate to run for governor as an Independent since Sam Houston. To get on the ballot as an Independent, he had sixty days to get 45,540 signatures from registered voters who didn't vote in a primary. With a grassroots team of volunteers and more than 268,000 square miles to cover, his "Save Yourself for Kinky" campaign generated 170,258 signatures.

When he ran in the 2014 Democratic primary for Texas Agriculture Commissioner, his platform focused on legalizing hemp and marijuana, as well as gambling, to provide a stream of revenue for schools in a state ranking thirty-ninth in education (that has since dropped to forty-third). He believed growing industrial hemp, which requires less water than cotton, would help farmers in the then drought-plagued state, and decriminalizing marijuana would free up jails for dangerous criminals. And this was before the Texas legislature even considered allowing marijuana for medical purposes.

"An artist is somebody who is ahead of his time and behind on his rent," is one of Kinky's favorite sayings, and he often laments that his careers, taste for Cuban cigars, and penchant for gambling have never left him financially set.

"Now the question is, 'Why ain't I rich?'" he says, putting on a thick Texas accent.

When told he's sitting on the porch of a 400-acre ranch in Texas Hill Country, and rich—if not in money—in the coin of the spirit, another one of his favorite sayings, he sighs.

His is the story of a man who has led an amazing life and is never satisfied.

2
Austin and the University of Texas

"My dad led a big civil rights march down the Drag.
It was the first one involving professors who could have gotten
fired for marching because no one knew
if it was going to cause a riot."
—Kinky Friedman

When the camp was heading into its seventh summer, Tom Friedman knew it was successful and he could pursue another one of his dreams. He moved his family to Austin and enrolled in the graduate program in the Department of Psychology at the University of Texas. Laying the groundwork for a career as a college professor, he worked as a special instructor and teaching assistant in the psychology department as a graduate student and also worked as a social science research associate in the Department of Sociology.

Today Austin is a bustling metropolis, appearing on "Best City to Live" lists by *Kiplinger, Forbes, CNN, U.S. News and World Report*, and other sources. In 2014, the U.S. Census Bureau estimated Austin's population as more than 912,000. Two years later, it had increased to 932,000. But when the Friedmans arrived in 1959, Austin was a charming little city with a population of 86,000.

"Austin was beautiful, lots of hills, a great little sleepy place," says Kinky, who remembers riding up Congress Avenue towards the state capitol in the back seat of the family 1953 Plymouth Cranbrook convertible with his brother Roger. "We lived in a house in Northwest Austin with a big deck looking out over the hills; now it's looking over a whole bunch of houses," he says. "It was on twenty acres in the middle of Austin, a beautiful little place on Mountain Climb Drive with a windmill."

Austin had an even smaller Jewish population than Houston, but that didn't impact Kinky's teenage years.

"I was in some Jewish youth group, a social group," he says. "My social life at that time was pretty pre-puberty. I had one girl I really liked, but we never accomplished much—never consummated our love. It's just as well," he deadpans.

Although he hadn't started high school in Houston, Kinky entered Stephen F. Austin High School as a sophomore.

"I jumped a year when I started high school; I was moved up because of my grades," explains Kinky. "If you could advance a year, people did it, but that was a big mistake. I was very socially immature—as I remain today because of a state of arrested development," he adds without skipping a beat. "But I was very immature and a year younger than everybody else. I was socially awkward, and at that age in high school, it didn't help."

Despite his youth, Kinky had no problem making friends and getting involved in extracurricular activities, including the *Maroon*, the student newspaper.

"I was sports editor of the newspaper," says Kinky. "Don't ask me how I got that. I reviewed a football game in Latin. Publishing it in Latin was probably the high point of my work as sports editor. I went to the games as little as possible."

Several high school teachers still stand out in Kinky's mind—Mrs. Hodges, an English teacher who gave him poems to encourage his development as a writer; and biology teacher Floyd Potter. "I liked him a lot," says Kinky. "He ended up running the nature study program at Echo Hill Ranch for many years."

Kinky was also inspired by the passion of John F. Kennedy, who broke through two centuries of prejudice in 1960 when he became the first Catholic and thus the first non-White-Anglo-Saxon-Protestant elected president. Kennedy's challenge to young Americans to serve their country by working in developing countries appealed to Kinky's social consciousness and would later change the course of his life.

Like Kinky's dad, JFK was a war hero and a socially conscious, forward-thinking individual. His concept of a New Frontier that would explore uncharted areas of science and space, and eradicate poverty, ignorance, and prejudice, also appealed to the teenager.

"He was a very inspirational man," says Kinky. "I liked him—I thought he had a wit, he was funny, charming. Personally, he was out of control, but nobody knew it. In spite of the many flaws he may have had, he inspired young people. That's what the Peace Corps was all about; that's what putting a man on the moon was all about. Bobby Kennedy was also very inspirational."

As it did for most of his classmates, music played a role in Kinky's high school years.

"The Beatles didn't hit till I was a freshman in college, but rock and roll was already there," he says. "I liked Buddy Holly, Fats Domino, and Sun Records artists like Carl Perkins, Jerry Lee Lewis, and of course Johnny Cash."

Although Buddy Holly died in a plane crash when Kinky was only fourteen, the Lubbock-born musician had quite an impact. More than thirty years later, Kinky wrote a full-length feature entitled "Buddy Holly's Texas" for *Rolling Stone* magazine. He also made sure filmmakers included a visit to Lubbock when he hosted a four-part documentary on Texas music for the BBC.

"Buddy Holly was really an original guy," says Kinky. "It wouldn't have happened out of New York or California—he was a special Texas guy. Lubbock is more isolated than any other city—you have to go hundreds of miles to get there. Nobody came through except Bob Wills and Elvis, who came through Lubbock at the very beginning and never came back.

"I think he made it because of the absolute lack of input he had. He just had his native talent—he didn't have the folk scene there, he didn't have other influences. He'd listen in his car at two in the morning to *Stan's Record Rack* [a radio show that played blues artists] out of Shreveport. Buddy saw *She Wore a Yellow Ribbon* with John Wayne; it's a very inspiring movie that I liked very much, too. After he saw it, he went home and wrote 'Not Fade Away.' He also did 'Oh Boy,' which is one of my favorites. He was a great one, and by virtue of his association with him, Waylon Jennings was touched by greatness too."

At home, Kinky's parents listened to folk music from the 1950s and early '60s, including Burl Ives, Paul Robeson, and Joan Baez. "My dad was pretty close to a socialist, especially when he was younger," says Kinky. "He and my mother were very humanistic people, very into people, and kids, and animals." Folk and rock and roll dominated popular music in the late 1950s, but Kinky's musical heroes were country and western artists.

In fact, he picked up the guitar because, like other Texas musicians—including Johnny Winter and Townes Van Zandt—he wanted to learn how to play "Fraulein."

"I started with an accordion, moved to guitar, and after I got over the Burl Ives, Paul Robeson, Joan Baez folk thing, I got into country," he says. "I was into country pretty damn early. I listened to early Johnny Cash, songs his fans today are not familiar with: 'Come In Stranger,' 'Teenage Queen,' 'Guess Things Happen That Way,' brilliant stuff. 'Pickin' Time,' a beautiful song, was my dad's favorite. I saw Ernest Tubb at the Skyline Club in Austin when I was about twelve or thirteen. I really liked Slim Whitman, Jimmie Rodgers, and Hank Williams. Real country acts. Willie [Nelson]'s song "Hello Walls" was speaking to me as a teenager. When I heard that song, I thought, 'What a great idea—this guy who is a mental case literally talking to the walls.' And it's so beautiful lyrically and musically; another one is 'Pretty Paper.'"

Folk became Kinky's first musical outlet, with his acoustic guitar the perfect vehicle for writing songs. Once he'd mastered the basics, he decided to put together a band with Joe Rude and Gary Nelson, two high school classmates who lived in his neighborhood.

"I knew Richard [Kinky] because he lived down the street, and Gary Nelson lived very close to him," remembers Rude, who is a radiologist in Atlanta. "My house was the most western house in Austin at the time; we lived near Mount Bonnell, which overlooks Town Lake. We didn't have mail service or any utilities except electricity. We were way out; now it's in the middle of town because Austin has grown so much."

Rude, like Kinky, doesn't quite remember why they put a band together. "It was fifty years ago; there's a little haze over that now," he says with a laugh. But he remembers being influenced by the Kingston Trio, the Limeliters, and other small folk groups popular at the time.

"Richard and Gary were very musical, and I wasn't," Rude says. "We'd get together and practice and cut up, and basically have a good time. Kinky played the guitar, Gary played the guitar, and I was endeavoring to play something and sing at the same time. They demoted me to washboard because that was about all I could handle," he adds, laughing.

"My first band was an acoustic band called the Three Rejects," says Kinky. "On the day Moshe Dayan died or around that time frame, I remember Gary's father saying, 'Well, it looks like one of your countrymen died,'" Kinky adds in a deep southern accent, before laughing.

"I remember that. I don't remember much about the Three Rejects except singing a song about 'Passengers will please refrain from using the toilets while the train is in the station, darling I love you.' We played a few parties, that was it—the Rejects didn't go very far."

"We played folk songs by the Kingston Trio, but the songs we were singing were Kinky's creations," explains Rude. "He was obviously the most musical person in the group. Gary wasn't bad and I was terrible."

Rude's most vivid memory of the band's performances was a pep rally in the Austin High School gym. "The acoustics were horrible and it wasn't loud enough because we had the typical speaker system for a basketball game in a high school gym," Rude says. "It was fun to get up there, but nobody could hear what we were singing."

Although the Three Rejects, or simply the Rejects, which is how Rude remembers the name, didn't go far, their shows were Kinky's first performances in front of people outside of Echo Hill Ranch and a harbinger of things to come. He hadn't yet adopted his Kinky name or persona; he was still Richard Friedman in both name and personality.

"He was a lot more serious and reserved back then," says Rude. "He wasn't always coming up with jokes, but he'd come up with wise-cracks and he was clever in coming up with songs. Most people in high school don't remember him because he wasn't a big performer. He was just one of the kids and less of an extrovert than he is now."

Kinky believes being much younger than most of his classmates contributed to his reserve. "I was a participant/observer in high school," he says. "I was too young; another few years would have done me better. But I did drive a green Plymouth convertible in high school with a wolf whistle and a 'ding dong' Bermuda bell. It was made out of brass, had a foot-activated plunger, and made a loud 'ding-dong' sound," he says, smiling at the memory.

"There were about 2,000 kids in my graduating class," he adds. "I knew a lot of kids weren't going to go to college—high school was the end of their life. They were big shots in high school, like football quarterbacks, and went right from that to pumping gas. I was looking forward to going to college."

Kinky never looked back after graduation or attended any high school reunions, but he hasn't been forgotten by his classmates. The Austin High School Class of 1962 website proudly claims an unnamed alumnus who became a Peace Corps volunteer.

Kinky began his studies at the University of Texas that fall, when his dad was in the final year of his doctoral program. He enrolled in the Plan II Honors program, a competitive multidisciplinary major that only accepted the top applicants. The program encouraged creativity, analysis, and critical thinking, and had challenging requirements that included courses in literature, philosophy, the social sciences, the arts, math, and the natural sciences that were typically open only to students within those majors.

When asked how he got into such a prestigious program, Kinky's initial response is modest. "Just lucky, I guess," he says before explaining the process. "You apply to it and do interviews. It's difficult to get into—you have to be reaaaally [sic] smart because its curriculum can be compared to the Ivy League colleges. It has very small classes and very pointy-headed intellectual professors."

College classmates of Kinky's tell conflicting stories about his study habits; some say he buckled down and kept his nose to the grindstone while others say he aced his courses without having to study. According to Kinky, they were both right.

"If it's a field you're comfortable with and something you like, you didn't have to study too hard," he says. "If it's a grind you don't understand, then you have to study. I took a psychology course but got out of that pretty fast. I was never a psychology major, although I see that written in a lot of places. It's not true, but because of the wonderful Wikipedia and Internet, it stays that way. I graduated with what is called a Plan II degree—a liberal arts degree with no rhyme or reason; it does not prepare you for anything. I've said it prepares you to run for governor or agriculture commissioner of Texas or to sleep under a bridge. It prepares you for them, but not much else, unless you're going to teach at a college."

Kinky was only seventeen when he entered college and had no idea as to what he wanted to do after graduation.

"There are all kinds of people in college," he says. "Those that know they're going to work for their father's business after they graduate and they drink and play cards all the time. As long as they don't flunk out, they'll go to work for their father. Or people that go to Harvard and drink and play cards all the time. As long as they don't flunk out, they'll be fine, and they usually don't flunk out because they don't like to flunk people at Harvard."

When Harvard's most famous graduate—President John F. Kennedy—was assassinated as he rode in a motorcade through downtown Dallas on November 22, 1963, the nation went into shock. People stayed glued to their televisions as the surreal story evolved live with the real-time assassination of Lee Harvey Oswald in full view of the TV cameras. The mood at the University of Texas, as throughout the nation, was somber.

"JFK's assassination was heavy," says Ken "Snakebite" Jacobs, a college friend who later played sax and flute in the Texas Jewboys. "I remember people staying at their apartments and watching TV for two or three days straight. I was in class and somebody came in screaming, 'They shot the president.' We all walked out of class and people were crying. There was a lot of crying and screaming on the campus."

Kinky's recollections of the Kennedy assassination are not as lucid. "College was a blur—the time JFK was killed and Lee Harvey Oswald was killed and Jack Ruby came into the picture. I slept that whole fucking time. I don't think I saw any of that after Kennedy was shot."

He says he was sleeping off a beer party from the previous night. Once he sobered up, he too was shocked and numbed by the horror and the reaction of some of his fellow Texans. "Since then I've been to the Petroleum Club in Houston, the place where they cheered when Kennedy was killed," he adds. "That happened in a lot of places, but that one for sure. There were a lot of eyewitnesses—black waiters—that saw the place erupt in cheers."

As a Jew transplanted to Texas, Kinky felt a sense of kinship with Jack Ruby, the nightclub owner who killed Oswald. Born Jacob Rubenstein in Chicago, Ruby moved to Dallas in 1947 and quickly became assimilated in Texas culture.

"Jack Ruby was very Jewish and also very Texas, a flamboyant, colorful guy who tried to be accepted as a real Texas type," Kinky says. "He was also a good friend of Hank Williams, and continued to book him in his club after almost nobody else would."

Kinky dubbed Ruby a "bastard child of twin cultures" in a September 2003 *Texas Monthly* article and explained why.

"Like the first real cowboy spotted by a child, Ruby made an indelible impression upon my youthful consciousness," he wrote. "He was the first Texas Jewboy I ever saw. There he stood like a good cowboy, like a good Jew, wearing his hat indoors, shooting the bad guy who killed the president, and doing it right there on live TV. Never mind that the bad guy had yet to be indicted or convicted; never mind he was a captive in handcuffs, carefully 'guarded' by Dallas cops. These are mere details relegated to the footnotes and footprints of history. Ruby had done what every good God-fearing, red-blooded American had wished he could do. And he was one of our boys!"

"I think Ruby was a real fan of JFK's and wanted to show he was a good American," Kinky says, sitting on an Adirondack rocker on the porch of his ranch, amid the melodic backdrop of chimes blowing in the Hill Country wind. "It's very unlikely Lee Harvey Oswald did that on his own. But now we'll never know."

The civil rights movement was in full swing during Kinky's high school and college years. But even though Congress passed the Civil Rights Act in 1964, the majority of Southern congressmen and senators voted against the bill, with many Southern states refusing to enforce integration. Kinky had been opposed to segregation since 1954, when he wrote the "White Citizens Council Marching Song" about that racist organization that officially renounced the use of violence, while encouraging white violence against blacks, and boycotting businesses and services with owners supporting and actively pushing for desegregation.

"I was always against segregation," Kinky says. "I thought it was very unfair, very un-American. Especially in a place like Texas where we celebrate outlaws. We're a different kind of place; we do what the hell we want to do in Texas. It's where the Alamo came from—that's where Texas was born, with a sense we're not going to be like the others. So we should have fixed it—we did eventually."

"Eventually" took a while, and it was not without repercussions. "Most of the blacks I knew were very bitter," says Kinky. "I knew one guy in high school and a few in college, very nice guys who eventually got fed up with it. It was amazingly late when those segregated places were shut down. Kennedy had been president and segregation should have been over."

Unlike many Southern towns and cities, Austin didn't have separate drinking fountains when Kinky attended UT, but a number of places, including drugstores, restaurants, movie theaters, and campus dormitories, were still not integrated. The public establishments didn't have the blatant "No Coloreds" signs seen in some Southern towns. Their signs read, "We reserve the right to refuse service," which would later inspire a song Kinky wrote as a Peace Corps volunteer in Borneo. The lyrics to "We Reserve the Right to Refuse Service to You" sound like it's about anti-Semites, but the song targets all racists. Those signs hung in the Rexall Drug store, which Kinky picketed because they refused to cash checks for black patrons, as well as the Plantation Restaurant, one of Kinky's favorite late-night hangouts.

"One place that was segregated was the Plantation Restaurant, a very popular after-hours place that I always liked," says Kinky. "Everybody would go except blacks. You'd see karate instructors, bowlers, bikers, folksingers, all kinds of people. They had a 'We reserve the right to refuse service' sign, but I don't think they even needed that. They wouldn't let blacks in. Blacks knew they weren't welcome, and the restaurant had people at the door.

"That was a twenty-four-hour home for me in college, so we picketed it, and encouraged people to just order coffee and tie up the tables and talk. After two or three weeks of that, the place caved in. I had friends that managed the place, but my sympathies were not with the restaurant. I wanted to integrate the place and we did. Today the Plantation is gone—a beautiful old place—and the street on the side of it, which was 19th Street, is now Martin Luther King Boulevard. We call that progress."

Another late-night college haunt was the Night Hawk, a popular restaurant on Guadalupe Street on the University of Texas campus. But the Night Hawk didn't need pressure to integrate. Owner Harry Akin, an equal-opportunity employer since 1935, was one of 100 businessmen from across the U.S. invited to Washington, D.C., in 1963 to confer with President Kennedy about the desegregation of public facilities across the nation.

Kinky spent many a late night drinking coffee, pondering his future, writing songs, or jotting thoughts in his ever-present notebook at the Night Hawk. "I used to hang out there a lot," he says. "I was writing songs late at night by the middle or end of college. It was a place where people went to sit up all night, drink coffee, and solve the problems of the world. And where I first contemplated joining the Peace Corps."

"Kinky loved the Night Hawk," says Jacobs. "The Night Hawk was very middle of the road, a Denny's type of place. Kinky talked about it a lot."

Kinky met Jacobs at Tau Delta Phi, a Jewish fraternity that lists Kinky along with Hubert Humphrey, Geraldo Rivera, David Sarnoff, and Jerry Stiller as notable alumni. When Kinky enrolled at UT, pledging to a fraternity or sorority was the way to go, despite the conformity those organizations expected. Sorority sisters wore bows in their bubble hairdos, circle pins (also known as virgin pins) on their blouses, skirts with white knee socks, and black suede loafers. Fraternity brothers wore button-down collar shirts, tan slacks or jeans, and black leather loafers.

"I probably joined because I knew a couple of older guys that were pretty cool and they were in the frat," explains Kinky. "I dressed like a frat boy for a while; after that I started dressing like Bob Dylan—I started listening to his music in college."

"I met Kinky freshman year of college," says Jacobs. "A friend told me he'd met this funny, hysterical guy named Richard Friedman, and kept talking about him. When I met Kinky a couple of months later, I thought, 'This guy is really an oddball, but he's funny.' We became friends right away. We took anthropology together. He was pretty quiet in class. He wasn't quieter in college than he is now, but he was quiet in class. In general, he was a young version of the same guy—up and down in his moods, rather extreme. Basically, he was a lot of fun."

"I wrote a monograph on the flathead Indians of Montana for that anthropology class," says Kinky. "The instructor was Chad Oliver, a very famous anthropologist. He gave me an A-minus on it and wrote, 'Your style has got to go,' because it was funny and had these witty little comments. He probably had no sense of humor."

Ironically, Symmes Chadwick Oliver, who taught under the name of Chad Oliver, also wrote fiction, including three westerns, eight science fiction novels, and short science fiction pieces. Luckily, Oliver's discouraging words about Kinky's writing style never impacted his writing career. With thirty-one books published to date, Kinky's literary legacy has surpassed Oliver's output in spades.

Oliver didn't make much of an impression on Jacobs, either; his fondest college recollections of Kinky were the times they spent together outside of the classroom.

"My best memories are going to his parents' ranch and going out for Mexican food," says Jacobs. "Kinky's parents had a place in the Austin hills—we used to go down there saying we were going to study but we ended up farting around. A real Texas ranch with dark wood inside with brick and stone—it was such a gas to go out there. He drove a 1948 Dodge pickup truck with an ooga ooga horn—Kinky was famous for that," Jacobs adds. "You could hear him two blocks away with the ooga ooga."

Kinky, who has owned a series of pickup trucks during his lifetime, doesn't remember that particular one but admits he probably had an ooga ooga horn. "Maybe so," he says. "I was pretty immature. That's one of my secrets—to remain immature. It's served me well; it has let me be a lot older than other people around me and still younger."

Although Austin hadn't become the "Live Music Capital of the World" in the early '60s, there was an impressive music scene during Kinky's college years. "Janis Joplin would sing at the [student] Union on the UT campus on Thursday afternoons in 1963," Jacobs says. "A lot of the musicians had hair down to their shoulders; I thought they were the coolest people on earth."

"I saw Steve Goodman [the folk singer/songwriter who wrote "City of New Orleans"] and Jerry Jeff Walker when I was in college," says Kinky. "I never saw Janis Joplin at the Union, but sure was an admirer of hers. The frat boys were running her for the ugly man contest when I was on campus, but it wasn't my fraternity."

Kinky is referring to a fraternity nomination for "Ugliest Man on Campus" when Joplin was an art student at the University in 1963. With her long unruly hair, torn-off jeans, tennis shoes, and bare feet, Janis didn't fit the UT mold. The public humiliation in front of the entire student body was too much to bear. She quit school and hitchhiked to San Francisco with fellow Texan and UT dropout Chet Helms, who introduced her to Big Brother and the Holding Company. UT's loss was the music world's gain.

The Tau Delta Phi fraternity parties never reached the level of chaos of the frat parties in *National Lampoon's Animal House*, the 1978 film featuring Kinky's friend John Belushi as John "Bluto" Blutarsky, a drunken degenerate in his seventh year of college. But Jacobs remembers the fraternity having parties "all the time" with getting drunk as the main event.

"We had wild parties where we would drink hurricanes and get blotto," he says. "They called them hurricanes but they were really Everclear, which is 190 proof grain alcohol, and grape punch so you couldn't taste the alcohol. We were trying to get our dates drunk so we could make out, but mainly we got sick at the end of the night—I did, anyway. One party we had the Crickets after Buddy Holly died and we had Jessie Hill with 'Ooh Poo Pah Do,' which killed us—people were singing 'Ooh Poo Pah Do' in the shower for six months. We brought dates and would drink and dance, but I don't think I ever saw Kinky dancing."

When he attended college, politics was closer to Kinky's heart than partying.

"I was politically minded in college," he says. "I ran a few campaigns in college; the only one I lost was my own when I ran for student council. Glad I lost. I got a friend of mine elected to the student council—Lee Hartman, a very bright guy. He promptly flunked out after that just from fooling around.

"The most exciting campaign was the one for Snakebite Jacobs— Kenny Jacobs," Kinky adds. "Ken was a very nice guy, very kind. I was the campaign manager when he ran for head cheerleader. The campaign picked up so much speed, the other cheerleaders, who I knew from high school, called me in and said, 'Richard, can we call this off? This is going to make a mockery of the whole thing,' which of course it was. We had these big sideboards on my pickup truck and he'd be in the back of the truck waving to everybody. That was pretty wild."

"Cheerleading is a big thing in Texas, so I ran for head cheerleader for a joke," says Jacobs. "I had a picture of myself on a big poster; it was a close-up of me with my beard, which was weird then. The poster was attached to a stick I carried around. Our slogan was, 'I can jump high.' Totally a goof. I still have a poster framed; it was one of the few things I got out of my house in New Orleans after Hurricane Katrina. It was the poster of my platform and the qualifications that Kinky helped me come up with.

"They were all really stupid. My platform was, 'Make Bevo a full professor.' [Bevo, a Texas longhorn steer, was the UT mascot.] My qualifications were, 'Grade-Point Average 1.2; Remedial English; Zero Health Rating; Round-Up Beard Contest; and Silverman Spurs,' a goof on the Silver Spurs, the students who brought Bevo to the games. I came in third out of five, although I came in first in both the graduate school and the law school. We thought that was really cool. I didn't want to be head cheerleader; I was going to quit if I got elected. When they first started counting the votes, I was four to one in the law school votes because they were older and they got the joke. That's when I got nervous—I'd be so embarrassed as a cheerleader. So I was trying to figure out excuses—maybe if I broke my ankle or something," he says with a laugh.

Although many states consider it a predominantly female extracurricular activity, cheerleading has helped some notable Texas politicians earn a varsity letter. Past presidents George H. W. Bush and George W. Bush were cheerleaders during their college years at Yale University, as was George W.'s grandfather Prescott Sheldon Bush. Texas governor Rick Perry earned his cheerleading letter at Texas A&M, where cheerleaders were called "yell leaders."

When asked about Texas's penchant for male cheerleaders, Kinky doesn't hesitate. "Latent homosexual Southern tradition," he says.

Jacobs remembers partying and football being "a big deal" during college. Yet Kinky, who has always been his own man, didn't drink or party excessively and was never a fan of football or of the Longhorns, the University of Texas football team. "Football didn't appeal to me because the Longhorns always won," Kinky says. "UT was the richest school; they had all the money, all the good teams."

In 1963, the University of Texas lifted its ban keeping black students from playing varsity sports, but it took another seven years for the football team to be integrated. Darrell Royal, the Longhorns coach, acknowledged pressure from the university regents to take his time admitting black athletes to the team.

"I became friends with Darrell Royal after college," Kinky says. "During college, he was a really big shot, the last man to coach an all-white team in the Southwest Conference. But he was a good man, a very nice man. He loved music and he helped Willie [Nelson] out a lot."

Bothered by the racist culture of all-white football teams and segregated dormitories, Kinky decided black students should be allowed to join his fraternity. He wasn't about to wait until a student lawsuit and the loss of a $257,500 Peace Corps training contract forced the Board of Regents to reconsider its stance.

"I tried to integrate my fraternity racially," says Kinky. "I had a number of black friends, but there were three I tried to get into the fraternity with disastrous results because no fraternity took blacks at that time. I wanted to be the first, but they didn't want them.

"There was a big fraternity party in Galveston, so we invited these three guys and they had their dates with them. Everybody is dressed up formal in tuxedos—ridiculous college fraternity stuff. The sheriffs were already there when we arrived and wouldn't let these guys in even though I had been assured they would. We boycotted that party— almost half of the fraternity left and just drank in a hotel room. It was definitely racial—they were worried somebody might bomb the fraternity. They were cowards, typical frat boys."

Concern about a racially charged bombing on the UT campus wasn't that farfetched. In 1960, two college students were indicted for setting off a homemade bomb outside an integrationist meeting at the University's YMCA. Once more, Kinky was way ahead of his time. It wasn't until 1967, when he was serving as a Peace Corps volunteer in Borneo, that an African American became the first pledge at a white fraternity at UT.

Nevertheless, that blatant act of racism was the last straw for Kinky. "The frat cost a fuckin' fortune and was a complete waste of time," he says. "I lived in the frat for maybe a year and a half or two years and left after the incident in Galveston. After that I was in the SDS for a couple of years."

Founded in 1960 at the University of Michigan campus in Ann Arbor, with activist Tom Hayden as national president, the Students for a Democratic Society opened a chapter at the University of Austin in 1964. Although the group eventually focused on antiwar protests, its early efforts revolved around joining black students at sit-ins at segregated restaurants.

Kinky wasn't the only Friedman to put his beliefs into action at the University of Texas.

"My dad led a big civil rights march down the Drag," he says. "It was the first involving professors who could have gotten fired for marching because no one knew if it was going to cause a riot. Tom was one of three untenured professors who marched. I remember a banker who was Tom's friend standing in front of the bank with his cohorts saying, 'Good God! There's Tom Friedman and he's leading this.'"

Although Kinky eventually became disgusted with his fraternity, he developed friendships with a number of musicians he met there, including Jacobs; Nick "Chinga" Chavin, who later played in the Texas Jewboys; and Shawn Siegel, who played in King Arthur and the Carrots and in the Texas Jewboys.

"I met Nick Chavin the first week at college," says Kinky. "Chinga gave me the name Kinky in college because I had an Angela Davis–style haircut. He got blackballed from the fraternity. Why? Because they were a very stupid fraternity. He was very much an individual and the fraternity didn't like that. They don't like rugged individualists.

"Chinga is a good man and a damn good poet. And, as Oscar Wilde said, a poet can survive anything but a misprint. Chinga survived being blackballed from the fraternity very well. I think it made him stronger, and made my opinion of him go up. It was the first year—he was either a member or a pledge. They also blackballed David Geffen, the founder of Asylum Records and Geffen Records, a few years earlier." Geffen, like Chavin, didn't let being blackballed affect his self-esteem or future plans. Geffen dropped out of UT, went on to produce *Dreamgirls* and *Cats* on Broadway, cofounded DreamWorks with Steven Spielberg, and now has a net worth of over $4 billion.

Jacobs shared an apartment with Chavin in San Francisco after he graduated.

"Chinga Chavin is really, really intelligent and he's another oddball," says Jacobs. "He got blackballed just for being different. He and I wrote 'Asshole from El Paso' together. Chinga loves Kinky; he loved his routine and tried to clone himself into Kinky after he came to our show [Kinky Friedman and the Texas Jewboys] at the Boarding House in San Francisco in 1974. Chinga wrote pornographic country tunes and had a band called Country Porn. He was famous for that and a toilet seat guitar someone made for him. Even today Kinky is his big hero, but he wouldn't admit it. He wanted to be like Kinky."

Kinky also met Siegel at Tau Delta Phi. Like most of Kinky's friends. Siegel, who refers to Kinky as Richard, is an extremely intelligent man. He played on Kinky's first single with King Arthur and the Carrots while they were both working at Echo Hill Ranch.

"I met him at the University of Texas frat house—we were roommates for one semester," he says. "Richard was a freer spirit intellectually than the other people in the fraternity. I liked his upfrontness, his whole family, and his relationship with Roger. Roger and Kinky had a real good relationship, which attracted me to the family and the lifestyle of having a camp for kids.

"Richard played guitar and I played piano," he adds. "That was the only reason I was in the fraternity. I was found—if you will—playing the piano by another frat member. We were freshmen and he was a senior. He rushed me to get me into the fraternity and I joined. When I look back at it, it was preposterous," he says with a laugh.

"Being in a fraternity was cool in the early '60s," adds Jacobs. "It was starting to be uncool after pot began to come onto the campus in 1964 and there started to be hip and square divisions. Frats started to seem corny and old school, so I moved out of the fraternity house and into an apartment. I hung out with a group that smoked pot and were semi-hippies, but I don't think Kinky ever smoked pot."

Kinky spent his high school and college summers working at Echo Hill Ranch. Siegel also worked there as a counselor from 1964 to 1967, so a musical collaboration was clearly in the cards.

When they got together to write songs in the summer of 1965, they decided to spoof the Beach Boys, who hit the pop charts with "Surfin' Safari" in 1962, then "Surfin' U.S.A." in 1963, and dominated the U.S. *Billboard* charts throughout the 1960s. To take advantage of the surf music craze, American International Pictures released a series of beach party movies, including *Beach Party, Muscle Beach Party, Bikini Beach,* and *Beach Blanket Bingo.*

"The Beach Boys were very popular at the time and we liked the music," explains Kinky. "I cowrote two songs in the same vein with Shawn, who is a very gifted musician."

"Schwinn 24," a parody of the early 1960s car songs ("409," "Little Deuce Coupe," "Hey Little Cobra," "G.T.O."), sings the praises of a bicycle. "Beach Party Boo Boo" pokes fun at the beach party movies.

"It was a total spoof on all the surfboard songs, with the same feel," explains Siegel. "The chorus 'One, two, three, four—I love Leslie Gore' on 'Schwinn 24' was real *Saturday Night Live* type of stuff. 'Beach Party Boo Boo' is about a guy who goes to the beach and forgets his pants. It's highly intellectual stuff," he says with a laugh.

"The songs are carefree, silly, almost impish," he adds. "We were twenty years old and didn't have a care in the world. I think they were written at camp because it was during one of the camp sessions that we drove to San Antonio and did the recording. Our dads chipped in and paid for the production. I think we got 500 45s [singles] for $500. Our dads put up $250 each and we got a bevy of records."

The single was recorded at a two-track studio on General McCullen Avenue, where producer Abe "Abie" Epstein helped create San Antonio's West Side Sound, a blend of doo-wop, R&B, soul, and rock and roll characterized by heavy reverb vocals and harmonies, triplets, and combo organ. Epstein is considered to be one of the early visionaries of Texas rock and roll, along with Houston's Huey Meaux, who produced the Sir Douglas Quintet, Freddy Fender, Johnny Winter, and several tracks on *Lasso from El Paso*, Kinky's 1976 LP on Epic Records.

During the 1950s and '60s, Epstein produced more than 900 songs released as singles on local labels such as Jox, Cobra, and Dynamic. "Schwinn 24 / Beach Party Boo Boo" was released on Epstein's Jox Records label in 1965 under the name King Arthur and the Carrots. Neither Kinky nor Siegel remembers how they came up with the name for the band, but Siegel still playfully refers to himself as a Carrot. To duplicate the four-part harmonies popularized by the Beach Boys, Kinky also invited Joe Kboudi, whom he knew from the fraternity, and Captain Dave Beers, another counselor at Echo Hill Ranch, to sing on the record.

"Kinky was King Arthur and we Carrots were standing together— either behind him or beside him," remembers Siegel. "Kinky played guitar and we all sang. 'Schwinn 24' had a bicycle horn—I was playing that holding it behind my back. When I held the bicycle horn in front, it was too loud in the playback. So I put it behind my back and played it towards the rear to get the right volume.

"We were set up in one end of a room in a small studio in downtown San Antonio," he adds. "It was relatively confined. Two-track reel to reel— if it was high-tech, it was stereo. The engineer room could have been a bathroom. We're talking about bare-bones here. A silly recording—semi-professional—with kids coming in, performing and recording, and going back to their regular lives. There was no King Arthur and the Carrots band and no gigs that came out of it. All there was, was a record."

Kinky remembers that record because it was his first time in a recording studio.

"The record we made in San Antonio was a real studio record—the first one we ever did," he says. "It was the only one we ever did, but it started getting airplay in Texas. In those days, it was a big deal to hear the record on the radio and people calling in to request it. Of course, the label wasn't able to promote the record, not that it was bound to be a smash or anything. I think the San Antonio guy—Abe Epstein—was a Jewish Mexican," Kinky adds with a laugh.

"They played it on KTBC in Austin, AM 590," adds Shawn. "I don't know how that happened; Kinky must've done it. They started playing 'Schwinn 24' on the radio, and kids in Austin who went to the camp started calling the station. The record was #1 that week, was #1 the next week, then fell off the list forever. If you looked at that week, we were probably ahead of the Beatles."

Despite the carefree atmosphere at the camp and in the recording studio, there was a darkness descending on the nation. The first U.S. combat troops arrived in Vietnam in 1965; by the end of the following year, 400,000 American troops had been deployed to do battle. For the first time in history, the CBS and NBC nightly news programs brought the horrors of war into America's living rooms. The antiwar movement had gained momentum, and by the time Kinky was in his senior year of college, the Vietnam War was on everybody's mind, especially young men eligible for the draft.

"I was never involved in antiwar marches or burning draft cards on campus, but I thought the war was something we got snookered into—that we made a mistake when we got into it," says Kinky. "I didn't think we should be there. I was certainly wondering what I was going to do, if I was going to bolt and go to Canada. At the time, going to Canada was a big deal. Once you went, you could never come back without getting arrested. I graduated in 1966 and the draft didn't come up until I got out of college." Held on December 1, 1969, the draft lottery determined the order of call for induction during 1970. Before that, draft boards called men ages eighteen and one half through twenty-five years old that were classified 1-A by age, drafting the oldest first.

Despite the uncertainty caused by the draft and the escalating war in Vietnam, Kinky's social consciousness and JFK's 1961 inaugural address to "ask not what your country can do for you; ask what you can do for your country" continued to resonate. It was the subject of late-night conversations and never very far from his mind. He still has vivid memories of the first Peace Corps volunteers invited to the White House in 1962.

"I remember well the first group of the Peace Corps that JFK met on the White House lawn," Kinky says. "They were a ragtag bunch and he met them all. They were really idealistic, and he pointed to them and said, "You are important people." That was a wise thing to say, because it's true. Of all the shipbuilders and hedge-fund fuckers and other people around, these were important people, these Peace Corps kids. They weren't doing it to get something on their résumé or dodge any wars. Their entire motivation was good and they were important people."

Like that initial group of volunteers, Kinky was also motivated by altruism.

"Kinky always talked about joining the Peace Corps," remembers Jacobs. "He had good idealistic reasons of helping poor people in underdeveloped nations. Idealism was always a big facet of him. I talked about joining it with him and I backed out. He was really mad; he went on a diatribe that I was chicken shit and went on and on and on."

He remembers giving Jacobs a hard time but doesn't blame his friend for having a change of heart. "That was a weird thing, too," Kinky says. "Speaking for myself, I knew it would take a lot of balls to join the Peace Corps. For me, it was JFK's spirit. It was a very good thing to do at the time, a very positive thing to do. And I liked the idea of making eleven cents an hour doing something that could be important work."

When Kinky graduated from college in June 1966, B-52 bombers were being used for the first time in the Vietnam War and the U.S. was intensifying its bombing raids. But an even more senseless form of violence was about to put the University of Texas in the headlines. Less than two months later, a UT student killed his wife and his mother, then climbed to the top of the UT Tower lugging a footlocker with a .35-caliber Remington rifle, a 6mm Remington rifle with a scope, a .357 Magnum Smith & Wesson revolver, a 9mm Luger pistol, a Galesi-Brescia, a 30-caliber M-1 carbine, a sawed-off 12-gauge shotgun, and 700 rounds of ammunition. Using the skills that had earned him a sharpshooter badge in the Marines, Charles Joseph Whitman began firing at random from the 231-foot vantage point of the Tower's observation deck. He killed seventeen people and wounded thirty-two others in a ninety-six-minute mass shooting rampage that shocked the nation before Whitman was finally shot to death by an Austin police officer.

Kinky and Siegel had the afternoon off from their jobs at Echo Hill Ranch when they heard about the shootings.

"We were driving to San Antonio and were listening to it unfolding on the radio," Siegel says. "People were coming out of Rexall and getting killed. The place was chaos. We wrote the first verse and the first chorus of "The Ballad of Charles Whitman" on the way back to camp—I think writing that song was a combination of shock and silliness. We wrote the chorus later, because it was well after the shooting that Whitman's note started the rumor of a brain tumor.

"We didn't write the whole thing together—just wrote the first verse or two and the chorus. Kinky added another five or six verses. First thing I noticed when he put it on his first album, my name wasn't there. I had a conversation with him one time and said, 'Kinky just give me my royalties I have coming—otherwise I don't care.' He said, 'Well, sure,' but I've never seen a penny."

Kinky's memory of where they heard the news and wrote the lyrics is a bit different.

"I wrote most of 'The Ballad of Charles Whitman' here at the ranch before I left for the Peace Corps," he recalls. "I was up here at the camp when the Whitman shooting happened. I seem to remember starting 'Charles Whitman' with Shawn and then cutting him out of it, saying, 'I can't give you half the song, you're not doing enough.' I always felt bad about that, but it could just be Jewish guilt or it could mean that I'm not an asshole. If I was a real asshole, I wouldn't remember it. But as a sensitive person, I've always thought he should have cocredit on that song. That song was never worth anything anyway, so it wouldn't have made any difference financially. It's impossible to tell how much money you've made on a particular song when you get a check for seventy-six bucks or $200 for all the songs you've ever written. The songs are not worth much unless they're a single and it hits, and I never had a hit single. But at least he would have cocredit for it because I had started writing it with him."

Kinky was and remains fascinated with the story of Charles Whitman for two reasons: there was no way anyone could have predicted that Whitman would commit such a horrendous act, and he believes there's a little bit of Charles Whitman in everyone.

"I knew some of the people that got killed; one of my brother's best friends was blown away out of a barber chair on the Drag—he was getting his hair cut," says Kinky. "Charles was looking and picking them out. It was amazing. I talked to people in his class that knew Charles and did homework with him. All of them say he's a great guy, never would have picked him to snap his wig. If you look at Whitman's résumé, you see a very interesting, successful man. He was a very good student, a Marine sharpshooter, an Eagle Scout. He married his first sweetheart. And he killed her.

"There were a lot of interesting things about the Whitman case. One was his confidence he was going to last up in that tower for many days. He brought lots of food and soap and weapons and ammunition—he brought a whole chest of things up there. Security wasn't anything back then. So immediately he was surrounded by all these guys in pickup trucks with deer rifles in the back, who lined the street and started shooting at him. It was very reminiscent of the Alamo. If Whitman had brought an accomplice with him he probably could've stayed up there for days."

The night before the rampage, Whitman shot and stabbed his mother to death, went home, and typed a note before he killed his sleeping wife. His note read "I love her dearly. . . . I cannot rationally pinpoint any specific reason for doing this." In another note found by the police after Whitman was dead, he asked to have his brain examined after his death to check for signs of physical cause of mental illness. The police autopsy showed "a small brain tumor in the white matter above the brain stem," but concluded, "No correlation to psychosis or permanent pains."

"I found it interesting they could find nothing that led to the killings in the autopsy," says Kinky. "The library was in the UT tower; you could go up into the tower to do your homework, get books, and study. One of the guards that was there when it happened told us, 'Well, it'll happen to you.' If I brought four people together and we sat and talked over drinks, you wouldn't know which one would be a serial killer. 'The Ballad of Charles Whitman' tells us there's a little bit of Charles Whitman in all of us. Having a psychologist do a profile of you and me is not going to tell us anything. You could flip out or I could and there's no trace of it.

"That song is making a few heavy points, one of which is very pertinent today. That's why NPR in Portland wanted me to play that song after the [December 2012] school shooting in [Newtown] Connecticut. You never know."

"The Ballad of Charles Whitman" continues to stir up controversy and caused the producers of *Saturday Night Live* to kill a "Sniper in the Tower" skit with Kinky, John Belushi, Dan Aykroyd, and Steve Martin hours before airing. But that was all in the future. With college behind him, Kinky was eager to follow his dream of joining the Peace Corps.

3

Peace Corps in Borneo

"I had monkey brains with the Punans
when we were really out in the jungle. I don't remember if
we cooked them or ate them raw."
—Kinky Friedman

When John F. Kennedy was assassinated less than three years after forming the Peace Corps, his death heightened Kinky's resolve to serve his country. "My main influence was JFK and his life," says Kinky. "The Peace Corps was a tribute to him and it really worked."

Kinky's parents supported his decision, but his friends told him he was making a big mistake. "Most of my friends went to law school or to medical school and they didn't think I should join the Peace Corps. I was the only one that did. They all thought I would come back broke and be way behind everybody. And they weren't far wrong," he adds with a laugh.

When Kinky signed on as a Peace Corps volunteer, he didn't know where that path would lead him. "You think, 'Hell, I'll sign up, see if they take me and see where I'd go,'" he says. "You had no idea where you were going. If you asked to go to Africa, you'd be sent to Africa, but you don't know if your village will have a war or if everybody is going to starve to death. I wanted to go to Africa, but I was deselected at the last minute after learning Swahili."

Kinky's initial Peace Corps training program, with several hundred volunteers, took place at Syracuse University in upstate New York in the dead of winter. Although Kinky had altruistic reasons for volunteering, his first attempt to serve in the Peace Corps was derailed by a Peace Corps psychologist who thought he wasn't serious.

"I'd been part of the program for three or four months and I'd done very well," he says. "Then I got deselected—deselect is the word they used—from that program. I think I told the psychologist too much. I talked about music and the record King Arthur and the Carrots had done. He thought I wasn't a serious young guy. I didn't think that would be enough to get me out, but I got deselected right toward the end. It's like the Gestapo; somebody comes by and calls you in. I'm pretty damn sure it was that red-bearded shrink.

"By that time, I had done very well in cultural empathy, living with very poor people that brushed their teeth with steel wool—really—in Vermont. It was great. I liked that family—it was a very broke family, just poor. I lived with them for a couple of weeks. There were a couple of teenage boys, and I stayed in touch with them for several years. The Peace Corps also taught me the language of Swahili—which I can speak a little bit of when I'm drunk."

Ironically, the program Kinky trained for was cancelled shortly after his deselection due to political upheaval in Tanzania. The abrupt ending of Kinky's plan to serve his country in the Peace Corps left him hanging and feeling ungrounded. It was a dream he had harbored since he watched JFK address the first contingent of volunteers at the White House. But once they told him he was out, he didn't waste time hanging around or trying to make the psychologist change his mind.

"I left in the middle of a snowy night and hitchhiked around the country, trying to find myself," he says. His travels made him even more determined to follow his dream. His determination paid off when he was accepted into another training program less than a year later.

"I got back into the Peace Corps; it was a training program in Hawaii to go to Borneo," he says. "Obviously they didn't think I was that bad, because they sent me on the next program and I became the fair-haired boy of the Hawaiian program. That one I really did well in because I'd done the fucking thing and I knew how to do it."

The combination of training in Hawaii and working in Borneo appealed to Kinky's sense of adventure. "Borneo sounded really exciting, with training in Hawaii," he says. "Hawaii in the '60s was more romantic than it is now . . . the big island was just gorgeous. Black sand beaches, white sand beaches, hitchhiking around the sugar cane fields; it was a delightful place. They taught me Malay [the language] for Borneo, and there was something very compelling about the three-month training program in Hilo. We all went for coffee and hung out at Paul Matsumoto's little country store. At night, we drank beer and hung out with Paul and his wife, Kay, who knew all the Peace Corps kids."

The reckless abandon of young love made a strong impact on Kinky when a fellow Peace Corps volunteer fell in love and followed her heart instead of her plans.

"Connie fell in love with Alberto, our Hawaiian flight attendant on the way from Honolulu to the big island," he says. "Alberto was a very friendly, big, colorful guy, smart guy. We're on the tarmac as we were leaving, and Alberto came on the plane, walked to the back where Connie was, and asked if she'd stay there and marry him. She said yes, everybody cheered, and they got off the plane and stayed in Hawaii. I was thinking, boy, if that was me, I wouldn't have done that, because we were really up for the Peace Corps thing. If I had a Hawaiian sweetheart, I would have said, 'Wait, I'll be back in two years; I'll be back in touch.' That's what I've always done, but Connie didn't; Connie married him."

Kinky called his journey to Borneo "a hell of a flight." After stops in Tokyo and Hong Kong, he arrived in the capital city of Kuching, "which means 'cat' in Malay," he explains. When Kinky arrived in Kuching in 1967, Malaysia was an independent country in Southeast Asia with a multiethnic and multicultural population. The federal constitution of Malaysia, which had been in force for ten years, had declared Islam the state religion.

"The country was a combination of Malay, who are the Muslims, the Chinese representation, the Indian representation, and the natives," says Kinky. "The natives always get the short end of the stick. After that, the Chinese and the Indians get beat up on. The Malay government that controls it is Muslim."

The Peace Corps assigned Kinky a job as an agricultural extension worker in Long Lama, a village of 200 people on the upper Baram River. The distance between Kuching and Long Lama was 320 miles as the crow flies, but the trip took days. There were no roads in or to Long Lama, and no flights. Long Lama was deep in the Malaysian jungle and could only be accessed by traveling upriver on a boat.

"The problem with the Corps is they have no idea where to put people," says Kinky. "They put me in the jungle because I was a water safety instructor and could swim and the whole place was navigated by rivers. The agricultural extension worker job was very vague and a job I had no particular knack for."

The Peace Corps volunteers assigned to jobs as agricultural extension workers were scattered throughout Borneo after the in-country training with a woman called the matron. "She was a large woman who was very nice," says Kinky. "She would make tea. At four o'clock in the afternoon, when it was like 190 degrees, she'd serve all ten of us tea and biscuits."

When Kinky served in the Peace Corps, it was still a fledgling organization with an admirable mission but little understanding of the needs of the volunteers or the native people.

"There wasn't a lot I did agriculturally," says Kinky. "There wasn't any improvement I could give them that might not ruin their whole economy," he adds, tongue-in-cheek. "The people knew what they were doing. They didn't need my help in agriculture, nor did I know much. I was put in a crash course for a month on how to grow peppers and other foods. I was issued a motorcycle, but there were no roads. You had to travel by river, so I couldn't have ridden anywhere."

Many people consider their Peace Corps years to be a life-changing experience where their efforts made a difference. But Kinky's taught him how to rely on his own wits, fortitude, and innate sense of humor to make the best of a bad situation.

"The Peace Corps experience can be a lot of things," he says. "Mine was sort of a soul-searching experience because I wasn't really in a community and I had no structure whatsoever. If I disappeared, nobody would miss me. We had a Peace Corps director, but being in the jungle, I never saw him. You'd see them if you flipped out and then a shrink would come in a helicopter and get you out of there. That happened [to volunteers] a few times.

"In these places, you just go with the river that flows by there," he adds. "I never was really bored. Then again, there never was anything official to do or anyplace or anyone to report to. They had old British newspapers and Chinese newspapers from twenty years ago; nothing is up to date in Kansas City. But there were some exciting times. There was an underground communist party, and you would hear motorboats go by in the middle of the night on the river. There was also political intrigue. I guess the Muslims won because they took over Malaya and Kuala Lumpur."

Rather than stay in Long Lama without a specific assignment, Kinky traveled down the Baram River, visiting the longhouses of the Kayan and Kenyah tribes and learning about the fascinating culture and peoples surrounding him. "They have wonderful traditions," he says. "Children stay up until they fall asleep, children can drink and smoke, and people can get as drunk as they want. They are fun-loving; as long as you keep drinking, they admire you. You can throw up as long as you have another drink. That's a real man to them and there's something to that. I don't have much use for a person that says, 'No, no, I know my limit.'"

Aptly named, Borneo longhouses are long, proportionately narrow, single-room wooden buildings raised off the ground on stilts. They are divided into a public area along one side and a row of private living quarters for families along the other side.

"It's like a little town or village but closer," explains Kinky. "To get into the longhouse itself, you have to walk up a pole, and the way to walk up that pole is not to look down. If you don't look down, if you keep walking up this angled log, you get there. There's a real knack to it and once you get it, you got it, and I got it.

"The longhouses are up high because pigs live underneath them. When people take a shit, the pigs all rush from underneath the long-house to get it. In fact, if you're going out in the woods to take a shit, the pigs will follow you. You have to have a stick to keep them away. Everything goes through the slotted floor of the longhouse. You can vomit through there, everything stays clean and the system works."

Even more frightening than walking up a pole to get to a longhouse are the relics of World War II adorning the front porches that run the length of the longhouse. Called the *ruai*, the porches can be as long as a football field.

"The Kayan tribespeople were former head hunters," explains Kinky. "The last heads taken were Japanese heads taken in World War II. They're hanging in baskets on the *ruai* of the longhouses. I've seen and touched the skulls on the *ruai*. The Japanese were the most recent, and as far as we know, most of the people in the Kayan and Kenyah tribes have renounced head hunting. They are very gentle people, but there are a lot of people who have taken heads. You can tell because the tattoos across their fingers and the tattoo on their neck indicate they have taken a head—cut somebody's head off."

Despite the isolation and what may seem like barbaric traditions, the Kayans weren't as out of touch with the rest of the world as one might be led to believe.

"I met a Kayan teacher who had a big picture of Bobby Kennedy on the wall of his longhouse that read, '*Perjalanan Selamat*, Bobby Kennedy'—'Safe Travels, Bobby Kennedy,'" says Kinky. "This was after he was shot. This guy knew about Bobby Kennedy and so did some of the people. They knew about JFK; they knew Hank Williams; they knew Ricky Nelson, who was very popular; and Cliff Richard, who was a big British pop star."

Several months after Kinky arrived in Borneo, he met a Peace Corps volunteer from Illinois. Dylan Ferrero and Kinky would become life-long friends, but their initial meeting was anything but encouraging.

"I met Kinky in 1967 in Kuching at this huge Chinese market where we used to eat when we were in town," says Ferrero. "I was with my girlfriend, who was a Dayak, a native tribal group. To be funny, she took off my shades and I ran after her, caught her and got my shades back. There were no Americans there except the Peace Corps. James, a friend of mine, was sitting with some guys that had just come in from the States. He introduced me to Rich—at that time he was Richard Friedman—who immediately got on my case about me running around with my Ray-Ban shades, and about my name, Dylan.

"He's talking about how wonderful Texas is and he knows a lot of people in Texas who are making records and are a lot cooler than I am. I'm thinking, 'Oh, my God, it's true, our stereotypical thoughts of Texans—they're loudmouth assholes.' I told him that and we got in this big argument."

Kinky's memory of that initial meeting is much foggier. "I met Dylan in this open marketplace where you order a chicken and they kill the chicken right there in the gutter. Fish, same way, everything is fresh. He remembers a lot more than I do. I remember we stayed in a place called the Nostril, a hostel with a lot of colorful types. I don't know how we actually became friends. It was rocky at first, but that always leads to beautiful friendships."

Ferrero's assignment was teaching twelve- and thirteen-year-old students in a boarding school in Kuching. He says he never experienced the language barrier, isolation, lack of structure, and lack of social connections Kinky did because he was surrounded by teachers and students.

"There were many regional languages but people there spoke real good English," he says. "In Sarawak, fifteen percent of the people were Malay, so we all learned Malay. All the teachers spoke to each other in English, even if they spoke Malay or Cantonese or Urdu or another language. They were all English trained, and the books were in English.

Kinky was completely misplaced, assigned to an agricultural group maybe because of his summer camp or because he was from Texas."

The Peace Corps provided additional in-country training for agricultural extension workers at a center outside of Kuching. When the instructors asked Kinky to demonstrate how to make a compost pile, his playful sense of humor cemented his friendship with Ferrero.

"Kinky's group was supposed to demonstrate to the local people what to feed the chickens to make them bigger," remembers Ferrero. "The rest of us went and were kidding around; we got blowpipes and were shooting darts at chickens. Kinky gave a demonstration on how to build a compost pile that was extremely funny. He called it Fast Eddy's School and was explaining the different layers on a chalkboard. To him it was a joke because he knew absolutely nothing about farming, but the locals thought he was terrific. Kinky put together these incredible skits that were funny as hell, almost like Sid Caesar. That's when we became close friends and started hanging out."

Ferrero never traveled to the jungle to visit Kinky; the two met only when Kinky made the trek into Kuching. "His post was a long, long way from mine; it was way upriver," says Ferrero. "You had a hard time getting to him. You had to fly somewhere else in Borneo, then take a boat. Sarawak was divided into five divisions; Kinky was in the fifth division, where they were no roads. I lived on the school compound in the first division by the capital city. I was not isolated in the jungle like Kinky was; I could take a bus, go to town, see a movie, eat a hamburger.

"He would come down and stay at my house. One time he hid out and the guy running the Peace Corps in Sarawak wondered where he was. He probably felt cut off and lonely, so he'd come out and hang with me and a couple of other guys because we lived near town."

When he wasn't making his infrequent trips to Kuching, Kinky spent time with the tribal people, enjoying their hospitality and learning about their culture.

"The Kayans have their *penghulus*, who are the chiefs, who are very wise," he says. "I like those people; they're very sharp and always very friendly. They've been through Japanese logging camps, and the government moving them from the jungle to fishing villages where they can't do much because there's no real hunting there. Even wilder are the Punans, the pygmies, who don't really have one place. They are true nomads. They travel through the jungle, and they bring in their pork and wild honey, or whatever they've got, and trade with the Chinese, who then trade to the natives, the Kayans, the Kenyahs, Ibans, or other tribes. It's charming; it's very, very much like something out of *Lord Jim*.

"But the people are wise and fun-loving. They have a three-stringed instrument called a *sape*, a traditional lute that is like a guitar and keeps a hypnotic sound going all night long. Malay is the trade language, but they also speak Kayan, Iban, and Kenyon. They're really beautiful people. I lived with them a lot of the time when I was on the road.

"They're not afraid of much except *hantu*, which are ghosts, and bees," he adds. "The bees are the most dangerous species in the jungle. They're not poisonous but there's no getting away from them. You can jump in a river, but there's nothing else you can do. If a swarm follows you, you are pretty much a dead man."

With so much free time for introspection, songwriting was never far from Kinky's mind. He had taken his acoustic guitar to Borneo, so he brought it and his notebook on his visits to Ferrero.

"He had his guitar and was very much into writing songs," Ferrero says. "He was extremely entertaining, extremely funny. His intent all along was to be a songwriter, not a performer. Kinky would come out and stay for several days or a week in my little house and be up till three or four o'clock in the morning writing songs. He was writing all the time. He always carried a pen and a little notebook and was constantly writing ideas, phrases, anything he heard. Phrases that are funny or he thinks are cool ended up in songs or books."

"I started writing more songs when I got out of college," says Kinky. "I wrote in Borneo at Dylan's place and did all through the time I was there. Mostly songs about America. 'Rapid City, South Dakota,' 'Sold American,' 'Silver Eagle Express,' and 'Ride 'Em Jewboy' were written there. Those are four pretty good songs."

Kinky never had a set method for writing songs; he followed his muse wherever it might take him. "Everybody writes a song differently, but the hard part is matching the music to the words," he explains. "Some come very fast, but 'Ride 'Em Jewboy' was written over a number of years. I had an idea and a melody but I didn't have lyrics that would work with it. So I wrote that song in increments in Borneo. After that, I wrote traveling, back when I had years not doing anything, just rambling around and staying up all night. I wrote 'Wild Man from Borneo' in Mexico long after I'd been back."

Kinky also grew close to two other Peace Corps volunteers, Joe Hollis and John Morgan. "Joe Hollis was terrific," says Kinky. "He went completely native. He dressed and acted native: he had earrings, tattoos, smoked opium all the time. He recreated a Borneo longhouse when he got back to North Carolina, where he had no electricity and drew his own water. I also met John Morgan, who was a dear friend of mine who died in Columbus, Ohio, an overdose kind of thing. He was the last good social worker, a very wonderful man. John was very special; he was a counselor here at Echo Hill Ranch for a number of years."

As a loving son, Kinky did his best to make his parents feel welcome during their weeklong visit to Borneo, which was part of a longer trip that included stops in Hong King and Israel. Yet he was struck by how much they had changed during his absence—or perhaps it was his view of them that had changed.

"They looked really older to me and also pretty out of it," admits Kinky. "You could see it really clearly in two years."

"When Kinky's parents came to visit, everyone was saying, 'God, whose parents come to visit them?'" says Ferrero. "It was unheard of. He had us do this routine he called 'the train'—it's like a conga line. We met Tom and Min in an open market in Kuching, and there were eight or nine of us lined up and marching in with our train. We didn't know this was a routine Kinky did at the camp, but they recognized it immediately."

Hollis, who was also stationed in the *ulu* near Kinky, traveled to Kuching to greet Kinky's parents but never made it to the open market. "Hollis had been up all night drinking or smoking joints," says Ferrero. "Kinky woke him up and said, 'Joe, my parents are here.' Joe rolled over and threw up. I don't think he was in the conga line," he adds, laughing.

When Kinky became bored with his vague assignment in the jungle, he called upon his experience as a counselor at Echo Hill Ranch and created a project for the Kayan children. "When I wasn't upriver, there was very little to do in Long Lama," he says. "I had to make my own fun, and did that with the kids. They already had a school, so I started a youth group and introduced Frisbee to Borneo. I don't know if my mom sent the Frisbees, but somebody did, and I used them for the youth club. That youth group went really gangbusters for a while."

Teaching Frisbee to the native children made Kinky immediately aware of the cultural differences in Borneo. "When you throw a Frisbee to an American or a Chinese kid, if he misses it, he runs after it and falls and grabs it aggressively," Kinky says. "A jungle or Malay kid will stand shyly back and not be able to catch it. He'll walk over and get it until it catches on what he's supposed to do. The whole culture is shy, but warm and intelligent."

The combination of shyness and warmth made the Kayan natives easy to get along with. "Kayans had a very easygoing attitude," says Kinky. "If they went fishing you would get *mabuk*—drunk—drinking this rice wine called *tuak*. The word for fishing means "visiting the fish." They rarely caught any fish because the current was too strong and everybody was too drunk. They'd go out with torches on their boats and have a great time. The Baram River is a beautiful river; it's a magical place with monkeys in the trees. One time I was with a friend who put his shirt up on a branch. We were swimming in the river and the monkeys came and grabbed his shirt, started tearing it up in little strips and tossing it back and forth. Monkeys are pretty common; you see the monkeys all the time."

Impressed by the sportsmanlike hunting traditions of the pygmies in Borneo, Kinky brought back several ten-foot-long blowpipes, which hang on the wall at his ranch. "They're handmade out of a single piece of bamboo," he explains. "You can't get them in a store; you had to barter for them up river. The Punan tribe—which is the pygmies— would never shoot an animal staring away from them. They thought that was unsportsmanlike, even though they were doing it for food. They want the animal to see them first to make it fairer, as opposed to hunting elk from helicopters and things we do. They had a moral code and a nice way of life."

Rather than offend members of the Punan tribe by not partaking of their hospitality, Kinky had his first—and probably his last—taste of monkey brains. But he enjoyed most of the native dishes he had in Borneo.

"I had monkey brains with the Punans when we were really out in the jungle," he says. "The monkey is dead, he's already been shot and they lop the top of his head off. I don't remember if we cooked them or ate them raw. In Borneo, you eat all the Chinese stuff, chicken feet, all kinds of Chinese delicacies. The Malay food was great, the curries, the Indian curries. The best soup I ever had in my life—and I am a big soup gourmet—was fish-head soup from the South China Sea. We were out on the boat and the fisherman cut the heads off the fish. Americans would throw those heads away, but they put the heads in a soup right away and salted the rest of the fish and put it away."

Kinky had no qualms about breaking a Jewish Orthodox prohibition by getting a Kayan tattoo on his forearm. He says he never got any flak for getting the tattoo but now has to "bury my arm in a gentile cemetery."

Unlike many familiar tattooing traditions dominated by men, tribal Kayan tattoos are done by native women using centuries-old methods. Dog designs figure predominantly in Kayan art, with tattoos serving to illuminate the darkness as the soul wandered in search of the River of the Dead. Tattoo designs are carved in high relief on blocks of wood smeared with soot or pig extract and then pressed on the skin to leave an impression of the design. The subject lies on the floor with the artist and an assistant squatting on either side. The tattoo artist stretches the skin to be tattooed with her feet, dips a nail into the pigment, and taps it with a hammer to drive the pigment into the skin. No antiseptic is used before, during, or after the painful process.

"The tattoo is pig fat nailed under the skin," explains Kinky. "It's nailed with a hammer and real nails, and done by ladies wearing magnifying glasses. I don't know where they got them, but they helped. They're all old ladies and have ears stretched down from metal earrings. All the older women have long ears, maybe a foot long; the idea is they can fly with those ears."

Taking his shirt off to display his tattoo, Kinky explains the significance. "That's the Kayan tattoo designed from a wood block," he says. "That's the dog, that's the eye of the dog, and those are the teeth. The idea is the eye in the middle is the eye of the dog and when you die, it becomes a torch and lights your way to heaven. That's how the meaning of the tattoo was explained to me, and that was a really cool thing."

The tattoo may have been cool, but the process of getting it was primitive and drawn out. "They wrap your arm in banana leaves and you chew betel nuts, drink *tuak*—which is very strong—and smoke a jungle cigar," Kinky explains. "A jungle cigar is big, but it's not marijuana; I don't know what it is. You smoke the cigar and drink the *tuak* and you hallucinate pretty much and it's painless. It's a very bloody process that took hours. I was lying on my back on the floor of the *ruai* in a longhouse with these ladies tip, tip, tapping with their hammers. It bled for a while. There's a high chance of infection so they put some kind of salve on it. I forget what they used, but everything's done like it's been done there for thousands of years.

"I was the only one that far up the jungle that got a tattoo," Kinky adds. "When you're deep in the *ulu*, a scratch could be really bad news. Any infection or illness can be bad news. When I was in the Peace Corps, I got malaria, dysentery, too. Dysentery is bad. If it stays too long, it'll zap all your energy. I don't know what we did for the malaria. I don't think much."

Ferrero and the other Peace Corps volunteers were impressed by Kinky's decision to get a tribal tattoo.

"I have a black-and-white photo of Kinky white as a sheet, lying on the floor of a longhouse getting the tattoo," says Ferrero. "It's amazing he didn't get blood poisoning from it. Guys thought, 'Wow, that took a lot of guts. I'm getting dysentery and I'm getting malaria; I would probably be dead if I got a tattoo.'"

Spending so much time living with the natives deep in the jungle, sharing their food, and taking part in the age-old ritual of getting a traditional Kayan tattoo on the floor of a longhouse gave Kinky a sense of kinship with the people of Borneo. It also dissolved any vestiges of racist attitudes he might have acquired growing up in the South.

"I'm sure I have been racist, but I think everybody is more comfortable with people who are like themselves," he says. "You have to get past that, which is one of the things the Peace Corps did for me. Living with tribes of people where you're the only outsider; living with black people and brown people and pygmies. For hundreds of miles around, you're the different one. You're the outsider, but you really are part of the tribe and you feel close to these people after a while. The missionaries never do—the missionaries eat their own food, they never become absorbed in the culture, they never find the culture beautiful. They just teach them how to sing 'Oh Susanna,' take their beads and any craven image or wood carving away, and cut their hair. The evangelical missionaries did their best to wipe out their culture. The British did, too—they would take one kid and bring him to Oxford, and then four years later spit him out back to Borneo. He'd tell people how stupid they were to follow the tribal traditions.

"But these people are not stupid at all. They are deliberately slow. Their motto is '*perlahan-lahan plahey plahey twan*'—slowly, slowly. The 'white' version is 'slowly, slowly catch your monkey.' I always say about the Far East—and it's true here, too—if you really want to do something, a brash attempt is usually unsuccessful. So if you want to find happiness, win political office, get rich, or whatever it is you wish to do, quite often it's 'slowly, slowly catch your monkey.' That's what they believe."

Borneo, which lies on the equator, has a tropically hot and humid climate with an annual rainfall averaging from 100 to 160 inches. Tropical rain forests, with numerous vines, flowering plants, and dense undergrowth, cover most of the country. Although Kinky found the rain forest beautiful, the tropical weather conditions were a major adjustment for all of the volunteers.

"The weather was extremely hot and extremely humid," says Ferrero. "During the monsoon season you could set your clock by the rain. You knew at three o'clock in the afternoon, every afternoon it would rain—really rain. I had a wooden house on stilts with a four- to six-inch-deep gutter around it. It would rain so hard in a half an hour the gutter would be full. It would just pour and then—boom—it would stop. If you're caught walking in it, steam would roll off your shirt as soon as it stopped raining. There was a lot of fungus; you were always ending up with something. I ended up with malaria."

"It was hot so you just wore Asian shirts, lightweight silk things, sandals," adds Kinky. "You didn't wear underwear or anything underneath them. It was tropical all the time, which made a real difference. It's hot and dry in Texas, hot as hell. It was tropical there and I liked it."

For someone stuck in the back of the jungle, being sick or injured during monsoon season could easily become a death sentence. Borneo experiences monsoons ten months out of the year: the northeast monsoon lasts from November to March; the southwest monsoon lasts from May to September.

"The monsoons go on and on and on," says Kinky. "Everything stops. There is absolutely no boat traffic, no anything, and it's flooding. You couldn't get out if it's an emergency. That's always a thought in your mind—that you can't get out."

Kinky ate most of his meals at a local market with the men who owned the shops.

"I really liked the Chinese restaurant owners in Long Lama. They were friendly and the food was great. It was like a coffee shop but with Chinese food, ducks hanging upside down. But it is way up river and ill supplied. When the monsoons hit for nine months, you may not get anything but what the natives can hunt around the jungle like wild pigs."

He conversed fairly well with the younger natives, especially Effendi bin Adis, a friend he made in Long Lama, but had a difficult time conversing with the older ones.

"We'd all be eating together, me and two or three Chinese guys," Kinky remembers. "I couldn't speak to them and they didn't know English, but they would take the best pieces with their chopsticks and put it on my plate. They were very, very sweet. Mr. Lee—all those guys are gone. I'm sure they're gone because it's been forty years and they were old then," he says wistfully.

Whether it was the climate, the Asian food, or the lack of processed food that tends to be a staple in the U.S., Ferrero and Kinky lost a lot of weight in Borneo. "We lost that layer of fat directly under your skin because we lived there so long," says Ferrero. "We were all skinny as hell. Kinky used to hunch his shoulders forward and the bones in his neck would bulge out. He called them his Jesus bones. I bet he weighed 138 pounds."

While living in the jungle surrounded by durian trees, Kinky developed a taste for that exotic fruit native to Southeast Asia. "If you eat a durian and drink alcohol at the same time, you'll die," he explains. "They're very pungent with a unique smell. Some airplanes and hotels have 'no durians' rules. You can see them at Chinese markets, like Chinatown in New York. You either like them or hate them; I've had them and like them a lot. They're shaped like a bowling ball with spikes on it. Durians fall from a huge height [durian trees range from 88 to 131 feet tall], and if one falls on you, it'll kill you. You would read in the newspaper that so-and-so was killed at Mile 7 [a location in Borneo] by a falling durian."

The isolation of Kinky's assignment packed a one-two punch. it put him out of touch with the U.S., and with other Peace Corps volunteers in Borneo.

"We saw some Brits occasionally drift through, but I never saw the people in my training program again," he says. "Had I been a certified teacher, I would have interacted with a lot of people, and been in a larger village. But I was in Long Lama, a village with a couple hundred native people way in the back of the jungle. There's a lot of lonely time there. You're out of touch with America. It's not like being in Vietnam, where you're up to date on television, movies, newspapers, and people around you are communicating with you. You're really out of touch, so when Bobby Kennedy dies, or Martin Luther King dies, it takes a while for the news to get to you."

Although Kinky heard the 1968 World Series and the Beatles album *Sgt. Pepper* on Ferrero's shortwave radio, he didn't have access to his friend's radio very often.

"I didn't see much of Dylan," he says. "Maybe a couple of times, but not regularly. Borneo is a big country and it's jungle. You can't fly into these places very easily. It was a real journey to get to the next town. Eight hours up the river, and the river is dangerous. It has waterfalls in places and dangerous whirlpools that suck you under."

To pass the time, Kinky began reading whatever books he could find in the *ulu*, but they were few and far between. "I guess people sent them or brought them in like Sgt. Pepperoni's [pizza delivery]," he deadpans, before answering seriously. "Somebody brings them by; it might be a mercenary or somebody coming through. There weren't many coming through then, but occasionally other people or volunteers would come along. I was reading Leonard Cohen's *Beautiful Losers*; *Naked Lunch*, and a couple of other things by William Burroughs; and John Rechy's *City of Night*. But they're all gay books. John Rechy was a homosexual; Burroughs was definitely gay; Cohen was bisexual. Cohen's book *Beautiful Losers* was very bisexual."

Kinky smoked cigarettes in Borneo but was troubled by waking images of smoking cigarettes, with the cigarette slipping through his fingers and going down his throat. He'd studied Sigmund Freud in college, and knew Freud considered all elongated objects to be phallic symbols.

"I had that image a lot and concluded it was a sexual thing," Kinky says. "I thought reading a lot of homosexual stuff was turning me into a fag. It's very strange I would have this conscious thought of being a fag, but it was a recurring thought: I'm turning into a fag out here in the jungle with nothing to do."

Concerned about those images, Kinky wrote to a psychologist and dream analyst in Chicago who was a friend of his dad.

"He wrote back and straightened things out for me right away," Kinky says with a grin, well aware of the double entendre. "He said, 'This has nothing to do with sex whatsoever. This has to do with your mother's breast. It is your lips, your cigarette, your mother's breast.

You're a gentle guy and you miss your mother. That's all it is; it's not bizarre at all.'"

The father of modern psychoanalysis would probably agree. When Freud, who smoked twenty cigars a day, was asked whether or not his trademark cigars were phallic symbols, he responded famously, "Sometimes a cigar is just a cigar."

Although Freud viewed phallic-shaped images as sexual in nature, the Hindu religion viewed the phallus as a symbol of creativity. Whether or not Kinky's proximity to Thailand exposed him to that tradition by osmosis, he used those waking images to spark his creativity. The Malay name for cigarette was rokok, so Kinky put together a satirical newsletter named *Rokok Loco.*

"*Rokok Loco* was all satire pieces," says Ferrero. "It was like *Rolling Stone* for the Peace Corps volunteers in Borneo. It was extremely funny. Kinky was editor and got all of us to write very funny stuff. He was going to have it mailed out to all the members of the Peace Corps in Borneo. It was real controversial, so they wouldn't let him put it out. One article was called 'Peace Corps Honky.' Kinky was always doing something innovative and entertaining."

"Dylan and John Morgan were very supportive," remembers Kinky. "There were a number of others who were and a number of others who wouldn't touch it with a barge pole. They knew this could be trouble. *Rokok Loco* was part real. A Peace Corps woman sent a poem about her boyfriend who was a pilot and died or something; it was a real cornball poem. We doctored the poem a little bit. It read, 'I still see him walking in the sun on the wing of the plane,' and we added, 'sporting a giant erection.' It was a pretty brilliant parody but it was very dangerous because it wasn't on some college campus. We made 500 copies, and if a government official saw it, the Peace Corps director would have some explaining to do."

Peace Corps volunteers received what the Corps calls a "living allowance" that came out to eleven cents an hour for a working day. The only opportunity volunteers had to spend it was on leave in Thailand. During his time in the Peace Corps, Kinky had several breaks from the isolation of Borneo. On one R&R leave, he took a train from Singapore, to Penang, to Thailand, up to the bridge on the River Kwai. On another, he stayed over in Penang, a Malaysian city known for its opium trade in the 1800s.

"We were there a night or two, and did opium," says Kinky. "I went to an opium den just like Sherlock Holmes. You put a little ball about the size of a pea in an oily opium cup of hot coffee. It was amazing. I saw Alice in Wonderland, people, colors, all kinds of images."

Two other incidents also stand out in Kinky's memory.

"There was a very strange-looking guy who checked me into my room at the hotel," Kinky remembers. "Dylan was at a different hotel nearby. As a joke, I gave this guy a note to bring to Dylan that said, 'Give me fifteen hundred *baht* [dollars] or I will kill you.' But Dylan didn't see it that way; he thought the note was from the guy and he was extorting him," he adds with a laugh. His other memory was not a laughing matter.

"The other incident happened in a bar," he says. "There were about four to five of us and we encountered about ten or twelve Green Berets on leave from Vietnam. The littlest guy was Hawaiian and he was a prick. If you're messing with a group like that, always go for the biggest guy, not the littlest. Dylan had beads on, flowers in his hair. The littlest guy looked at Dylan and said, 'Ain't you fucking cool.'"

"It started getting uglier and I could hear the big guy talking and he had a Texas accent," Kinky continues. "So, I went right over and said, 'Are you from Texas?' He said he was and asked if I was, too. I told him I was and asked where he was from. He says Dublin, Texas. I knew a guy named Chuck who was a wrangler here at [Echo Hill] camp, and his brother-in-law Lou Segal grew up in Dublin. So, on a real chance, I said, 'You know a friend of mine, Lou Segal?' He says, 'Sure, I know Lou.' So we got to talking.

"None of the Green Berets were from Texas, and none of my guys were from Texas. This taught me something. Had we both been from California or New Jersey, I don't know if it would have worked. But it's a real bond. The minute this guy made the Texas/Dublin connection, I knew we were totally in the clear. He was the biggest one there, and he was my buddy in a way different from the other people. That was the mythological power of Texas—when two Texans run into each other, it means something. I don't know if two people from Nebraska give a shit; maybe they do, but to a lesser degree. That bond was instantly made and it saved us. After that, buy the guy a drink and everything was fine. And it wouldn't have been fine, because those guys were really in a mood."

"We would meet all these GIs coming from Vietnam who were on

R&R," adds Ferrero. "They all hated us because we were in the Peace Corps and peace is equal to being wussy or un-American. The Special Forces guy wanted to beat the shit out of me because he didn't like my beads, my hair, and my tie-dye shirt, but Kinky cooled it off."

Ferrero believes Kinky's ability to make friends wherever he goes and defuse a tense situation goes much deeper than the Texas connection.

"Kinky has a natural charisma," he explains. "When we stopped at the island of Penang on the way back to the States, we stayed in a condemned hotel for free or a dollar a night. These Aussies were there and immediately gravitated to Kinky—there's something about him. I've been his friend for forty-five years and can't define it. One of them played the didjeridoo, a primitive instrument used by the aborigines of Australia. Kinky whips out his guitar and plays 'The Ballad of Charles Whitman.' We went to a Peace Corps Christmas party in Penang, and Kinky played his songs with these Aussies wherever we went. It's amazing—people are drawn to him."

Kinky never had any regrets about joining the Peace Corps but found it bittersweet to leave his native friends, whom he would never see again.

"I had a lot of friends over there, much younger people, and some people my age," Kinky says. "It was very poignant that some people, like Effendi and Dave, another native guy I knew over there, would have done very well if they had gotten over here. But they had no chance if they couldn't get out of Borneo. When I was saying good-bye to him, I knew I would probably never see him again. Effendi was stuck there; so was David. You had to leave all those people on the other side of the dream, right where they were. And *playhey, playhey twan,* slowly, slowly twan; that's the way it goes."

Although the Peace Corps provided comprehensive training before volunteers were sent to their assigned countries, the debriefing before returning home left a lot to be desired.

"They trained us for three months to go there and what they did was pretty damn good," says Ferrero. "When we left there was a three-day conference. My group boycotted the debriefing after the first day because we thought it was full of shit. They brought a guy from Nepal to talk to us and had us fill out all these forms. We were out there for two years and they're asking us questions that sounded like they were going to use the answers for their dissertations. I thought it was divorced from real life, so I walked out.

"They didn't help at all coming back to the States. When you left, nothing trained you to come back to your own country. Maybe because the historical period was unique. A lot had gone down that we completely missed out on. We heard about Bobby Kennedy and Martin Luther King's assassination in Borneo; we learned about hippies by reading *Newsweek*. I had major culture shock when I got out. America was completely insane at the time; this was after Kent State [May 4, 1970]. I left the country and was gone for a year and a half because I couldn't deal with anything."

"I don't remember attending a debriefing, but I talked to the Peace Corps director," says Kinky. "He was trying to get rid of me. Publishing the satirical newspaper put me on his bad side, but they didn't throw me out. I did close to two full years; that's a long time in the jungle. I might have left a few months early because I was coming unwrapped at that point, unraveled. I'm not sure if it was from the isolation, or just from not having any structure."

When Kinky returned to the States on October 16, 1969, he found himself in the middle of a ticker tape parade New Yorkers held to celebrate the Mets winning the World Series. The chaos of that historic moment was a far cry from the quiet of the Borneo jungle.

"I flew into New York and then came back to Texas," he says. "That started a lot of Woody Guthrie bumming around, in Texas and in Nashville, back and forth. Hell, I had a girlfriend in Chicago at the time, so I went up there, too."

Both Kinky and Ferrero suffered from reverse culture shock, a common reaction for people who have been out of their own country for years. Symptoms can include restlessness, rootlessness, boredom, depression, uncertainty, confusion, isolation, and wanting to be alone.

"Anybody that stays in the jungle for a few years and comes back will feel the culture shock," Kinky says. "It's like Davy Crockett riding in a car on a freeway today. Even though he was a brave man willing to embrace the future and to try anything, I think being in traffic or driving fast on the freeway would unnerve him. When I was with my friend the rabbi, I jumped out of the car. I hadn't been in a car in two years. The culture shock is very real. When your relatives come up to you and say, 'Well, did they have bones in their noses,' you have trouble explaining the experience to people who are just family and friends. I can see why somebody from a war zone thinks nobody understands that experience except people that have been in a war."

While Kinky weathered monsoons and lived among peaceful indigenous people in Malaysia, the atmosphere back home was filled with turmoil. Martin Luther King Jr. was assassinated, and within two hours, 125 cities across the U.S. went up in flames. Thousands marched against the Vietnam War, Robert Kennedy was shot to death in California, and riots broke out during the Democratic National Convention. But the shock of adjusting to changing times and fast-moving cars would pale when Kinky received his U.S. Army draft notice.

On December 1, 1969, the U.S. Selective Service System conducted two lotteries to determine the order of call to military service in the Vietnam War for men born from 1944 to 1950. Kinky's lottery number was nineteen, which guaranteed that he would be drafted. But returning to Southeast Asia—this time to kill, rather than to help the natives—wasn't something Kinky was willing to do.

"That's a tough one when you think about it," Kinky says. "I'd been in the Peace Corps in Borneo trying to help people, yet when I returned to the good ol' U.S.A., they wanted to send me back over to Asia to kill the same people. It was unconscionable."

Kinky's parents understood and supported his decision not to serve in the military. "Tom had been in World War II and was vehemently against the war in Vietnam," says Ferrero. "His mother said Kinky had come back a completely different guy and not for the better. I never knew what she meant by that, because I never knew him before he joined the Peace Corps."

"I don't think I got a draft notice as soon as I got home, but it was always hanging over your head," says Kinky. "By the time they tried to draft me, I had a phalanx of shrinks and lawyers. I was pretty fucked up. I might have legitimately needed a shrink by that time. I was able to stay out of the service—I think justifiably so; I was pretty fragile.

"Some of it was from seeing how everybody—the Muslim government, the British, the Peace Corps, and the missionaries—all tried to have an influence on the natives. These people survived for thousands of years on their own. Their longhouses should be preserved and the people should be encouraged and helped. But the Muslims have done everything they can to wipe them out. The government of Malaysia gets embarrassed by a photograph of a man with a spear or a man with a blowpipe. They want people to see their three-story office building in Kuala Lumpur [the federal capital] rather than show a guy with a blowpipe."

Despite the loneliness, the isolation, the monsoons, the malaria, and his dismay about how the indigenous people in Borneo have been treated, Kinky has nothing but praise for his opportunity to serve his country in the Peace Corps and to continue JFK's dream.

"It was an experience that affected us much more than the people that we were trying to help," he says. "They helped us. Millions of Peace Corps kids were fundamentally transformed when they got back to America. It brings out the best in you and you come back to America with more empathy for the human race.

"I'd advocate it for anybody graduating college, rather than going right into a job or graduate school. It expands your horizons enormously. You really see the world and see what people are like. You have an opportunity to think about your own country, which you're cut off from for a couple of years. My spiritual bond to America strengthened, but I realized that, if I had to, I could live anyplace. If I never saw America again, I'd be fine. America is a great country, but there's real charm and beauty to the lives of the people in Borneo."

4
Jewish Cowboy in Nashville

*"Not since the days of Bruiser Barton and the Dry Heaves
in Houston has Texas had so little to be proud of."*
—Rolling Stone, *December 9, 1971*

By summer 1970, Kinky had moved back to the family ranch and Roger had returned to Texas after graduating from Northwestern University. That fall, the brothers moved into Rio Duckworth, a 200-acre family property a few miles from the ranch.

Rio Duckworth's interior reflected Kinky's love of Texas history and his irreverent sense of humor. The head of a Texas longhorn that had hung in the first bank in Kerrville, founded by Jewish merchant Captain Charles Schreiner, a former Texas Ranger and Confederate Army veteran, was proudly displayed on the living room wall. Photographs of the Whitmans—mass murderer Charles Whitman and country artist Slim Whitman—hung side-by-side in the kitchen.

Both Roger and Kinky were at a crossroads in their lives. The majestic beauty and quiet of the Texas Hill Country was a perfect place to regroup and recharge their batteries.

"I had just broken up with a girl and graduated college, and he was still kind of reeling from the Peace Corps experience," says Roger. "I'd been in Nashville the spring before and Kinky was writing more and writing more country. He had a whole bag of songs he wanted to take to Nashville."

Kinky's mindset was establishing himself as a songwriter. His goal was to make a demo to get his songs recorded by other artists, especially Waylon Jennings. To include his brother in the project, Kinky suggested they write a song together. "I probably wrote most of 'Silver Eagle Express,' and Roger helped round out the lyrics," he says.

The musicians on the demo included members of Tiger Balm, an acoustic band based in San Antonio. Tiger Balm opened for Shiva's Headband at the Armadillo World Headquarters, where Shawn Siegel told them Kinky needed a band with recording experience. Band leader Hank Alrich arranged the sessions and set up two stereo reel-to-reel recorders at the ranch on a Friday afternoon.

On Saturday morning, the band started learning Kinky's songs, which were taped on one recorder, with what Alrich called "the finishing touches and weird stuff" overdubbed on the other one. Kinky played guitar and sang lead vocals; Alrich played guitar and mandolin; Thomas "Wichita" Culpepper played fiddle; Carl Aldrich played harmonica; Bill Brooks played guitar, slide guitar, and banjo; and all the musicians sang background vocals.

"We hadn't heard the material, we started in the middle of Saturday morning, and by the time I'm packing up in the middle of Sunday afternoon, we had twenty-two songs in the can," says Alrich. "That gives you an idea of how much material was ingested.

"Kinky and Roger put together the material, and I was the band leader and technical recording guy—what mic to use, how to structure arrangements, things like that. Kinky wasn't used to playing with a band, so all that had to be integrated. But they had great ideas and it was a lot of fun.

"I didn't know much about Kinky; just he was a friend of Shawn Siegel's," adds Alrich. "I remember him having a big cigar in his mouth, kind of a weird attitude, and a lot of songs that ranged from being really silly, like 'Ol' Ben Lucas,' to being really tender, like 'Ride 'Em Jewboy.'"

Although Roger was living and working as a probation officer in Austin, he spent long weekends at the ranch to help with the recording. "I was the engineer, and we set up five or six mics and made an acoustic reel-to-reel recording of all his material at the Echo Hill Ranch," he says. "That was the demo of virtually all the songs on the first Vanguard album. We recorded everything live. We found a one-track reel-to-reel we could jack multiple mics into, and it sounded freaking great to our ears.'"

"We did the demo here in the lodge by putting blankets over the windows," recalls Kinky at the family ranch. "Cully played on the demo—Thomas William 'Wichita' Culpepper—and a guy named Hank Alrich, who was a very good bluegrass musician. The original group was very bluegrassy. 'Ride 'Em Jewboy' was on there, 'Sold American,' 'Second Hand Nose'—it's an old bluegrass parody," he adds, singing, "Why do you bob your nose, girl, nah, nah, nah, nah, nah . . . I wish I had that tape. I hope somebody has it, because I don't know what happened to it." After his biographer hooked him up with Aldrich, who had the master, Kinky released it as *Lost and Found: The Famous Living Room Tape* on Avenue A Records.

Kinky didn't know how to find an established artist to record his songs, so he started at the Armadillo World Headquarters, Austin's version of San Francisco's Avalon Ballroom and Fillmore West. With its enthusiastic audiences and home-cooked meals for performers, the club attracted an eclectic lineup of artists playing all styles of music, from bluegrass, folk, blues, soul, country, reggae, jazz, and rock, to cosmic cowboy. Kinky started hanging around backstage, which gave him access to a variety of artists.

One of the artists he approached was George Frayne, who fronted Commander Cody and the Lost Planet Airmen. One of the first country-rock bands, Commander Cody and the Lost Planet Airmen mixed country, rock and roll, Western swing, rockabilly, and boogie-woogie piano. The band released its Warner Brothers debut album *Lost in the Ozone* in late 1971; by early 1972 the single "Hot Rod Lincoln" hit #9 on the *Billboard* charts.

Although Frayne was initially put off by his relentless persistence, Kinky's talent and personality soon won him over.

"I met Kinky at the Armadillo," remembers Frayne. "If you were in Austin at the Armadillo World Headquarters, he was always backstage. I thought he was very annoying and obnoxious until I started talking to him and heard his songs. When I heard the 'Ballad of Charles Whitman,' I knew he had some brain cells and was a really funny guy. Once I realized what he was doing was self-promoting, we became friendly, hung out, and I shared some of my weed with him."

Kinky's single-minded persistence is obvious in Frayne's description of how he acquired a copy of Kinky's demo. "He tried to force a tape on me because he thought it would be a good idea [for us] to record one of his songs," says Frayne. "I listened to it with the band. I liked that he was funny and had funny political songs, which was what I was trying to do at the time. But my band didn't want to do that, because nobody wanted to touch anything political after 1972. I thought he had a lot of balls to do that and I liked that about him. The only way to do a political thing and have anybody listen is to make it funny, and Kinky was pretty adept at doing that.

"Kinky was a hilarious character and a smart guy too. He's very, very clever, very thoughtful, and knows what he's doing," Frayne adds.

Never one to give up on a dream, Kinky spent most of 1971 traveling back and forth to L.A., trying to find a market for his songs.

"I had the songs and I had this quaint notion I could take them out to Hollywood," says Kinky. "The people that helped me were Pat Carlin and Jerry Rudes. Pat Carlin, who was George Carlin's smarter, older brother, was very friendly. Pat was bumming around L.A. like everybody else. He wasn't working for a record company officially, but was very well connected in the record industry.

"Jerry was a guy from San Antonio who went to L.A. with me. Jerry devoted a lot of energy. So did Roger, Dylan [Ferrero], and Cowboy Jack—Jack Slaughter, who later worked with the Jewboys as a road manager. The game plan was to play this demo for these idiots and see if we could get a record deal."

Although Kinky relentlessly made cold calls to all the L.A. record labels, record executives were put off by the Texas Jewboys name.

"They were definitely interested and they all had the same problem with the Jewish thing and kicked us out," says Kinky. "That was a real problem. These record company executives were Jewish and it bothered them. Like the Jewish guys that owned the chain record stores; they weren't going to sell records with the word 'Jewboy.' They didn't get it, but a lot of younger people and a lot of counterculture people did; [they understood] 'Ride 'Em Jewboy' was a badge of honor. Lenny Bruce espoused this decades ago—if you say, 'You can't say this . . .'" it lends power to racial slurs.

"Joe Smith of Warner Brothers was the classic case that famously said, 'What would I tell my mother if I signed a band called Kinky Friedman and the Texas Jewboys?'" Kinky adds. He was referring to the Warner Brothers press release explaining why the label passed on him after his debut album was critically acclaimed by *Rolling Stone.*

Although Kinky's father wasn't thrilled by the band's name (he called it a "negative, hostile, peculiar thing"), his parents stood behind him 100 percent.

"You have to understand Kinky was my father's alter ego," says Roger. "Kinky was everything my father wanted to be. Although my father loved to argue with him and would argue that 'Jewboy' wasn't the most salable name for his band, he thought it [Kinky's collection of songs, including

"Ride 'Em Jewboy" and "They Ain't Makin' Jews like Jesus Anymore"] was the most important American writing since Isaac Bashevis Singer was translated into English. My mother was a mother—she loved him and thought whatever he did was wonderful. From 1972 until my mother died in 1985, she would play all of his records every Sunday afternoon. It was sort of a shiva, kind of a ritual," he adds with a laugh.

Joe Smith was obviously a pseudonym for a Jewish man in an era where anti-Semitism was still a strong force to be reckoned with, and played a major role in motivating some people to hide their ethnicity.

In fact, during the 1950s, '60s, and '70s, and well into the '80s, Jews played a behind-the-scenes role in the music industry. They were accepted as songwriters (Jerry Leiber and Mike Stoller, Burt Bacharach, Irving Berlin, the Gershwin brothers, Marvin Frederick Hamlisch) and as DJs (Alan Freed). Many attained great success in artist management, most notably Albert Grossman, who managed Bob Dylan; Janis Joplin; Peter, Paul and Mary; Todd Rundgren; Gordon Lightfoot; and the Band. Brian Epstein managed the Beatles; Andrew Loog Oldham managed the Rolling Stones. Many record company owners and/or producers, including Leonard and Phil Chess, Chris Blackwell, David Geffen, Jerry Wexler, and Phil Spector, were of Jewish descent.

Yet many Jewish musicians adopted stage names to hide their ethnicity, including Bob Dylan, Ramblin' Jack Elliott, Peter Green (of Fleetwood Mac, John Mayall and the Bluesbreakers), Joey Ramone, and Kiss cofounders Paul Stanley and Gene Simmons. Asleep at the Wheel founder Ray Benson didn't acknowledge his Jewish roots for nearly forty years. Kinky was in-your-face. He performed under his own name, called his band the Texas Jewboys, and wrote songs that skewered prejudices, stereotypes, and sacred cows. Captain Midnight, a Nashville DJ and close friend, captured Kinky perfectly when he wrote, "He wears his Jewishness like a backstage pass."

Even before Kinky found a label, he had an ace in the hole in Chet Flippo, a friend and fellow University of Texas graduate who freelanced for *Rolling Stone*. Flippo wrote a tongue-in-cheek article titled "Band of Unknowns Fails to Emerge" for the December 9, 1971 issue. The article told of a clandestine gathering of "certain key rock personalities" in an "anonymous garret in a down-at-the-heels Austin neighborhood for the first playing of the only existent copy of Kinky's quasi-legendary living room tapes."

Although the piece was littered with anonymous quotes like "That's the most repulsive, disgusting crap I've ever heard," and "Not since the days of Bruiser Barton and the Dry Heaves in Houston has Texas had so little to be proud of," it created a stir and gave credence to Kinky's music. Flippo mentioned several songs by name and included the kudos of a "Coast radio personality," who reportedly said, "The music's good and the words are good, but isn't that guy a little warped?"

When the underground buzz generated by that article began, Kinky returned to L.A. and booked two solo gigs: one at Rancho Park, the other at the Palomino Club in North Hollywood. Although the latter club was dubbed "country music's most important West Coast club" by the *Los Angeles Times,* Kinky's gig at that venue was a bad experience.

"That was a little bit ugly," Kinky told Flippo in a 1973 article in *Rolling Stone.* "The place was full of drunks and Merle Haggard's band was there. I was wearing a red fringe outfit and did 'Biscuits' ["Get Your Biscuits in the Oven and Your Buns in the Bed," Kinky's song poking fun at women's lib]. They hated it and started yelling 'bullshit.'"

The trip to L.A. wasn't a total disaster. Although Smith at Warner Brothers wouldn't touch Kinky's music, his secretary saw potential in Kinky's tape. She brought it to the attention of Chuck Glaser, who was in town pitching songs. Chuck and his brothers Tompall and Jim owned Glaser Publishing and Productions in Nashville, and represented country artists including John Hartford, who wrote and recorded the Grammy-winning "Gentle on my Mind," and Jimmy Payne, who cowrote "Woman, Woman" with Jim Glaser.

Chuck Glaser has Parkinson's disease, which makes speech difficult, so his son Louis Glaser spent many nights with him drawing out the story of that fateful meeting and his father's working relationship with Kinky.

"When my dad came out of Joe Smith's office, his secretary said, 'You need to listen to this guy, because Warner's will never sign him,'" says Louis Glaser. "She gave him her telephone number and asked him to call her that evening."

The savvy secretary took Kinky's tape home with her and, when Chuck called, invited him to her apartment to hear it. Without telling Chuck, she also invited Kinky. Impressed with Kinky and his music, Chuck offered him a deal and told Kinky to meet him in Nashville to discuss a contract.

An established country music artist in his own right, Chuck performed with Tompall & the Glaser Brothers, a trio that recorded ten studio albums, and charted nine singles on the Billboard Hot Country Singles charts between 1960 and 1975. When the Nebraska-born brothers moved to Nashville, they formed Glaser Publishing, which negotiated the rights to "Sitting in an All Nite Café" (which hit #4 on the country charts in 1964) and "Streets of Baltimore," which was written by Tompall Glaser and Harlan Howard and covered by Bobby Bare, Tompall & the Glaser Brothers, Charley Pride, Nancy Griffith and John Prine, the Flying Burrito Brothers, and Gram Parsons.

In 1969, determined to gain more control over their careers and the careers of the artists they represented, the Glasers bought an apartment building at 916 Sixteenth Avenue and converted the space into a sixteen-track recording studio with offices. The Glasers' state-of-the-art studio and twenty-four-hour-a-day open-door policy turned it into *the* hangout for Nashville musicians. Waylon Jennings made recordings at all hours of the night, and a yet-to-be-discovered Kris Kristofferson slept on the floor of the studio later dubbed Hillbilly Central and Outlaw Headquarters.

"One morning my dad's bookkeeper turned on the light and tripped over a body lying on the floor of Tompall's office," recalls Louis. "She looked down and said, 'What you doing here?' and Kris Kristofferson looked up and said, 'What are you doing here?' They eventually put in a shower because there were too many people sleeping there."

"Musicians hung out at our studio because it was against the system—it was for artists having a say in their careers," explains Jim Glaser. "Our door was open. Waylon came to our studio and Captain Midnight lived in one of our offices. In those days, it was hard to get any doors open, especially if you're new and different. We let people in and we listened to them. If they were a little different, so much the better."

"Hillbilly Central was fabulous—it was one of the coolest places," recalls Will Hoover, a country artist who recorded in Nashville in the late '60s and early '70s. "Captain Midnight was a fixture at Outlaw Headquarters—one of the funniest satirical characters there ever was."

When the Glasers signed songwriters to a publishing deal, they offered a production deal to artists with the potential to be successful performers, and pitched them to major record labels. "We were trying to get more artists' rights—for where they recorded, even their own album covers," says Jim Glaser. "When we were fighting our [Tompall & the Glaser Brothers] contracts, the artist didn't have any control. You didn't have any say as to what your album cover looked like, where you recorded, or the mastering of your product."

The Glasers were perfect for launching Kinky's career; as outlaws, they enjoyed bucking the Nashville music establishment and weren't put off by his in-your-face persona.

Chuck says he loved Kinky's "insanity" and explained why he signed him in an unpublished memoir. "Kinky was an off-the-wall character during a time when the public seemed to love that sort of thing," Chuck wrote. "He called his group 'Kinky Friedman and the Texas Jewboys,' a handle that sent shock waves through the staunch establishment in Nashville and shivers of fear through the higher powers in New York and L.A. His idea of calling his first album *Ride 'Em Jewboy* met with even less enthusiasm with the establishment, but the media, and much of the public, loved the whole idea as well as the outrageous character who was indeed a rare find."

Signing an in-your-face Jewish character like Kinky in a Bible Belt town where the biggest industries are life insurance, printing Bibles, and music was a bold move. Ironically, it took three Catholic brothers with the foresight and open-mindedness to recognize talent without bringing their own baggage into the equation.

Jim Glaser, like his brothers, didn't have a problem with the controversy over Kinky's band's name or his lyrics.

"Even though I hadn't grown up Jewish, I sure as hell respected his writing and whatever he wanted to say," Jim explains. "I trust the voice of someone intelligent who is saying things they feel need to be said."

Working for the Glasers, who bucked the Nashville studio system and treated their artists with respect, was a great opportunity for any artist.

"The Glaser Brothers were hot stuff, one of the hottest acts in country music," says Hoover, who was "under contract, lock, stock, and barrel" with the Glasers. "When Chuck got me the deal with Epic in 1969, I didn't know how unusual it was at the time. He said, 'I've got you booked in Columbia Studio. Who you want to back you up?' I started rolling off all these A-list pickers—Charlie Daniels, Charlie McCoy, and Danny Buttrey [both played on Dylan's *Blonde on Blonde* and *Nashville Skyline* albums]. Chuck said okay and got them. That was unheard of. Back then Waylon was pissed off he couldn't pick players to back him up. He wanted his road guys, and RCA and [RCA producer] Chet Atkins was saying, 'No, that's not how the system works.'

"Before Waylon finally broke the Nashville studio system in 1972, no major artists had total artistic control," he adds. "Not Johnny Cash, Marty Robbins, Elvis Presley. When these guys signed contracts, the A&R man picked out the music, and the studio had total control of every aspect. The singer was just a talent. But even back in the late '60s, the Glasers didn't do things like anybody else; they were very independent."

Kinky's original goal had been to get his songs recorded by respected country artists. But when Chuck Glaser approached him about performing his own material, he decided it was the next logical step.

After moving to Nashville, Kinky stayed in close touch with his brother, keeping him updated in long phone conversations. When he mentioned money was tight, Roger began sending him $150 a month from his salary as a juvenile probation officer. Kinky tried working a day job, but that ended almost as soon as it began.

"I worked as a busboy briefly at Shoney's in Nashville," remembers Kinky. "I lasted maybe a week or two. I don't know where I got my money, but I guess most of it was from my dad and my mom. It's a hardnosed business, the business of music. I never thought of myself as poor when I was in Nashville—I was broke. I was broke a lot of the time, but so were a lot of the people."

When Kinky signed the production deal, Roger quit his job in Texas and got an apartment on Music Row in Nashville with country music writer Dave Hickey and Tompall Glaser. Roger supported Kinky's decision to become a performer, but he knew it wouldn't be an easy transition for his older brother.

"By the time I moved there, we were thinking band," Roger says. "He would be a lead singer, blend Lenny Bruce with the Flying Burrito Brothers and Hank Williams and blow people's minds. He had to work real hard emotionally because it was way out of his comfort zone to perform. That was a big transition."

Hooking up with the Glasers, who saw his potential as a performer, was the best thing that could have happened to Kinky. They didn't go along with the Nashville cookie-cutter mentality or take advantage of their artists. Even his publishing and production deals were more generous than the norm, with a fifty/fifty split on his recordings and fifty percent of the royalties on his songs. He was a novice to the music industry, but Kinky knew he had lucked out.

"Before the Glasers, Nashville was a Southern Christian boy network of musicians, a close-knit good ole boy society that didn't even like Hank Williams," says Kinky. "The studio musicians ran the town and the producers decided everything. Can Willie use this picker? No, he has to use this one. Can he record this song? No, he has to record this one. Good Lord, look at Willie writing these monster #1 hits for other singers and all of Music Row is convinced this guy can't sing. Great writer but he can't sing. Put a turtleneck on him, and we'll try some strings. They didn't have a clue, and they didn't see it coming.

"The Glasers paved the way; they opened their hearts and their studios. Chuck is a very good guy and did something really different for the *Sold American* record that reached a lot of people. Tompall had the right idea—he wasn't as big as Willie or Waylon, but he got it. And Tompall was a rich and powerful guy; he didn't have to do that. He was a major player in the Nashville establishment. He introduced me to Jack Daniels—which is putting it mildly—brought me closer to Waylon, and gave me an understanding of what they were doing."

Kinky still has fond memories of his first meeting with Waylon.

"When I first came to Nashville, I was walking in an alley on Music Row," Kinky says. "Waylon knew who I was—maybe because he'd seen me with Tompall. Waylon's driving his black Lincoln Continental down the alley in a cloud of dust, stops, and says, 'Hop in Kink, walking is bad for your image.' Very clever, and for a really big star like Waylon, that was pretty cool. Waylon was the first country star I ever saw wink at the audience as if to say, 'This is so bullshit and I know it. I've given the Big Bopper [J. P. Richardson] my seat on the plane and after that this is all gravy.'" Kinky is referring to the plane crash on February 3, 1959, that took the lives of Buddy Holly, Richardson, Richie Valens, and the pilot. Richardson had the flu, so Waylon, who played in Holly's band, gave up his seat on the plane and traveled by bus.

Kinky knew the importance of image, even before his fateful meeting with Waylon. Knowing he and Roger needed a professional environment in which to work on promotion, he cut a deal with the Glasers in exchange for a piece of his publishing.

"We were in an apartment and needed an office in Nashville with phone lines and copiers," Roger explains. "So we struck a deal with the

Glaser Brothers to give us office space and absorb all the phone, clerical, and copy expenses in their overhead. That was a really smart deal. Even though we were broke and didn't have anything to eat, we had this very nice office in the Glaser building and all the resources we needed. For the outside entertainment world, we looked very successful."

Despite the professional office space and a production deal, it took quite a while for Chuck Glaser to find a label for Kinky. The Nashville labels all passed on him, as did a number of labels in New York.

Meanwhile, unknown to both Kinky and Chuck, Vanguard Records A&R man Dave Wilkes had heard about Kinky through the grapevine and read "Band of Unknowns Fails to Emerge" in *Rolling Stone.* Wilkes was intrigued by the band's name and approached his boss, Maynard Solomon, who owned Vanguard with his brother Seymour. Maynard gave him the go-ahead to check out Kinky, but Wilkes couldn't find him.

"I kept looking around, asking people about Kinky, and wasn't getting anywhere," remembers Wilkes. "Then I saw another article in *Rolling Stone*—in a gossip column like 'Random Notes'—that said Kinky had signed with Columbia Records. That was a real downer."

However, as fate would have it, Wilkes regularly traveled to Nashville on Vanguard business. He had signed several acts in Nashville, and Vanguard artists Joan Baez and Buffy St. Marie had recorded in the Music City. In fall 1972, Wilkes was in a Nashville restaurant with Audie Ashworth, a producer who worked with J. J. Cale and Leon Russell, when Chuck approached him.

"I was having dinner on a Saturday night, going back to New York on Sunday, when Chuck Glaser walks over and introduces himself to me," says Wilkes. "He said he had a great act he wanted me to hear. I told him I was going back to New York the next day but if he wanted to pick me up at my hotel the next morning, take me to his studio, then take me to the airport, I was game.

"He picked me up around 10 a.m. on Sunday and took me to his office. We're talking in his office and behind him stood an old oak credenza, maybe six or seven feet tall. He opens it to take a tape out, and I see a painting the size of an album cover—a painting of a western saddle embossed with a Jewish star. I'm thinking in New York, Glaser would be a Jewish name; maybe they're Jewish and don't want anyone to know about it. I wasn't looking for a menorah," he says with a laugh, "but that was going through my mind."

"When I heard 'Sold American,' it made my day. I told Chuck, 'That's a great song,' and he says, 'Yeah, Kinky writes a lot of great songs.' The light bulb goes off in my head and I say, 'Kinky who?' He says, 'Kinky Friedman.' I heard only one song and it wasn't even him singing. It was Jimmy Payne, who the Glaser Brothers were producing. So we drew up a contract for Kinky and I also signed Jimmy Payne."

Neither Wilkes nor anyone else at Vanguard had heard Kinky's demo tape or any of his other songs when they offered him the contract.

"We signed him just on the strength of that Jimmy Payne recording and the buzz at *Rolling Stone*," says Wilkes. "I could hear his writing ability, and he had an association with Nashville's outlaw elite . . . even before that term was coined. Tompall & the Glaser Brothers were highly regarded. They were rebels from Nebraska, rough and ready guys; they weren't the normal, sweet-talking Nashville kind of guys."

In October 1972, Vanguard's foray into country music made head-lines in *Billboard Magazine.* An article titled "Vanguard in Country Buy" announced the signing of Kinky, Payne, and Bill Carlisle to the previously folk, blues, and classical music label. The article also noted that Payne's "first rush release single will be 'Western Union Wire' written by Friedman." A photo depicting a smiling Kinky with a big Afro and wearing a white shirt and string tie, posing with Roger, the Glaser Brothers, Wilkes, and Carlisle, ran in *Billboard's* "Nashville News" column. Kinky was truly on his way.

Wilkes was especially pleased to have finally found and signed Kinky, whom he described as "a singing George Burns with Will Rogers thrown in."

"Kinky's a character and I like characters," he says. "I wanted Kinky because I figured anybody who could come up with a name like that had something on the ball. The name had already generated publicity, so there was a certain trademark value to it. Nashville labels wouldn't sign an act with a name like Kinky Friedman and the Texas Jewboys, but nobody at Vanguard took offense, because they knew it was a play on Bob Wills and the Texas Playboys.

"There was never an issue with the names of his songs, either, although the publicist had an issue with 'Get Your Biscuits in the Oven and Your Buns in the Bed,'" Wilkes adds. "Maynard didn't have any issues with the songs because he owned a label with a history of fighting against censorship."

Both classically trained musicians, Maynard and Seymour Solomon founded Vanguard Records in 1950. Within five years they were challenging the politics of the McCarthy era by signing artists, including Paul Robeson and the Weavers, who had been blacklisted by the House Un-American Activities Committee.

"Seymour started the classical side of Vanguard; Maynard started the folk side of the label," explains Wilkes. "Maynard was also very political, so the folk music movement, which included left-wing politics and civil rights, fit right into his political beliefs. They signed acts other people would have dropped, which led to other folk artists who were politically simpatico with Maynard."

Kinky, however, remembers Vanguard as a label without the foresight to sign Bob Dylan. "When Joan Baez tried to bring them Bob Dylan, they didn't want him," says Kinky. "They had Joan Baez, who had a big hit with 'The Night They Drove Old Dixie Down,' but in general Vanguard was a folk collector's label."

Even before signing with Vanguard, Kinky traveled back and forth to the Music City, trying to establish himself in the Nashville scene. He didn't know a soul when he moved there, but started making friends as soon as he found a place to live.

"I got an apartment in the building where Billy Swan lived," says Kinky. "He had just finished touring with Kris Kristofferson and his Band of Thieves. He put that band together, so he knew the ropes. Willie Fong Young—an old friend of mine and my bass player—lived in that apartment building. There was a cadre of friends—pilled-up songwriters. Billy was one of the first ones I knew in the business. Another one was Hoover. I met Billy Joe [Shaver] in Nashville—our first records were snowplows to the outlaw movement. They didn't have the big commercial success of *Wanted! The Outlaws*, but they were way ahead of their time."

Kinky has met hundreds, if not thousands, of people in his lifetime and is rightfully cautious before making the leap from acquaintance to friend. When he does, his friendships stand the test of time. He has an inner circle of close friends he has stayed in touch with throughout the years; many of those friendships began in Nashville in the early 1970s.

Hoover is one of Kinky's long-term friends. They still talk regularly and get together in Hawaii, where Hoover settled and became a respected newspaper reporter after he left the music business. He met

Kinky in passing in Glaser Studios, but really took notice when Kinky stopped by his apartment near Vanderbilt University.

Never a man to waste time on small talk or social niceties, Kinky got down to business as soon as Hoover opened the door.

"Kinky just breezes into my apartment with a guitar without saying hi, talking the whole time," remembers Hoover. "'I got some stuff here that I want you to listen to,' says Kinky. I go, 'Oh, shit, now I have to listen to somebody playing their stuff.' Ninety-nine percent of the time it was insufferable, and you had to listen and act like you think it's good.

"He sat down on a hassock and played 'The Ballad of Charles Whitman.' I'm listening, going, God, this is great. He had a great melody and lyrics and the song was funny. I was totally stunned and asked him if he had any more songs. I had never done that before, but his songs were totally unique and I was blown away. So we started hanging out. Me, Kinky, Billy Swan, and Willie Fong Young were always hanging out together."

Although Kinky initially met Shaver in Austin, it was the time they spent together in Nashville that forged their forty-year friendship.

"I met Kinky much earlier in Austin when I was playing at Castle Creek, a good-sized place that has long since gone away," says Shaver. "It was just me playing my guitar. His dad, Tom, came by and introduced me to him, and it was weird, because Kinky was mad about something. My wife knew Tom and knew Kinky's mother, too. We were all good friends."

Shaver had moved to Nashville in 1966, so when Kinky moved to town, he approached him to reconnect. "We all Texans hung together," adds Shaver. "We all hung out at the Burger Boy with a pinball machine that everybody played. I don't think Kinky played it, but Waylon would come in and play it. I worked right across the street as a songwriter for Bobby Bare. I made fifty bucks a week and sometimes the checks would bounce. I lived in Bobby Bare's office. There wasn't much to it but I had me a number three washtub. I'd take a hose bath every once in a while," he adds with a laugh.

When Kinky moved to Nashville, he began using his college nickname rather than his given name.

"I didn't think the name Richard Friedman was a good name for a struggling country artist of the outlandish type I had imagined," Kinky says. "I would have liked being like Porter Wagoner or Little

Jimmy Dickens," he adds, referring to the popular singers in the Grand
Ole Opry and Country Music Hall of Fame. Known as "Mr. Grand Ole
Opry," Wagoner was famous for his flashy Nudie and Manuel suits and
blond pompadour. Dickens was well known for his four-foot-eleven-
inch frame, rhinestone-studded outfits, and humorous novelty songs.

Both Shaver and Kinky found a feeling of camaraderie between
Nashville songwriers, who Kinky says "were trying help to each other."
Hoover remembers it differently.

"For the writers and performers, there was a little more competi-
tion than with studio musicians," Hoover says. "None of us would ever
admit it, but, if somebody would say—you heard about such-and-such
and he OD'ed, he's dead—there was a very, very tiny part of your soul
that would go, 'Yay!' because that's one less. When I got in my car and
drove out of Nashville in 1974, I'm sure nobody cared."

Although Nashville attracted dozens of songwriters from all over the
country, Kinky stood head and shoulders above the crowd. Brian Clarke,
a bass player who later played in the Jewboys as Skycap Adams, moved
to Nashville from St. Louis. Clarke paid the bills by working at a pinball
arcade frequented by Waylon Jennings, and hung out at publishing companies to learn the music business. He had what he called "an early bird
internship" at Combine, Kris Kristofferson's publishing company.

"I was around a lot of really great writers at Combine, but Kinky
was different," says Clarke. "Nobody was writing like that. He was not
part of the Nashville songwriting clique, and he didn't hang around
with other musicians or other writers. He was a very good writer and
he did it in a vacuum. He just showed up with this collection of songs.
He was different but very good, and everybody knew it."

"Kinky mingled a lot socially but did not mingle a lot musically,"
explains Roger. "My impression is he didn't really like the song-swap-
ping culture there—I'll play a song, you play a song. I think he was
uncomfortable with that, whether it had to do with feeling competitive
or generally being less social than those guys. Socially he hung out with
Billy Joe, Tompall, Kris Kristofferson, Billy Swan, Captain Midnight—the
whole crowd. There was a lot of mutual respect. We were all great fans of
Billy Joe Shaver and Waylon. Kinky had a lot of respect from that crowd,
too. They had heard his material and saw him as a serious writer."

Impressed with Kinky's craftsmanship as a songwriter, Clarke
explains why. "He was very articulate and funny, and knew how to write

songs that made their point with a sense of humor," Clarke remembers. "For a guy who didn't know a lot of chords, and didn't know his way around the different progressions extremely well, he still knew how to write songs that worked. He was working with simple elements in terms of the number of chords he could use, and was able to position them in ways that made really great songs. That adds to his brilliance because it means he knew about structure, and balance, and phrasing."

"Country music is three chords and the truth," a phrase credited to Nashville songwriter and artist Harlan Howard, captures the essence of the genre. Kinky grew up listening to Hank Williams, who used three and sometimes only two chords, and was a big fan of Woody Guthrie, who said, "Anyone who uses more than two chords is just showing off."

Kinky's songs blended that basic country music formula with insightful social commentary and his offbeat and sometimes tongue-in-cheek sense of humor. He never learned to read music. He created his own shorthand of writing music—using arrows going up and down to indicate a change in the chords or the melody.

Inspiration can't be planned or forced, which is why Kinky rarely sat down to write with other songwriters. For him, inspiration usually happens serendipitously in a manner he calls "just magical."

"It's like Roger Miller seeing the sign that said 'Trailer for sale or rent,'" he says. "That's when the song emerges. Merging the music and the lyrics is the hard part. When I write a song, it can take a while."

Just as he did as a college student and a Peace Corps volunteer, Kinky kept his ears and eyes open for inspiration, jotting his thoughts and observations into a little notebook.

"If I heard a phrase I liked, I wrote it down," he explains. "We had a bum in Nashville, who was our pet bum and our friend—Patrick O'Malley. He was a homeless guy and a raging drunk. He wasn't a songwriter, but he was a poet who said, 'If there's two things I can't stand, it's a shitty baby and a crying man.' That is poetry and I wrote that one down, but I didn't get a chance to use it. Later I read where a British poet said writers vampirize their friends and strangers. [Country artist] Tom T. Hall always had the same melody, and that's where I got the line from Captain Midnight, 'I love Tom T. Hall's songs and both of his melodies.' I always loved Tom's music, especially 'Old Dogs, Children and Watermelon Wine.'"

Although Kinky wrote most of his songs alone, he collaborated on a couple of songs in Nashville. He wrote one of his most beautiful love songs with Sharon Rucker, who later married Harlan Howard.

"He and Sharon Rucker were good friends, and they wrote 'Marilyn and Joe,'" remembers Shaver. "I love that song; it's a really great song. I liked Sharon, too, but she told me I wasn't her type because she liked Kinky. But I liked them both, and was just happy to be part of the Nashville scene."

Kinky wrote "I'm the Loneliest Man I Ever Met" with Hoover. They initially battled over the songwriter's split.

"Kinky came over to my place high as a kite, and wrote most of that song," Hoover says. "I told him, 'If you want to work on it together, we can, but it's fifty/fifty.' It's all about Tompall holding court: 'Last night he had them in his hand, he had them laughing till they left him with a bottle and a bill.' That's how those things always wound up—he spent five hundred, six hundred, seven hundred dollars for dinner and after everybody was done drinking and eating, they'd get up and leave and he'd be there by himself."

Because he had written the bulk of the song, Kinky wanted a bigger cut, but Hoover wouldn't budge. "I had a big fight with Hoover and said, 'I have to have sixty percent; it's my title and it's my idea,'" he explains. "He said, 'No, it should be fifty percent each,' and of course he was right.

"I screwed a couple of people in my time where I was writing something and didn't include them in the credits for the song—everybody's done that. So, as a result, if I'm writing a song that's almost finished and you make one little suggestion or change a word, I put you in and give you half. You feel guilty after a while. Then there's people like Bob [Dylan] who never had a problem. Bob doesn't screw everybody, but Bob thinks, and he's right, a lot of the songs have been around forever [are in the public domain]."

Never one to bring in lawyers and spend thousands of dollars on drawn-out legal battles, Kinky adapted a philosophical approach, which he calls "a Willie attitude."

"If Willie [Nelson] and I do a song together and I cut him off out of it or do something not kosher and make a lot of money with it, he doesn't waste a lot of time suing me or blaming me," Kinky explains. "He just doesn't work with me again. He Frisbees something else out there. He's always embracing the future. That's his method, but there are some people that spend their entire life trying to get back the money the record companies screwed them out of or complaining, 'This guy stole my song.'"

With songwriting playing a major role in Kinky's life, he made the rounds nearly every night to the all-night coffee shops and restaurants that sparked his creativity.

"At night, Willie and a lot of people went to the bars and drank and got stoned," Kinky says. "I went to the all-night diners and restaurants, which were so beautiful. Just like heaven. I wrote songs and hung out with different people; I did most of my writing in coffee shops."

"Kinky was and still is a night owl, so he knew all the all-night places," says Hoover. "There were places we both liked to go; one was Linebaugh's, a twenty-four-hour-a-day restaurant. Linebaugh's was next to the Merchants Hotel, which bordered on being a flophouse. The main floor was a restaurant and you could get a decent meal for next to nothing. Those places were lower Broad with Tootsie's [Tootsie's Orchid Lounge] and Ernie Tubbs Record Shop on the same block. He would hang out in Linebaugh's, at Merchants, at the Bump Bump Room, which had alcohol. Lots of times we would end up hanging around Kinky's apartment. Kinky never was much of a drinker. If he felt like drinking, he drank whiskey or scotch or maybe an occasional beer. I've never seen him inebriated.

"One time we're at the Bump Bump Room. He had a big Afro and was wearing a big ten-gallon hat, walking around smoking his cigar, throwing out one-liners. He meets some woman and tips his hat to her and his hair is completely in the shape of the Stetson hat. That cracked me up. He would make me laugh and he would infuriate me—he was very combative. If Kinky wasn't pissing you off, he was making you laugh so hard you couldn't believe it. He was like a walking comedian—like hanging out with Lenny Bruce."

Tompall Glaser, a Nashville friend Kinky called a mentor, was another member of the late-night crowd. Both Kinky and Tompall traveled with an entourage that, depending upon the night and who was in town, could include Bobby Bare, Kris Kristofferson, Captain Midnight, Billy Joe Shaver, Waylon Jennings, Willie Nelson, Hoover, Billy Swan, Donnie Fritts (Kristofferson's keyboard player), and Roger Friedman.

Clarke remembers Kinky's Nashville entourage and the magnetism that surrounded him even in the early years.

"With Kinky there's always plenty of energy," Clarke says. "When he walks into a room, the magnetic field of the room changes. He's the North Star no matter where he goes. But there was a bit of a wall; he wasn't a real open guy. I don't think my conversations with him were much of anything except as a booster to his small entourage wherever he was. He had his own traveling village. They just existed in a bubble— whether it was an airport, a hotel, or wherever I met him—at the pinball arcade, the restaurant attached to the arcade, or at a restaurant nearby."

According to Hoover, Kinky and Tompall had such strong, similar personalities that he enjoying going what he called "roaring" with them, hoping to witness a clash of wills.

"Tompall and Kinky are both masterfully aggressive and can be very argumentative," Hoover says. "The word 'asshole' is frequently associated with both of them, although most of the time it was Tompall. Very difficult to get along with, but he's also like Kinky. Kinky has a charming, endearing side to him that trumps all the other stuff if you're strong enough to put up with the shit in order to find the gold—the gold that lies beneath the shit. I used to love to hang around with Kinky and Tompall; they were a little uncomfortable with each other. They were friends, but they were two guys who held the cords—they didn't hang out with others. Kinky and Tompall were the ones footing the bill and the people were gathered around them. Kinky's still like that."

Although Tompall was generous, concerns about the lack of money were always lurking in the background. "Once a week Tompall would take us to the Peddler, an expensive steakhouse, and buy us all dinner," remembers Roger. "It was a fun lifestyle, but there were lots of times of worrying where the hell all this was going to go. You have to remember—my brother and I had no income. And everybody we were dealing with has lots of income, the Glasers, the studio musicians. We really had nothing and it's hard over a long period of time to be around people with a lot of money when you've got nothing.

"At the time, the only major names were Bobby Bare and Kris Kristofferson and the Glasers, who were known in pure country circles. Billy Joe Shaver and that whole crowd were not big names. They were like us—they didn't have any fucking money for anything. We all tried to keep each other going and cheer each other up."

Despite financial concerns, Roger and his Nashville buddies enjoyed the Music City.

"Billy Joe and I were friends; we shared the same Dexedrine prescription," adds Roger. "I loved his music and wrote one of the first articles about him for the *Texas Observer*. We used to do the town together. Nashville was still very old-school. On Thursday evenings, you could get in free for the Johnny Cash show tapings. That was fun."

"To be a Texan in Nashville was great because all us Texans stuck together," explains Shaver. "Waylon helped me and Kris helped me and Willie helped me. Everybody that seemed to have anything to do with me were Texans or people who wanted to be Texans. I'd give them my hats and make cowboys out of them."

Wearing a favorite hat and giving your hat to someone as a gesture of friendship was almost a rite of passage in Nashville in the early 1970s.

"Of the three hats I have, that's the one I love," Kinky says pointing to a black Stetson sitting on a rustic chair in the writing room at his Texas ranch. "Jerry Jeff [Walker] has a hundred hats; he's got them all mounted on things—fucking ridiculous, like a hat store. He gave me one—it was a really nice one and I gave it to somebody I cared about—I don't remember who. That's what happens. Because giving hats away was the way we worked. If you met somebody that was really good, you give them your hat, and they would take on a little bit of you. I had Waylon's hat at one point. Bob Dylan gave me a lot of stuff. I had some heavy shit, but I don't have any of it left, except for the vest Waylon gave me. I still wear Waylon's vest."

The Nashville Texans, as well as the rest of the late-night crowd, would inevitably end up at Glaser Studios after an evening of roaring. Danny Finley, a guitarist who played with Shaver and later joined the Texas Jewboys as Panama Red, remembers those late nights.

"Tompall, when he got loaded on booze, would hold forth in the middle of the night in his office," says Finley. "Glaser Studios was the place to be; there was a lot going on that was fun. There was a knife-throwing area, and you always had Captain Midnight to talk with."

Kinky has fond memories of hanging out at Glaser Studios with Shaver, Jennings, Tompall, Chuck, and Captain Midnight. He remembers crashing there on occasion, and Midnight sleeping there on a regular basis.

"Midnight either stayed with me, or stayed with Waylon, or stayed with the Glasers," says Kinky. "He always tied his bandana over his eyes [to sleep] on a couch someplace, or in somebody's office. He stayed for months in Jim's office or Chuck's office, and then he would go to the all-night restaurants with me, the twenty-four-hour hillbilly heaven—the Holiday Inn. That was where Midnight claims he first met me. He says I was nailed to a cross outside of the Holiday Inn on one cold wintry night. Midnight used to eat the sugar out of the sugar bags like a hummingbird. He lived without writing songs, but he was the inspiration for many of them. He was the inspiration for the lifestyle, and the lifestyle was beautiful."

When asked about his relationship with Captain Midnight, Kinky quips, "He's dead, so it's great," before seriously answering the question.

"He was sweet," says Kinky, smiling at the memory. "Captain Midnight was a disc jockey who had been fired about ninety-seven times and was very, very close to a lot of the seminal people, especially Waylon. Midnight played 'They Ain't Makin' Jews like Jesus Anymore,' 'The Ballad of Charles Whitman,' a bunch of songs like that that Nashville didn't want, and they fired him. He was one of many disc jockeys that got fired, and it wasn't just my music. 'Charles Whitman' got more people fired than anything else. That song is a masterpiece, if I say so myself, because of the happiness of the music and the somberness of the lyrics."

"The Ballad of Charles Whitman" was one of the songs on *Sold American*, Kinky's debut album on Vanguard Records. The sessions for that album were Kinky's debut in a professional studio. He respected his producer, so he followed Chuck Glaser's lead during the Nashville sessions.

Vanguard's recording budget was only $10,000 to $15,000, rather than the $100,000 budget Columbia Records allotted. But Chuck was an experienced producer who knew how to guide musicians to shape the sound he wanted in a short period of time.

Chuck played Kinky's demo to give the musicians a reference for the first takes. After he had the basic tracks on tape, he helped them fine-tune the sound. "When they finished one take of a song, Dad would go in on the buzzer and say, 'Okay, drums up here, guitars come in here,' and shape it to the way he wanted it to sound," explains Louis Glaser. "After going through it a couple of times playing it with Dad tweaking it, he would bring Kinky and the musicians in to listen to it. Then he'd send them back in [to the recording area] and they would collaborate on tweaking it some more. Once they got the base of what he wanted, it was very collaborative. My dad has fond memories of those sessions."

Finley, who played on that album, remembers the dynamics of the sessions.

"Kinky was really, really edgy," he says. "That never changed later, either. That's the way he is when he's recording. There was some kind of buzz, as I recall, spreading around Music Row about what we were doing. The Kinky blitz, managed by Roger, was on."

The lineup of musicians on that record reads like a who's who of Nashville studio players. Kinky's guitar was joined by guitarists John Buck Wilkin, Danny Finley, Doyle Grisham, Dan Moose, Norman Blake, Chuck Glaser, Jim Glaser, and Bill Holmes. The rhythm section included John Harris and David Briggs on piano, Bill Holmes on bass, and Fred Pierce and Ken Malone on drums. The sessions also featured Norman Blake on mandolin, John Hartford and Buddy Spicher on fiddle, Paul Craft on banjo, and Jimmy Payne on harp.

Kinky choose Billy Swan and Willie Fong Young to join him on vocals; other vocalists included Benny Whitehead, Jim Glaser, Chuck Glaser, Jack Ross, and Captain Dave Beer. Roger and Tompall did the voices of the redneck highway patrolmen in the song "Highway Café."

The song list for *Sold American* consisted of almost all the songs from Kinky's demo tape, including "We Reserve the Right to Refuse Service to You," "Highway Café," "Sold American," "Flyin' Down the Freeway," "Ride 'Em Jewboy," "Get Your Biscuits in the Oven and Your Buns in the Bed," "High on Jesus," "The Ballad of Charles Whitman," "Top Ten Commandments," "Western Union Wire," and "Silver Eagle Express."

Roger remembers the excitement of his brother cutting an album at a top Nashville studio. "The sessions lasted until two or three in the morning," he says "My brother had a hard time getting the vocals, but I also remember being very thrilled by it. It was exciting for all of us gathered in the studio to hear these amazing tracks played back on these huge speakers—our first introduction to what was then very cutting-edge recording technology."

Dave Wilkes was also thrilled when he heard the final tracks. But, having signed Kinky on the strength of another artist's recording of one of his songs, he was taken aback when he heard Kinky's vocals and guitar playing.

"Chuck Glaser was a real good producer and he had no problem delivering a great record," says Wilkes. "I was kinda disappointed with Kinky's singing and guitar work, but it was his personality and songs that were so great. The songs were amazing. I'm glad I heard Jimmy Payne sing 'Sold American' first. Maybe I wouldn't have been as astute if I'd heard Kinky sing it."

"I never thought of myself as much of a singer until fairly recently," says Kinky. "I'm mostly a songwriter or a performance art type of performer. I try to deliver the song because I don't have a natural country style. I don't have the voice to do a Hank Williams or a Dwight Yoakam or a Willie Nelson, but very few people do. Those voices, especially Willie's, are not considered good voices. It's the same for Bob Dylan and Johnny Cash. The three of those—particularly Willie and Bob—are not good voices, but great voices. I don't have a good voice or a great voice, but I have kind of a sweet one," he adds with a laugh.

Kinky doesn't have any delusions of grandeur about his guitar-playing ability either. If he did, his friends would be delighted to help keep his feet on the ground, especially well-known radio and TV personality Don Imus and country music legend Willie Nelson.

"When I play a song on his show, Imus says, 'I'm gonna take a chainsaw to your guitar,'" Kinky says, laughing. "What Willie says is really true—'Kinky thinks he's a guitar player, but he's not really a guitar player.' But that hasn't held back other people who play worse than I do."

The Vanguard crew in New York was also delighted with the final product, but balked at Kinky's idea of naming the album *Ride 'Em Jewboy*. Kinky caved and agreed to name it *Sold American*, after his song was selected as the single. "Sold American" was also recorded by Glen Campbell on his 1973 album *I Knew Jesus (Before He Was a Star)*, which hit #13 on the *Billboard* country charts.

"I remember what the A&R guy told me," says Kinky. "I can't remember his name, but he was a Jewish guy, a really cool cat from New York. He told me, 'Kinky, you're an aaartist, you're an aaartist.' He would always say that; he was really kind now that I think about it."

Kinky had his own promotional machine for that record, consisting of Roger, Jim Glaser and Hazel Smith from Glaser Studios, and the publicist at Vanguard Records.

"I did promotion for the Glaser Brothers and our publishing company, and was involved in promotion of Kinky's record," says Jim

Glaser. "I divided the country into six different sections according to radio play and reporters. I did mailings to stations in each of the areas every week, and listed their charts. Roger used my list of DJs to call radio stations."

Kinky was fortunate to have a brother with the savvy and ambition to promote his record and career, because Vanguard relied on the product to generate its own sales.

"Vanguard was not a super marketing machine," explains Wilkes. "Their belief was the artist was so good and the record was so good, you wouldn't have to hype the record. You'd send it to radio stations, and in those days, we actually charged the radio stations for DJ copies—at a reduced rate. But we didn't send out hundreds of records to radio stations. In Kinky's case, they probably called Vanguard and asked for it. So we'd say, 'We'll send you one and invoice you for it,' at maybe half the retail price of a single or LP.

"We got very good FM airplay for Kinky. It didn't get pop airplay, but those were the days of underground radio stations like WBIA. Although some radio stations may have taken offense at the name and not played it."

Roger worked tirelessly in their office in Glaser Studios, calling radio stations and generating press coverage, including several stories in *Rolling Stone*.

"Chet Flippo had just begun working for *Rolling Stone*, and he got some of the early word out," Roger says. "We helped him get connected to the Nashville scene, and in turn, Chet promoted Kinky because he was an interesting part of the scene."

"Kinky got tremendous press," adds Wilkes. "Everybody knew who Kinky was, one way or another. Maureen Orth interviewed Kinky at the Chelsea Hotel and wrote a major article about him in *Newsweek* magazine."

Although the publicity gave Kinky his initial exposure, it was his intelligence, unique perspective, and offbeat sense of humor that made him—and continues to make him—a media darling.

"Kinky had this persona that he carried through his life," says Wilkes. "It wasn't like he talked one way in an interview and another way in person or on the stage. He always talked in Texas parables or slogans. He was like a good ole boy, only the words that came out of his mouth were not the normal good ole boy type of talk.

"Kinky wants to keep everyone guessing and keep them off-balance," adds Wilkes. "His career took a longer trajectory and lasted longer because he couldn't be the apple pie pop star that lasts three weeks or three years. The more people heard him, the more people talked about him and flocked to his shows."

To introduce Kinky's music and persona to the radio stations, Glaser Productions threw a promotional party and invited 1,000 people, including station managers and DJs, to listen to *Sold American*. Chuck Glaser remembers having so many people in the second-floor studio, he wondered if the floor would cave in from the weight.

The name "Texas Jewboys" kept Kinky's album out of some record stores. But Wilkes did what he could to convince the owners to carry *Sold American*.

"When record stores had an issue with the band's name, I'd tell them, 'This is not a negative thing for being Jewish,'" Wilkes explains. "You have to be able to say who you are and not be afraid of repercussions. Kinky wanted to ring people's bells and said outrageous things about everybody. If anybody took Kinky 100 percent serious that would be crazy, although there was a kernel of truth in everything he said."

Despite the flak, Wilkes remembers Kinky's debut album as a big seller. "In the early 1970s, sales were nowhere near what they were ten or fifteen or twenty years later when you had mass record chains and sold hundreds of thousands of records," he explains. "In those days, Sam Goody's and Tower Records were your big sellers. *Sold American* had to sell 40,000, 50,000, or 60,000 records. If you look at Vanguard's roster at that time, probably only Joan Baez and Country Joe McDonald and the Fish might have sold more."

With the buzz in the media and the records in the stores, Kinky was ready to put together his touring band of Texas Jewboys and take the show on the road.

5
On the Road with the Texas Jewboys

"I've only been with two acts that got bomb threats:
Elvis and Kinky."
— Randy Cullers, drummer for the Texas Jewboys

Not one to forget even the smallest slight, Kinky still resented the Jewish record company executives and record store buyers that wouldn't touch his music because of "Ride 'Em Jewboy." What better way to insult them than by calling his band the Texas Jewboys? His father's impassioned objection didn't change his mind. "I told Kinky, 'That's a terrible name,'" said Tom Friedman. "It's a negative, hostile, peculiar thing. If you call somebody that, it's an insult. Kinky said, 'That's great, that's what I wanted.'"

When he put the Texas Jewboys together in early 1973, Kinky chose friends from Texas—Jeff "Little Jewford" Shelby, a childhood friend from Echo Hill Ranch, and Thomas "Wichita" Culpepper, a local musician. Classically trained at Tulane University and the California Institute of the Arts, Jewford played keyboards, accordion, clavinet, and kazoo. Culpepper, a self-taught musician, played lead guitar. "Wichita taught me a little bit about the guitar, or tried to, anyway," Kinky says. "He was a very good natural guitar player."

He also handpicked friends from Nashville. Willie Fong Young, whom Kinky called "the singing Chinaman," played bass, Lanny "Major" Bowles played drums, and Billy Swan, who played bass for Kris Kristofferson, played rhythm guitar and served as his musical mentor.

"Guys like Willie [Nelson] have been playing dance halls and beer halls since they were eight or ten and knew country music," says Kinky. "I didn't and relied a lot on Billy Swan because he toured with Kristofferson. Billy knew what clubs to play, how to put a set together, the ins and outs of touring. He was also top of the line as a harmony vocalist."

When Roger spotted an eight-room Greek Revival antebellum

house for rent in Nashville, he knew he had found the perfect band house. With its majestic white pillars, ornate cornices, and fragrant magnolia trees lining the walkway, it was hard to imagine the fireplaces and ceiling-high windows covered with Goodwill mattresses to absorb the sound during rehearsals.

"Once we pulled the band together for a tour, we stayed there for three months," says Roger. "It was the informal rehearsal. Performing was a big transition for Kinky, and that's why he put together such a talented band around him—great musicians and singers that carried him musically. He developed his confidence as a performer on that first tour from being with those guys who were musically very sophisticated."

Kinky's brother continued to work on the press as well as bookings for the *Sold American* tour. "We had a press kit from Vanguard, but did all the mailings ourselves," Roger says. "I booked about half of the first tour. A little bit with Vanguard's help; a little bit with William Morris."

Although Roger laughs about it now, his meeting with the agents from William Morris was neither pleasant nor helpful.

"At my first meeting at William Morris, this Jewish agent looked at me and said, 'Texas? Jewish? What a peculiar juxtaposition.' I didn't know whether to throw up, hit him in the face, or walk out," he says, laughing at the memory. "I realized I shouldn't do any of those things because we needed these fuckers. But they didn't do much. They set up the Max's Kansas City show and album party, a show at the Quiet Knight in Chicago, and one in San Francisco. I did bookings in Texas and the logistics of setting up the tour, getting them there, trying to figure out how to collect the money, getting friends to do the roadie stuff, getting a vehicle, figuring out the travel and where they would stay."

It was a complete career change for a man with a bachelor's degree from Northwestern University and a background as a juvenile probation officer.

"The booking process was complex," he says. "Kinky played on the Grand Ole Opry twice, but he never got into the country circuit. He was too quirky and his material was too quirky. And the commercialized progressive country scene created by Willie, Waylon, and Jerry Jeff Walker didn't happen until three or four years later."

Kinky has always been a visionary, so it's not surprising the first Jewboy gig was in Luckenbach, Texas, a town Waylon Jennings immortalized four years later when "Luckenbach, Texas (Back to the Basics)" hit #1 on the *Billboard* country charts. But when Kinky played the tiny wooden stage in the town's open dance hall, it was just a ghost town in Texas Hill Country owned by two eccentrics.

Kinky freaked out when he saw German farmers among the cosmic cowboys and cowgirls smoking joints and drinking Lone Star beer. "I don't think it would be a good idea for me to play for these Krauts," he told a *Rolling Stone* reporter as he waited nervously backstage. The Jewboys finally took the stage, but not before Kinky told a friend, "Get your .38 [revolver] and cover the front row."

With only two quick rehearsals at the ranch, the band sounded sloppy and some of the audience found their songs offensive. "Highway Café," which mimicked redneck highway patrolmen, drew drunken catcalls; "Get Your Biscuits in the Oven and Your Buns in the Bed" generated "oinks" from the audience. Despite his reluctance to play "The Ballad of Charles Whitman" after an Austin radio station received angry complaints and threats for playing it, Kinky charged ahead. His chutzpah was rewarded with rebel yells from the audience that danced a two-step while he sang about the UT sniper.

"Our gig in Luckenbach was bizarre," remembers Jewford. "The energy was exciting, but you had a 'What the hell are we watching?' from the stage and from the people watching us. Everybody was enjoying it, but it was a strange energy. It was a mix of hippies and German people and we were extremely irreverent."

"They still tie their shoes with little Nazis there in Luckenbach and they liked us," says Kinky. "They were all dancing around in little schottisches and different kinds of dances. We were walking a fine line at that point; a lot of people thought we were a put-on."

When Rabbi Jimmy Kessler, a friend of the Friedman family, set up their next gig at the Jewish Student Center at the University of Texas in Austin, Kinky was torn between his religion, his family, and his driving ambition.

"I can't be the good Jewish boy and also make it as cowboy star," he told Chet Flippo in an interview for *Rolling Stone*. "It makes it difficult for me in Austin when my parents and my little sister come to the fucking thing. I can't be what I really am until I get away." Conflicted by the stereotype that comes with being Jewish and his newfound image as a Texas country artist, he spoke candidly during the interview. Probably because the reporter was Chet Flippo, a friend from Texas who had shared Roger's apartment in Nashville.

"I'm very torn between the Texas trip, which is pretty neat, just being a bullethead," he said. "The idea of a Jew trying to be country is ludicrous. Texas Jews are basically nerds. Texans have an attachment to Texas; Jews have an attachment to Jewish shit. Both are as repellent as they can be to everyone else. I don't dig country folks, don't like hanging around the truck stop, but I don't feel at home with Jews, either."

Despite his reservations, and the attendance of his parents and his thirteen-year-old sister, Marcie, the Jewboys played for a well-dressed audience of Jewish college students who were either what Kinky calls "Jewish polite" or fawning at the gig at the UT Hillel chapter.

Jewford remembers the audience reaction as odd.

"It was like when you look at a painting and you're not sure, so you say it's 'interesting,'" Jewford says, laughing. "They were polite and everything went over well. But it was an odd reaction; it wasn't flat but it wasn't 'yee ha!'"

Not all reactions were positive or polite. One pretty, dark-haired coed told Kinky his music was "negative Jewishness." After Kinky's parents sent a letter to several hundred friends and colleagues extolling "our son, the recording artist," negative articles and letters began appearing in Jewish publications. A letter in the *Jewish-Herald Voice*, a statewide Texas newspaper, condemned Kinky as a "shanda" (disgrace) and read, "Nothing he has to say is so profound it would justify his selling out his people by putting the derogatory word 'Jewboy' back into circulation." Jewish papers from Tel Aviv to Los Angeles printed nasty reviews, but Kinky didn't care. He had begun to create his persona as a provocateur and was laying the groundwork for the Kinkster brand.

After two gigs, Kinky called on his old Peace Corps buddy to help with logistics.

"Kinky said he really needed a road manager, and I said, 'I don't know what that means,'" remembers Dylan Ferrero. "He said, 'I don't know, either, but we'll find out together.'" Ferrero learned quickly. After Roger set up the gigs, Ferrero joined the band on the road. To maintain his own image, Ferrero wore a python jacket custom made in India from the skin of a snake his students had killed in Borneo, Ray-Ban sunglasses, and snakeskin boots. A wiry, high-energy individual, he drove the band to gigs and sound checks; collected the money at the venues; paid the musicians, bar tabs, and hotel bills; and drove Kinky to interviews set up by Roger. Texan Jack Slaughter joined on as tour manager and jack-of-all-trades.

"It would be like a scene in *Spinal Tap*, where we'd arrive at LaGuardia and I'd watch the bass amp rolling off and getting broken and I'd have to get it fixed for that night," says Ferrero. "Having nine of us wedged in the station wagon in three sets of seats, pulling a U-Haul, and having the wheel bearings going out when I'm driving to Philadelphia."

Dealing with the personalities in the band and crew wasn't easy. "You're constantly dealing with relationships in the band," he says. "With the band living in close quarters, there are always arguments and difficulties. Somebody won't room with somebody else, and somebody's pissed off at something or other. I've had friends ask me how I could go from road manager to elementary school teacher, and I tell them there's a lot of similarity between that and working with fourth graders."

Then there was the hair-raising gig on a snowy evening at SUNY-Buffalo at the height of the Women's Liberation and feminist movements. Not surprisingly, some members of the audience were offended by the lyrics of "Get Your Biscuits in the Oven and Your Buns in the Bed," Kinky's male chauvinist anthem.

As soon as he sang the first two lines—"You uppity women I don't understand, Why you gotta go and try to act like a man"—catcalls of "pig" and "asshole" filled the auditorium. Kinky, who enjoys provoking people to get a reaction, looked straight into the audience and yelled, "Lick my salt block." Almost en masse, nearly a dozen outraged women charged the stage and started knocking over amps and pulling out cords.

"They weren't just feminists, they were lesbians—bull-dykish and pretty scary," says Jewford. "There was a lot of tension and some very, very angry women. When they stormed the stage, it was pretty scary. One or two of them got hauled off by the cops."

"It was a lesbian coalition of radical feminists," adds Kinky. "They were fighting with the Jewboys—and they were winning. They were wrecking our equipment when the police came in and gave us a police escort off campus."

Kinky laughed when the police car escorted the Jewboys off the campus, and is still proud of the "Male Chauvinist Pig of the Year Award" he received from the National Organization of Women in 1974.

The Jewboys made their New York City debut at Kinky's record release/press party at Max's Kansas City, a trendy nightclub on Park Avenue South. Andy Warhol held court every night from midnight to dawn in the club's back room. The Ramones, Velvet Underground, and New York Dolls made rock and roll history upstairs, while Iggy Pop, David Bowie, and Lou Reed sat together at a table checking out each other's eye makeup. "You knew even the assholes were going to be famous. It was that kind of place," said Aerosmith's Steven Tyler.

Heavily advertised in the *Village Voice*, Kinky's run of six shows attracted a sell-out crowd, chaos, and controversy. A sloppily painted swastika or Jewish Star of David appeared on the club's window, and somebody called in a bomb threat prior to the show.

NYPD detectives searched the club several hours before the show. They didn't find any explosives but weren't taking any chances. By the time the club opened, it was teeming with security and plainclothes cops. Detectives demanded IDs and frisked everyone—no matter who they were—under the sidewalk canopy before they let them in the club. Journalists, record-label people, celebrities, rabbis, members of the Jewish Defense League (JDL), and fans all had to wait in line until the cops deemed them safe for a Jewboys concert.

Kinky's Jewboy moniker drew flak from the JDL, other New York–based Jewish organizations, and anti-Semitic groups. Members of the JDL had been involved in four incidents involving bombs in the previous year, so it wasn't far-fetched to think they were involved in the Max's Kansas City bomb threat. But a member of the Jewish Defense League approached Kinky before the show to assure him the JDL had nothing to do with the bomb threat.

"We invited the JDL backstage and they realized the Texas Jewboys *were* Jewish, we *were* from Texas, and we were very intelligent," Jewford says. "Once they started listening, they realized it was satire, and went to dinner with us at the Carnegie Deli after the show."

Walking through the standing-room-only crowd wasn't easy. The entire Vanguard Records staff, Tompall Glaser and the Glasers' publicist Hazel Smith, friends, fans, and celebrities—Abbie Hoffman, actor Michael J. Pollard, Johnny Winter, Townes Van Zandt, and Blood Sweat and Tears—had all come out for Kinky's debut. Noted music journalist Lester Bangs, who called Kinky "the Lenny Bruce of country music," was also in attendance. A big Kinky fan, Bangs reviewed *Sold American* in *Rolling Stone*, and *Kinky Friedman*, a second LP, in *Creem*.

"We were very trendy back then, and attracted Abbie Hoffman-ish people," says Kinky.

Randy Cullers (a.k.a. Rainbow Colors), the Nashville studio player who replaced Bowles when the original drummer took time off for surgery, remembers that show.

"I've only been with two acts that got bomb threats: Elvis and Kinky," says Cullers with a laugh. "Opening night was crazy with all these people swarming around backstage. You had record company functionaries trying to act cool mixed in with underground fans and assorted crazies. I remember some greasy little guy with cocaine in a bread sack offering it to folks. I doubt there were many takers, but, for crying out loud—a bread sack! It was the kind of chaos Kinky enjoyed."

"Max's Kansas City was small so it was an intimate room," says Jewford. "There was so much energy and electricity in the air. Each of the nights at Max's was amazing because everybody in New York wanted to be a part of that scene."

Divine, a drag queen who launched his own and John Waters' film career by eating fresh dog feces in the movie *Pink Flamingos*, strolled in wearing a skin-tight red dress. Keith Richards, his dark hair in a shag haircut and a cigarette dangling from his lips, sat in the back.

Kinky's buddies Willie Nelson and Leon Russell jumped on stage one night, and lanky albino guitarist Johnny Winter joined the Jewboys on another occasion.

"Johnny Winter came up to do 'Fraulein,' used Cully's amp, turned it up to eleven, and blew it out," says Ferrero, laughing. "There were sparks flying out and a lot of smoke. It was funny but too bad, because he sounded good before he blew out the amp."

As electric as the energy was at Max's Kansas City, it paled in comparison to the excitement Kinky felt during his first performance on the hallowed stage of the Ryman Auditorium in Nashville. He had dreamed of being a country artist from the mid-1950s, when he first heard Johnny Cash, Jimmie Rodgers, Slim Whitman, and Ernest Tubb. That childhood dream became a reality when he appeared on the Grand Ole Opry in May 1973. Having Tubb, Hank Snow, Barbara Mandrell, and Marty Robbins on the same bill made it even sweeter.

Kinky hit the stage in a patterned shirt, two-tone pants, a white hat, a cigar, and a lineup that included Culpepper, Swan, Young, Jewford, and Bowles. Kinky smuggled a couple of forbidden beers backstage to calm his nerves. "Carryin' the Torch" drew compliments from Snow and Bill Monroe and wild applause from the audience when Bowles played the final chorus with American flags attached to his drum sticks.

Jewford remembers that day as nerve-racking. "When they announced Kinky Friedman and the Texas Jewboys, you could tell they weren't sure what the hell was going on—especially after we went out on stage," he says. "I remember a tentative reaction. A polite reaction. But as soon as they realized the song was about the Statue of Liberty, they loved it and went nuts. There was something magical about playing at the Ryman in 1973. It was very cool—a great, great moment. The Glaser Brothers played there a lot and Tompall made it happen."

The media blitz and the buzz accompanying the band's debut were just beginning.

A three-column review of *Sold American* in the *Chicago-Sun Times* deemed it "the most exciting country debut album since John Prine's" and called "Sold American" the best song on the album, "a beautiful, haunting ballad . . . as good as the best things Kris Kristofferson ever wrote."

Journalist Maureen Orth interviewed Kinky at the Chelsea Hotel for "Star of Texas," an article in *Newsweek*. She also compared Kinky's songs to those of John Prine and called "Ride 'Em Jewboy" his anthem. With responses ranging from honest answers to Kinky's shtick, the article ended with Kinky's plans to showcase his album in a New York delicatessen, where "There's going to be a chopped liver bust of me, and all the critics can eat me up."

The Max's Kansas City show generated reviews in the *New York Times* and *Variety*, which called it "a most-unusual program as the fun is often biting with taste sometimes questionable" and concluded, "Most questionable is 'Ride 'Em Jewboy' with its veiled concentration camp references." Many critics and audiences didn't know what to make of an in-your-face Jewish country artist performing songs that included both irreverent, laugh-out-loud humor and serious social commentary. With his humorous songs overshadowing his poetic and serious songs, Kinky was cast into a narrow stereotypical category his audiences, as well as the media, had trouble getting around.

"Kinky had been worried about being a novelty act . . . he was afraid he was going to get caught up in the *My Son, the Folksinger* genre," Danny Finley says, alluding to the live comedy album by Allan Sherman filled with Jewish culture references. "He wanted to avoid that but still felt compelled to write more of those songs, like 'They Ain't Makin Jews like Jesus Anymore.' People loved it, they were great songs, but it was self-limiting. These songs, good as they were, overshadowed 'Wild Man from Borneo,' for instance, which is brilliant *and* more universal."

"I never found any of his songs offensive; I thought they detracted from his other material," adds Dylan Ferrero. "I got a lot of feedback from club owners and from watching the audience response. They would crack up, and they couldn't turn around and follow something more poignant with serious lyrics because they had difficulty changing gears. Kinky would do a song like 'Asshole from El Paso' and follow it up with 'Ride 'Em Jewboy.' They're laughing at 'Ride 'Em Jewboy'—not getting that this is a song about the Holocaust. For years Kinky would insist on doing songs I didn't like. He still insists on doing 'Ol' Ben Lucas.' I think it's a shitty song but he gets a laugh out of the audience."

When asked if humor hurt his career as an artist and a songwriter, Kinky doesn't hesitate. "Absolutely—it killed it," he says. "I call it the curse of being multitalented. We do not accept a hockey player who's also a concert pianist—we don't think he can be any good. Once we accept somebody in one category—once you think Kinky is outrageous and funny, it's hard to take him seriously. Humor doesn't sell, and if it does, it's very limited. What sells is a serious guy, whatever the fuck he is; a guy who is caught up in his own bullshit. Self-pity sells. Warren Zevon and I tried humor. Warren wrote some really beautiful songs and his really beautiful stuff was downgraded because of his humor. If I had to depend on the [money from the] music, I would not be here—you'd be talking to a skeleton in a cowboy hat and a cigar."

Kinky never had a problem getting press; it was the lack of airplay that kept him in clubs rather than larger venues. According to the manager of Max's Kansas City, Kinky had more print media than the Rolling Stones, but you still couldn't hear his music on the radio.

"The exposure was there and the hip people in every town came out to see what it was all about," explains Kinky. "Part of the problem was me; part of it was there was really nobody working the songs. 'Sold American' was top ten all around the country. But it wasn't what it could have been—it should have been a mainstream hit. The honest-to-God truth is, if you think about it—or, as Willie says, if you look it straight in the eye—there wasn't going to be any big commercial success there. The Jewboys were playing songs that went completely over or under the heads of most of the people in the country.

"I was just successful enough as an artist not to be taken seriously as a songwriter," he adds. "I got the songs out there. People knew about them and talked about them—especially 'They Ain't Makin' Jews like Jesus Anymore.' But they missed 'Rapid City, South Dakota' and 'Wild Man from Borneo.' My lyrics were a little too sophisticated for Nashville and the music wasn't that well understood in New York, which did get the lyrics."

As he had done even at the age of ten with "White Citizens Council Marching Song," Kinky used songwriting as social and political commentary.

"Bob Dylan told me he originally picked up a guitar to get laid—I did not," he says. "I have a lot of friends in the band who would fuck some waitress or some patron every single night. That's what they did, like smoking cigarettes. I got into music because I wanted to express my ideas," he says bursting out in laughter, embarrassed by the admission. "It's ridiculous.

"I'm not playing just to get laid," he continues. "If you notice songs, most of them—whether it's Bob Dylan or Leonard Cohen, or Tom Petty or Neil Young—are aimed at women. Mine were social commentary; I was writing with a social conscience. There were some love songs—'Marilyn and Joe,' 'Lady Yesterday'—but they got lost. Kris's songs, with the exception of 'Billy Dee' and a few others, are songs written to women. My songs weren't written to women; my songs are stories. 'Rapid City, South Dakota' is a story about this kid that knocks up this chick and leaves. I've been that kid; I know that story."

Kinky's most haunting song—"Ride 'Em Jewboy"—tells the story of the Holocaust with vivid imagery and poignant lyrics. Intrigued by the song and eager to meet the artist who wrote it, Bob Dylan wandered into the club barefoot and wearing a white robe before Kinky's show at the Troubadour in L.A. Intimidated by Dylan's unexpected appearance, Ferrero downed a quick drink before offering to take him to the dressing room. Not wanting his presence to affect the band's performance, Dylan said he'd rather meet Kinky after the show.

"I go upstairs not saying a word, and Kinky looks at me and says, 'I hear Bob Dylan is here,'" says Ferrero. "Bob Dylan came up after the show. He's very, very short, and without his boots, he's really short. I'm only five foot eight and I'm taller than him. Our band was very intimidated by him—everyone is intimidated by his presence. But he liked the show, and Kinky and I shot the bull with him and had a lot of fun."

Several weeks later, Dylan's people called Kinky so he could hook up with Bob at a party at Roger McGuinn's house at the end of Point Dume overlooking Zuma Beach in Malibu. To keep the exact location under wraps, they instructed Kinky to meet them late at night at the end of the Santa Monica pier, where he'd be picked up by a blue 1962 Cadillac convertible and driven to the party.

"We went on a long, winding route and Kinky says, 'Maybe we're going to Charlie Manson's house'—it was very scary in the middle of the night—right out of the movies," says Ferrero. "The house had a big wrought iron gate that opened electrically. When we walked into the kitchen, Bob Dylan is sitting on the kitchen counter. He sees Kinky and starts playing 'Ride 'Em Jewboy'—it was a mindblower. He hands Kinky the guitar and Kinky says, 'This isn't a hootenanny. What am I supposed to do? Play one of your songs? I'm not like Kristofferson or one of those guys.'"

Kinky has a much vaguer recollection.

"I don't remember much of it except getting in a baby blue Cadillac convertible, driving all around, and finally ended up at Roger McGuinn's house. I do remember seeing Kris there with a groupie. Kris said, 'Kinky,' and the girl and I both said, 'Yeah.' That was funny. Bob was in the kitchen, drunk, singing 'Ride 'Em Jewboy.' He asked me to play, but I didn't—I had kind of an attitudinal problem."

Much of Kinky's "attitudinal problem" is caused by his "best defense is a good offense" way of dealing with situations that make him uncomfortable. Kinky only knew three chords; Dylan's songs have at least five. It was his inability to play Dylan's songs and his fear of looking foolish in front of his hero that caused his rude reaction.

Refusing to miss even a minute of that night's surreal experience, Ferrero stayed in the kitchen with Dylan after Kinky walked out.

"After Kinky left, Kris Kristofferson walks into the kitchen," Ferrero recalls. "Then everyone walks out and it's me and Bob Dylan, and he starts talking to me about doing something meaningful. He says, 'I don't know, man. I got to get him into it. Nobody's saying anything with their music; nobody's doing anything. What are they doing? Seeing how many people they can get into a Volkswagen? I'll tell you what's wrong, man. It's post-World War II existentialism. There are too many people here into existentialism.'"

A drunken Roger McGuinn soon staggered in and admonished Dylan for laying his familiar rant on Ferrero. "McGuinn says, 'He doesn't need any of that shit,'" remembers Ferrero. "When I turned around to talk to Bob, he was on the floor—completely conked out. A couple of guys had to haul him off to his bedroom."

Although it couldn't compare to meeting Dylan, Kinky's other West Coast dates provided a wild mix of excitement and celebrities. In August, after a week of successful gigs in the Bay Area with Commander Cody, the band played a live show at the Record Plant recording studio in Sausalito for an audience that included Ken Kesey and Jerry Garcia. That show was broadcast on KSAN-FM on *Live from the Plant*, a Sunday night radio show that featured popular artists, including the Grateful Dead, Peter Frampton, Jimmy Buffett, Bonnie Raitt, and Fleetwood Mac. It was a prestigious gig with great exposure.

Jewford released that performance as *Mayhem Aforethought* on his Sphincter Records label in 2005. Dubbed a unique time capsule that allows the listener to travel back to 1973 and hear a complete, uncut, and uncensored performance of Kinky Friedman and the Texas Jew-boys, the show opens with the theme song from *Exodus*, a 1960 epic film on the birth of Israel. That theme song became Kinky's musical intro and followed him into the mid-'80s.

Mayhem Aforethought is also a time capsule of Kinky talking with a thick country hick accent. Although Kinky was "struck by it too" after listening to the CD years later, he wasn't quite sure where his accent came from. Roger pegs it to their time in the Music City.

"The recording at KSAN at Berkeley was the band at its best," says Roger. "A great fucking show. The band and Kinky wanted to make a big splash, and Pacifica underground radio was *the* early FM world. Kinky maintained a Nashville country demeanor throughout. Some of it was put on; some of it was real. At that time, he wanted to keep his persona connected to the traditional country music world."

Jewford remembers the celebrities in the KSAN studio. "I walked in and went, 'Wow, that's Jerry Garcia, and there's Ken Kesey leaning back in a chair holding court with some people,'" he says. "We had played a gig or two in San Francisco and there was a buzz surrounding those shows. Garcia lived in town, and Ken Kesey came in from Oregon, where his Merry Pranksters lived in a commune. We heard they wanted to meet us and vice versa, but we didn't meet them because they were gone when we finished."

Like the crash that follows snorting a good line of cocaine—which had not yet come into the picture—that high was followed by a gig with the club owner refusing to pay because the band didn't draw a large audience. Ferrero found out where he lived and showed up at his door the next day.

"I had to be super aggressive as a road manager," Ferrero says. "When we got stiffed, I went to the owner's house in L.A. to get the money. My python jacket and shades served me well. Kinky gave the impression I was his bodyguard and people thought I was a tough guy carrying heat. If I acted like that now I'd be gunned down."

That ugly incident was quickly forgotten when Kinky and Ferrero spent a few nights at the infamous Continental Hyatt House on Sunset Strip in L.A. before returning to the ranch to regroup. A favorite haunt of rock stars, the hotel was dubbed the Riot House after Led Zeppelin rode Harleys down the hallway, tossed TVs out the windows, and hosted orgies with drugged-out groupies.

When Kinky resumed that tour with dates in Nashville and Dallas in mid-October, Chet Flippo chronicled his journey in a *Rolling Stone* article titled "One Week in the Life of Kinky Friedman: Triumph at the Opry, Showdown in Big D." Kinky's initial Nashville gig was opening for Jerry Lee Lewis at the 27,000-seat stadium at Vanderbilt University. Having just come out on the losing end of a bar brawl with Arkansas rednecks in Memphis, Lewis didn't look like much of a killer when he took the stage.

"He was wearing bandages; he either got beat up or he got married again, I don't remember which," says Jewford.

"Jerry Lee came out with a splint on his nose—the word was he had been in a bar fight the night before," remembers Ferrero. "We were cracking up because he was leaning back at the piano and playing with his foot with all these bandages on."

After the show, the six band members and three-person crew squeezed into their faded gold 1971 Plymouth Satellite station wagon. Stuffing the band's instruments and equipment into a rented U-Haul, they embarked on the grueling 670-mile trek to Dallas for the next gig. What should have been a ten-hour drive took more than twelve hours because the U-Haul wobbled and threatened to tip over if they went faster than sixty miles per hour.

When a cranky and exhausted Kinky walked into the tiny office to get the key to his one-star motel room, a Dallas TV crew approached him about filming a "Day in the Life of Kinky Friedman" segment for a feature story. Kinky immediately perked up. Thrilled to get TV coverage, he invited the crew to his gig at The Western Place, a country-and-western bar with four pool tables and a big dance floor. The Jewboys delivered a balls-to-the-wall first set for an appreciative audience, including several Dallas Cowboys. Although Kinky's not much of a football fan, he couldn't help smiling when wide receiver and two-time Olympic gold medalist Bob Hayes stopped him on the way to the dressing room to say how much he had enjoyed the show.

That crowd-pleasing set included Kinky's joke, "I never say fuck in front of a C H I L D." The audience cracked up, but Vernon Gatlin, a good ole boy in a suit and tie who owned the club, was livid about Kinky's use of profanity. Gatlin stormed into the dressing room and screamed into Kinky's face.

"You can't talk like that," he yelled. "There's a place for your act, but not this place. We have kids come out here all the time; and families and Christian people come into this club all the time, not that you're not Christian. I don't know what you are . . . But y'all better get the hell out of my club unless you clean up your act."

When Kinky responded with silence and a penetrating stare, Jewford knew the Jewboys would be packing up and leaving early.

"Dylan said, 'We're not playing anymore tonight; get in the car quick,'" remembers Jewford. "Kinky was pissed and said, 'I'm not changing anything for anybody.'"

Before they left, Ferrero made sure Gatlin knew he was holding him to the band's three-night contract that called for two sets a night and paid $6,000.

"I whipped the contract out of my pocket and said, 'It doesn't say a fucking thing in there about saying the word "fuck"—you owe me money,'" recalls Ferrero with a grin. "The guy blanched, but he met me at his bank the next morning and paid us in full."

Although that gig turned into what Kinky calls a "tension convention," serendipity in the guise of the club manager led to an introduction to Willie Nelson and a friendship that's lasted forty-plus years. The club manager, who liked Kinky's act, called Willie from the dressing room and handed Kinky the phone. That impromptu conversation led to an invitation to visit Willie at his home. Willie enjoyed Kinky's music and sense of humor and invited the band to perform at Willie's Homecoming Concert in Abbott, Texas, in November. Having Willie's blessing and playing the forerunner of his Fourth of July Picnic concerts was an amazing break and great exposure. When Kinky performed for 10,000 country music fans in a lineup including Waylon Jennings, Billy Joe Shaver, and Jerry Jeff Walker, he felt like he was finally on his way.

Three-night gigs at a venue were common in the 1970s. Hippies and cosmic cowboys loved the Jewboys at the Liberty Hall in Houston and the Armadillo World Headquarters in Austin. The band wasn't so blessed in Temple, Texas.

"I don't think it was a specific joke, but for some reason I only got half the money," says Ferrero. "Kinky was furious. I told him it was the owner, not the manager, but he didn't give a shit. He said, 'The guy's an asshole.'"

In October 1973, Kinky resurrected his role of civil rights activist by bringing Dobie Gray as his special guest to his performance on the Grand Ole Gospel Show in Nashville. His attempt to integrate his fraternity at the University of Texas ten years earlier had failed, but now he had the clout to bring a black artist to center stage. Prior to that, only two black artists had performed on the Grand Opry stage—Deford Bailey, who played harmonica for the Opry from 1927 to 1941, and Charlie Pride, who wasn't invited until he won a Grammy in 1967.

Country artist Tex Ritter, who had appeared in fifty-plus "singing cowboy" movies, was a founding member of the Country Music Association, and had been inducted into the Country Music Hall of Fame, wasn't thrilled with Gray's inclusion on the bill. When he ran into Hazel Smith backstage, he didn't attempt to mask his feelings about Kinky or Gray, whose single "Drift Away" was #5 on the Billboard charts.

"So you work for Kinky, do you?" he said. "I thought you'd be Jewish or in blackface. Kinky's a fine boy, though. But he ain't homegrown and sugar-cured Texas. He went up to Chicago and came back like that other Texan—the one that killed the guy that killed Kennedy . . . Jack Ruby."

Jewford wasn't surprised by Ritter's comment.

"There was a black and Jew thing with rednecks in Nashville in 1973, and religious tensions were very prominent," he says. "I let some of that stuff bounce off. Being the only other Jew in the band—the guy named Little Jewford—I had to have a lot of Teflon around me. I had to smile a lot during many of those instances. It's the way the world was in 1973—especially if you're pushing the envelope at all levels."

Unaware of Ritter's comment, Kinky was nervously pacing in the dressing room, drinking a beer, and flinging handfuls of silver glitter over Swan and Gray while they rehearsed "High on Jesus." When Reverend Jimmy Snow introduced him as "the first full-blooded Jew to ever appear on the Grand Ole Opry," and his band as the "Texas Jews," the predominantly Baptist audience didn't know what to expect.

"The reaction was, 'Who are these people, and why are they here?' and 'We're religious and we don't know if we like Jews or not,'" says Jewford. "But once we began singing the chorus to 'High on Jesus,' the crowd went nuts and it didn't matter what the rest of the lyrics were."

As to whether "High on Jesus" is a serious song or satire poking fun at fundamentalist religion, Kinky's response is cryptic.

"The answer is both," he says, pausing to relight his cigar. "You come to see what you want to see. Quite often, what's written between the lines or left to the imagination is the most important thing. I'm not a 'Jews for Jesus' or a guy like that, but Jesus is a hero of mine. I always thought Moses and Jesus were two good Jewish boys who got into a little trouble with the government."

Although Kinky doesn't always enjoy talking about his past, he still has fond memories of that performance and of the Temple Evangelical Choir.

"The Reverend Jimmy Snow had a choir made up of large-busted women," he says laughing. "There were about a dozen of them, very religious, and very out-there fundamentalist. We went over very well and were coming off stage when one of the women grabbed Dobie. She hugged him and hung onto him and said—I remember exactly what she said—'Honey, you were pure nigger and I love you.' That was nice. So we had our first full-blooded Jew and Dobie Gray."

But the Reverend's remark after the show reflected the true Nashville mindset. "He came up to Kinky and said, 'This is the first time we're having a real live Jew and a nigger play at the Grand Ole Opry,'" says Ferrero.

High on the buzz from that performance, Kinky headed to Hillbilly Central the next day to record a single and fulfill yet another dream. With Waylon Jennings producing, Kinky was confident his "Carryin' the Torch" single would top the charts. But he's forgotten or purposely repressed any memory of that session, and Ferrero's memory is sketchy.

"I think it was one of those 'in and out the door quickly' things," says Ferrero. "Although it's somewhat of a blur, we were all very excited about Waylon coming over to the Glaser Studio to work on it." Whether it was internal struggles among the Glaser brothers or the lack of support from the Vanguard label, that single was never released.

Talent buyers aren't always familiar with the artists they book; hence the legendary mismatch of Jimi Hendrix as the opening act for the 1967 Monkees tour. The Jewboys opening for Mott the Hoople, a British glam rock band with cascading hair and thigh-high boots, was another incongruous pairing. Ian Hunter, who strutted in a sequined black velvet suit when he sang "All the Young Dudes," was infuriated.

"I was checking the mike at sound check when this very tall guy with big hair and a British accent comes out screaming," says Ferrero. "He's yelling, 'America is such a country of extremes—why do you have these cowboys playing country music opening for a rock band?' I said, 'Well it's like Cliff Richard and Keith Richards—don't you think that's an extreme?' He just glared at me and walked off in his platform shoes."

An equally odd pairing was Billy Joel opening for Kinky when he returned to Max's in November for another six-night run. Joel's debut single "Piano Man" had become a big hit, and he'd just come off the road as an opening act at coliseums. But Joel's agent had booked the gig a year earlier and couldn't get him out of the contract.

When Clive Davis, the president of Columbia Records, joined Joel in the dressing room, Kinky wasn't impressed with either of them.

"Clive Davis came over to me and said, 'You know you guys are going to make it,'" recalls Kinky, who resents Davis for signing Joel but passing on the Jewboys. "Billy Joel was busy blow-drying his hair."

He wasn't the only bitter performer at that gig. "Billy Joel was furious and wouldn't even talk to us," says Ferrero. "When Willie Fong Young ran into him on the street months later, he apologized, saying he had been doing two sets a night at small clubs and was exhausted."

Perhaps. But it's more likely he resented being upstaged by Kinky and his raucous fans.

"Sadly for Billy, the appearance of Kinky in New York drew out all the underground fans and assorted rowdy crazy people who didn't give a damn about Billy Joel or his piano," says Cullers. "Abbie Hoffman was one of the rowdy fans in the crowd that night."

Attracted to Hoffman's intelligence and reputation as a rabble-rouser, Kinky had become friendly with the Jewish counterculture hero the previous year. "I don't know where I met Abbie, but I hung out with him at the Chelsea Hotel," Kinky says. "I played the show at the Village Gate the night before he skadoodled. [The club held a fundraiser before Hoffman went on the lam to avoid serving time for a cocaine bust.] That was a great night. I'm not sure if [the home movie of] his vasectomy was the opening act, or if I opened for the vasectomy."

By late 1973, Kinky began to have second thoughts about Vanguard and its ability to promote his songs. He also had grown close to Waylon Jennings and wanted him, rather than Chuck Glaser, to produce his follow-up album.

According to Chuck Glaser, he produced and recorded the songs "Nashville Casualty and Life" and "Tramp on the Street" with Kinky for the second album. But when he brought them to Maynard Solomon at Vanguard, Solomon told him Kinky had called from Texas to say Waylon was producing his next album. When Chuck called Kinky and discovered his brother Tompall had steered Kinky to Jennings, he knew it was over. He blamed his brother's "constant interference" for ending his own professional relationship with Kinky.

"Chuck thinks he was squeezed out; he was mostly squeezed out by Tompall," says Kinky. "They hated each other. I became much closer with Tompall and realized he totally ran the company and made all the decisions. Chuck really did a good job producing that first record. But the next one went to another label, which changed everything."

"Tompall had an agenda because he and Waylon were good buddies," says Louis Glaser. "That's why Glaser Publications, Glaser Productions, and the Glaser Brothers as a group began to fall apart.

It wasn't too long before they broke up and pretty much dissolved in 1974."

The fallout from the infighting among the Glaser Brothers, and the stress of living off his dwindling savings, made Roger question his future in the music management business.

"During that first year we weren't making any money, but with the notoriety and press coverage, it was all moving beautifully," says Roger. "Then it started going crazy with Tompall and those guys and I realized how irrational the music business was. The band was making money from gigs but not enough to throw anything back to me."

With Roger working behind the scenes in Nashville, and Kinky on the road, their once-close relationship began to erode. "He and I didn't connect real well," admits Roger. "We had a bunch of fights about different strategies, and he didn't include me in any of the production discussions with Chuck and Tompall. What had started as a fun labor of love was becoming a business and I needed to get out of it without messing up Kinky's career."

Enter Steven H. Weiss, a formidable and aggressive New York entertainment attorney. Called "one of the toughest lawyers I've ever encountered" by Ahmet Ertegun, founder and president of Atlantic Records, Weiss represented Jimi Hendrix, Led Zeppelin, Swan Song Records, Bad Company, and Vanilla Fudge. His relationship with Hendrix went far beyond business. When Weiss mentioned how much he liked the brown velvet and gold silk brocade vest Hendrix was wearing at the Royal Albert Hall in February 1969, the guitar legend took it off and handed to him as a gift. Weiss flew to Canada to help Hendrix when he got busted for possession of heroin in Toronto and represented Hendrix's estate after he died.

Roger met with Weiss in his office in New York and asked him to find an aggressive manager to take Kinky's career to the next level. But it was Kinky's song about the Holocaust that first got Weiss's attention and his playful charm that sealed the deal.

"Kinky was never outwardly the least bit self-conscious about being a Jew," says Finley. "But he also had the ability to schmooze the old Jews in the communications business right out of their socks. He was the nephew they'd never had and hadn't known they missed until he came along. Charming, charming boychik"(a Yiddish word of endearment for a young man).

Kinky's relationship with Weiss went much further than charm and the ability to schmooze. He has nothing but respect for Weiss and his efforts on Kinky's behalf. In fact, Kinky immortalized Weiss's unusual pronunciation of "Aristotle Onassis" in "They Ain't Makin' Jews like Jesus Anymore."

"Steven H. Weiss, the great lawyer in New York, loved the song 'Ride 'Em Jewboy,'" says Kinky. "He picked me up as a result of that, got a couple of record deals for me, and hooked me up with Jerry Weintraub. Steve had a white Rolls-Royce Silver Cloud with flower vases inside and his own chauffeur; it was very impressive. He loved me— he was a guy who really tried. I learned to appreciate him—because if you're handling Led Zeppelin, it doesn't seem like you'd want to pick up Kinky Friedman and do it for the right reasons."

Roger didn't leave Nashville until Weiss put together a management deal with Weintraub. An aggressive manager and promoter, Weintraub managed Bob Dylan, John Denver, Neil Diamond, Wayne Newton, the Beach Boys, and the Moody Blues. His promotion efforts were equally impressive. By booking Frank Sinatra in Madison Square Garden and billing it as "The Main Event," he revitalized Sinatra's career. And he had no misgivings about calling Elvis Presley's manager every day for a year until he had a contract to "present" Elvis Presley on a nationwide concert tour.

Although Kinky respected Vanguard and the people working there, he knew he had to leave the label. "I thought Vanguard dropped the ball," he explains. "They had great spirit, but they'd never done a country record. We got into Montreal and there were front-page stories in every newspaper, but no records—they hadn't gotten there yet. It was clear they didn't have the manpower for promotion. Vanguard was what it was: people that could appreciate and understand what we were doing, but not commercial enough to make it happen."

To keep himself from any further involvement with the label, Kinky dragged his feet about going back into the studio. "My brother was avoiding doing another album for Vanguard—pulling a moody, saying, 'I'm too crazy to play; I've got to calm down,'" says Roger. "Dragging it out until Weintraub could work a deal with the Solomons and ABC Dunhill."

But Kinky didn't sit back and wait for Weiss or Weintraub to get him out of the deal; he went directly to Maynard Solomon. "Whenever

Kinky had something important to do, he did it himself," says Wilkes. "When Kinky wanted to get a release from Vanguard, there was a lot of fighting with Maynard about it. I'm not going to get into specifics, but there was a big argument between Maynard and Kinky. Kinky won and got the release, and Maynard sold the contract to ABC Dunhill Records."

In addition to what Kinky felt was a lack of promotion, he never received any advances against sales or help with the expenses for the tour following the record's release.

"Vanguard didn't pay us to be on the road like ABC Dunhill did," says Ferrero. "We were seriously nickel-and-diming it, and the person who was underwriting it all was Kinky's father. I bet he lost a fortune on that album. Not the production, but he ended up paying the hotel bills, and for gas for all the cars. I don't think Vanguard paid shit.

"The only money we got on the Vanguard tour was what we got on the gig. Once I paid the hotel—we'd be five to a room—we'd be lucky if we could give everybody in the band lunch money. It was a rough go with the guys in the band yelling at me, 'This is all there is, man?' with a couple of guys ready to punch me out. Jack's [Slaughter] motto was 'Score or the floor.' You had to find a woman at the gig because we couldn't afford hotel bills."

"The money was a problem," agrees Kinky. "We depended upon my father's Phillips 66 credit card to get hotels, gas, and just about everything all around the country."

"I'd have to talk to Tom when we got back," remembers Ferrero. "He'd show me this big stack of receipts from Nashville—Kinky's phone bills, Holiday Inn bills. I'd say, 'Tom, this isn't even the band. It's all Kinky's because he stayed another month while we dispersed.' His father was stuck with a lot of bills."

Pleased his son had found his calling, Tom Friedman didn't mind helping him financially.

"After he graduated college, he was in the Peace Corps and we visited him there," the elder Friedman said in *Kinky Friedman — Proud to Be an Asshole from El Paso*, a 2001 Dutch documentary by filmmaker Simone de Vries. "The first thing he showed us was three or four country-and-western songs. He had written them in the *ulu* in Borneo—it was quite touching. When he came home, I asked him what he wanted to do—if he wanted to go to graduate school. He says no, he wants to be a songwriter.

"I thought about it for a while," he said, reflecting upon his decision. "Then I figured, why should he have to wait until he retires at the age of sixty or sixty-five to write his songs? So I told him, 'I'll give you a fellowship,'" he added with a twinkle in his eyes.

While Tom Friedman was helping his oldest son, Roger was living on his own savings in Nashville, hoping for some remuneration from the band for his efforts. That scenario was bound to create even more friction for Ferrero, and didn't help the brothers' shaky relationship.

"I remember having an argument with Roger on the phone when we got to Austin," says Ferrero. "I hadn't slept in days and Roger is calling from Nashville asking how much money I have to send back. I was pissed. I said, 'Are you fucking kidding me? We arrived in Austin on an empty gas tank and don't have enough money to buy a cheeseburger. What do you think we're making with gigs?' We weren't making shit. Five hundred bucks and you got six or seven guys, a hotel bill. And the band would drink a hundred dollars of the take because in those days the clubs wouldn't give you free drinks."

Kinky regretted leaving Nashville and losing the artistic control that came with recording in Glaser Studios, but felt it was the only viable option.

"When a big guy like Jerry Weintraub and a lawyer like Stephen H. Weiss in New York all say, 'We've got you a quarter-of-a-million-dollar contract,' you have to leave Vanguard, whether it's one record or ten. Because they're paying you nothing and it would be stupid to turn it down."

Once Weiss and Weintraub got Kinky out of his Vanguard contract, they negotiated a lucrative contract with ABC Dunhill Records for Kinky's second album, which included money for touring and promotion. Weintraub planned to mold Kinky into a pop/folk/country artist like his successful client John Denver, so he suggested Milton Okun, Denver's producer, to oversee the sessions. Okun had produced chart toppers for Peter, Paul and Mary, and helped Denver score a string of hits in the '70s, including "Take Me Home, Country Roads," "Rocky Mountain High," "Sunshine on My Shoulders," "Annie's Song," "Back Home Again," and "Thank God I'm a Country Boy." But Kinky had his doubts about moving in that direction or working with Denver's producer.

"I had a choice between Willie and Leon Russell coproducing it for me—they wanted to work together and do it in Nashville—or with John Denver's producer," Kinky explains. "John Denver was huge at the time, but pretty sappy compared to Willie Nelson. I naturally gravitated to Willie. John Denver was a good songwriter, but his whole thing 'Thank God I'm a Country Boy'—I don't know," he says with a sigh.

"Maybe I didn't see it coming when I said I'd rather work with Willie than with John Denver's people. But those were decisions I wasn't really qualified to make. I had never been on the road. I had never been in a studio until Chuck Glaser. If I had gone with John Denver's producer, those songs might have gone mainstream, might have broken big. But at the time it was more soulful to have Leon and Willie do it."

Released in late 1974 on ABC Dunhill Records, the *Kinky Friedman* LP included "Rapid City, South Dakota," "Popeye the Sailor Man," "Homo Erectus," "Lover Please," "Wild Man from Borneo," "Before All Hell Breaks Loose," "Somethin's Wrong with the Beaver," "When the Lord Closes the Door (He Opens a Little Window)," "Miss Nickelodeon," "Autograph," and "They Ain't Makin' Jews like Jesus Anymore."

"The second album was a hodgepodge of two different albums," explains Kinky. "The first with Willie, which was good stuff but way ahead of its time. The second was with Steve Barri in L.A., the guy who did 'Billy, Don't Be a Hero,'" he adds, referring to the 1974 #1 hit by bubblegum pop group Bo Donaldson and the Heywoods.

Held in Glaser Studios, the initial sessions for the *Kinky Friedman* LP featured Willie, Jennings, and Tompall Glaser singing background vocals on "Miss Nickelodeon" and "They Ain't Makin' Jews like Jesus Anymore," along with Swan and Young. But it wasn't long before ABC Dunhill pulled the plug and moved the sessions to L.A.

"When we got to Nashville, we had everybody in the studio at one time," says Kinky. "With Willie, there would be a song that was sixteen minutes long because everybody's stoned out of their mind. Dolly Parton would come by to visit the studio, all kinds of people stopped by, and it was great fun," he says with a laugh. "I realized Willie—as far as a business head to please the record company—wasn't going to do it. Sure enough, after two songs with Willie, they came and took the project away . . ."

Cullers remembers feeling uneasy with the lack of musical direction.

"I was the Nashville guy, so I called Ron Oates for keyboards and Alan Rush on bass," he says. "The other studio guys were Glaser friends. Music-wise, I was uncomfortable. Usually the producer is in charge and works closely with the artist and session pickers. In those sessions, nobody was in charge. Willie was just there, sitting behind the board, smiling and stoned. I didn't think we did the 'They Ain't Makin' Jews like Jesus Anymore' track justice. But it was nice having Waylon come by to horse around and sing with us."

Kinky has always followed his heart and instincts. It was only natural he'd choose Willie over a mainstream producer.

"We were kindred spirits; I liked what he was doing," Kinky explains. "But ABC Dunhill thought the sessions with Willie were getting out of hand. I thought we were ahead of our time and were making a very interesting record. But back then they didn't see it as being commercial. It was the same thing when Willie did 'Blue Eyes Crying in the Rain.' He did the whole *Red Headed Stranger* record for $20,000 in four days. Some of it was so sparse, like 'Blue Eyes Crying in the Rain'—just Bee Spears on bass, Mickey Raphael on harp, and Willie. Columbia Records thought it was a joke and maybe a good collector's record but said, 'This fucking thing wouldn't even make a good demo.' Columbia's top producers in Nashville said, 'This is shit; we'll put some strings and background vocals on it and try to save it.'

"Willie said no, and it was the first record he got to produce himself. All the producers, the record company brass, and a lot of artists didn't take 'Blue Eyes Crying in the Rain' as the hit. But the disc jockeys did, and it became the song of the year and crossed the pop charts just like Willie sent it to them. So when you're faced with that kind of thing, who knows how good that Willie [produced] record might have been if they'd let it happen?"

Choosing Steve Barri to produce Kinky's second album made as much sense musically as hooking him up with Okun. Dubbed the "King Midas of AM Radio," Barri was a successful pop producer who produced six singles for bubblegum pop star Tommy Roe, including "Dizzy," which topped the *Billboard* charts. Riding on that success, he produced the Grass Roots; Jan and Dean; Hamilton, Joe Frank and Reynolds; and Johnny Rivers. Barri also produced blues artists B.B. King and Bobby "Blue" Bland, and several R&B artists, but had never produced a country artist.

Although Barri tried his best to produce Kinky in a way that would please both the artist and the record company, Kinky hated the way he handled the L.A. sessions.

"Tons of attention was paid to the sound of the L.A. bass player, and none to the vocals," he says. "It wasn't even in the right key for me. Steve Barri was a pop hit producer and that's what he wanted to do. He was polishing his nails with clear polish in the control room while we were playing. He was a nice guy, a Hollywood guy who had that hit. This was right after 'Billy, Don't Be a Hero,' and everybody thought, 'Wow, if he can get another one like that!' He did charts and arrangements and got some good L.A. pickers. I brought in good players from Nashville, but they didn't play—they put the Hollywood guys on."

Kinky brought Swan, Young, and Finley, and also invited his old college buddy Ken "Snakebite" Jacobs to play horns on those sessions. Jacobs renewed his friendship with Kinky after he began playing sax and was attending the Berklee School of Music.

"I went to see him at a bar outside of Boston with his first incarnation of the Jewboys," says Jacobs. "I flipped; it was the funniest thing I ever saw. After that, I bugged him for about a year. Steve Barri wanted horns on the *Kinky Friedman* record and eventually I talked my way in. I played flute and all the saxophones and was the first and only horn player."

Finley, who cowrote several songs with Kinky for that record, remembers the competitive atmosphere during those sessions.

"There was a lot of tension initially between the L.A. musicians and the ones Kinky brought with him, including me," says Finley. "The way sessions were run in those days, you had a team, a bunch of guys who always recorded together as a unit. They were the band of choice for whoever was the producer. There was a struggle going on, all very sotto voce and polite, of course, but still there.

"What I brought was an ability to communicate Kinky's vision to the other players. The studio guys wanted to have Kinky just play guitar for them and sing "Wild Man from Borneo" so they could work out the feel of it on their own. Me and Kinky had made a demo of the tunes in Austin, but they didn't want to reference it . . . again that thing of territory. So they struggled with it for about an hour. Finally, I said to Steve, 'You know, it's right there on the demo.' So he played it and the Hollywood guys got it right away because it was on the demo and so easy anyone could get it. After that, they gave me my propers and the rest went smoothly."

ABC Dunhill was a pop music label with a stable of artists including the Mamas and Papas, Three Dog Night, and the Grassroots. Signing Kinky was an anomaly and a financial risk for such a straight-ahead label. But ABC Dunhill's president, like Weiss and Weintraub, was intrigued by him as well as his songs.

"Jay Lasker liked Kinky; he heard 'They Ain't Makin' Jews like Jesus Anymore' and decided to sign him," says Barri. "They weren't surprised by his material. But they were used to recording pop artists and knew it would be difficult to get his songs played on AM pop stations. We kept them to three minutes to fit the format. 'Rapid City, South Dakota' got the most airplay—some FM stations played it. We used horns on some songs and strings on one; I didn't want anything to overshadow the music."

Although Kinky still has bad feelings about the sessions in L.A., Barri remembers him as a respectful professional who always kept him laughing.

"Kinky was easygoing in the studio," says Barri. "He would play the songs on his guitar so the musicians would know what he wanted. Then they built the songs around that with drums and bass. I can remember laughing a lot. Every day, he'd give a news report with an offbeat comical slant that was always funny.

"He brought tracks he'd made in Nashville. I don't remember if the songs with Willie Nelson, Waylon Jennings, and Tompall Glaser were complete or whether we remixed them. But we used those songs as a guide as to the way they wanted the record to sound. It didn't involve many takes because the musicians were all studio players. We had to do Kinky's vocals a number of times to get them right. I thought it came out good."

Kinky, however, hated the album and refused to play any the songs from it on the tour following its release. Yet, unlike some artists, he hid his displeasure during the sessions. "Maybe I should have thrown a fit," Kinky says in retrospect. "Dwight [Yoakam] will throw a fit to get what he wants, but he knows studios and production. I don't."

Despite his dissatisfaction with the *Kinky Friedman* LP, Kinky's deal with ABC Dunhill was more lucrative and inclusive than his deal with Vanguard. The label paid for plane tickets, rental cars, and hotel rooms, and gave band members a weekly salary during the tour. That tour would include death threats and tense moments with club owners, Weintraub's underlings, and a Native American fellow artist, who were all outraged by Kinky's irreverent sense of humor. But it led to a forty-year relationship with Don Imus, a controversial and often-fired nationally syndicated radio personality who understood and could match Kinky's role as a provocateur.

6

Banned at Austin City Limits

"There I was in the spotlight, wearing an Indian headdress,
big blue aviator glasses, a furry blue guitar strap, and a
sequined pair of bell-bottom trousers—and this was almost
thirty years before Queer Eye for the Straight Guy.*"*
—Kinky Friedman

Kinky put together a second incarnation of the Jewboys in January 1975 for a tour to support the *Kinky Friedman* LP. He kept Jewford, Culpepper, and Cullers, hired Jacobs to add horns and flute to the mix, and hired Brian "Skycap Adams" Clarke to replace Young, who had left to write musicals. He chose Finley to replace Billy Swan, who left the band shortly before his single "I Can Help" reached #1 on both the *Billboard Hot 100* and the *Hot Country Singles* charts.

Finley had cowritten a number of songs with Kinky in exchange for a position in the studio and in the band. "Autograph," "Homo Erectus," "Popeye the Sailor Man," and "Somethin's Wrong with the Beaver" appeared on the *Kinky Friedman* LP; "The Boogie Man," "Rock 'n' Roll Across the USA," and "Mama, Mama, Mama (Let Me Jump in Your Pajamas)," written with input from Roger, were added to the live show.

"Everything between Kinky and me was always the result of some back and forth, tit for tat, give and take," explains Finley. "Kinky wanted me to come and write with him. This was a year before the album was ever made. In nearly all of our songs together, I provided the chord changes and Kinky provided most of the words. We wrote 'Homo Erectus' in Mazatlan [Mexico] when we went down there to write."

B.B. King said that when he hires players for his band, the *man* is more important than the *musician*. He knew he could always find talented musicians, but if they couldn't get along and fit in with the band, he wouldn't hire them. Kinky didn't audition new players; he tested them during two weeks of daily rehearsals at the ranch.

Kinky still likes to put people through the wringer before accepting and respecting them as colleagues. "I know I can irritate—I'm good at getting under people's skin," he admits. "I haven't lost my touch—even today."

Most of the players were used to Kinky's temperament. But Clarke, who at twenty-four was the youngest and newest member, had a tough time adjusting.

"During the first week or two, they put you through some changes to see how you are personally and whether you're a good fit culturally," says Clarke. "I think Kinky liked me pretty fast. But his brother was making remarks like 'This guy's barely heterosexual' that would come completely out of left field. It was constantly like paintball with words.

"It was a little bit intimidating, because they were very fast. Jewford was pretty good and Roger was really good with the barbs—he'd nail you. I came from an athletic background where there was a lot of good-natured taunting, but these jokes were coming out of some pretty high-end academics who were verbally very adroit.

"I think they were testing me because once you are accepted, you couldn't play yourself off the team. You had to do something heinous, something socially or spiritually bankrupt, to be removed. Who you were as a person was probably more important as long as you had enough expertise to handle the parts, which weren't difficult musically."

Kinky took a roundtable approach as a band leader during rehearsals and on the road. "He was very open to other people's ideas," says Clarke. "Sometimes they'd come late at night at a Waffle House–type place after the gig. When we rehearsed at sound check, there was an element of Mickey Rooney—'Let's try this.' He was very open to throwing something into the show we hadn't studied a lot.

"Somebody would come up with something really off the wall. If he liked it, we'd start developing it. Sometimes those ideas stuck. For example, 'Carryin' the Torch' was stuck in the middle of the show. Me and Lanny [Bowles] said that song should close the show, and Kinky said, 'Maybe you're right.' We tried it the next night and it worked, and it stayed at the end of the set every night. The American flag was Lanny's idea. Smart and really astute about appearances, he knew flags on his drumsticks would look great. Kinky was never a control freak, and was a pretty confident guy. Somebody not liking him didn't bother him at all. It didn't change his idea of who he was."

Kinky modeled his "colorful band leader style" after Bob Wills, and attributes his democratic way of interacting with his musicians to the kind of person he is and the way he was brought up. "There are all kinds of bandleaders—there was Spike Jones, who was apparently an asshole and very controlling, and micromanaged and fined people for cussing or missing a note," he says. "Bob Dylan will hire and fire very quickly. With my pal Dwight [Yoakam], the people in his band are employees. With Willie, they're old friends that have been with him for forty years."

When the Jewboys began touring to promote the new CD, Weintraub was busy producing Robert Altman's film *Nashville*, and sent an underling to check out their show. "Weintraub's guy came to Nashville to watch us and was blown away by the act," says Ferrero. "He spent a lot of time with me one-on-one; they wanted to make sure I was good enough to be on the road with Kinky. He was a very, very nice man and had gone back to the days of Milton Berle."

The Jewboys' gig opening for Don Imus at the Bottom Line in New York was another story. "Weintraub came to that show, and Sal—one of his top guys—was there, too," he adds. "I introduced the band, there's a huge roar, and the band didn't start playing because something fucked up. I'm in the wings and Sal's yelling, 'Dylan, get out there. Kick them in the ass; they've got to get going.' Panama broke a string or had a problem with his amp—there was a several-minute delay between my introduction and when the band started.

"When Kinky came out, everyone's timing was off. The whole set was off, and we got all this negative feedback. After that gig, Weintraub's guy said he was disappointed, the show didn't look professional, and they didn't think we were ready for the big time. At the time, and for years after that, Kinky thought that one specific gig cratered his relationship with Weintraub."

The bright spot of that disappointing evening was Kinky meeting Don Imus, who would become a lifelong friend. But there wasn't much bonding going on that night because of Imus's altered state.

"Imus had written a book [*God's Other Son*] and was doing a standup comedy routine based on a character in his book, Billy Sol Hargus, a

Southern TV evangelist," remembers Ferrero. "That night Imus was completely coked out and alkied out and fucked up."

After the Bottom Line gig, the band embarked on a cross-country tour, playing 300- to 500-seat listening rooms in major cities. They also played selected larger venues: the Great Southeast Music Hall in Atlanta, which held 1,000; the Texas Music Hall in Houston, which held 1,200 people; and the Armadillo World Headquarters in Austin, which held 1,500.

"We did a lot of two- to three-night gigs," says Jacobs. "The Troubadour in L.A., the Bohemian Caverns in Georgetown, the Boarding House in San Francisco, nice upper-end music clubs in every city—Chicago, New York.

"The first gig was two nights at the Great Southeast Music Hall in Atlanta. Liberty Hall in Houston also went crazy. It was packed, we were on the radio, and the Mayor of Houston came back to meet us. We played the Armadillo many times; that was always great. People were packed in, they loved us, and they fed us really good Mexican food. That was my favorite Kinky gig because it was like home and we got called back onstage for a lot of encores. We played a club in Toronto where they went crazy for us, too."

The band played a gig in Baltimore with Cheech and Chong, a duo known for its irreverent, counterculture, and drug-related comedy routines. Not surprisingly, that gig was sponsored by NORML, the National Organization for the Reform of Marijuana Laws, which gave Kinky et al. T-shirts with a marijuana leaf incorporated into the logo.

"Their set was hilarious," says Ferrero. "They had a rack full of clothes they changed into on stage for various bits. We didn't get to hang out with them, but Kinky and I had lunch with Cheech when he was in Austin."

Not all shows were fun and free T-shirts; an ugly night at a club in East Texas stands out in Jacob's memory. "I remember not getting paid in Nacogdoches, Texas—the club refused to pay us," he says. "Another band thought we had taken their spot and were threatening to kill us—that all happened the same night."

Playing Willie Nelson's annual picnics and outdoor festivals provided exposure to larger and more welcoming audiences. Kinky and the Texas Jewboys played for 25,000 fans at Nelson's Fourth of July Picnic at the Texas Motor Speedway in 1974, in a lineup with Willie, Waylon

Jennings, Leon Russell, Doug Sahm, Jimmy Buffett, Michael Murphy, Bobby Bare, and Townes Van Zandt.

They later played the Son of Cosmic Cowboy Festival at the Hofheinz Pavilion, a 10,000-seat stadium at the University of Houston. The festival was a benefit for KPFT-FM, an independent, listener-sponsored radio station that had its transmitter bombed twice by the KKK during its first year on the air. Kinky's band joined a notable lineup including Willie Nelson, Jerry Jeff Walker, David Bromberg, Asleep at the Wheel, and Freddy Fender.

The cerebral aspects of Kinky's music earned him a fan base that went beyond the cosmic cowboy, hipster, and country music scenes. Best-selling novelist and screenwriter Larry McMurtry, music publicist/author Howard Bloom, and Art Garfunkel all made their way to Kinky's shows. "Larry McMurtry came to our show at the Cellar Door in Washington, D.C.," remembers Kinky. "He brought his little kid, James, who was about eight at the time and later became a musician."

"Kinky knew all the writers, and knew how to work the phone," says Clarke. "There was always something in the press. I met Howard Bloom at the Bottom Line—turns out he's also a well-known physicist and a regular guest on the radio show *Coast to Coast.* People around Kinky were very smart people."

At one gig, a representative from the Wham-O toy company, which manufactured Frisbees, presented Kinky with a gold Frisbee because he often talked about teaching the Borneo natives how to play Frisbee during his stint in the Peace Corps. "It wasn't actually gold; it was goldcolored," remembers Ferrero. "They gave it to Kinky because he used that line all the time."

No matter where the band was performing, Ferrero stayed in close touch with Kinky's management throughout that tour. "Jerry Weintraub's people would call the room and say, 'We couldn't get through because the desk clerk said no calls,'" recalls Ferrero. "I'd say, 'Yeah, no calls because we've been up from eight at night to five in the morning. I never met him, just met his underlings. I remember going to his offices in New York and L.A. Instead of his name, he had 'Under Assistant West Coast Promo Man' from the Rolling Stones song on the door."

The playful spirit of Weintraub's pseudo title disappeared after Kinky shared a bill with folk singer/songwriter Buffy Sainte-Marie at the Boarding House in San Francisco. When she began her career in the early 1960s, people in the music industry didn't know how to market a Native American female musician and wanted her "to appear like Pocahontas in fringe," she said. Whether it was that background, or her belief the band was poking fun of Native Americans with Kinky's headdress, Little Jewford's buffalo head, and their onstage antics, she became enraged watching their act.

"The night with Buffy Sainte-Marie was unfortunate—like an accident that we should have foreseen," says Clarke. "Kinky had a gigantic headdress he wore for the song 'Miss Nickelodeon.' Buffy was still in the audience when he put it on. This was as offensive to her as anything she had seen in her life. She walked right up on stage and grabbed it. I still remember the visual—she came up the right aisle, and came up on stage walking really fast. She was a short girl—probably five foot one with jet-black hair. It was quite a sight."

"We did a morning radio show in downtown San Francisco to plug the show," says Jacobs. "We played a tune on the radio—Tom Hayden was on the same show. We did two or three nights at the Boarding House. I wore feathers, Jewford wore his buffalo head, Kinky wore a huge headdress, and we danced around and went 'woo woo woo' when we did 'Miss Nickelodeon' the first night. Buffy Sainte-Marie was fuming backstage—I've never seen anything like it. She got all her friends to come the next night; the first three rows were filled with 250-pound Indian guys that looked really mad. We didn't do the Indian song that night."

"Kinky put on a gorgeous Indian chief headdress; it's the real deal," adds Ferrero. "The band put on little toy ones. As soon as they start that song, Buffy Sainte-Marie runs up screaming, takes the headdress off of Kinky and rushes backstage with it. She was seriously pissed off. Apparently it was a sacred headdress and she felt Kinky was mocking Native Americans. The song is nothing like that, but the Jewboys had to have their shtick.

"The next day Weintraub's guy called me at the hotel furious about it. There were two San Francisco newspapers—the *Chronicle* and the *Examiner*. One thought Buffy Sainte-Marie had overreacted, and one thought Kinky was a complete shmuck. When Weintraub's guy called, I'm thinking, 'Can't you get it, this is good publicity?' but they were very concerned."

Whether that incident on top of the Bottom Line show led to Weintraub losing interest in managing Kinky is anybody's guess, but it didn't help. That loss of interest was apparent to the brass at ABC Dunhill, who expected Weintraub to use his considerable power in the industry to help the *Kinky Friedman* LP.

"We would have liked for it to be more successful," says producer Steve Barri. "We really felt, with all of Jerry Weintraub's clout, he would do a lot to promote the record, get us gigs and good exposure. Kinky had to be seen and heard. But that never did happen."

Part of the record's disappointing sales may have been linked to Kinky's refusal to play any of the songs during the tour. "Kinky was upset with Barri for years," says Ferrero. "We tried to get Kinky to play the songs from that album's set list—'Wild Man from Borneo,' 'Autograph'—and he wouldn't play them. Kinky was so turned off by that record he avoided those songs."

As for Weintraub's lack of support for the album and the eventual dissolution of their business relationship, Kinky pegs it to a number of reasons. "He managed me for a while, but it didn't work," he says. "We liked each other and Jerry Weintraub got what we were doing, but we just didn't fit there. He really didn't do anything and didn't have time; he was busy with John Denver and Frank Sinatra."

Roger has his own theory on why that relationship never worked. "I never met Weintraub, but from afar, it appears that the two of them never connected," he says. "He wanted to take him into a John Denver pop/folk world, and that certainly wasn't where Kinky should be. They wanted different things."

Even without Weintraub's backing, Kinky managed to build a diverse fan base one gig at a time. "The norm was maybe about twelve people in the audience and eight of them would be Jewish psychology majors," Ferrero says laughing. "Our drummer kept saying, 'Where are all the groupies? All we have is academics.' But it built up and eventually got more and more people to come."

"Genderwise, the audience was split right down the middle," says Clarke. "There was always an element of the Jewish community, a lot of academicians, college kids, music fans, and the hip kind of people who kept up by reading *Rolling Stone*."

Again, the lack of airplay contributed to what Ferrero calls the lack of "meat in the seats." "We played the best clubs, but musically we were going in too many directions at once," says Kinky. "We had songs that could have been hits, but we didn't have airplay."

What the band did have was the ability to attract celebrities, especially on the West Coast. "L.A. was very exciting, and the kind of people we met there were soulful musicians," adds Kinky. "I lived there for a while and liked it. There was a certain frisson at that time with people like Bob Dylan and a lot of other celebrities coming out to see us."

Dinah Shore and Burt Reynolds came to see Kinky at the Troubadour, as did Dennis Hopper and character actor Warren Oates, who starred in *The Wild Bunch* and numerous epic westerns directed by Sam Peckinpah. Richard Dreyfus came to a gig in Montreal, where actor Randy Quaid hung out with the band for a week.

"Randy Quaid introduced us—a hysterical and perfect introduction for Kinky—when we played the Troubadour because Randy and Dennis Quaid went to high school with Jewford," says Jacobs. "Kinky would attract these people in L.A. Iggy Pop hung out with us backstage. Backstage Iggy Pop was just one of the guys; he was very nice. Rowan and Martin, the famous comedy duo, used to come to the gigs."

Kinky tried to introduce Jacobs to two of his musical heroes, but the demons that often accompany celebrity got in the way.

"Kinky knew I loved Paul Butterfield and took me to the bar next door to the Troubadour to meet him," says Jacobs. "But Paul Butterfield was lying dead drunk on the floor. Same thing happened with Kris Kristofferson. Kinky took me to meet him, and he was completely passed out in the dressing room of the Exit Inn in Nashville."

Kinky also started hanging out with the musicians in Three Dog Night, and is still close with Danny Hutton, one of the lead vocalists. An L.A.-based rock band made up of three lead singers, a guitar player, an organist, and a drummer, Three Dog Night had twenty-one consecutive Top Forty hits and twelve consecutive gold LPs, and sold nearly fifty million records. But they too struggled with their demons.

"They were enormous and a very important band in terms of hits and records and money, which pretty well wrecked all of them," says Kinky. "They were the first band I met like that. They had to eat Vaseline to keep the cocaine from completely robbing their voices and were traveling with registered nurses—it was ridiculous."

Although Jimi Hendrix died before Kinky formed the Jewboys, the band did a live radio broadcast in Electric Lady Studios, Hendrix's studio in New York. The eleven tracks recorded on that 1975 show were released twenty years later on *From One Good American to Another* on

Fruit of the Tune, a label owned by Nick "Chinga" Chavin. "That was a good show with a lot of energy," says Jewford. "We had just done a gig and gone there late at night to do it."

Kinky traveled with Led Zeppelin on their private plane to their concert at the San Diego Sports Arena that same year. The Starship, which appears in the film *The Song Remains the Same*, was a former United Airlines Boeing 720B passenger jet modified for rock stars. Owners invested $200,000 to reduce the seating capacity to forty and install a bar with a built-in electronic organ, seats and tables, revolving armchairs, a thirty-foot-long couch, a TV set, a video cassette player, and a video library. Modifications included two back rooms in the rear of the plane: one with a low couch and pillows, the other with a bed, white fur bedspread, and shower.

"That was because of Steve Weiss, who knew Peter Grant, the former wrestling promoter who managed them," says Kinky. "It wasn't my thing, but I went and everybody seemed very deferential—I don't know why—and the guys were very friendly. Their plane had a fireplace and we drank Black Marys—a Bloody Mary with a hell of a lot of Worcestershire sauce.

"We flew from L.A. to San Diego, your typical rock star thing. They're in limos, have women running after them, people trying to get to them, girls showing their tits in the audience on guy's shoulders."

Although Kinky was nonchalant about the rock star trappings, he acquired one claim to fame during that trip. "I did urinate backstage with Jimmy Page," he deadpans.

"The guy I liked best was the guy who died—John Bonham," adds Kinky. "I love drummers and get along well with them. I liked him, Keith Moon of the Who—he was crazy and really good. Levon Helm [Kinky's close friend], Corky Laing's another great one."

Bonham couldn't dress too fancy behind his elaborate drum kit but was a dapper dresser offstage, known for his black bowler hat, gray pinstriped suit, and red boutonnière. Although the Jewboys started out wearing traditional country and western attire, they quickly evolved into dapper dressers in outlandish outfits Roger called "country drag."

Kinky's outfits were modeled on the costumes of country artists Little Jimmy Dickens, known for his rhinestone-studded outfits, and Porter Wagoner, famous for his flashy Nudie and Manuel suits. Manuel also designed Elvis Presley's signature gold lamé outfit, made Johnny

Cash the man in black, made suits for the Rat Pack, and created outfits for Roy Rogers and the Lone Ranger. Known as the "Rhinestone Rembrandt," Manuel designed a number of flashy, rhinestone-studded outfits for Kinky during his Texas Jewboys days. Kinky also used Nudie, who created outfits for Cher, Elton John, Hank Snow, Hank Williams Sr., ZZ Top, and the Flying Burrito Brothers.

Dubbing himself "the man who put the glitter on Loretta Lynn's titter," Kinky's penchant for glitter, sequins, and custom clothing helped him create his style. He still uses Manuel to design the black thigh-length western preacher coats synonymous with the Kinkster persona.

Kinky was the most outlandishly stylish member of the band, but the other players did their best to give him a run for his money.

"My attire was cowboy-esque for the early gigs: cowboy hat, vest, cowboy shirt, and handlebar mustache," says Jewford. "Then it evolved into the top hat, jacket, and buffalo hat I wore for *Austin City Limits*."

"We tried to look as weird as possible," says Jacobs. "Brian Clarke wore anything wild and weird that clashed: plaid pants, orange shirts, and a huge pimp hat. I always wore black with cutaway black tails and a cowboy hat with a rattlesnake headband handmade at Texas Hatters. Kinky wore a number of bizarre customized cowboy shirts—one had a Star of David; another had a menorah. He wore wild boots, a horseshoe diamond ring on his pinky, and a weird thing around his neck that looked like a miniature gold purse. He had his pills in it; he called them L.A. turnarounds, which is a strong speed you can use to drive to L.A. and back."

"The outfit I wore on the *Austin City Limits* show is really regrettable," Clarke says, laughing about his velvet pimp hat, plaid shirt, and clashing plaid pants. "We would pick things that were off-the-wall. There was a sense about that act that made it hard for people to tell exactly where it was coming from. Some people complained it wasn't taking a committed step in any direction; it was always vague. The outfits were the same way. For a while I wore an orange jumpsuit—something a really pathetic lounge lizard might wear. Kinky loved it. He liked things that threw people off balance."

Jacobs and Jewford spent hours shopping for outrageous outfits and accessories. "Me and Jewford were very conscious of our look," Jacobs says. "Jewford always wore a felt top hat in a really weird Mad Hatter shade. Weird, colorful, and cool. He had a maroon velvet sport jacket.

Jewford would spend the days we were on the road shopping for weird clothes, going to weird shops, getting weird sunglasses. Sometimes I'd go with him and we'd get matching sunglasses. Wichita wouldn't dress up; he just wore cowboy clothes."

Part of the Jewboys' style, and their charm, was the onstage banter between Jewford and Kinky, and the choreographed dances by Jewford and Jacobs. Much of the banter evolved from routines Kinky and Jewford had worked out as counselors at Echo Hill Ranch. The rest of their shtick evolved during the tour.

"The tricks and dances came about on the road," says Kinky. "Jewford and Snakebite had a little thing they would do together. I had a lot of tricks—little hat flips, stepping into my guitar strap—that I really liked."

"I think life is a setup line," explains Jewford. "I've always reacted and commented about everything. Kinky would make a comment and I would react and make my own comment on his comment. It was a natural evolution that happened and worked in favor of what we were doing. Most of the time we improvised. I never tried to overshadow Kinky, just complement what he was saying. My way of looking at it was you needed some comic relief in all the BS."

However, the dance steps Jewford and Jacobs did during the show were rehearsed ahead of time. "Jewford and I had a lot of steps worked out," says Jacobs. "We used to stay up till six or seven in the morning working on steps in front of the mirror in his hotel room. Then we would laugh hysterically."

"As for the dancing, I had to call Bob Fosse several times," says Jewford, his tongue planted firmly in his cheek. "We did some serious choreography, but in all truthfulness—at least in my mind with my theatrical background [he studied theater and music at CalArts], even as ill as this may be or if someone wants to perceive it as stupid, I wanted it right," he says laughing. "It may be basic but I'd like it to look like good choreography. It was funny to see two insane Jewish guys up there doing their choreography with weird glasses—Snakebite with his sax and me with a kazoo sax. We spent endless nights on choreography. It worked because it was funny and the crowd loved it."

The band was never on a nonstop tour; they'd get together for a string of dates and then return to their respective home bases. "We go on tour and then I'd go home," says Jacobs. "Then they'd say, 'We're gonna tour Texas next month' and give me the dates and fly me in. It would come in spurts."

If the dates were one- or two-nighters in a number of cities across the US, the band would fly. If they had a string of dates in Texas or Colorado, they traveled together in a rented van.

"We had one van in the summer in Texas that wasn't air-conditioned," says Jacobs. "I thought I was going to pass out most of the time. I remember driving all night from Houston to Dallas, get to the hotel, shower, and go to the gig. It was rough, but we were thirty—we were young and it was exciting."

Ferrero and the rest of the band shared Jacobs' excitement. "The label actually paid for plane tickets, rental cars, and hotel rooms," Ferrero says. "We were thinking, 'Oh, my God; we're high on the hog.' We would each get 100 bucks a week, which was huge money in the mid-1970s. That was a short-lived tour, but everybody in the band was happy because we knew we were actually going to make money."

"There was great support from the record company—which is something that doesn't exist these days," agrees Clarke. "By the time I got there, he was on Epic [a subsidiary of Columbia], and ABC Dunhill was in the mix, too. Columbia dumped a lot of money into it, because we were flown all over the place."

Even with all that support, Kinky never sat back and rested on his laurels. An energetic and ambitious person by nature, he excelled (and still does) at self-promotion.

"We were doing a lot of traveling, but when we had days off, Kinky slept till two or three, then was on the phone doing business," remembers Jacobs. "He was always doing business, talking to journalists. He was great at it—did it all himself, and look how famous he got. Kinky is always doing something; I admired his business abilities and his ambition."

Considering the amount of time they were thrown together in close proximity, most of the band members got along. But, as one player observed, "We weren't the Monkees," so they did have their moments.

"Everybody loved performing," says Clarke. "The guys who were chiefly musicians—and there were four of us—understood everyone else's roles and what we were doing. We were there to be part of what Kinky was doing. There weren't a lot of musical arguments. If there were, Panama [Danny Finley] was the source. He was like a rooster and would get in your face about things—I think unnecessarily. He was the most combative. If there was any tension at any particular moment, he usually had something to do with it. Otherwise there wasn't any."

"Most everybody got along well," says Jewford. "Everybody had their little idiosyncrasies and made fun of each other a little bit, but mostly we all hunkered down to what we were trying to do—to make it happen."

Drinking and heavy drugging, which can often lead to short fuses and frayed tempers, wasn't a problem with the Jewboys.

"I don't remember anything heavy drugwise, and drinking didn't seem to be anybody's style," says Clarke. "Kinky might drink some Jack Daniels, but it was mostly a prop. Drinking is not his personality."

"Just me and Wichita were the potheads," says Jacobs. "We were constantly smoking pot at Kinky's ranch. We were taking speed after a while but not serious, just taking a pill once in a while. But the pills were strong; that's why Jewford and I were up till six in the morning doing dance steps. I don't think I slept for a year. Not everybody—I think maybe just Jewford and Kinky and me. We were the comedy part of the show, especially Kinky and Jewford. I was also lumped with the musical part."

Kinky would eventually develop an addiction to cocaine—which he calls Peruvian marching powder—but just toyed with it during his stint with the Jewboys.

"Cocaine came in during the latter part of my tours with Kinky," says Jacobs. "We'd do it after the show and stay up all night. I wasn't high when I was playing; maybe on speed, because I couldn't play on coke. I tried it at Liberty Hall and couldn't feel my lips. It's a little hard to play the horn when you're doing coke; my whole mouth was numb."

Bruce Springsteen's E Street Band was in the audience when the Jewboys played the Texas Music Hall. That show was a month or so before Springsteen appeared on the covers of both *Time* and *Newsweek* in the same week (October 27, 1975).

"After the show, the guys from Springsteen's band came backstage," says Clarke. "Nobody knew who they were yet, but they came and watched and came backstage to talk about it. They really liked the show; they were positive about that, very friendly, nice guys. The next thing I know, [Springsteen's album] *Born to Run* exploded."

Towards the end of 1975, the band landed a dream gig playing a live show for *Austin City Limits* (ACL), shot in Studio A of the Communications Building on the University of Texas-Austin campus. The concept of the *Austin City Limits* live TV broadcast began in October 1974, when PBS affiliate KLRU (then KLRN) program director Bill Arhos, producer Paul Bosner, and director Bruce Scafe responded to PBS's call for original programming. They shot a pilot with Willie Nelson, which was a successful fundraiser on a PBS pledge drive. Thirty-four stations aired the Willie pilot, and PBS gave *Austin City Limits* its blessing for an initial one-year run with the stipulation at least five stations support the series.

Videotaping for the 1976 season began in September 1975 with Asleep at the Wheel and a reunion of Bob Wills' Original Texas Playboys. Kinky and the Texas Jewboys were taped in November. The set list included "Amelia Earhart's Last Flight," "Rapid City, South Dakota," "Homo Erectus," "Men's Room L.A.," "Highway Café," "Wild Man From Borneo," "Carryin' The Torch," "Miss Nickelodeon," "Lover Please," "Rock 'n' Roll Across the U.S.A.," "Mama Baby Mama," "Asshole from El Paso," "They Ain't Makin' Jews like Jesus Anymore," and "Ride 'Em Jewboy."

The band was in top form and gave an inspired performance. But the show was never aired, and still isn't included in the official history on the *Austin City Limits* website.

"Kinky and I went in the day before, and Kinky promised to tone down the show and not to say the F-word," remembers Ferrero. "Then they did a very toned-down performance, and they never played it. We didn't understand it, since we agreed to all their demands prior to going on."

"They didn't tell me, but they told the press," adds Kinky. "At the time I remember thinking, 'Oh, fuck. I've done a real Lenny Bruce thing here, because they said 'Show Banned.' They told me quite clearly, 'Don't edit. Just do your show; we'll edit for you.' And then they became morally outraged. If I wanted to be careful, 'Men's Room L.A.'—a very funny song, I must add—may have done it; maybe it was 'Ain't Makin' Jews.' Actually, that show was pretty tame. So I blew it off and put a Biblical curse on *Austin City Limits*."

"Men's Room L.A." was an irreverent song written by Buck Fowler, who gave it to Kinky saying that if he didn't play it, no one would. Although Kinky's expressions were playful when he performed it on ACL, it's easy to understand how a deeply religious person might get offended. The song tells the tale of an empty toilet paper roll, a picture of Jesus, and a man's dilemma deciding whether to save his pants or his soul.

It was thirty-two years before the hour-long show was released on DVD as *Kinky Friedman: Live from Austin, TX*, with liner notes calling it "the only *Austin City Limits* program in over thirty years that has never aired on TV anywhere." It's a priceless look at Kinky and the Texas Jewboys in their prime: the Marx Brothers meet (a tamed-down) Lenny Bruce in a tight country band playing a repertoire that included a mix of humor, satire, and social commentary well ahead of its time. Dressed in a royal-blue cowboy shirt with white piping and mother-of-pearl buttons, a silver lamé scarf, and sequined jeans made of large frayed denim patches, Kinky is clearly in his element. Add a black hat, dark blue aviator shades, a single gold earring, a blue fur-lined guitar strap, and Kinky's falsetto on "Wild Man from Borneo," and you knew this wasn't your father's country music band.

Holding an unlit cigar, he tosses out one-liners: "Thank you for being Americans," "They must have gotten the heebee jeebees" (about three people who left early), and "Pretty hard to tune when you have a tampon on the guitar," referring to his capo. He introduced "Men's Room L.A." with "This is in the area of the old man, the boy, and the spook [referring to the Father, Son, and Holy Ghost]—in your religious area—we hope the baby Jesus will smile upon us with this particular number."

"We were afraid the *Austin City Limits* show wouldn't be aired, and we were right," says Jacobs. "But it was a good show at the height of the band. When you watch it, you can see Kinky was really nervous until he gets some reaction from the home crowd. Then he warms up and it's funny as hell. 'Ride 'Em Jewboy' was the last tune during our shows and blew people's minds. On *Austin City Limits* you get the best reaction you'll ever get, because those people are ready [to listen]."

Jewford remembers that night as one of the band's memorable gigs.

"Playing the *Austin City Limits* gig was wonderful—it felt great," Jewford says. "Just getting an *Austin City Limits* gig was a major deal. Besides being in Texas, we thought it would catapult the band into a situation even higher and better than we were in. Not knowing," he adds with a laugh, "that it would never be aired."

"Nothing was ever said—it wasn't until afterwards they made the decision it was way too edgy and not what they were going for," says

Jewford. "I saw a basement tape many years later and thought it was a little edgy but not worth canceling."

When Bill Arhos got the word the show was "too outrageous" to air, he proposed offering it to affiliates as an extra program.

"There were thirteen programs, and a station didn't have to run a program if they didn't want to; they could opt out of them," explains Arhos. "PBS called them hard feeds, made a schedule for thirteen weeks, and that was what everybody played no matter what it was—*Masterpiece Theatre, Sesame Street.* After I saw the performance, I wanted to offer it as what they call a 'soft feed.' [Let affiliates] Play the first thirteen and give them that [the Jewboys show] as a fourteenth week. They wouldn't even do that, which I thought was odd. That wasn't like them to not offer it to the stations with the option of not playing it. As program director, I played a lot of things I didn't want to air, but [if you don't] then you become a censor.

"I knew it would be controversial, but I personally didn't have a problem with it. I've seen worse things on public television as far as controversy. One of them—a play with Bill Bixby called *Steambath*—took place in a steam room with Jose Perez playing the role of God."

Arhos is referring to the play by Bruce Jay Friedman depicting the afterlife as a steam room, with God as the Puerto Rican attendant. That PBS production, controversial due to its language, satirical take on religion, and brief female and male nudity, was only carried by twenty-four affiliates.

In his role of program director at KLRN, Arhos had seen controversial programming. When KLRN was about to get its first two-hour satellite feed, he traveled to Washington, D.C., for a preview screening.

"All the program managers were at the Waldorf, and the play was called *Day of Absence*," he says. "The cast was all black people in white-face. The premise was all the domestics in town had disappeared and they didn't know how to change their babies' diapers, wash dishes, iron clothes, or do anything. They were all wailing and crying because all the domestics had disappeared. All of us managers looked like we had been machine-gunned. Having seen that, I couldn't understand why they had a problem with Kinky."

According to *Austin City Limits*, a history of the program by Clifford Endres, many PBS network executives felt it crossed the line of "community standards" but would send it to affiliates with a flag to signify that it might contain objectionable material. Although split on whether or not it was objectionable, KLRN's management felt a flag might jeopardize the continuation of the series after the initial one-year run.

"I don't think it had anything to do with anything other than they were scared to death of the repercussions they might have from the community," says Arhos. "It seemed like they would do what they did for a lot of things—get a room full of 200 to 300 people, show it to them, and see what they thought. But they didn't."

Howard Chambers, KLRN's director of development, told the *Daily Texan*, the University of Texas newspaper, that management felt nearly half of the 114 PBS affiliates wouldn't air Kinky's segment due to "questionable taste." But KLRN president and general manager Robert Schenkkan, who helped found KLRN and Austin's KUT-FM, told Endres he was "personally offended" by the decision.

"For years we [ACL cocreators Bill Arhos, Paul Bosner, and Bruce Scafe] kept getting consistently and wrongly blamed for killing the Kinky Friedman performance," says Arhos. "Nobody knew the real story, and even I don't know all of it. I don't know what possessed PBS not to do it, but my boss became apoplectic when he found out the first song in Rusty Wier's show was "I Heard You Been Layin' My Old Lady." He got Bosner to move it to the second song. What did it matter when Rusty Wier's old lady was getting laid? First song, second song, fifth song," he adds, laughing. "That's crazy."

Kinky's songs that tended to create the most controversy were "They Ain't Makin' Jews like Jesus Anymore," a satirical tale of a redneck racist and a Jew who refuses to turn the other cheek, and "Ride 'Em Jewboy," a poetic and haunting ballad about the Holocaust.

Kinky wrote "They Ain't Makin' Jews like Jesus Anymore" after watching an incident with a bully in a bar in Texas Hill Country. "I saw it go down in a bar around Kerrville near a place called Five Points," Kinky remembers. "It was a very redneck scene; anybody from out of state or definitely any black person is going to get it. Like the scene at Sarge's Place in the movie *Giant* where Rock Hudson fights Sarge to the music of 'The Yellow Rose of Texas.'"

"They Ain't Makin' Jews like Jesus Anymore" is Kinky's most misunderstood song and has caused people to label him a racist—a false accusation to anyone who knows him or his history—for more than four decades. Anyone who listens to the lyrics would understand the song as satire aimed at an "ethnocentric racist," but many people just hear the song's racist calling Kinky a "country nigger" and accuse him of racism.

"They don't listen to the words," says Kinky. "Like in Don McLean's song 'Vincent'; they weren't listening then, they're not listening now, and they don't get the song. A song like 'They Ain't Makin' Jews like Jesus Anymore' has a lot of different ways of being misunderstood. After a while, if you're going to be misunderstood, you identify with those people, some of the greatest that ever lived, that were misunderstood. We remember in Van Gogh's time, there was a Barry Manilow and a Justin Bieber, and probably somebody like Jimmy Buffett. They may have been commercially successful, but not a scrap of their paintings or canvases are left, and we don't even know their names. But we know Van Gogh. He lived in a mental hospital with his pet cat, and we've all been there."

Kinky sighs, exasperated that the charge of racism still won't go away. "With 'They Ain't Makin' Jews,' it got to the point where bigots—real racists, not people we call racists like Bill Clinton or Kinky Friedman or Mark Twain—real racists really liked some of my songs for the wrong reason. But you can't educate these people if they don't listen to the songs and try to understand them. A number of cool blacks in L.A. got it: Odetta, who is a friend of mine; Taj Mahal; Richie Havens; Lou Rawls."

Although Kinky says he never experienced anti-Semitism growing up in Texas, he relates an incident in Westchester County when he was in his thirties.

"It happened in New York of all places, up in Chappaqua," he says. "That's the only time I remember anyone saying anything. This very well-dressed couple that was going to a formal affair called me a dirty little Jew. That enraged me. They were old, but not quite elderly. It happened in a bar I used to hang out in all the time. I went after them through the door, smashed the glass door on my way out, chasing them into the parking lot with blood in my eyes. My head hit the door, my arm, too—this was not a suicide attempt," he says, displaying the scar on his arm. "They took me to the hospital and the doctor sewed me up. I still have a scar on my forehead which I believe is in the shape of a swastika. I don't know what this tells us.

"At any rate, when you're doing songs like 'They Ain't Makin' Jews like Jesus Anymore,' it can really enrage a Christian if they didn't

Kinky with his younger brother, Roger. *(Photo courtesy of Kinky Friedman)*

A two-month-old Richard Friedman on New Year's Day, 1945. *(Photo courtesy of Kinky Friedman)*

Kinky as a toddler with his parents in front of their Houston home. *(Photo courtesy of Kinky Friedman)*

Second-grade class photo at Edgar Allan Poe Elementary School in Houston. A very dapper Kinky is on the far right in the first row. *(Photo courtesy of Kinky Friedman)*

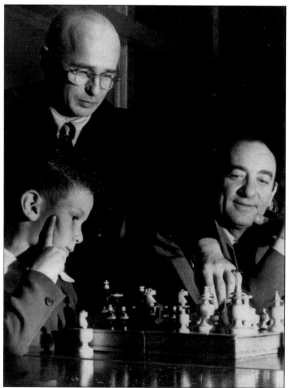

At age seven, Kinky was the youngest of fifty competitors to play grandmaster Samuel Reshevsky in a marathon match in Houston.
(Photo courtesy of Kinky Friedman)

Class photo at Pershing Middle School in Houston.
(Photo courtesy of Kinky Friedman)

Commissioned as an officer, Kinky's father, S. Thomas Friedman, piloted a B-24 (Liberator) bomber with the Eighth Air Force and flew thirty-five successful missions over Germany. *(Photo courtesy of Kinky Friedman)*

Kinky's mother, Minnie Samet Friedman, was the only Jew and one of very few women in graduate programs at Northwestern University when she earned her master's degree. *(Photo courtesy of Kinky Friedman)*

Kinky's yearbook photo at Stephen F. Austin High School, where his first band, the Three Rejects, played a pep rally in the gym. *(Photo courtesy of Kinky Friedman)*

During his stint in the Peace Corps, Kinky was assigned to Long Lama, a small village in Borneo that could only be accessed by traveling upriver on a boat. *(Photo courtesy of Kinky Friedman)*

Kinky Friedman and the Texas Jewboys always enjoyed the crowds at
the Armadillo World Headquarters in Austin. *(Poster © Micael Priest 1975)*

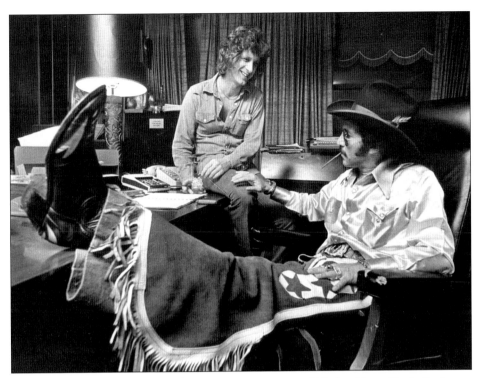

Kinky in his trademark chaps with Bill Simonson, owner of Mother Blues (the hottest nightclub in Dallas from the '70s to the early '80s) after a Jewboys show in 1975. *(Photo by Ron McKeown)*

With his lifelong friend Larry "Ratso" Sloman during the 1977 Rolling Thunder Revue tour. *(Photo © Marcia Resnick 2016)*

Kinky in his Jesus jacket and Star of David belt buckle with (left to right) John Cheateau (and his pickled herring ice cream) and iconic Austin poster artist Jim Franklin backstage at the Armadillo World Headquarters.
(Photo © 1977 Ken Hoge [www.kenhoge.com])

In one of very few photos of him without his mustache, Kinky poses for a glamor shot that appeared in *Punks, Poets and Provocateurs, NYC Bad Boys 1977–1982* (Insight Editions).
(Photo © Marcia Resnick 2016)

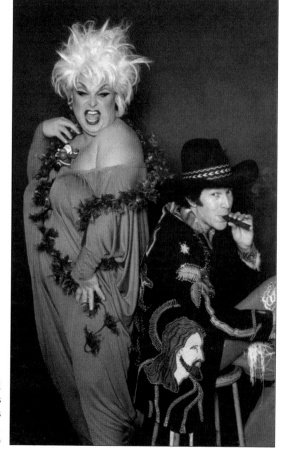

Divine, a drag queen who launched his film career by eating dog feces in *Pink Flamingos*, attended Kinky's 1973 debut at Max's Kansas City.
(Photo © Marcia Resnick 2016)

Kinky drinks a toast at Joseph Heller's birthday party at the Lone Star Café with Heller, Speed Vogel, and Michael Simmons. *(Photo courtesy of Kinky Friedman)*

John Belushi often joined Kinky on stage at the Lone Star Café. *(Photo by Beverly Cusimano)*

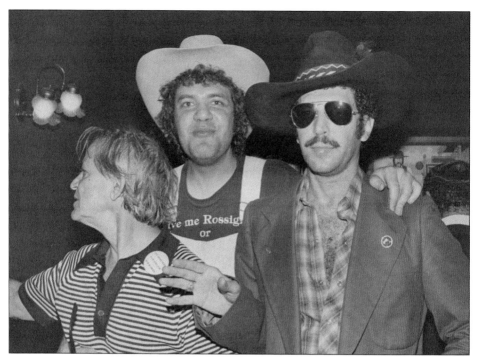

Hanging out with Mike Bloomfield and Professor Irwin Corey at the Lone Star Café in the late '70s. *(Photo by Beverly Cusimano)*

With Townes Van Zandt and Guy Clark before a show at McCabe's Guitar Shop in Santa Monica in February 1992. *(Photo by Gary Glade)*

understand it, or a Jew, or a black, or a liberal, or a conservative. It has lots of racial slurs in it. In fact, it is pretty evenhanded, and has become kind of an anthem.

"It skewers a false morality, but there's no time to discuss that in life or in politics," he says, referring to the charges of racism leveled at him by his opponents during the 2006 Texas gubernatorial race. "So when my opponents get ahold of that song or have a YouTube video of me singing it in lower baboon's asshole or wherever I am—it could be thousands of miles away— 'Here's Kinky singing this song and there's the N-word,' even though there are a lot of other things in there, too. All through my career, if there is one thing that is consistent, it's skewering false morality. This does not seem to be understood in America very well. It's understood in Europe and Australia; there's a history of it and people like me who do that."

"Ride 'Em Jewboy" is another misunderstood song that generates a kneejerk reaction from critics and the morally outraged that are unable to get beyond the title or the subject. For those who actually listen to the lyrics, it's a poignant reminder of the Holocaust with touching imagery that brings tears to their eyes.

"That song bothered Jewish record executives, and many Jews are uncomfortable with it," says Kinky. "It's the Christians—the Christian men that you see cry." Willie Nelson, who recorded that song on the 1999 release *Pearls in the Snow: The Songs of Kinky Friedman,* and played it during his own shows, observed the same reactions.

"I remember being in the studio with Willie and Imus doing an early morning radio show," says Kinky. "Imus played Willie's cut of 'Ride 'Em Jewboy' and I was watching both reactions. You get to lines like [now Kinky sings] 'Dead limbs play with ringless fingers,' and I see Imus look at Willie and Willie nods and smiles, kinda like a Buddha. He understands that line."

But many people didn't, including a Jewish woman who worked at KLRN. "I showed her Kinky's *Austin City Limits* show and she was terribly offended," says Arhos. "I don't think she was listening, because she thought it was a slam on the Holocaust."

The critics joined in with the knee-jerk reactions. "Satirizing Mom, apple pie, and other cherished dreams of the middle class was not enough for Friedman: he had to put the Holocaust in a song . . ." wrote Enders in *Austin City Limits.* In a round-up of "The Best Texas

Music-Ever-On CD" in *Texas Monthly*, Joe Nick Patoski recognized *Sold American* as a progressive country landmark, but wrote, "He skewers his own religion."

Kinky's first introduction to *Texas Monthly* readers was more off-base. In an article titled "Kinky Friedman's First Round-Up," the writer called "Ride 'Em Jewboy" a "country-western variation on the myth of the Wandering Jew," quoting selected lyrics but omitting the line "When on your sleeve you wore the yeller star." She quoted but did not catch the reference in the line "I'm with you, boy / If I got to ride six million miles," referring to the number of European Jews killed during the Holocaust.

Kinky's father, whose family emigrated from Poland, where three million Jews (ninety percent of the Jewish population) were killed by the Nazis, understood and was rightfully proud of the song.

"'Ride 'Em Jewboy' is the greatest," he said. "For the first time, Kinky wrote a song for popular tastes on the Holocaust. I know of no other song written this way. They would sing it in bars; they would sing it in taverns; they would sing it in clubs. He was bringing the Holocaust to these people and it was great."

The *Austin City Live* performance, which ended with a haunting rendition of "Ride 'Em Jewboy," was one of the last shows with the second lineup of the Texas Jewboys. The band dissolved shortly afterwards. Although there wasn't a dramatic or defining moment leading to the breakup, Jewford was the first to call it quits.

"That kind of situation grinds you—not to a bad place, but to a nothing place," he says. "It's like any relationship when the dynamic stretches at a point where you wonder why. On my side was complete burnout from everything. I think everybody was burned out on each other, personalities, the road, the lifestyle, and everything that goes with it.

"Kinky never said, 'I don't want to do this anymore,' but you could see it was going in that direction. I told him, 'I'm so thoroughly burned out on all this—I need distance. It's not as much fun anymore, it's hard work.' I felt bad about it, but I needed a break. He went on a little bit and then said, 'Screw this.' I can't believe he disbanded everything because of me; I would hope I wasn't the lead catalyst. But it wasn't fun for him anymore, either."

"The dynamics between Kinky and the band would change all

the time," says Jacobs. "Sometimes it was, 'You guys are great; this is wonderful.' Towards the end he talked about firing the band all the time, and he finally did. It was all Kinky—his up-and-down moods, his quirks. I think he was sick of it and sick of us. I guess I can't blame him," he adds with a laugh.

According to Kinky, it was the lack of money and gigs, as well as the pressure of keeping the band together, that led to the breakup. "Sometimes Danny wouldn't show up for shows," he says. "Or Jewford decided he'd had enough—he came and went. I don't blame him, because we weren't being paid. We paid him as much as we could pay him. Then the wives or girlfriends said we needed more gigs. It was a lot of pressure. Willie went through the same thing; he had many years where he couldn't pay his band.

"I didn't enjoy it as much as I could have because I was too worried about the Panamas and Jewfords, Billy Swans, and everybody else. We never had money, at any time. I remember tennis-shoeing hotel bills pretty often. Not being able to pay and not paying. Flat tires and problems with the vehicle all the way down the highway on these long-ass drives; getting stiffed on promotion or by different club owners, which happens all the time. I'm glad we didn't have a monster hit or anything—I'd probably be dead."

Despite the pressure and the financial woes, Kinky has fond memories of the Jewboys years. "It was fun and very, very exciting," he says. "There were times my band was terrific—nobody could doubt it. No matter how critical you were musically. These guys weren't the virtuoso guys in L.A.; they weren't like the studio guys that played with Warren Zevon. But they were very, very good at what they did. When we first went out, the crowds were excited. We got headlines in the *L.A. Times*, so did Elton John—but I knew we weren't gonna be Elton John."

Kinky talks about the Jewboys years as if he was a failure, but he tends to be hard on himself when he looks back over his life. He doesn't seem to understand that remaining true to himself and his musical vision—when everybody wanted to homogenize him to fit into the latest musical trend—was the ultimate success. Although he may not have known it at the time, he was following the sage advice of another Texas musician he has always admired. "Don't compromise yourself. You're all you got," said Janis Joplin. Kinky never did.

Lyle Lovett, four-time Grammy Award–winning country singer-songwriter and actor, says it best. "Who says Kinky Friedman and the Texas Jewboys never made it big?" he asks in the Dutch documentary. "Kinky's music reached and reaches so many people. To say that they never made it by commercial standards is to underestimate his music's impact. I used to buy his records as I was learning to play and sing myself."

Kinky's impact spread well beyond Texas and the country music scene. "Ride 'Em Jewboy" might have gone over the heads of the knee-jerk reactors who didn't listen to the lyrics, but it had caught the ear of a singer/songwriter who understood and respected a fellow artist with a social conscience. It wouldn't be long before Bob Dylan invited Kinky to join his traveling caravan of musicians on the Rolling Thunder Revue.

7
Bob Dylan and the L.A. Scene

"Bob was really a sweetheart. Just think Howard Hughes,
and you've got Bob Dylan."
—Kinky Friedman

An addictive personality who craved the excitement and star treatment of touring with the Jewboys and the chaos he created provoking people from the stage, Kinky moved to L.A. in search of his
next fix. He found it when he hooked up with Tom Waits and Chuck
E. Weiss. Feeling an immediate kinship with the two gravelly voiced
singer/songwriters, he hung out with them at Duke's Coffee Shop, a
funky late-night haunt below the Tropicana Hotel. Ben Frank's Coffee
Shop on Sunset Strip was another favorite all-night stomping ground.

Both were outsiders. Waits, who bore an uncanny resemblance to
Kinky's hero Woody Guthrie, wrote songs about the seamy side of life
and named his band Nocturnal Emissions. One critic described his
voice as sounding like "it was soaked in a vat of bourbon, left hanging
in the smokehouse for a few months, and then taken outside and run
over with a car."

Kinky and Weiss shared the commonality of music, as well as
growing up in the early 1950s in what Weiss called "Jew-hating towns."
"I grew up in Denver, which had a million people and only three
synagogues," he says. "When I took the Hebrew school bus, we went
through neighborhoods where adults in their fifties and sixties threw
rocks at the bus. Between the Rosenberg executions, the McCarthy hear-
ings, and the A-bomb scare where you had to 'duck and cover,' it was a
scary time for an alienated Jewish kid to grow up."

Weiss and Waits lived at the Tropicana Hotel, which Kinky remembers fondly as "a really soulful dive." Weiss, who inspired Rickie Lee
Jones's first hit song, "Chuck E.'s in Love," described it as "a combination of a weird dormitory for crazy oddballs and a demilitarized zone."

Truckers spending the night would innocently wander into the lesbian bar across the street and get rolled. A coked-up drug dealer ran a juice bar that didn't open until 3:00 a.m. When a drunk left his car suspended between the two tiers of spaces in the hotel's parking area, it hung there for a month before anyone bothered to move it. And the rent depended on the mood of the person working the front office.

"The rent was six dollars a night, but they told me that the sign was upside down and it was really nine dollars," says Weiss. "That was the kind of place it was. There was always something crazy going on. I saw William Burroughs beating up a woman at Duke's Coffee Shop. She was interviewing him at the table next to us. He got up and slapped her and walked out the door after she fell off of her chair.

"Sam Shepard lived there; the Dead Boys and a lot of punk rockers lived there," he says. "The Ramones and Blondie lived there when they were in town. It was a weird conglomeration of nuts, with a lot of unknown people off the beaten track—like porn stars and people just trying to make a buck."

One of the porn stars that hung out with Kinky, Weiss, and Waits was Tom Baker, a handsome Irishman with no inhibitions and a penchant for drinking and drugging. Although he started his acting career on the New York stage, Baker's good looks, thick head of hair, and muscular physique landed him more roles in porn films than on Broadway. His starring role in *I, a Man*, the 1967 Andy Warhol film modeled after *I, a Woman*, a Swedish film about a nymphomaniac, chronicles his lecherous adventures with six women in twenty-four hours.

Kinky enjoyed the company of people living on the edge. When he heard about Baker's close friendship with Jim Morrison and their arrest by four FBI agents for drunk and disorderly conduct and interfering with the flight of a plane, they too became fast friends.

"Tom Baker was my heart, my spiritual older brother," says Kinky. "He was older, had been around Hollywood and New York and really knew the scene. A very tough guy—a whore with a heart of gold. I started picking a fight with a guy that was bigger than me and Baker pushed me aside and said, 'You're the writer; I'm the fighter.' That guy probably would've killed me."

"We all looked up to Tom Baker," adds Weiss. "Tom was really a great guy, so full of life. He had a great sense of humor; he was smart as a whip, a great-looking guy, just a man's man."

Another one of the characters Kinky gravitated to was gonzo journalist Hunter S. Thompson. "I met Hunter Thompson there, too," he
says. "We both had the same girlfriend at different times—Laila Nabulsi.
She worked for *Saturday Night Live* and later went to Hollywood and
produced *Fear and Loathing in Las Vegas*. When I was seeing her, I was
too coked out to appreciate what a great person she was."

Kinky only stayed at the Tropicana a night or two, but often stopped
by to hang out. "We had a bunch of crazy people hanging around,
and he'd come over with his girlfriend Twinkie [Caplan]—Kinky and
Twinkie," Weiss says with a laugh.

Kinky met Caplan during the Jewboy days when she interviewed
him for her talk show on WEEP-AM, a Pittsburgh country music station. Falling in love immediately, as he tends to do, he later set her up
in L.A. and took her on the road with him when he joined Bob Dylan's
Rolling Thunder Revue.

"He talked about her incessantly; it was always Twink, Twink,
Twink," says Ferrero. "As for money, I don't know how he was doing it.
He was fronting her money for an apartment in Hollywood and buying
her bags of weed."

In any case, the arrangement was short-lived.

"It really didn't work out," says Kinky, who is uncomfortable
talking about the relationship. "It was kind of unrequited . . . part of the
loneliness of a Sunday night in L.A."

Kinky and Weiss often made the scene at L.A. hot spots, including
Dan Tanna's, a celebrity hangout, and the Troubadour, the legendary
300-seat club where Kinky met Bob Dylan during his first Jewboys tour.
During the club's colorful history, police stormed the stage and arrested
Lenny Bruce on obscenity charges, and artists including the Byrds,
Buffalo Springfield, Joni Mitchell, Neil Young, Tom Waits, Cheech and
Chong, and James Taylor made their debuts.

Working as a fry cook at the Troubadour in the early 1970s, Weiss
experienced some of the club owner's craziness. "Doug Weston was a
crazy man; he was out of his mind," says Weiss. "He'd get hopped up
and go on stage. One night he got up on stage with a twelve-gauge
shotgun—everybody ducked. He had everybody under contract from
the early days of folk. Even though they had become big stars playing
arenas, Linda Ronstadt, Jackson Browne, and Elton John were still under
contract with him for the same money he paid them in the late '60s."

While Kinky was hanging at the Troubadour, Dylan was planning the fall 1975 leg of the Rolling Thunder Revue. Designed as a traveling caravan of musicians, the lineup included Joan Baez, Joni Mitchell, Roger McGuinn, Ramblin' Jack Elliott, Bob Neuwirth, T-Bone Burnett, Mick Ronson, and an array of backing musicians. McGuinn, who became friends with Kinky during the spring 1976 tour, met Dylan in 1964 when he stopped by the Byrds' rehearsals for *Mr. Tambourine Man*, their 1965 debut album.

"We were rehearsing some of his songs in L.A. and he didn't recognize them," says McGuinn. "Because we change the time signatures and the arrangement so much, sometimes even the melody and the lyrics. We took great liberties with Bob's work," Roger adds, laughing. "But he liked us and gave us his go-ahead to do 'Mr. Tambourine Man,' even though Albert Grossman—his manager at the time—hated the idea. He tried to get Columbia records to pull it, but it was too late because it was already climbing up the charts."

Their friendship started to evolve in 1973, when Dylan contacted McGuinn through his real estate agent and asked to buy McGuinn's house in Malibu. Covered with bright red bougainvillea flowers and built out of an old Santa Monica dance ballroom, the house had spectacular ocean views. "Roger's house was a cool, funky old house," says James Mazzeo, a tour manager who was a friend. "You could sit in the living room and watch whales scratch barnacles off their bellies on rocks 150 feet out from the beach."

When McGuinn wouldn't sell, Dylan purchased a large piece of property on Bird View Drive, down the street from Roger's house. After commissioning a $2 million domed mansion overlooking Zuma Beach, Dylan began visiting him during the construction.

"We'd watch old movies or play guitars, even shoot baskets in the backyard until we were friends and hanging out," says McGuinn. "That's when he told me he was thinking of doing something unusual. I thought, 'Wow! For Bob Dylan to say something unusual it could be anything—like Fellini.' When I asked him what he had in mind, all he said was 'Something like a circus.'

"Six months later I had some time off from touring with my band, so I went to the Village to hang out and ran into Ratso—Larry Sloman—who at that time was a reporter for *Rolling Stone*. We had dinner in Chinatown and he said, 'I think Bob's at The Other End.' When we got there, Bob and Jacques Levy—we wrote 'Chestnut Mare' and a lot of songs together—were sitting at a little table in the back drinking brandy.

"When we walked in, they stood up and knocked the table over and the drinks went flying. They said, 'Hey Roger, we were just talking about you. We're going on a tour and want you to come along.' I said, 'Ah, man, I've got all these dates booked with my band that I don't think I can get out of.' But I changed my mind the next day, canceled all my dates, and joined the Rolling Thunder Revue."

Sloman met Dylan when he wrote a preview piece about Dylan's album *Blood on the Tracks* for *Rolling Stone*. Pleased with the article, Dylan invited him along to cover the tour. The self-named Ratso chronicled the tour in *Rolling Stone* and in *On the Road with Bob Dylan*, a book published in 1978.

A longtime close friend of Kinky's, Sloman met the Kinkster at his New York debut at Max's Kansas City at the urging of Mike Bloomfield. "Mike had seen Kinky in San Francisco and L.A. and told me, 'You got to go see this guy; this guy's the greatest,'" explains Sloman. "I met Kinky upstairs after the show and that was it: the beginning of a wonderful relationship. When I was in graduate school I got my master's in deviance and criminality—that's one of the reasons I like Kinky so much," he deadpans.

When Sloman invited Kinky to a Rolling Thunder Revue show in Hartford, he met Rick Danko, who was hanging out, and hit it off with Ramblin' Jack Elliott. But Kinky wasn't comfortable with the position of hanger-on and only stayed for one night.

"Kinky felt like I was pushing him on those guys and he didn't want to seem like he was so anxious to join," says Sloman. "Kinky was reluctant, but Dylan was very receptive. That was the spirit of the Rolling Thunder Revue—whatever town you went to, whoever was there would come and play. In Toronto, Gordon Lightfoot came and hung out. Joni Mitchell came in for one day and stayed for four weeks. Bob was a big fan of Kinky's work and told me to call Kinky and get him to come."

Before Kinky joined the spring 1976 leg of the tour, Dylan invited him to perform at the January 25 benefit concert for boxer Ruben "Hurricane" Carter at the Houston Astrodome. Dubbed "Night of the Hurricane II" (the first benefit concert was held in Madison Square Garden in December), the lineup included Dylan, Stevie Wonder, Carlos Santana,

Stephen Stills, Ringo Starr, Isaac Hayes, Dr. John, Richie Havens, and the Rolling Thunder Revue.

Rehearsal for the Astrodome show, held at the S.I.R. soundstage in Hollywood, included Ringo, Dennis Hopper, Santana, and members of the Band. Dylan bankrolled a shopping spree at Nudie's for stage attire for the entire entourage, and provided four-star rehearsal buffets and unlimited room tabs at the Sunset Marquis.

When Levon Helm and Rick Danko signed on for the Houston gig, Mazzeo, the tour manager for the Band's 1976 farewell tour, was hired as lighting director. Mazzeo, who also went by the name of Sandy Castle, started his career doing psychedelic light shows for Buffalo Springfield, Moby Grape, the Animals, the Beach Boys, the Mothers of Invention, the Doors, and Andy Warhol.

He became friendly with the Band in 1974, when he was tour manager for the Crosby, Stills, Nash and Young world tour, which had the Band and the Beach Boys as opening acts. He deepened that friendship the following year, when he lived with Neil Young in his Malibu ranch down the street from the Band's recording studio.

"Bob had me take everyone down to Nudie's Rodeo shop before the gig and they bought tens of thousands of dollars in rhinestone clothes," says Mazzeo. "Kinky may have gotten the sombrero and probably the Jesus jacket. I got Rick a really cool jacket that he never wore. That's when Kinky and I started to be pals, during rehearsals for that gig."

After the rehearsals and buying spree, which was rumored to cost $50,000, Dylan flew the entourage to Houston on his chartered plane. Although the exact circumstances of when and how Kinky obtained the Jesus jacket depends on who's telling the story, Kinky did wear it to the Houston benefit. Kinky's performance, which included leading a sing-along on "Asshole from El Paso," gave credence to McGuinn's observation that "he stood out as a character and made an effort to do so." If his choice of "Asshole from El Paso" wasn't enough to capture the audience's attention, his stage attire sealed the deal. A bearded Kinky performed in aviator sunglasses, a sequined sombrero, the Jesus jacket over his Grand Ole Opry satin menorah shirt, and dark-blue white-fringed chaps emblazoned with three red stars on a white background.

"Bob bought this gorgeous Jesus coat with Jesus's head and rainbows and palm trees," remembers Kinky. "God knows what it's worth today. He got it from Nudie's, wore it for a show or two, and then gave it to me. I wore it for a little while, kept it for some years, and eventually the jacket was sold at auction. I told Bob years later that I had hit some hard times and sold the coat. He said, 'Bad move, bad, bad move.' It was a bad move."

Kinky thought Dylan made a bad move when he championed the cause of Carter, portraying him as innocent in his song "Hurricane" on his 1976 recording *Desire*, and headlining fundraisers to get him out of prison. But he could understand Dylan taking up the boxer's cause.

"That's Bob's folk-singer naiveté side," he says. "The guy is out [of prison] for one minute and he beats somebody up and just about kills her," he adds referring to the incident with the national director of Carter's defense fund. Carolyn Kelley said Carter punched her in his hotel room, and then kicked her in the back after she collapsed on the floor. Although Carter denied hitting her, Kelley left the hotel with two black eyes and a massive lump on her cheek. She also spent a month in traction for her back injuries.

Eager to enjoy the lifestyle of a hip and happening artist, Kinky splurged on an apartment in Sunset Tower on Sunset Boulevard. Inviting friends to the fifteen-story art deco hotel, he regaled them with tales of celebrities—Frank Sinatra, John Wayne, Marilyn Monroe—who lived there during Hollywood's golden era. He also had stories about his new friend Iggy Pop.

With Pop's lust for life and drugs, and intelligence masked by his wild stage antics, Kinky had found another kindred spirit. "I used to hang out with Iggy Pop at the Sunset Tower and the Sunset Marquis, too," he says. "He was great—a very bright guy. Iggy was extremely talented and a lot of people vampirized his natural style."

Pop also had a habit of jumping off the balcony of his Sunset Tower apartment and into the swimming pool. When Kinky told Baker about Iggy's wild antics, he couldn't resist. The actor's naked leap from Kinky's third-floor balcony soon became part of the "Tom Baker, Troublemaker" mystique.

Kinky enhanced his own mystique by throwing a Hollywood party with his own star-studded guest list.

"Everybody came—Bob Dylan, Joni Mitchell, Jack Nicholson, Elliott Gould, and hundreds of people—it was a cool fucking party," says Kinky. "It was like you died and went to heaven. Everybody you could think of was there—big stars, little stars. About 500 of them all crammed into this room. Bob Dylan played guitar in one room; Jack Nicholson is in the other. People watching Bob sleep on the floor. Everybody, Tom Waits, Art Garfunkel—on and on. I knew them all.

"Dennis Quaid was sleeping on my floor, crashing at my apartment because he'd just gotten to Hollywood and didn't have a place to live. Randy [Quaid] was around—he was already famous. I played chess every day with Dennis, who was trying to get into commercials.

"Dennis said it was the best party he ever went to in his life. He wanted to meet Elliott Gould, so I introduced him. I really liked Elliott, but he wouldn't shake hands with Dennis Quaid—he looked at him like he was a cockroach. It was bad. After that, Elliott's career went over a cliff. So be very careful about not shaking hands with somebody."

Weiss, who had his own cheeky sense of humor, enjoyed his role of gatekeeper.

"Kinky invited the who's who of Hollywood and had me operate the intercom to see who was buzzed in and who wasn't," he says. "I was screwing with a lot of people trying to come in. I'd say, 'Who is it?' He'd say, Elliott Gould.' I'd say, 'Who?' Or, 'Jack Nicholson.' I'd say, 'Who?' I eventually let them in after I screwed with them for a while.

"Joni Mitchell and Bob Dylan ended up in Kinky's bedroom doing a mini concert. Everybody was reverent and I farted in the middle of one of Joni Mitchell's songs," he adds. "It was like they were in church and I farted. The girl I came with got so appalled she never talked to me again. It's not something I do now, but back then it was my thing—to be as irreverent as I could."

It was through Kinky's friendship with Abbie Hoffman that he met Nicholson in L.A. "Me and [Dennis] Hopper and Abbie were at Jack's house," says Kinky. "Jack was saying he was in about fifty biker films in Hollywood and nobody ever wanted him for a good movie. They just wanted him for bad B movies, so he got known as the B-movie guy. Nobody would put him into a legit movie, so he finally moved to Montana or Wyoming and lived in a cabin for a while. He was one of the first guys who left and turned his back on Hollywood.

"People in Hollywood are all afraid to leave. They think they'll miss their big break. The same with New York—it can be horrible. You'd be bartending or doing something and nothing's happening. You're out of control and losing it, living in squalid conditions, but you're afraid to leave because you might meet a big director or you might meet somebody at a party. But Jack left Hollywood and said it was when he turned his back on Hollywood, it came to him.

"Peter Fonda called him and said, 'We've got this movie *Easy Rider*, and I want you to play this supporting role.' That fucking supporting role made Jack a big movie star. Every movie after that was a great film like *Chinatown*, *One Flew Over the Cuckoo's Nest*, *The Shining*. There's a real lesson there. If you can walk away and turn your back on your passion, sometimes it will come to you."

Ferrero, who shared Kinky's apartment, remembers Nicholson and a number of celebrities dropping by and hanging out. "When Randy Quaid was doing *The Missouri Breaks* with Jack Nicholson, he came in one day and said, 'I just got off the set,' and Nicholson said, 'Another day, another $36,000.' Danny Hutton was always hanging out at Kinky's apartment, and Bobby Neuwirth came over drunk one night and threw hamburgers in the pool."

Although Kinky has no recollection, Ferrero has vivid memories of another celebrity-studded party that almost cost Kinky his life.

"Kinky is such a magnetic personality that one day, he said, 'I bet by tonight I can get this place packed with people,'" says Ferrero. "He told about four people in L.A. and the party was packed. Bob Dylan showed up. So did Lowell George, Robbie Robertson, Levon Helm, and most of the Band. It was incredible. Kinky did so much blow [cocaine] that night, he was passed out in the bedroom and I thought he was gone. He was that zombied out—it was scary.

"David Cassidy was in the bedroom putting a teaspoon of blow under Kinky's nose. We thought Kinky had ODed on blow, and these guys are mixing it with ludes [Quaaludes] or giving him a joint because they thought it would take you out of that. I said, 'You got to get out of here; Kinky doesn't need that shit.' I had my friend Squid stand in front of the door so nobody could get in to give him any more drugs."

When Kinky came to the next morning, he had no memory of the party or his near-death experience.

"The next day Kinky is pissed off at me because I didn't introduce Robbie to Lowell George," says Ferrero. "I told him, 'They met and were playing guitars with each other. Sorry you missed it.' Each picked up one of Kinky's piece-of-shit guitars and they played together in a corner. Lowell took a beer bottle and played this great slide guitar on blues songs. It was amazing. Levon came over to listen, but there were about 100 people roaming around the apartment stoned, not even noticing it."

Before the tour started, Dylan invited Kinky to join him; Hopper; his road manager, Gary Shafner; and his tour manager and old friend Louie Kemp for a month in Mexico. They stayed on the island of Yelapa off the coast of Mazatlán. Intrigued by Kinky's songwriting ability, Dylan wanted to write songs with him. Although Kinky enjoyed the getaway, he passed on the songwriting, a move that he now regrets.

"I found that some of the people I admire very much—Woody Guthrie is one, Churchill is another—blew a lot of opportunities," he says. "I've seen the pattern in myself. I've hung out with Bob a lot and been with him in Mexico when he wanted to write songs with me. He said, 'Let's write some songs together,' and I said, 'Nah, I don't know.' Whatever it was, I didn't do it," Kinky says with a laugh, before explaining why he passed on an opportunity most songwriters can only dream about.

"A lot of people who were not musicians—the road-traveled, street-savvy road management types who worked for Bob—were very charming and I became very close to them. They had worked with everybody, and knew more about the music world and rock and roll than the star does. They're good people that babysit the artist. Quite often the artist is just an artist, and not a real attractive human being.

"It would have been great to write some songs with Bob and today I would have done that. And I should have. But I hung out with the cool guys—the road managers and tour managers . . . although that wasn't really the point of it. The point of it was to get with the stars, write some songs with them, and get a catalog going. I didn't and I ended up like an aging black blues artist whose catalog is disseminated all around."

Even though they never wrote songs together, Kinky and Dylan did spend one-on-one time getting to know each other.

"One day I'm on a deserted beach with Bob; it was almost like a movie, a surreal movie," says Kinky. "We sat out there and talked for a while, about the king of the gypsies and other things like that. He was feeling like the king of the gypsies then because all his wives and children were leaving him. He had a guitar case and was wearing a leather jacket and it was fucking 190 degrees. We're kidding around and he opens up his guitar case. By the time he had the guitar out and was strumming it, he's got a crowd. In the fucking middle of an empty beach. Then he puts his guitar away, and says, 'I liked it a lot when people would be eating dinner or talking when I was playing—when there was a little noise.' That's something he never gets anymore."

Curiosity may have also spurred people to gather in an open-air marketplace to watch a high-stakes chess match between Kinky and one of the locals. Aware of Kinky's reputation as a virtuoso chess player, Dylan and his managers put Kinky up against the Yelapa champ.

"I was really good in Mexico; I had to be," Kinky says. "There were hundreds of dollars bet between Louie Kemp and Bob Dylan and some local business guys. Louie put $200 on Kinky to beat the Mexican champ. I wore my Jesus jacket and a big cowboy hat and played one game. I played this Mexican guy and beat him. I hadn't played in years and was very lucky, because this guy was good. I don't know if I could ever do it again, but the pressure was really on—and I won!" he says with a playful inflection.

"Louie gave me a $100 to sing 'They Ain't Makin' Jews like Jesus Anymore' at the anniversary of his seafood partner many years ago," he adds, laughing. "They were all old Jewish people, and of course I did—a hundred bucks is a lot."

When Kinky returned from his getaway with Dylan, he began hanging out with members of the Band in L.A. and Malibu. "A lot of people I hung around with were really cool," he says. "I spent a lot of time with Levon, Rick Danko, Richard Manuel, and their road manager, James Mazzeo. I hung out with them at the Shangri-La, too. That was a great bunch of guys, wonderful guys. It's rare that people with such raw talent as that can make it, and they did."

Two years earlier, the Band had leased a small seaside ranch in Malibu and built a recording studio in the master bedroom. The Shangri-La Studio, which included a game room with pool table and built-in bar, was built to the precise specifications of Dylan and the Band. Mazzeo, who lived in a bungalow attached to the main building, describes the scene.

"You can look right out the bungalow window to Zuma Beach," he says. "Elvis used to live there, Johnny Carson owned a place—it had gone through a series of transformations. There were three bedrooms in the main house, a kitchen, living room, and studio and three bungalows attached to the house overlooking Zuma Beach."

During studio sessions, artists stayed on the property, which included the corral where *Mr. Ed*, the 1960s TV show, was filmed. "You had to drive up a hill to get to Shangri-La, which had a horse corral and a little stable at the bottom of the driveway," says Mazzeo. "Roses grew along the fence in the backyard and Bob had a tent by the roses."

If the studio sessions and parties went well into the night, or he'd had a fight with his wife, Sara, Dylan slept in the tent. When his tent wasn't pitched, he'd crash on the mattress in the back of Mazzeo's 1951 Pontiac hearse ambulance. The night he slept in the hearse in his gauze turban almost took ten years off of Mazzeo's life.

"Every Monday morning I had to drive into town to meet the Band's business manager at Capitol Records," Mazzeo says. "One morning I'm driving for fifteen or twenty minutes and was south of Topanga Beach when I looked up and saw a ghost looking at me from the back of my hearse. A guy all wrapped in gauze. When I looked in the rearview mirror, and saw this gossamer ghost looking at me, it scared the shit out of me. It's Bob; he was sleeping with his turban on and it had come undone and fallen down over his face. He said, 'Where are we? Sara threw me out last night so I slept in here.' When I told him we were by Topanga Beach, he said 'Let me out, I'll hitchhike back home.' I wanted to turn around and take him home, but he insisted he did it all the time. So I let him out and he hitchhiked home."

It was during that same time frame that a serendipitous meeting at a legendary L.A. nightclub hooked Kinky up with an amazing talent for his third album. "One night I was hanging out at the Troubadour, where a lot of musicians hung out," Kinky says. "I was at the bar drinking a diet hemlock, I believe, and a guy comes in wearing a riverboat gambler's hat. He had a wispy red beard and sideburns; I'm not sure about his pubic hair. He looked very familiar and he comes up to me, sits down next to me, and says, 'Kinkster, let's have another round.'

"We're talking there already for too long for me to admit I don't know who he is. I think he's a Texas singer-songwriter, maybe Ray Wylie Hubbard or Rusty Weir or somebody. I know it's not Jerry Jeff Walker, because he's the second-biggest asshole in Texas. And I know that because I'm the first. So after a few hours of drinking with this guy, I'm really fishing for clues to who he is and hesitating to bring it up.

Then we go into the men's room at the Troubadour and did some long lines of Peruvian marching powder.

"We came back to the bar, me and this guy, and it's a couple more hours, about five hours of hanging out together. Like the beginning of a beautiful friendship at the end of *Casablanca* and I still didn't know who the guy is. So I'm struggling with this. Do I want to not hurt this guy's feelings, or do I want the truth? The best thing was to find out the truth. So at some awkward moment, I turned to the guy and said, 'Look, I hate to ask you this, but what is your name?' 'Eric Clapton,' he said. That's how I met Eric, and a week later he was playing slide Dobro on 'Ol' Ben Lucas,' and Dr. John, the Night Tripper, was playing piano on it at Shangri-La Studios. Levon was involved, Lowell George was involved, Van Dyke Parks . . . there were some great ones."

When Kinky recorded "Kinky" and "Ol' Ben Lucas" at Shangri-La Studios for his Epic LP *Lasso from El Paso*, Clapton was recording *No Reason to Cry*, and Danko was recording a self-titled LP. Clapton, Helm, and Danko joined Kinky on those two tracks with Clapton on Dobro, Danko on bass, and Helm on drums. Helm and Danko also sang backup vocals on "Kinky," which included Manuel on percussion and Ron Wood on slide guitar. Dr. John played toy piano on "Ol' Ben Lucas."

"I remember Clapton being so fucked up," says Ferrero. "He was sitting on a high stool with the Dobro when he nodded out. This muscle guy—he looked like an English boxer—came over and woke him up. Clapton woke up and plays these incredible riffs. He staggers out and says, 'That's the hardest note I've ever played, mate.'"

Kinky met Dr. John at the Night of the Hurricane in Houston and was thrilled to have him play on his album. "Dr. John was great," he says. "He had a little daughter who loved 'Ol' Ben Lucas' and was singing in the chorus. So he brought a little toy piano and played it on that song."

Ringo Starr, who Kinky also met at the Night of the Hurricane, improvised his role as the voice of Jesus in "Men's Room, L.A."

"Ringo, he came down from L.A. to do it," says Kinky. "Ringo was very spontaneous; he ad-libbed. He may have had a few notes, but he didn't read anything," says Kinky, who recites Ringo's ad-libbed lyrics in an English accent: "Well, I may seem to come from Liverpool. And then on the other hand I may come from France. But if you don't get off that toilet, well I'm just gonna have to dance."

"That's pretty clever," Kinky adds with a laugh. "Ringo wasn't there the whole time, but various people popped in, including Ronnie Hawkins. Members of the Band played in the Hawks [Hawkins' band] in the late '50s and early '60s. I did his song 'Kinky.' He was one of the most colorful guys on the planet."

"Ronnie Hawkins was great," agrees Ferrero. "He had this big gallon of tequila on his shoulder. When Clapton came out, Hawkins says, 'You're good, boy. You're one of the best, but you ain't the best.' Clapton was cool about it."

But Clapton's bodyguard was not amused and attempted to throw Hawkins out.

"Clapton's bodyguard told Ronnie, 'You're gonna have to leave the studio, fellow,'" says Kinky in an English accent. "Ronnie said, 'You better be the baddest motherfucker in California if you think you're gonna get me out of here. No way.' Hawk was laughing at him.

"That's when I gave Eric a cigar and a butt cutter and he just bit the end off of it. Eric met everybody in the place, every friend and every musician there. He was so nice until I introduced him to Steve Popovich, the producer at Epic Records. The record company guy was the only guy Eric wouldn't shake hands with. He said, 'Piss off, mate, piss off.' Eric doesn't like record company executives. He doesn't like the business side of it, and that is understandable. "

Kinky was invited to Clapton's impromptu birthday party during the *No Reason to Cry* sessions. In his 2003 biography *Crossroads*, he describes the sessions at Shangri-La Studios as "an intensely creative period, where all-night jam sessions and wild parties were the norm."

Friends who joined the jam to celebrate Clapton's thirty-first birthday included Bob Dylan, Ron Wood, Jesse Ed Davis, Billy Preston, Van Morrison, Robbie Robertson, Rick Danko, Levon Helm, Richard Manuel, and Garth Hudson. That jam was released twenty-two years later as *Happy, Happy Birthday Eric!*, a ten-track bootleg CD on Dandelion Records. A quote attributed to Clapton is included on the CD artwork:

"I had a magnificent birthday party right in the middle of the sessions and we decided to record everything and everybody that came into the studio. There's Billy (Preston) singing a couple of Ray Charles songs with the Band backing him along with Jesse Ed Davis, me, Robbie (Robertson), and Woody (Ron Wood) on guitars. Bob (Dylan) showed up about eight o'clock in the morning and it went on from there."

When Ferrero arrived at the party with Helm, Dylan was flipping through a stack of records. "Everybody is walking around him—tiptoeing around him—including Clapton and Ronnie Wood," says Ferrero. "Levon with that great accent goes over and says, 'Are you having a good time there, are you, Bob?'

"Levon introduced me to Ronnie Wood and Ronnie was blown away by my python jacket. He takes me out in the hall and took out these fifty-pound notes, rolled them up, and brought out some blow. We did some blow, and later I put him on the phone with a friend of mine in Texas who was a big fan. Ronnie was happy to do it. He said, 'If it wasn't for the man in the twenty-seventh row, where would we be?'"

Ferrero was also impressed with the way Clapton conducted himself at that party. "Some drunk came up to him and said, 'I hate McCartney. He's not as good as John; he has no talent.' Clapton didn't even raise his voice. He said, 'Paul is a very good friend of mine and I appreciate you not talking that way about him.'"

"I sure liked Eric," adds Kinky. "You like the consistent people. Bob is consistent. Dr. John is consistent, Eric Clapton has been consistent. I got a call at the ranch one night from Eric in the months after Eric's kid died. [Clapton's four-year-old son, Conor, died in March 1991 after falling out of an open bedroom window on the fifty-third floor of the Manhattan apartment building where he lived with his mother.] I hadn't talked to Eric in maybe five or ten years. Just a sweet call, how's it going? We made plans to get together at his show and I couldn't fuckin' make it—it was during some bullshit. I sent people to shows like the dead love of my life; Kacey Cohen went to Eric's show using a Kinky guitar pick. She showed it to the security guy and got in with her friends and went backstage. Here's a guy that maybe I hadn't seen in twenty years. I wouldn't know how to call him; I don't know if he still knows how to call me, but some of these people you have a special kindness for."

Kinky's song list for *Lasso from El Paso* included a live version of "Sold American" from a Rolling Thunder Revue gig in Fort Collins, Colorado, "Twinkle," "Ahab the Arab," "Dear Abbie," "Kinky," "Lady Yesterday," "Catfish," "Men's Room, L.A.," "Bananas and Cream," "Ol' Ben Lucas,"

"The Ballad of Ira Hayes," and "Waitret, Please, Waitret." Kinky wrote six of the tracks and cowrote another with Lanny Bowles.

Between guests, friends, studio players, and the Rolling Thunder Revue entourage playing on "Sold American," *Lasso from El Paso* included nearly three dozen musicians.

"There were a lot of legendary artists on that record, a hell of a lot of talent," says Kinky. "I did the vocals, but there must have been fifty musicians. Teddy Jack Eddy—that was the music name of [actor] Gary Busey. Richard Manuel also played drums; he's an all-around spinning genius. Lowell George on guitar; he's a fuckin' genius. He played on a beautiful version of 'Catfish' produced by Van Dyke Parks," he adds, referring to the Bob Dylan/Jacques Levy song written as a tribute to Baseball Hall of Fame pitcher Jim "Catfish" Hunter.

Although he has fond memories of the artists on that album, Kinky doesn't remember who negotiated the deal with Epic Records. "I don't remember if Weintraub was still involved or how I got hooked up with them for *Lasso from El Paso*," he says. "I'm foggy about that, and that's part of the problem. But I remember Merle Haggard was friendly and helpful—he was great."

Haggard, who wrote "Okie from Muskogee," the song parodied by Ken Jacobs and Chinga Chavin in "Asshole from El Paso," had no problem with the parody. But country artist Buck Owens, who owned the publishing to Haggard's songs, refused to let Kinky record the song or use *Asshole from El Paso* as the name of the album.

"There was a big fight to call it *Asshole from El Paso*," remembers Kinky. "Merle very much liked the version of the song and wanted me to record it. He was very happy about it, enough to call me up and invite me to go on a tour with him. The problem was his publisher, Buck Owens. Buck and Merle didn't get along. You get a publisher and you're locked into it—it's like having a wife you hate."

The legal injunction arrived at the eleventh hour, which had Epic scrambling to come up with another name for the album and new artwork for the cover. The name became *Lasso from El Paso*, and the artwork a parody of the Camel cigarettes logo with Kinky riding a camel, a cigar in his mouth and a lasso in his hand. It was a clever solution that played on Kinky's chaotic rendition of Ray Stevens's 1962 hit "Ahab the Arab."

After Kinky cut two songs at Shangri-La Studios, he travelled to SugarHill Studios in Houston to record the other eight songs. Hawkins and Rick Danko's brother Terry Danko played on those songs; Richard Manuel was the only Band member at the Houston sessions.

Since founding the studio in 1944 as Quinn/Gold Star Studios, producer/owner Bill Quinn had helped launch the careers of Lightnin' Hopkins, the Big Bopper, George Jones, the Sir Douglas Quintet, Willie Nelson, Roy Head, and Freddy Fender. When Huey P. Meaux took it over in the early 1970s, he renamed it SugarHill and produced records by Fender, as well as Todd Rundgren, Asleep at the Wheel, Ted Nugent, and a live Little Feat broadcast for the Pacifica Radio Network.

Kinky wrote "Dear Abbie" for Abbie Hoffman, who went into hiding from the authorities in 1974 and didn't turn himself in until 1980. During Hoffman's years on the lam, Kinky gave his friend sanctuary at the family ranch in Medina, and at his rented house in Chappaqua, New York. Hoffman lived in the infirmary building behind the Echo Hill Ranch lodge—where Kinky currently resides—when Kinky recorded those cuts.

"Abbie Hoffman went with Kinky to Huey Meaux's studio in Houston for the *Lasso from El Paso* recording sessions," remembers Ferrero. "He was there when Kinky cut 'Dear Abbie.' Abbie talked about himself a lot. But when we went to Huey Meaux's studio, they didn't know who he was."

Meaux, like Hoffman, had secrets very few people knew about. In early 1996, Meaux was arrested and charged with child pornography, sex with a minor, and drug trafficking. He was found guilty and given a fifteen-year jail sentence in the summer of 1996. "Twenty years later we found out about the porn," says Ferrero. "We were all in shock; we didn't believe it."

Despite Meaux's personal proclivities, Kinky believed in his talents in the studio. "I knew Huey Meaux pretty well; he was a very good producer," says Kinky. "If he'd been there from the beginning . . . if I had any producer who knew what he was doing like Huey did . . . Huey was a very troubled guy. He was fucked up, but that doesn't take away from the fact that he had a good ear. He created a guy like Freddy Fender, and he could've done that with me. He worked with Doug Sahm, too."

Although the information came in too late for the artists to be credited on the liner notes, Little Feat members—Kenny Gradney on bass, Richie Hayward on drums, and Sam Clayton on percussion—joined Kinky and Lowell George for the "Catfish" session in Haji Sound in L.A.

"Those Little Feat members did play on the session with—as Kinky will attest—some inspiration from Irving Berlin," says Van Dyke Parks, who produced the song. The Irving Berlin comment alludes to the "White Christmas" of cocaine in the studio.

Airplay for *Lasso from El Paso* was minimal; a warning label on promotional copies ("ATTENTION Radio Station Programmers! Contains some provocative material which may be objectionable") didn't help. The cuts were uneven; the styles ranged from tender ballads like "Twinkle" and "Lady Yesterday" to raucous tunes like "Ahab the Arab," the irreverent "Men's Room L.A.," and "Waitret, Please, Waitret," where Kinky extols his server to "come sit down on my fate" because "eatin' ain't cheatin', Lord it ain't no disgrace." Whether it was the content or lack of airplay, Epic dropped Kinky from the label.

Kinky didn't know about the warning label and called his lack of awareness "one of my blessings and curses. The record company is usually only good for one thing—to support the band and the tour," he says. "But once you've been on the road a few years, the new comes off the crystal chandeliers. If you don't have a hit record, you've got a problem. Keeping a band up is very expensive; to travel with any band costs a fortune. Then cocaine came into the picture and it becomes impossible.

"It was the music business that I didn't understand or relate to," he adds. "Being in a studio, mixing songs—that all bored me—my eyes glazed over. I liked the human interaction—the people, the excitement of it. That was fun, but it wasn't commercially successful."

Even without a label, Kinky's career was hardly at a standstill. He was going on tour with Bob Dylan, and his friends in Nashville were thrilled for him.

"Kinky got the deal—he got in front of Dylan and Dylan was king of all kings as far as everybody was concerned," says Billy Joe Shaver. "Kinky was a big hero of ours. Back then, nobody was doing all that great. He was the first one of our gang of people that got to sing on the Grand Ole Opry. Then Bob Dylan took him out and let him front him on a big tour.

"We were all happy and would say, 'One of our guys did it.' It was a big deal. I was real happy about Kinky playing in front of Bob Dylan. He was doing his nasty stuff—doin' all that Women's Lib stuff, and 'eatin ain't cheatin'—stuff like that, trying to shock you," Shaver says laughing. "I'm not trying to shock you, but it's true. He said if a night went by and he didn't get a bunch of tomatoes or something [thrown at him], it wasn't a good night."

The spring 1976 leg of the Rolling Thunder Revue consisted of twenty-two shows in five weeks. That lineup included Dylan, Joan Baez, Joni Mitchell, Roger McGuinn, Ramblin' Jack Elliott, Bob Neuwirth, Eric Clapton, Ringo Starr, Allen Ginsberg, Mick Ronson, and Scarlet Rivera. Kinky opened the show with Neuwirth and McGuinn, who introduced him as "the original Wooly Bully from Austin."

Kinky is a bit foggy as to how he got picked to join the Rolling Thunder Revue. "I'm trying to remember, but I don't know," he says. "But Bob took me on and paid me well—it was a real good gig. When Bob Dylan picked me up, I wasn't doing much."

McGuinn didn't know why Dylan picked Kinky either but thought it had to do with his respect for Kinky and his music. "Bob picked people he liked at random, and he and Kinky liked each other," says McGuinn. "They're both Jewish; they have that in common. That was really important to Bob at that time—to be Jewish. That was probably a factor, though I'm not sure it was the whole thing. Kinky did his own songs—he was doing whatever he wanted and Bob was fine with that."

Sloman, who is also Jewish, didn't think Kinky being Jewish had anything to do with getting chosen for the tour. "Look, Bob was nudging me," he says. "There's a scene in my book in Montreal where I'm calling up Leonard [Cohen] to come on the show 'cause Bob is a fan of Leonard's and wants him to come on the show. Bob appreciates good work—he liked Kinky because he was writing great songs. It's the same reason Mike Bloomfield called me and told me to go see him. When you listen to Kinky's first album—every song on *Sold American* is a great song.

"Of course it's more; camaraderie and 'I want to get to know this guy,'" adds Sloman. "It was such a great combination of Lenny Bruce and Hank Williams to be writing songs like this. That's why musicians were attracted to him. I don't think it had anything to do with being Jewish. One of the charming things about Bob is he can be as big a fan as anybody. Bob was really into hanging out with Kinky—they're kindred spirits in a lot of ways."

The tour started with a run of gigs in Florida. Traveling in private Greyhound buses, the entourage then headed west for shows in Alabama, Mississippi, and Louisiana. They took a three-day break before hitting the Lone Star State, where they played six shows. They wound up the tour with shows in Oklahoma, Kansas, and Colorado.

"We had a lot of fun on that tour," says McGuinn. "The camaraderie was amazing. We were all friends and all hung out together. Riding these buses at night . . . I used to sit right next to Joni Mitchell and I even bummed a song off her for one of my albums. It was a great time."

Kinky also enjoyed the camaraderie. "Joan Baez and Joni Mitchell were great," he says. "Ringo was terrific. Clapton was great; he was there a little bit. Then Roger McGuinn. Allen Ginsberg was great. He's terrific. That's a lot of talent there. I met Scarlet Rivera. I didn't know Scarlet well but I liked her. Very talented, a gypsy fiddle player; that's pretty cool. Then there was Ramblin' Jack—he and Bob started the whole folk music thing. Two Jewboys from the Midwest. Ramblin' is the real goods."

Kinky and Dylan hit it off from the time Dylan caught his Texas Jewboys gig in 1973. "We have some of the same interests and have a certain curiosity about each other," says Kinky. "I brought a girlfriend backstage to a show that Bob later took out. He did have one of his guys call me and ask if it was ok for Bob to call her. I said, 'No problem.' When Bob went out with her, he asked about me—he wanted to know if I was funny all the time.

"Bob is pretty funny most of the time when I'm with him. We don't sit there and talk about Kierkegaard [a Danish philosopher known as the father of existentialism] or anything like that. He's a witty guy and we clearly like each other. Bob was very charming, and he's said some really nice things. Especially in Ratso's book," he adds, referring to a conversation in *On the Road with Bob Dylan*. When Sloman told Dylan many people considered him a great lyricist who didn't understand music, Dylan agreed. "Well, I don't understand music," Dylan said. "I understand Lightnin' Hopkins. I understand Leadbelly, John Lee Hooker, Woody Guthrie, Kinky Friedman. I never claimed to understand music, Ratso. If you ever heard me play the guitar you'd know that," he added with a laugh.

Playing the Rolling Thunder Revue tour with Dylan was a big jump from the club tours that Kinky played with the Texas Jewboys. But he knew he had better not outshine the star, and was clever enough to suggest a change in format when he did.

"With Bob we played coliseums; we played some big venues," says

Kinky. "Being on that tour with Bob, when you walked on the stage you were a star. It was an experiment—some of the guys were really cool, some weren't. I was opening with 'Ain't Makin' Jews like Jesus Anymore' for a while. Then going into 'Sold American' and then doing 'Asshole from El Paso.' It wowed them in Florida.

"I came on before Bob and Roger McGuinn—Roger's great—he's a genius. When I tried that new set format in Florida, 'Asshole' brought down the house. It was so good; the crowd was cheering and raucous. Then Bob comes wandering out in a turban—they didn't even know who he was. He starts his first song, which was 'Visions of Johanna,' which takes about twelve minutes. The crowd was laughing and talking throughout the first half of his song. I said, 'Man, I'm in trouble,' and I was.

"It was my suggestion to invert the songs—to do something familiar and start with 'Mr. Tambourine Man.' We did 'Asshole from El Paso' right into 'Mr. Tambourine Man' and that took it up about twenty decibels as soon as he sang the first line. That worked and I saved my job. And my job was easy because on the Bob Dylan tour, even the security guys were gentle. People didn't get hurt, but they knew how to handle real troublemakers and assholes."

During the Florida dates, the band stayed at the Belleview Biltmore Resort and Spa, a historic luxury hotel in Belleair looking out over Old Clearwater Bay and the barrier islands.

"We camped out there for a couple of weeks because they had a big ballroom that we set up as a rehearsal area," says McGuinn. "That was where they filmed a *Midnight Special* TV show that Bob didn't like so it never got aired. Bob was very generous at that tour. We always stayed at fine resorts, we all had big hotel rooms, and he took care of all our meals. We had a hospitality suite; it was like a rolling party the whole tour. It was great."

It was during that tour that Kinky and McGuinn became friends. "He was at my house when I had parties with Bob Dylan, but we were all doing a lot of stuff [drugs and alcohol], so it's hard to remember those days," says McGuinn. "I remember him distinctly from the Rolling Thunder tour because I'd see him every day. I remember hanging out one night with Bob, Kinky, Ratso, and Mick Ronson. Bob was driving a motor home at night with his sunglasses on. That was quite interesting," he adds laughing.

"Kinky and I had a lot in common with music and hung out a lot. He was a lot of fun; I've always had a good time with him. I didn't take any offense in any of the so-called offensive things that he said—I thought it was funny. He wasn't offensive to me, but he could be towards women. He had a habit of calling them 'slits,'" he adds laughing. "'You know, she's not a bad person for a slit.' I found him amusing and I liked him. I think sometimes he says and does things simply for shock value."

After the gigs in Florida, the Rolling Thunder Revue played the Warehouse in New Orleans. Kinky was appalled several decades later when he listened to a bootleg tape of the show. "That was when I lost it on cocaine," he says. "I was shocked at how bad it was. I could do the song 'Asshole from El Paso' right now on a stage alone and bring down the house—just with spirit, energy, and a little humor. The way the band did it there—this great band—was with all these false endings. They produced it all wrong—they took all the excitement, the climax, out of it, dragging all these slow choruses around."

Kinky's harsh impression of that performance wasn't shared by friends at that show.

"I brushed over the drug taking because I don't think it's my place to say who did what when," says Weiss. "But I can tell you from the feed-back from Tom Waits—who went to the New Orleans Rolling Thunder Revue show—that Kinky saying it sounded terrible was probably all in his head. He probably was coked up, but I don't think it was anything that embarrassing because I would have heard about it if it was."

Five days after the Big Easy gig, the Rolling Thunder Revue played the Hofheinz Pavilion in Houston with Willie Nelson. Dubbed the Rolling Smoke Revue, Nelson and his touring band followed Dylan's set and joined Dylan and his entourage during the sixteen-person finale. When the Revue rolled into Austin for their May 12 show at the Municipal Auditorium, Kinky and his family gave Bob and his entourage a heaping helping of Texas hospitality.

"We had a party at our house in Northwest Austin that was terrific," says Kinky. "It was for everybody in the Rolling Thunder Revue. We had twenty acres and a big deck looking out over the hills. Joan Baez was there and Joni Mitchell. We had a friend there who was one of my fathers' colleagues—Warren Bachelis—he was dying of cancer. He came to the party but he elected to stay in the bedroom. He wasn't feeling that well, but he wanted to see if he could meet Bob Dylan or Joan Baez.

Bob wouldn't go back there because he doesn't like to be around death or whatever—it brings him down. But Joni went and sang a song for Warren, which was great."

Kinky made up for Dylan's' slight of his father's colleague—who died two months later—by including and attributing one of Bachelis's quotes in his 1999 novel *Spanking Watson*. Dylan apparently had other things on his mind.

"I think Bob may have screwed Joni Mitchell in the other bedroom during this party," says Kinky. "But Bob was charming. He told my parents, 'I'm sure you're very proud of your son,'" he adds with a laugh. "He's funny; he's got that kind of thing where he was trying to be Jewish polite. They were already very proud of their son, even before I did the Bob Dylan tour. But it was still nice. My dad liked Bob, so we brought him up to my dad's office on the University of Texas campus. He worked in educational psychology and the chairman of the department had never heard of Bob Dylan. Most people had, but he had not. The halls started filling with people who were waiting to see Bob Dylan. That was great.

"My dad got along well with Allen Ginsberg, too," Kinky adds. "Al is wonderful; he came down here to speak at UT and went out to dinner with me and my dad. He's a really interesting man who can relate to everybody. It was incredible how well he did with bikers, for instance. Bikers loved him. They liked him more than they liked Hunter Thompson. Rednecks liked him. Hippies liked him. His life and his poetry were perfectly intertwined."

Kinky enjoyed that tour, as well as the time he spent with Dylan.

"Bob was really a sweetheart. Just think Howard Hughes, and you've got Bob Dylan," says Kinky. "He can be very funny because of circumstances. Just traveling with him, and him being Bob Dylan, makes it very funny because there are some straight people that don't know who he is. Like we're in some dive or little motel on the highway and he's locked himself out of his hotel room and can't fucking find the key. And the guy who runs the place is a local redneck who wants to see an ID because has no idea who he is. That's always funny.

"Bob's been through ups and downs, through all kinds of shit, but has a strong sense of humor. One time we had to book a flight at the last minute and there was nothing available in first class. When we got back to coach, there were only a few seats left and Bob ended up sitting next to a young female fan that got hysterical. 'I can't believe it,' she screamed. 'I'm sitting next to Bob Dylan—I can't believe it.' Bob just looked at her and said, 'Pinch yourself.'"

Although Kinky's and Dylan's careers have taken different paths, Kinky tries to catch up with his friend whenever his schedule allows. When Dylan played the Municipal Auditorium in San Antonio, Texas, on April 14, 2006, Kinky, who was then running as an Independent in the Texas gubernatorial campaign, was in the audience.

"We saw Bob backstage and he just lit up," Kinky remembers. "As Mae West would say, he was very happy to see me and I was happy to see him."

When Kinky returned to L.A. after the tour ended, he continued to spend time with the Band, backstage at their shows and hanging out with them in Malibu and Santa Monica. One of the shows Kinky attended was a June 1976 concert at the Santa Barbara Bowl, a natural amphitheater carved into a hillside and surrounded by oak trees. When he talked about that show late one night at the ranch, the Kinkster disappeared and you caught a glimpse of Richard Friedman, who was like any other fan awed to be in the company of his musical heroes.

"I remember that concert in Santa Barbara," says Kinky, his deep brown eyes lighting up as he shared the memory. "I was really close to Dr. John at that time, who I love. He's loaded with talent. From his fingertips to his toenails, he's brilliant. It was a cobill with the Band. That was really cool, being backstage and involved with the Band and Dr. John. That was a great double header, and I felt like part of it hanging out with those guys."

Kinky's natural charisma, sense of humor, and larger-than-life persona attracted many people to him, but not everyone became a lifelong friend like Levon Helm.

"Rick and Richard were close to Kinky, but with Kinky and Levon there was a simpatico," explains Mazzeo. "They were both from the South; they both had that Southern way about them. They both had the Dylan connection. For Levon, Kinky would be almost like an alter ego. Kinky is pretty outspoken, and Levon was a little more diplomatic.

"Levon was a real country gentleman, just a Southern gentleman of the highest order," Mazzeo adds. "He made everybody feel comfortable and was a wonderful guy. You just fell in love with the guy—he was such a kind and amazing person."

Kinky often stayed at the Miramar Hotel in Santa Monica, where Levon lived when he wasn't staying in Malibu. "Levon called it 'The Crest of Good Living,'" Kinky says with a laugh. "I lived there for a while; so did Richard Manuel. God knows who else lived there."

"Kinky would stay in a small bungalow from time to time," remembers Mazzeo. "The place was filled with beautiful airline stewardesses. You get a bungalow close to the swimming pool and you're in like Flynn."

Kinky also stayed with Mazzeo at McGuinn's house in Malibu, where Mazzeo was living with a film scout/drug dealer. Having an endless stream of coke, with the inevitable crashes after the highs, was bound to lead to some cranky moments, especially with a provocateur like Kinky.

"Kinky stayed with me out there for about a month, or maybe it was a couple of weeks that seemed like a month," says Mazzeo. "I was 'Mr. Easygoing' in high school because I don't get riled up easily. But when we had been doing cocaine for two-plus weeks, we got on each other's nerves. We were sitting around the kitchen one day and I went off on him about something. He took it really casually and said, 'I knew I'd be able to ring your bell sooner or later.' That's how he measures up who's who—on how you handle it.

"You have to remember it was the '70s and the whole world was doing coke," Mazzeo adds. "Everybody who smoked pot in the '60s was snorting cocaine in the '70s. Judges, lawyers, district attorneys, everybody. Doctors were saying cocaine was healthy; it was totally nuts."

Mazzeo isn't exaggerating. When cocaine regained popularity in the 1970s, it was glamorized by celebrities and the media and viewed as a harmless recreational drug. Cocaine wasn't considered addictive until the 1985 emergence of crack.

Although Kinky sometimes glosses over that period of his life, he is well aware of the adverse impact of his drug use. But the excitement of the times and the camaraderie with famous friends led him to embrace the lifestyle.

"I don't remember when cocaine came into the picture—I just remember it was pretty tragic," says Kinky. "Bob did it a little early on, but not during the tour. That was the problem with being with Bob. The coke dealers hit on me wanting to get to Bob. The whole cocaine thing was impossible to stay away from because there was somebody you loved—here's Rick Danko and he's got cocaine. Eric Clapton is there—what are you gonna do, turn Eric Clapton away from having a little snort with him?

"Danny Hutton was one of the kings of drugs," he adds. "He had a pool table covered with cocaine and lived in a mansion with barbed wire and remote cameras—he was very paranoid. It was exciting hanging out with Danny during the drug era.

"I don't think cocaine did you any good, but when everybody else is doing it, it's hard not to. One night Lowell George came up to me with a stethoscope and had one [ear tip] in each nostril," Kinky adds with a laugh. "That was New Year's Eve in Houston—probably '76. We used rolled-up hundred-dollar bills, rolled-up anything. Rolled it up with dreams—it didn't matter."

During the '70s and early '80s, celebrities from all walks of life—actors, musicians, writers, and comedians, from Tim Allen to Robert Downey Jr., Steven Tyler to Stephen King, John Belushi to Robin Williams—used cocaine to fuel their creativity and lifestyle. And that lifestyle usually included sharing coke with their friends.

"With John Belushi and Lowell George it was all free," says Kinky. "And if you're hanging out with Danny Hutton, and he's got a pool table full of it, why would you pay for it? I guess there was a little bit of coke whore in the Kinkster, but I did pay for a lot of it. Then you get to where you're doing it alone at home, and that's like the final days of alcoholism. The trouble with cocaine—boiled down—is it distances you from your dreams. It truly does. You don't have the will power to do what you could have done."

Aware of the impact of drugs, especially heroin, on some musicians in the Revue, Dylan scheduled an impromptu intervention of sorts. "One time Bob insisted that everybody stay at this hotel in Colorado for a week or two weeks; he didn't want anybody going back to New York or anyplace," says Kinky. "My friend Howie Wyeth, who is one of the best drummers alive—he later played with me at the Lone Star—needed heroin and didn't have it. So he couldn't stay for the week and we lost him."

Drug overdoses led to the deaths of four of Kinky's friends from that period of his life: Lowell George died on June 29, 1979; Mike Bloomfield died on February 15, 1981; John Belushi died on March 5, 1982; and Tom Baker died on September 2, 1982. Looking back, Kinky sees a heartbreaking waste of talent and potential.

"I went through this with a lot of people—Lowell George, Mike Bloomfield—both were close to me, and Belushi—there's talent in all three of those guys. Lowell George is up there in the Eric Clapton category as a guitar player, and he had more imagery as a songwriter. He had great potential, and Bloomfield was a genius. You look at that and you look at the Barry Manilow moment and it can be kind of depressing . . . ."

Kinky often talks about the "Barry Manilow moment" to explain his philosophy on the difference between "important" and "significant" people.

"Important people would be like Rick Perry, the [former] governor of Texas, and Barry Manilow, who is important to his publishers, the record company, his fans, and the casinos," he says. "Manilow is a very talented man that makes more money than God. He also writes and sings songs that make you feel good for a short period of time.

"I try to be like Willie [Nelson] or Kris [Kristofferson] or Merle [Haggard] or Bob Dylan or Billy Joe Shaver or Levon Helm and write songs that make you think and stay with you for a lifetime. That's not nearly as profitable as what Barry Manilow does because the culture demands it. We have an entire ADHD culture that doesn't listen to a full song or a full album anymore. It's usually the ones that fail that are more significant: the Jesuses, the Mozarts, the van Goghs, the Warren Zevons, the Van Dyke Parks, the Gram Parsons, and the Kinky Friedmans."

One of the reasons Kinky refers to himself as a failure is a haunting thought that Dylan put into his mind more than thirty years ago.

"Bob told me my biggest fault was getting started too late as a singer and songwriter—that I got into music too late professionally," adds Kinky. "He dropped out of college and was already playing in Greenwich Village when he was nineteen. If you count the Peace Corps, I didn't get into it until my late twenties. Hank Williams and Gram Parsons were already dead [by that age]. So was John Keats. Bob said, 'You were thirty or thirty-one before you ever hit the stage or had a record. Just know you got in too late and that's part of the problem.'"

Kinky took Dylan's words to heart, and the concept of starting too late still bothers him. But they may have been motivated by Dylan's propensity to treat musicians as inferiors to ensure his status as top dog.

Roger McGuinn experienced a similar reaction when Dylan came into the studio where the Byrds were recording several of Dylan's songs in 1964. "He was always kind of superior because he was Bob Dylan and we were just a fledgling band trying to make it in the music business," McGuinn explains. "He was a year older than I was and I was the oldest guy in the Byrds. It was like in high school, when you're a junior and how seniors feel about you—that's always been the relationship with Bob."

When the Band was slated to play the final show of their 1976 tour at the Winterland Ballroom in San Francisco on November 25, Kinky and Ferrero took a train from L.A. Advertised as the Band's "farewell concert appearance," the Thanksgiving Day show was filmed by Martin Scorsese and released as *The Last Waltz* in 1978. Special guests included Paul Butterfield, Bob Dylan, Neil Young, Emmylou Harris, Ringo Starr, Ronnie Hawkins, Dr. John, Joni Mitchell, Van Morrison, Muddy Waters, Ronnie Wood, Neil Diamond, Bobby Charles, the Staple Singers, Mike Bloomfield, and Eric Clapton.

But Kinky was the sole spectator at a private show put on by Bloomfield and Clapton.

"No one was in the place—it was like the rehearsal before the rehearsal," says Kinky. "We were the only three people there. Bloomfield was outrageous and shouting at Clapton, saying, 'You know that my licks are better than yours.' Bloomfield was going crazy, just going off on Clapton. Clapton was saying, 'You're right mate, I agree.' We were both agreeing with Mike that his chops were more original, that he was the first. But he wasn't having any of that either and kept going off on Clapton. Mike is a great guy; he was just fucked up, as a lot of us get.

"I thought, here are arguably the two greatest—you can count Lowell George in there, maybe Jerry Garcia; Mick Ronson was great, too. But Clapton and Bloomfield—you can't get much better than that. I'm the only other guy in the place, and I'm not even refereeing. I'm just standing there. I wish I had a witness or a tape recorder."

Kinky and Ferrero watched the concert with a number of the Band's special guests. "We saw the show from the side of the stage with Neil Diamond, Neil Young, and all these guys that were in the show," says Kinky. "Muddy Waters was in the show, too. He's the one Robbie wanted to cut out of the show; he didn't want to pay airfare for Muddy Waters. But he wanted Neil Diamond, who didn't really fit in it. Robbie wanted Neil Diamond because he was producing one of his records. That's the kind of guy Robbie was.

"Levon told them, 'You cut Muddy Waters, you're cutting me, pal— I'm not gonna be in the show.' Robbie really was the runt of the litter and I think he financially and spiritually screwed those guys. Because they all created the songs and the big ones were all of Southern origin —'The Night They Drove Old Dixie Down,' 'The Weight,' 'Up on Cripple Creek.' To put his name after every song on that record and say that was what the accountants wanted for simplification.

"He had deals going with Al Grossman, who was a crook— Grossman was the manager who screwed them royally and played right into Robbie's hand. That's the way it went and Levon and Rick and Richard were spinning ghosts. They were out of control for the most part and they didn't stop it. I've had that experience myself; I tend to let people get away with things. If I lend a guy $10,000 and he says he'll pay a little back, I'll say okay. There are other people who would make sure they get the money back. I let things go."

One of the things that Kinky let go after recording *Lasso from El Paso* and touring with Dylan was finding new management to guide his career. After he was dropped from Epic Records, the ensuing dark mood led him to spurn a fan—a well-known fan—who wanted to meet him.

"Kinky and I were walking through the parking garage at the Sunset Marquee one night when I spotted Jon Landau, who I became friends with at Duke's," explains Weiss. "Jon managed Bruce Springsteen, so I tried to introduce Kinky to Bruce. But Kinky refused to shake his hand and didn't want to meet him."

"I had just gotten dropped by my record label, and was really feeling sorry for myself," Kinky explains. "I was depressed, hooked on cocaine and everything else. Chuck E. says, 'Say hello to Bruce Springsteen,' and I said fuck it. I didn't much like Bruce Springsteen, although I didn't know him at all. Then later Chuck E. said, 'Bruce really likes you—he's a fan of yours and wanted to say hello to you,' which made me feel worse. I never met him again to tell him I felt bad about that. I normally would never do that to somebody—I would shake hands with Bruce or anybody. To refuse to shake hands with somebody unless it's Hitler brought me seven years of bad luck."

8

Running Wild in the Big Apple

"I snorted a long line of what I thought was cocaine at
the house of a woman who was selling drugs. And it was heroin.
I was in a bed in that place—pretty much a shooting gallery—
semiconscious for forty-eight hours."
—Kinky Friedman

Kinky's luck seemed to be changing when he was invited to perform on *Saturday Night Live* in late October 1976. Although no one remembers who invited Kinky to appear on the show, most likely it was John Belushi and head writer Michael O'Donoghue. Known for dark comedy and black humor, O'Donoghue wrote for *National Lampoon*, created the *National Lampoon Radio Hour*, and played "The Ballad of Charles Whitman" on that weekly radio show. He wanted a "Sniper in the Tower" musical skit with Kinky, Belushi, Dan Aykroyd, and Steve Martin based on the Whitman song.

"We had rehearsals for a week and they cut it at the last minute," says Kinky. "It really pissed me off because we had a great version of 'Charles Whitman' in the can. It was hysterical, fucking great, and they pulled it because of legal problems with the victims or the family of Charles Whitman or some bullshit like that. So they threw the ball to me. At that point I wasn't really adept at performing solo, but I did 'Dear Abbie,' which was a message to Abbie Hoffman because at that time nobody knew where he was.

"'Whitman' was the song that might have [taken off]," he adds. "That was a great opportunity and the skit was hilarious. You have a very narrow window when you're hot and people are buzzed about you; you've got to take advantage of it. It was a major production number and would have been killer. But I was left doing a ballad by myself about Abbie Hoffman, and it was kind of weak."

"It was really bad," agrees Jacobs. "He had fired the band a month or two before; he didn't even have Jewford. It looked like he was so nervous, he couldn't even sing. I don't know why he did '"Dear Abbie'; he should have done something funny."

Kinky's irreverent sense of humor and larger-than-life persona were perfect for *Saturday Night Live*, but his tepid performance and self-indulgent behavior after the show killed any chances of being invited back. "When they canned the skit I went into a petulant snit and gave the producers a hard time," he says. That hard time lasted a week.

Saturday Night Live put him up at the Marriott Essex House, a forty-four-story luxury hotel in Manhattan. But a night or two on *SNL's* tab evolved into more than a week when Kinky, still fuming about the last minute change, began throwing parties with bowls of cocaine.

"I started inviting all these people," says Kinky. "I bought 100 plastic gun-shaped toothbrushes for little kids; you could do a baking soda freeze—put baking soda and cocaine together and put it on your gums. That's when I met [journalist and longtime friend] Mike McGovern in the closet. The room was packed, so I was snorting cocaine in the closet.

"*Saturday Night Live* picked up the party that went on for a week because I refused to leave the hotel. I'm surprised they didn't summon the police, but they didn't. The hotel kept billing me for a year or two. I didn't pay for it; maybe nobody paid for it."

Disgusted, Kinky returned to Hollywood and began playing offbeat comic roles in B-rated films. His first role was in *American Raspberry,* a 1977 release spoofing TV shows and commercials. Based on the premise that an unknown source is taking over the airwaves and broadcasting crude and tasteless programs, the film includes sketches for a Die Tough Battery that powered executions, and Stay Down, a spray that prevented unwanted erections.

Determined to include a sniper like Charles Whitman in the film, Kinky invited Warren Oates. Kinky became friendly with Oates at a Texas Jewboys show in the early 1970s, but had known him much longer as an actor in two TV western series he had grown up watching: *The Rifleman* and *Have Gun—Will Travel.*

In *American Raspberry,* Oates played the celebrity guest on a show called *Celebrity Sportsman Presents: The Charles Whitman Invitational.* In a tasteless parody of the 1966 shootings at the University of Texas, Oates and the show's host climb a tower to shoot their limit on the students below. When he shoots a beefy football player, Oates proudly proclaims, "Must be a 280-pounder!"

"I don't remember much about the movies I was in, but I remember that one," Kinky says. "Warren Oates was terrific. He was an enormously talented actor. I got him to play a character in the movie for a case of tequila and something else, which I can't remember. I played a kiddie show host who snorts this huge line of cocaine—it's about four feet long—and sings the song 'Ol' Ben Lucas.'"

That skit opens with a close-up of Kinky snorting the cocaine with a male voiceover asking, "Hey, kids, who's the guy with the bloodshot eyes?" Two cute eight-year-olds dressed in cowgirl outfits yell, "Ol' Ben Lucas!" and dance alongside Kinky as they sing the chorus about the hapless character with "A lot of mucus comin' right out of his nose."

Kinky also appeared in *Loose Shoes*, a sketch comedy composed of trailers for nonexistent movies. Played by a big band with a Cab Calloway–style leader, the title song appeared in "Darktown After Dark," a sketch filmed in sepia that came from a racist remark by Richard Nixon's then Secretary of Agriculture Earl Butz: "The only thing the coloreds are looking for in life are tight pussy, loose shoes, and a warm place to shit."

Other sketches included "Billy Jerk Goes to Oz," a *Billy Jack* parody starring Tom Baker; a biker film satire called "Skateboarders from Hell," and a horror flick called "Penis Snatchers" ("They came in empty-handed and left with a fistful"). In "Three Chairs for Lefty," Kinky is sitting in a prison cafeteria with candelabras on the tables. Bill Murray, who later dies in the electric chair holding a roast for the warden, throws a fit because the quiche is subpar, the bouillabaisse is made from tripe, the wine is domestic Chianti, and the chocolate mousse wasn't made with real cream. The 1977 film wasn't released until 1980, when the then-unknown Murray had achieved fame on *Saturday Night Live* and in *Meatballs* and *Caddyshack*.

In 1978, Kinky donned a light-blue fedora with a red visor; a red, white, and blue striped jacket; a satin shirt emblazoned with musical notes; and his fuzzy royal-blue guitar strap to play himself in *Record City*. One reviewer pegged it "Like *Empire Records*, only raunchier"; another called it a "day-in-the-life of a Los Angeles record store that plays like *Carwash* meets *Caddyshack*—with lots of characters, episodic scenes and slob humor."

Asked about *Loose Shoes, Record City,* and his roles in the 1983 horror flick *The Being* and *Texas Chainsaw Massacre 2,* the 1986 gory and camp sequel starring his pal Dennis Hopper and directed by his college buddy Tobe Hooper, Kinky laughs. "I don't remember—these are very forgettable movies," he says. "But I like Bill Murray."

When a career as a comic actor failed to materialize, Kinky flew back to New York to try to resuscitate his music career. The Lone Star Café, a country music venue at the corner of Fifth Avenue and Thirteenth Street, had opened in 1976, and Kinky figured he was the perfect artist for the Texas-themed nightclub. So did Mort Cooperman, who ran the club with his partner, Bill Dick. Cooperman saw Kinky on *Saturday Night Live* but didn't meet him until more than a year later, when Kinky and Ferrero walked in wearing shades and long black Navy pea coats on a freezing cold day in the winter of 1977.

Cooperman remembered that moment when he talked to a reporter twenty years later. "He arrived with his road guy, the two of them looking like Texas anarchists," he said. "Starting the next year, he began playing every Sunday night for a period close to ten years."

Kinky didn't have a band when he started playing the Lone Star in the summer of 1978, so he used his charm to recruit musicians hanging out at the club. One of the early musicians was Sredni Vollmer, who played harmonica and became a good friend.

Cleve Hattersley, who currently books Kinky's tours, became a manager at the Lone Star after Kinky began his weekly shows. Hattersley, who fronted a band in Austin called Greezy Wheels (and still does), met Kinky at Austin's Soap Creek Saloon in the mid-1970s. Kinky's backup band for that gig was a blues band called Paul Ray and the Cobras, with a lineup that included Stevie Ray Vaughan as second guitarist.

Kinky didn't spend time with Vaughan until nearly a decade later, when they hooked up at the Berkley "Cowboys for Indians" benefit for the SEVA Foundation in October 1985.

"I met Stevie Ray and hung out with him with Wavy Gravy at a show in San Francisco with Bob Weir," Kinky says. "I liked him—he was a real gentleman, a very nice man."

Shortly after Kinky began performing at the Lone Star Café, Austin artist Bob "Daddy-O" Wade, who graduated from the University of Texas-Austin a year before Kinky, created a forty-foot sculpture of a giant iguana. Iggy, as the sculpture was affectionately called, was lifted in sections by cranes onto the top of the club on Halloween 1978. Iggy was the perfect place to smoke a joint, snort a line, or try to get lucky when someone caught your eye.

"Daddy-O Wade's iguana was a cool place," says Kinky. "You could get into it, underneath it, on top of it. When you went out on the little portico of the Lone Star, that's what you saw and you would walk down there and hang out and drink. The iguana pretty well defined my life there for a number of years."

Kinky has always been a celebrity magnet, so it wasn't surprising the Lone Star Café became a celebrity hangout once he began his Sunday night gigs. "Kinky started playing the Lone Star before it was hip," remembers Ferrero. "After he started playing, people like Belushi, James Taylor, and Keith Richards started hanging out there."

"Kinky was the only act that could play every week—even the good-size acts had to wait six months to come back in," says Hattersley. "He had a full band behind him, all hotshot New York players, with all manner of stars sitting in."

"The Lone Star had a lot of Texas talent, but lots of musicians who played that place were from New York," says Kinky. "We always had a full band that was constantly in motion and revolved around Sredni 'Nigger Lips' Vollmer. He played with me quite a bit—later he played with Rick Danko. Washington Ratso would sit in when he was in town. Michael Simmons, who was a friend and a good singer, would sit in on acoustic rhythm guitar and harmony vocals. Howie Wyeth, Bob Dylan's drummer, worked with me. Larry Campbell, who later worked with Bob [Dylan] and Levon [Helm], played guitar and steel guitar. Buddy Miller, who worked with everybody, played guitar with me first. They all learned my songs."

"The band could play any way Kinky named it; that's why Kinky brought in these top guys," says Hattersley. "Kinky's rhythm is very Jewish—you have to be in time with him to catch exactly where he's hitting you with a song, or which fucking song it may be. Kinky is not an improviser; they played Kinky's songs. But he also had to follow Larry. Although Kinky wrote the songs, sometimes he had to look at Larry to know where to come in."

Other regular musicians included Buffalo Bill Gelber [the Lesley West Band] on bass; Scarlet Rivera or Sweet Mary Egan [Hattersley] on violin; Parks or Wyeth on keyboards; Jim Rider, sidekick to Ramblin'

Jack Elliott, on mandolin and vocals; and Corky Laing [Mountain, the Lesley West Band] on drums.

Laing was introduced to Kinky by Wyeth, who put together musicians behind Kinky. "Howie was in rough shape," says Laing. "He was working with Keith Richards and John Phillips and said he couldn't keep playing with Kinky every Sunday night too."

Laing wasn't sure he could handle the gig, either. "I was broke and going through a divorce, so I told him, 'I'm way too depressed to play with anybody,'" he says. "Howie said, 'No, you want to play with Kinky; you want to play with someone who is more depressed than you. He'll make you feel good about yourself. When I went to see Kinky, he said, 'What the hell does a celebrity rock and roll drummer want to do with me?' I said, 'Nothing; Howie said you'd make me feel good.' Kinky said, 'I don't have enough cocaine to make anybody feel good these days.' But I played with them for years and it was some of the most fun I had in my life."

The 1980s were rough on established musicians. MTV and music videos made youth and good looks as important as musicianship. New wave, techno-pop, and heavy metal topped the pop charts; the success of the 1980 film *Urban Cowboy* caused what Simmons called "fake country bars" with mechanical bulls to open up across the country.

"The Lone Star days were golden, but it was probably the worst era for everybody," says Laing. "These were the '80s—everybody was turning thirty and forty years old, going through midlife crises. All the performers—Van Dyke Parks, Johnny Paycheck—were totally depressed. I used to refer to Kinky as the Super Bowl of Misery. But it was funny seeing him on stage putting everybody down equally, whether you were black, Jewish, white, or Indian."

Kinky could be especially rough on women.

"When I went with my wife, he used to say, 'So that's your main slit.' She'd look at him like she was going to lay into him physically—'What did you say?' He'd say, 'Why? You don't like the name "slit"? I'd say, 'Oh, boy—you may as well use the C-word.' She'd come down to have a good time and he'd embarrass her all to hell. She would come to me crying, saying, "I can't stand this anymore; I have to get out of here.' And she really wanted Kinky to like her."

Band names, which were more amusing than some of Kinky's antics, included the Entire Polish Army, the Exxon Brothers Band, the

Bird Band, the Young American Hose Company #5, the Frogman Band, and the Anti-UnAmericanism Crusade.

"The name of the band was a joke," says Simmons. "Kinky used to change the name of the band every night, but everyone called us the Texas Jewboys."

According to Mary and Cleve Hattersley, Kinky had to drop the name "the Entire Polish Army" when it caught flak from the Polish community and made Page Six in the *New York Post*. Simmons was skeptical.

"The Polish community?" he asks. "What, some guy named Krukowski on East Second Street, Avenue B? That sounds like publicity. How do I get my name in the press? By saying some Polack is outraged by the band's name, even if it's true."

Nevertheless, Lone Star Café calendars continued the buzz by promoting his shows with an array of eclectic taglines, including "the Kinky Friedman post-Jewish New Year celebration"; "Kinky Friedman with a real Kinky Sunday"; "Kinky Friedman receives the Buford T. Fusser Walking Tall American Award"; "Bro. Kinky's cleansing"; and "Bro. Kinky's ordination and bar mitzvah." And there was always the feeling anybody could show up and anything could happen.

"There was a period when you never knew who was going to come to a Kinky show because he became the darling of all the other famous musicians," says Sloman. "Keith Richards came to one of Kinky's shows and was hanging out by the stage watching the show and upstairs. He was the most down-to-earth guy you can imagine. I met John Cale there and wrote songs with him over a four-album stretch. To this day, Cale is always emailing me—'What's the Kinkster up to?' You really felt you had your finger on the pulse of what was happening in the city."

"We had people coming into the Lone Star—Robin Williams, Don Imus, Bob Dylan, Sally Struthers—you name it," remembers Laing. "There was a lot of celebrity action. Peter Wolf would come with his wife, Faye Dunaway. Peter Frampton, Hall and Oates. Everybody came through on Sundays, because that's when a lot of people—including all the Broadway people—had the day off. The *Saturday Night Live* people—John Belushi , Chevy Chase, Gilda Radner—came down to see us, too, because it was their day off and it was always a party."

Laing knew Belushi years before he joined *Saturday Night Live*.

"John was a big fan of Mountain—he and Leslie [West] got along, so he used to hang with us," remembers Laing. "We knew him when he was just starting—doing [*National Lampoon's*] *Lemmings* with Chevy Chase. Leslie and I went to see the first *Lemmings* show at the Village Gate. Leslie loved to dress up and had this bright orange suit on. Belushi came out and said, 'What the fuck are you doing? You look like a fuckin' basketball.'"

Like West's wild outfit, Kinky's shows always offered something unexpected. "Every Sunday became 'God knows what happens this Sunday,'" adds Hattersley. "Whether it was Don Imus getting up with him regularly, or Don Imus and Robin Williams getting up with him and doing crazy shit."

"One night Imus did dueling evangelists with Robin Williams—an Elmer Gantry kind of thing—while we played gospel songs," remembers Kinky. Hattersley missed the dueling evangelists but has vivid memories of the first night Williams performed on the Lone Star stage.

"One of my bartenders came down with Robin and said, 'I've got some really great blow; can we come into your office and do a line?' remembers Hattersley. "I said sure—we were all doing it then. So Billy rolls out three big fat lines of really good cocaine and Robin sits down, does two of the lines, and then goes up and does the funniest fifteen minutes you've ever heard. Just rapid-fire fifteen minutes, while Kinky was hiding somewhere else in the club."

Part of Hattersley's job was to get Kinky back on the stage after a guest star got up. "Kinky would always disappear," Hattersley says. "Where I found him depended on his mood. He was doing mountains of Peruvian marching powder, so he was usually in some corner doing blow."

Laing also remembers that night with Robin Williams. "That was right after *Mork & Mindy* and he was running around the city doing all the comedy clubs," he says. "He jumped on the stage and took over the Lone Star. Bob Dylan's manager was trying to manage Robin Williams and wanted to impress him, so he called Bob Dylan. I was sitting near the phone and I could hear Robin Williams saying, 'No, it's fuckin' Mork, Bob. I'm fuckin' Mork.' He's screaming at Dylan, who didn't believe it was him.

"People jumped off and on the stage quite a bit," he adds. "Not necessarily singing. Just acting up. Johnny Paycheck would get up and sing. Larry Coryell got up a couple of times and played guitar. Lester Chambers of the Chambers Brothers got up. Leon Russell came in and replaced Van Dyke Parks on keyboards for a couple of numbers. Every time Kinky showed up, there were lines around the club. You couldn't move in there, and you couldn't walk in. When Levon was on tour doing his solo thing, he pulled up his bus just to go in and party. I remember Joe Heller being there. A lot of people really loved and respected Kinky."

Not everyone who jumped on the stage had a right to be there.

"A lot of sports people would come in," says Laing. "John Davidson was a huge fan. I think he was a frustrated country singer, because he came up a couple of times and sang some songs—embarrassed himself. The sports guys are all frustrated singers. John McEnroe came in all the time; he was a frustrated guitar player. He'd come up and play guitar—fucking awful."

Kinky loved that I played with Meat Loaf," says Laing. "He had a lot of fun joking about the Meat Loaf name, like saying, 'Does he refer to his wife as Mrs. Loaf?' All these really corny jokes—that was one of his things. He also made up names, and always talked about people in the third person. My name was Corkster. The third-person thing was very popular with Kinky and was charming. Kinky can be very, very charming."

Kinky credits the success of the Lone Star Café to Mort Cooperman for having the right idea at the right time. "Mort got real Texans coming to his club, as well as people that wanted to be to be Texans," he says. "He had John Belushi, John Matuszak of the Oakland Raiders, the New York Rangers hockey team, Nolan Ryan, Mickey Mantle, and all kinds of pointy-headed intellectuals drifting through that club."

Prior to opening the club, Cooperman was a successful advertising executive who managed two prestigious accounts—Datsun and Pepsi—at Wells, Rich, Greene, a top New York agency known for its innovative "I Love New York" campaign. Cooperman had a soft spot for Kinky and helped him in a number of ways.

"Mort was great," says Ferrero. "We ran out of money when we were staying at the Chelsea, so I told Mort I need 500 bucks. He took me downstairs, and his partner, Bill Dick, gave me a stack of crimped five-dollar bills. In those days in New York, the club would charge the bands for drinks; he never did that to us. He gave us a tab so we could eat there, too."

Kinky, who was already heavy into cocaine, used his tab to fuel his habit. "I had a deal with the waitresses where I would tip them when I got one hundred dollars on my credit line," he says. "They would kick back eighty dollars in cash and I would get a gram of cocaine. That worked pretty well for a while. Everybody in New York thought I was one of the owners. I had a credit line there for a quite a while before they shut it off."

Cooperman also set Kinky up with two managers; neither panned out. One was the trophy wife of a wealthy man in Scarsdale; she had no background in show business but was bored and wanted something to do. The second was a charismatic con man whose past caught up with him before he and Kinky struck a deal.

"Mort set Kinky up with a manager who was managing a rock band in Manhattan," says Ferrero. "He said he'd pay Kinky a grand a month and pay me one hundred dollars a week—which was a huge amount of money in those days. We were staying at the Gramercy Park and the guy came over with all these great ideas for promotion. He was going to take us to Vegas, everywhere, and keep us on retainer when Kinky wasn't playing."

But those grandiose plans evaporated when undercover cops caught up with the con man.

"He was at the club during sound check when these scruffy guys came in, slammed him against the bar, put cuffs on him, and walked him out," recalls Ferrero. "The lead guy looked like Serpico. Kinky and I went back to the Gramercy laughing about the irony; we finally get management and the guy is hauled off in cuffs."

Kinky's would-be manager went directly to Rikers Island, New York City's main jail complex, on charges filed by his father. "He had ripped off his own father for huge amounts of money," says Ferrero. "His father got stuck with the hotel tabs of the band he was managing. He was covering all their expenses and paying them—like he was going to pay Kinky and me—on his father's credit cards."

Although Cooperman's attempt to find a manager to take Kinky's career to a higher level didn't work out, Kinky's irreverent and magnetic personality continued to attract an array of stars and friends eager to share the stage.

"Dr. John played with me at the Lone Star," says Kinky. "John

[Belushi] got up and sang with me a number of times. The Band, Paul Butterfield. All kinds of people and a lot of bands. I played with Dougie [Sahm], too; he was a great one who died way too soon."

"The Band played with Kinky a lot," adds Sloman. "Delbert McClinton played with him every now and then. Ramblin' Jack [Elliott], Johnny and Edgar Winter."

When it was time for "They Ain't Makin' Jews like Jesus Anymore," anybody—from Abbie Hoffman, who was still on the lam, to *Catch 22* author Joseph Heller (who called it his "all-time favorite song") and John Davidson, star goalie for the New York Rangers—would jump up and join Kinky on stage.

Kinky met Heller in the mid-1970s and visited him in the hospital in 1981, when he was almost completely paralyzed with Guillain-Barre syndrome. Heller had to be fed through a tube in his nose, and needed months of rehabilitation to be able to sit up in bed.

"I took Imus to see him in the hospital; that's when Imus first met him," Kinky says. "I knew him before he went in the hospital through Speed Vogel. When Joe was in the hospital, Speed lived in Joe's house, used Joe's credit card, and wore Joe's clothes—it was very funny. They were lifelong friends. Speed was also roommates with Mel Brooks; that's what inspired Neil Simon to write the *Odd Couple*."

Kinky wrote about his friendship with Heller in "Catching Heller," an essay for *George*, a glossy political/lifestyle magazine cofounded by John F. Kennedy Jr. Heller's daughter, Erica, wrote about their friendship in her 2011 memoir *Yossarian Slept Here—When Joseph Heller Was Dad, the Apthorp Was Home, and Life Was a Catch-22*.

"Two other favorites of Dad, apart from the old guard, were Kinky Friedman and Don Imus," she wrote. "The friendship grew and Kinky and his band played once at a party for Dad, and this was followed by some late nights they spent together, in the company of Don Imus, downtown at the Lone Star Café." During one of those late nights Heller joined Kinky on stage.

"There's a great photo of me and Kinky, the band, and Joseph Heller and Speed Vogel on the stage," remembers Simmons. "People would get up to do 'Ain't Makin' Jews' cause it's a great sing-along—it's not like they had to have good voices."

"We'd do that song with Lee Fraser, the black manager of the club, and my friend John Walsh, an albino and a head executive at ESPN," Kinky says. "There's that line where the bigot in the song would say, 'Is there anyone I missed?' and John would shout out, 'Albino.'"

Kinky still catches flak for the use of the word "nigger" in "They Ain't Makin' Jews like Jesus Anymore." Although his father tried to discourage him from using that word in his act by telling him he wasn't Richard Pryor, he never listened. "There was a big black guy [at the Lone Star] who wore a cowboy hat and Kinky would say, 'That's one of my favorite nigger Americans,' and he'd get away with it," recalls Simmons. "Nobody cared. It was totally politically incorrect by today's standards. Kinky said whatever he wanted to say and always got away with it."

"He would call people names like 'you Jewboy,' and nobody gave a shit," adds Laing. "Kinky had a lot of good friends. If you really know Kinky, you let all that stuff slide off your back. I worked with some of the biggest assholes in the world. Kinky was nowhere near that—he didn't even run a close second. The guys in rock and roll—forget about it."

Laing's initial impression of Kinky was not as forgiving and got even worse after a gig in Philadelphia.

"I thought he was an asshole when I met him, but at the time I was in no position to judge anyone," Laing says. "The Jewish thing was always very funny, but he's half Jewish—he doesn't go the whole route. At the same time he drops Jewish when he needs Jewish. (Laing wouldn't play on Yom Kippur when he toured with Mountain; Kinky makes no bones about spending Jewish holidays gambling in Las Vegas.)

"Then I played with him at a Hadassah party in Philadelphia where he was putting these old people down," he says. "I don't know how we got the gig; maybe they thought Kinky Friedman was a nice Jewish boy. He was so adverse and irreverent about everything. I know a lot of people like to be beat up, but these were nice little Jewish ladies. He talked about masturbation and all that shit . . . It was one of the most awkward moments; it made Louis C.K. look conventional."

Kinky also had no empathy when Laing showed up for a gig after breaking his leg in California.

"I came back with a cast and on crutches, and told Kinky, 'I'm really sorry, but I don't know if I can play.' He said, 'Get your fucking leg up on the tom-tom and play with your left foot.' When I got up on stage on my crutches, he introduced me as the Special Olympics drummer.

Then I realized everything was going to be all right," he adds laughing at the memory.

Comedian Professor Irwin Corey, who ran a mock presidential campaign in 1960 with the slogan "Irwin will run for any party and he'll bring his own bottle," brought his own brand of chaos to the Lone Star stage. Known for his rants and rambling diatribes in a skit called "The Insane Professor," he loved joining Kinky on stage and talking gibberish.

Jackie Mason and Henny Youngman also stopped by the club. "I had lunch with Jackie Mason and really admired him," says Kinky, who stayed loosely connected. Both Kinky and Mason made multiple appearances on the same episodes of *The Joan Rivers Show*. In a review of Michael Chabon's novel *Yiddish Policeman's Union*, Kinky expressed his respect for Mason and the way he took pride in his Jewish heritage.

"Jackie Mason, whom I admire intensely, reports that old Jewish ladies come up to him after almost every show," he wrote. "Like Reform harpies, they whisper in his ear, 'Too Jewish, too Jewish.' Mason never listens to them. I hope Chabon doesn't either."

Mason enjoyed razzing Kinky in the Carnegie Deli, a favorite comedian hangout. "Me and Kinky and Ratso were eating at the Carnegie Deli and Jackie walks by Kinky," says Laing. "They all knew Kinky and he said, 'Hey Kinky, I heard a lot about you.' Kinky said, 'Thank you.' Jackie says, "No, it wasn't good.' Then he'd come back by us and say, 'I see you haven't gotten linen yet.' At the Carnegie Deli, if they give you linen instead of paper, it means you're a star. Another dig was, 'One day, Kinky, you'll get linen.'"

When Kinky wasn't performing, he spent a great deal of time at the club. "I'd hang out and see other artists there: Delbert McClinton, Billy Joe Shaver, Freddy Fender, Doug Sahm," he says. "Bob Dylan used to hang out there a bit; so did Mike Bloomfield. Doctor John and Doc Pomus lived at the Lone Star. Johnny Paycheck came to see me, and I met Keith Richards there. I met Nolan Ryan, a great pitcher who was the owner of the Texas Rangers, and met Mickey Mantle there, too. Tom Baker introduced me to Mick, who was more fucked up than either Baker or me."

"Everybody came at one time to kiss the feet of the Kinkster," says Hattersley. "Kinky and John Belushi really respected each other. Belushi got up with him occasionally and the Blues Brothers rehearsed at the Lone Star Café."

The Blues Brothers, which consisted of Belushi and Aykroyd performing "I'm a King Bee," dressed as bees, made its *SNL* debut in January 1976. Unsure of how a blues band fronted by comedians would go over, Belushi asked Kinky and Ferrero what they thought of the concept.

"Belushi floated the idea by me, and I thought it was a pretty bad idea," says Kinky. "But he could have done a bluegrass band and it probably would have worked."

"When John asked me and Kinky if we knew any blues players because he wanted to do some blues music, Kinky and I are going, 'Is John crazy? He's a comedian; what a stupid idea,'" remembers Ferrero. "Kinky knew some incredible blues players in Atlanta and they said, 'We would never do that—it's disrespecting the blues—the guy is a comedian.'"

Luckily, Belushi didn't listen. Within two years, the Blues Brothers' live album *Briefcase Full of Blues* reached #1 on the *Billboard* charts and went double platinum. The 1980 film *The Blues Brothers* is still a classic.

"Belushi was greatness—I know that," Kinky says. "He was the most talented guy they ever had on *Saturday Night Live*. He could do any fucking thing. If he had not been so strung out . . . I spent a lot of time with him in L.A., too. He could've played roles in movies that weren't comedic—he could've been a big actor. That's what he wanted to do."

Although Dan Aykroyd never hung out with Kinky like Belushi did, he remembers their friendship and mutual respect.

"Kinky Friedman was a big part of John Belushi's New York experience," Aykroyd says. "John enjoyed Kinky's anarchic view of life, his boundary-pushing humor, and his formidable musical talent. Belushi enjoyed the company of brilliant, skilled artists who put out their own message. Kinky certainly is one.

"Kinky was among a group of creative Texans who arrived in the mid-'70s and impacted the culture and society there greatly. We went to Kinky's Sunday night shows often. It was a fun time to be in New York and our interactions with Kinky were memorable. I remember Kinky playing in the Blues Bar at Hudson and Dominic, where we kept an abundance of house axes for visiting players," he adds.

Aykroyd is referring to the corner bar he and Belushi rented on 282 Hudson Street in a late-1800s four-tenement building. Dubbing it the Blues Bar, they established it as a private (and unlicensed) after-hours hangout for friends and members of the *SNL* cast. Sloman, who considers his approach to drugs as being "the shy one at the orgy," remembers incredible amounts of cocaine at the Blues Bar.

"We'd hang out at Belushi and Aykroyd's bar on the West Side," says Sloman. "When we walked into the bar Belushi walked up to greet us with a baggie full of cocaine and would scoop out coke in his palm and shove it in your fucking face. The other friend of Kinky's who did that was Johnny Paycheck. Johnny Paycheck was a little guy who did enormous amounts of blow. We would go see Paycheck at the Lone Star—go backstage, then go to his dressing room in the basement. He'd whip out this baggie and start stuffing it up your nostrils."

Kinky's memories are not as vivid. "I don't remember hanging out at Belushi's bar very much, but I stayed at Belushi's apartment in the West Village a lot when he was out of town," he said. "Me and Dylan stayed there when he was gone for a couple weeks; he went to some secluded island. He rented a house and there was only one other house a quarter mile down the beach. Nobody else was supposed to be around or know John was there. He was just going to take it easy. He didn't want anyone around, or anybody coming up and asking for his autograph.

"The only people he saw were his neighbors—an Oriental woman with a hippie-looking guy. John saw them walking on the beach and was very concerned they'd find out his identity. Some of it was him getting off of drugs, but he just didn't want any fans around. So he avoided these people for the better part of a week and it turned out to be John Lennon and Yoko Ono," Kinky says with a laugh. Amused by the irony, Kinky asked Belushi if he'd gotten Lennon's autograph.

At that point, Belushi was growing tired of doing *Saturday Night Live.* As one of the original "Not Ready for Prime-Time Players" when the show started in 1975, he complained to Kinky and Ferrero that his pay in 1978 didn't reflect his role in the show's success. "Belushi said he was getting screwed by *Saturday Night Live,*" remembers Ferrero. "He said, 'They're paying me fifty grand a year and that's ridiculous. I'm gonna get out and get into movies.'"

Although Belushi also appeared in *Goin' South* with Jack Nicholson in 1978, it was *National Lampoon's Animal House* that launched his film career. Kinky and Ferrero attended the premiere as well as the opening-night party at the Village Gate.

"Belushi invited us to the first showing of *Animal House* in Manhattan," says Ferrero. "Kinky was friends with Doug Kenney, the guy who wrote it. After the movie, John came over to us—he was very nervous and was always chain-smoking. He said, 'What do you guys think?' I said, 'Are you kidding me? It'll be a monster. This is the funniest damn movie I've ever seen.'"

"I don't remember much about that," adds Kinky. "I just remember it was real good. John was more talented than everybody else put together and Doug Kenney was a genius."

Like Kinky, Kenney wrote for his high school newspaper and used humor to fit in. He developed an eclectic circle of friends at Harvard and used his absurdist sense of humor to become an editor at the *Harvard Lampoon*. Four years later, he and fellow editors Henry Beard and Robert Hoffman founded the spin-off *National Lampoon*.

Given Kenney's irreverent sense of humor, writing talent, and eclectic taste in friends, he and Kinky were bound to hit it off. "We hung out in New York, and later in L.A.," Kinky says. "He and I got turned away from Studio 54. Then we got turned away from a Hare Krishna center."

Studio 54 was a hot Manhattan nightclub during the disco era. Owner Steve Rubell screened the long lines of people outside the club, admitting only celebrities and media darlings. Regulars included Michael Jackson, Cher, Dolly Parton, Andy Warhol, Truman Capote, and Woody Allen. Bianca Jagger rode a white horse through the club on her thirtieth birthday, and ex-husband Mick and his new paramour, model Jerry Hall, were always there.

Kinky wrote a song about his and Kenney's exclusion from Studio 54 for the soundtrack of *Skating on Thin Ice*, a Canadian documentary on hockey. Recorded in 1982, "People Who Read *People* Magazine" was released on *Under the Double Ego* on Sunrise Records. Kinky changed the name of the song to "God Bless John Wayne (People Who Read *People* Magazine)" for his 1985 performance on the Playboy cable channel show *Country Blue*.

Kenney, like many of Kinky's friends, died young with drugs as a contributing factor. Strung out on cocaine and despondent that his 1980 film *Caddyshack* met with mixed reviews, the thirty-three-year-old writer traveled to Maui with his friend Chevy Chase to try to kick cocaine. When Chase returned to the mainland a month later, Kenney went to Kauai, where his body was discovered at the base of a lookout thirty feet beneath a cliff. It was never clear whether he fell or jumped to his death.

"He was an extremely good writer, very funny guy, very seminal," says Kinky. "I think if he had lived he'd have really. . . . ," he begins, before the thought of his friend's untimely death leaves him speechless.

Kinky, however, has only happy memories of his friendship with New York Rangers goalie John Davidson, whom he calls "a great guy." His introduction to the New York Rangers was orchestrated by Sloman, a self-proclaimed "big hockey fanatic," who immediately recognized players Davidson and Ron Greshon when they stopped by the Lone Star after a game. Calling himself "the semi-official custodian of Kinky's guest list," he "grabbed the Rangers as soon as they came in, sat with them throughout the set, and dragged them backstage to meet Kinky," Sloman wrote in his book *Thin Ice: A Season in Hell with the New York Rangers*. "Soon the whole team was coming down," adds Sloman. "They loved music, and after attending a few games, Kinky loved hockey."

Sloman and Kinky started hanging out with the Rangers and became their cultural ambassadors to New York. They took the Rangers to Chinatown for dim sum and to Luna's in Little Italy, and showed them the bullet holes outside Umberto's Clam House, where New York mobster "Crazy Joe" Gallo was gunned down in 1972. They also made the scene together at rock clubs, Soho bars, and City Limits, a country bar in the Village.

"Ratso knew New York and I knew the funky places," explains Kinky. "Ratso was a denizen of New York; he'd been there forever. He was very connected to the Rangers, and I was, too, by the end of it. I hung out with the Rangers a lot. Hockey players are tough; they're a cool breed of people."

Bill Brownstein, a Montreal filmmaker who made documentaries for the National Film Board of Canada, met Kinky and Sloman when he started filming a documentary about two Canadian players and their difficulties handling fame.

"We focused on Mike McEwen and Pat Hickey, who were playing for the Rangers at the time," said Brownstein. "We wanted to not only get into hockey, but the lifestyle they had plunged into. It's hard enough for seasoned pros with street smarts to deal with, but for some kid from the boonies in Ontario, it was especially tough. One of those guys was married to a runner-up for Miss America; the other one was married to an Ice Capades star. You could see how hard and bizarre life was for them.

Everybody wanted a piece of them—from Madison Avenue types, Upper West Side restaurateurs, and all the rest."

When Brownstein met Kinky and Ratso at the Lone Star Café, he decided to include them and the Lone Star Café in the film.

"I knew Kinky by reputation from the Texas Jewboys," says Brownstein. "I always thought he was an eccentric, wild, lovable character. He is definitely a character; you couldn't invent a guy like that. For all the bravado with the cigars, the big cowboy hat, and the tough talk, Kinky is a good soul. His heart is in the right place, yet he's funny as hell."

Brownstein drew on Ratso's knowledge of hockey and Kinky's talent for songwriting in the film. "Kinky wasn't hockey, but Ratso was, so we thought we'd get their unique views and perspective on the Canadian sport because these guys are as far from being Canadian as possible," he explains. "I had the brainstorm Kinky could write a great soundtrack for the film. He came up with 'Skating on Thin Ice' and 'People Who Read *People* Magazine' in about a day.

"The lyrics are amazing. For a guy from Texas who knew next to nothing about hockey, he was able to compose a song that said everything about hockey. He never got the respect as a songwriter he really deserves. Everybody gets hung up on the name of Texas Jewboys."

The lyrics to "Skating on Thin Ice" are pure Kinky.

> *They say that even Jesus hates a loser,*
> *And when you die you go to hockey hell*
> *And when your soul gets sent down they'll be*
> *The devil skatin' round*
> *And an interview with Howard Cosell.*

Brownstein shot the songs at a packed show with a number of Rangers in the audience. Decked out in his Jesus jacket, sequined pants, and two-tone boots made of "fine brontosaurus foreskin" with fancy toe taps, Kinky was accompanied by an eclectic cast of musicians including Scarlet Rivera on violin, Larry Campbell and Chinga Chavin on guitar, Corky Laing on drums, and Vaughn Meader (best known for his JFK impersonations) on piano.

The following day, the film crew followed Kinky and Sloman on a stroll through Chinatown. "We liked the idea of filming in Chinatown instead of shooting the usual New York imagery," says Brownstein. "It didn't really have much to do with anything, but it worked. Kinky and Ratso were walking around making typical New York observations on Chinatown with a jaded edge and talking about hockey. It [the film] was a wonderful juxtaposition having guys from the boonies of northern Ontario with Kinky from the Texas Jewboys talking about hockey in Chinatown—it made it surreal and it worked out very nicely."

When the film was released in 1982, it did well in movie theaters in Montreal and several other Canadian cities. After the initial theatrical run, it aired on The Movie Network, the Canadian equivalent of HBO.

Although the Rangers had become fast friends with Kinky, his crass sense of humor didn't go over well with their wives, especially the night they stopped by the Lone Star to celebrate the team making the 1979 Stanley Cup playoffs. Hattersley remembers that night vividly.

"Kinky was insane in those days," says Hattersley. "One night the entire New York Rangers hockey team was sitting at a big table in the back of the club with their wives. Everybody is dressed to the hilt. Kinky walks in wearing his hockey jersey, which comes down to his knees, and is wearing no obvious pants under the jersey. He's ripped and he takes a bottle of Lone Star beer, shakes it, and sprays the whole table."

Kinky may have picked up the crude gesture from Belushi, who shook a beer and sprayed the audience when he sat in with Roomful of Blues at the club. Belushi, like Kinky, was acting spontaneous with no thought of repercussions. Unlike the Rangers and their wives, Belushi's audience shook their beers and sprayed him back. Disgusted by the beer and foam on the instruments and band, guitarist Duke Robillard yelled at Belushi to get off the stage. In retrospect, that wasn't a very smart move, either. Belushi had planned to hire Roomful of Blues for the Blues Brothers band, but that rift led to him hiring musicians from the *Saturday Night Live* band and the Stax Records house band.

During that year, Bob Dylan became a born-again Christian and released *Slow Train Coming*, an album of gospel songs. He released *Saved*, another gospel album, the next year and performed only gospel tunes on his 1979 and 1980 tours. Although Kinky never mentioned his friend's renunciation of the Jewish faith, he joked that Dylan wanted his Jesus jacket back now that he was born-again. Dylan, however, had plans for recruiting both Ratso and Kinky to his newfound religion.

"I'm one of the few people who consistently defended Bob during his born-again period, and he invited me on those tours," says Sloman. "When I went on the bus after one of his shows, Bob says, 'Ratso, you and Kinky could be powerhouses for the Lord.' He thought he'd convert me and by proxy Kinky," Sloman says, laughing. "His bus takes off and is circling the arena while Bob is haranguing me. It was hilarious."

When Ratso didn't bite, he was in good company. When Dylan tried to evangelize producer Jerry Wexler during the *Slow Train Coming* sessions at Muscle Shoals Studio, Wexler replied, "Bob, you're dealing with a sixty-two-year-old Jewish atheist. Let's just make an album."

Then there was an unknown politician in town for the 1980 National Democratic convention who stopped by the Lone Star Café. Impressed with Kinky's act, he made his way to the dressing room to pay his respects. Nobody had any idea Bill Clinton would be elected president in 1992. Or that he would read his first Kinky Friedman novel in 1994, and invite Kinky and his dad to a gala dinner at the White House in January three years later.

"This young up-and-coming politician from Arkansas gives a rousing speech at the Democratic convention; then he comes to the Lone Star to see Kinky," says Sloman. "We were hanging out with Clinton in Kinky's dressing room and nobody knew who he was. He was the governor of Arkansas but had no national exposure at that point."

"It wasn't any big deal when Clinton came by," adds Kinky. "He was just the governor of some Southern state and nobody was even sure what state it was. That was the first time I met him—I forgot about that. I talked to him and he was fine; he was a nice Bubba."

Another one of Kinky's serendipitous meetings in New York was with writer and musician Michael Simmons. As leader of the band Slewfoot, Simmons was dubbed "the Father of Country Punk" by *Creem* magazine in the 1970s. He was an editor at the *National Lampoon* in the '80s and often mentioned Kinky in his popular column "Drinking Tips and Other War Stories." He won a Los Angeles Press Club Award in the '90s for investigative journalism; has written for *MOJO*, *LA Weekly*, *Rolling Stone*, *Penthouse*, *High Times*, *Los Angeles Times*, the *New York Times*, *CounterPunch*, and the *Progressive*, and scribed liner notes for Bob Dylan, Michael Bloomfield, Phil Ochs, and Kris Kristofferson.

Simmons, who clicked with Kinky when they met at the Lone Star in 1977, has been a key player in Kinky's life ever since.

"We hit it off and we started improvising and bantering and talking about country music—we both were extremely passionate about the history of country music," says Simmons. "Kinky used to call me the walking country music encyclopedia because I could say, 'So-and-so played the Opry for the first time in 1951.'"

Even before they became friends, Simmons sang Kinky's praises to his colleagues at *National Lampoon*, where he was working as Michael O'Donoghue's assistant when he caught Kinky's Max's Kansas City show in 1973. His father, Matty Simmons, was the publisher of *National Lampoon*, so he began working there in various positions at an early age.

When he was seventeen, he did underground/rock press and radio PR for *National Lampoon's Lemmings*, a 1973 off-Broadway show billed as "a satirical joke-rock mock-concert musical comedy semi-revue theatrical presentation." *Lemmings* helped launch the careers of John Belushi and Chevy Chase, and led to Simmons' friendship with Belushi and his taste for cocaine.

"John Belushi gave me my first line of cocaine—it was my eighteenth birthday present," Simmons remembers. "He looked at me, put his hand on my shoulder, and said, 'Today you are a man.'"

After Simmons began playing and hanging out with Kinky in the late 1970s, he became "one of Kinky's coke buddies."

"Cocaine was everywhere. It had a lot to do with Kinky staying in New York, and it's also why he left New York eventually," Simmons says. "He was into blow the way he's into gambling now. He obviously has an addictive personality."

Simmons recalls going on what he called "three-day cocaine odysseys, where we wouldn't sleep and went from apartment to apartment in New York, always south of Fourteenth Street. We'd score a bunch of blow and do the blow with the people that lived there. After they went to work, we would just sit there all day and talk to each other really coked up out of our skulls.

"Kinky had a crib in Chinatown with Sredni and Sredni's girlfriend at the time, who later jumped off a building and killed herself," he adds. "We would hang at their place in Chinatown all coked up to five in the morning. I would play guitar or we would read Agatha Christie to each other to amuse ourselves. One night I was reading an Agatha

Christie novel to him and the word 'agitato' appeared. I said, 'What a great word, "agitato."' He says, 'Agitato.' Then he starts writing books and 'agitato' is in every goddamned one. That is the genesis of Kinky and that word. These tears, where we would go from apartment to apartment, were like a John Cheever novel—it was fun but there was desperation about it."

In addition to cocaine, Kinky and Simmons would also snort speed and stay up all night. "I had access to industrial-strength crystal methedrine [methamphetamine] and I would share it with him," Simmons says. "That stuff was great because you didn't have to go to the bathroom every half-hour and snort another line. You snort a line and you were up for sixteen hours.

"Kinky would pace, but actually he got more peaceful, which might mean cocaine served as a diagnostic drug like they give Ritalin to kids [with ADHD]," Simmons adds. "He would get serene almost—not almost—he would get goddamned serene on it."

Although he was never officially diagnosed, Kinky most likely has ADHD—Attention Deficit Hyperactivity Disorder. Symptoms in adults include trouble focusing or concentrating, restlessness, impulsivity, difficulty completing tasks, disorganization, low frustration tolerance, frequent mood swings, hot temper, trouble coping with stress, and unstable relationships. Even today Kinky tends to be wired and has a difficult time sleeping.

Sloman describes Kinky's reaction to cocaine as a combination of agitation and calm.

"Kinky was always a funny guy, although it can be incredibly trying to be around him, especially when he was doing blow," says Sloman. "When Kinky would do cocaine, he would turn into the hunchback of New York and literally start pacing the floor, talking out loud about what career choices he should make—'What am I going to do now? Should I do this?'" he adds, laughing. "'All right, Kinky, enough.' In some respects the cocaine had the opposite effect on him. So if it slowed him down, you can imagine how it made him more self-obsessed, and what it was like being around him."

Ironically, Kinky didn't like the way cocaine made him feel, but he couldn't stay away from it.

"Keep in mind it was the early '80s, there was a lot of cocaine, and everybody was doing it upstairs all the time," says Laing. "Most of the people hanging around with him were coke freaks. He had a lot of drug dealers coming in, regularly going up to the iguana on the roof. Everybody would hang out in the iguana's ass and do blow. The thing about Kinky is he hated cocaine. It would make him feel so bad, but he did it anyways. He'd always say, 'I can't stand the shit—you got any?' He's paranoid anyway, and it just enhanced and exaggerated his paranoia. He would obsess totally about things. But everybody felt the same way—everybody was totally paranoid of everybody."

Sloman recalls doing coke and hanging out with Kinky at Don Imus's penthouse at Astor Place in the Village. "Imus was doing as many drugs as Kinky was at that time," Sloman says. "Drinking copious amounts of vodka and doing a lot of blow. Everything centered around it."

"That was Imus's low ebb," adds Kinky. "Not that I was doing that well, but once again Imus had the ability to really fuck himself up good, and he did."

Despite his "low ebb," Imus's novel *God's Other Son* was published in 1981. It's a clever story that starts out funny, but takes on a darker edge. A Southern televangelist who believes he's the son of God, Hargus was sexually molested by his stepmother at an early age and tormented by her for his sinful pleasures. His attempts to eliminate his sexual desires include slamming a window on his penis and hitting it with a hammer.

Determined to turn his novel into a Broadway musical, Imus asked Kinky to write the musical score. Kinky began writing the music, not the least bit concerned that the darkness of the story line might impact their ability to launch a successful production.

As executive producer, Laing set up, produced, and played on the *God's Other Son* demo sessions at the Record Plant. Musical producer Larry Campbell also played on the sessions. Imus did the speaking parts and financed the project. With booze and drugs flowing, Imus slipped Laing $15,000 instead of $1,500 to pay the players for the first week.

"Don was doing his standup shows and everything was in cash," Laing says. "He packed auditoriums for a hundred bucks a seat and he'd have thousands of dollars on him. He gave me an envelope and said, 'Here's the money for the band and yourself.' When I got back to Westport and opened it, there was $15,000. I remember thinking, 'Shit, maybe it's a tip.' I didn't know Don that well at the time. We were all starting to get to know each other during the production."

When he went back to the Record Plant to ask Imus if the extra cash was a tip, the shock jock was lying on the bathroom floor, passed out in front of the toilet with his pants down.

"The door was sort of open and I looked in and thought, 'This is such a bad scene. Here's a million-dollar DJ lying on the fucking floor just like Steve Tyler used to do in the '70s. When he woke up, I told him, 'You look just like Steve Tyler on the floor,' and he went, 'Really? That's cool!!' I don't think he showed up in his head one night during the whole session."

Imus quickly recovered his senses and acerbic tongue when asked if the extra $13,500 was a tip.

"He said, 'What are you talking about?'" recalls Laing. "I said, 'You gave me $15,000.' He said, 'Holy shit, you're telling me a rock and roll drummer has-been—as he liked to put it—is coming back, being an honest American citizen and giving me back my change?' I said, 'I'll keep it if you want, Don.' He said, 'No, but that's fucking amazing.' Don and I were friends for a long time. Any time I needed him for promotion he was always glad to do it."

Not everyone was impressed with Laing's honesty. "When I told Kinky, he said, 'What the fuck did you give it back to him for? He would have never missed it because he was drunk.'"

Simmons also sang on the demo, playing the role of a pedophile who runs an orphanage in one of the darker songs.

"They brought in a children's choir for the song about the pedophile," he says. "I led the children's choir and sang a song about schtupping [Yiddish word for having sex] with these children. Talk about dark. Kinky wrote a bunch of songs for *God's Other Son*; I sang two or three songs. There's a tape of those songs somewhere. It's really a never-heard masterpiece." Yet, like so many things in Kinky's life, the tape is lost to posterity.

Kinky didn't perform on the demo, but he stopped by the sessions to have a few drinks, hang out, and talk to Earl Shuman, a song publisher/songwriter who Laing wanted him to meet. A prolific and popular songwriter with songs recorded by Meat Loaf, Patti Page, Barbra Streisand, Patsy Cline, Nina Simone, Perry Como, Ella Fitzgerald, Sammy Davis Jr., k.d. lang, Tom Jones, Bobby Vinton, and the Mills Brothers, Shuman immediately recognized Kinky's songwriting talent.

"Earl Shuman goes back to the Brill Building and knows good music when he hears it," says Laing. "Earl was working with Paul Simon, Simon and Garfunkel—and considered Kinky to be one of his favorite writers. He loved Kinky and was the only one Kinky ever showed respect for or was polite to. Earl would show up in his Brooks Brothers shirt and tie—just a real classy guy. He became Kinky's publisher and got Kinky's song 'People Who Read *People* Magazine' recorded by the Irish Rovers."

Although Imus approached Tony Award–winning Broadway director Jerry Zaks, among others, the project never got off the ground. "*God's Other Son* was hard to launch as a Broadway musical," admits Kinky. "I wrote the music and lyrics and we expected to have some homosexuals tap dancing years earlier, but it never happened."

"Don put a lot of money—a couple of hundred thousand dollars— into it," adds Laing. "He had all the Broadway theater owners because Don was huge at the time. It could've been bad timing [not getting it to Broadway], but it was very close. Kinky thought it was going to be his ticket, because Willie Nelson was gonna cover one or two of the songs, too. It was happening at the time; it just never clicked in. That's the thing about music; you just never know."

Following this most recent disappointment, Kinky's drug use continued to escalate. Once again, he almost died from a drug overdose. He credits Rickie Lee Jones, who battled her own demons, for helping him survive an inadvertent overdose of heroin.

"Only time I met Rickie was when I snorted a long line of what I thought was marching powder at this woman's house who was selling drugs in New York," Kinky says. "And it was heroin. Rickie said, 'Oh, my God, Kinky, that's way too much and it's not cocaine.' That grounded me—I was in a bed in this place; it was pretty much a shooting gallery. I was there for forty-eight hours, semiconscious. Every time I'd wake up Rickie Lee Jones was there or somebody else was there. There was a parade of people coming through. But it wasn't like they were watching over me . . . although maybe John Belushi was."

In 1981, he lost Kacey Cohen, an heiress he calls one of the loves of his life, to a drug-laced lifestyle. He had known Kacey for three years and fallen in love almost instantly.

"She was Jewish, from Canada, and her father owned a chain of something in Canada," says Ferrero. "Kinky talked about her incessantly. She was really a knockout and very nice, but she was stoned all the time."

"We were together three years—on and off," says Kinky. "We weren't actually seeing other people, but we were both fucked up in different parts of the city. When you're doing cocaine, you'd do cocaine with Heinrich Himmler rather than be with the person you love, and that was on both sides. Kacey and I often talked about going somewhere without cocaine—the two of us—getting away from it, and we never did. It [coke] defined our lives. She was the only rich girl I've ever loved. All the others, I was able to take care of in some way or another."

Chuck E. Weiss thought Kacey was "somebody really special," but after spending time with her and Kinky in the Tropicana, he knew she would die young.

"We were all partying and it was five or six in the morning," he remembers. "She was high as a kite and she jumped into a sports car—it could've been an XKE or a Porsche—and just flew down Santa Monica Boulevard at about 110 miles an hour. When we saw her speed off like that, I looked over at Kinky and we both knew that was how she was going to die," he says.

Kinky still has vivid memories of that fateful night. "That was when Kacey and I were really in love, and she drove off in her little convertible," he says. "She drove it fast, the way she did things, dangerously, recklessly. Chuck E. just shook his head. He knew it was a dead-end street and she wouldn't be around long. She walked on the wild side and ultimately went through three windshields in Vancouver—kissed three windshields and the third one got her.

"Her world was kind of crumbling and I wasn't there. Somebody else was, and they weren't particularly good for her, either. Kacey always said, 'Not a long time, but a good time.' That was one of her mottos. She was twenty-seven when she died."

He dedicated his 1988 novel *When the Cat's Away* to her; Kacey's self-portrait still hangs in his writing room at the ranch. Although he lamented not being able to save her in another novel, he knows it was just wishful thinking.

"I don't think it could have been done," he says. "It's a world full of death-bound passengers, and some of the most beautiful and charming are the most death bound."

Another death-bound passenger was Belushi, who died of an

overdose of a mixture of cocaine and heroin. And, like the glimpse of Cohen's future that night in the Tropicana Motel, Kinky remembers an eerie foreboding of Belushi's death when the comedian visited him in his suite at the Miramar Hotel in Santa Monica.

"Belushi was up in my room, and one of us had Quaaludes and one of us has something like speed or Molly [Ecstasy]," he says. "I don't know what we had or whose it was. Except I went in the dumper, and when I came out he was laying on the floor with Quaaludes spread out all around him as a joke. He might have been telegraphing to me what was to come. You don't know.

"Then, when he was dying, Robert De Niro and Robin Williams and other people came by when he was still alive. That stunned me because number one: it's a terrible loss. Belushi had been a mentor to me in a lot of ways. I looked up to John for advice. And number two: I wondered what I would have done if I had dropped by there looking for cocaine or whatever. Would I have just gone off to let him die? Could I have even known he was dying? It looked like he was dying, he was really fucked up, but maybe you just don't know and scoot out of there— 'Bad scene,' you know? One would think I would've called 911 and done something.

"I just don't know what I would have done if I had drifted by that night and seen him in such bad shape. Would I have been sharp enough to say, 'We have to get him help now—get out of here—John, come with me'? You just don't know what the fuck you'd do. That's one of the things about cocaine; you have totally no willpower whatsoever. You see a guy getting killed or you fuck around on somebody you love. You tend to spend time with really marginal people. Somehow I came out of that—by dumb luck or something—and John didn't. And I still wonder, if I'd had his money and success, would I have come out of it?"

Six months later, almost to the day, Kinky's close friend Tom Baker died of a drug overdose after attending one of Kinky's shows at the Lone Star Cafe. There was always a lot of traffic in Kinky's dressing room; that night was no different. Amongst the musicians, friends, and acquaintances, there was a drug dealer who had just gotten back from a trip to Thailand.

"Apparently he not only had cocaine but he had this incredible heroin," says Sloman. "Baker was into junk and loved doing heroin. From what I remember, this guy was so stoned he dropped a little packet of heroin on the dressing room floor."

When Kinky later found the packet and showed it to Baker, his friend grabbed it. Baker crashed that night at the home of his good friend Robert Brady, an acting coach and casting director with a stage for students in his loft on Fourteenth Street. When Brady discovered Baker passed out on the stage, he called Sloman's apartment, where Kinky was crashing on the couch. But nobody picked up.

"We were up late doing coke," says Sloman. "He may have called at ten in the morning or before that, because I remember vaguely hearing, 'Ratso, Kinky. It's Brady—you there? It's important—pick it up.'" But they slept through the call, and when they returned Brady's call, it was too late.

"I didn't get the call till later the next morning—it was not clear whether he was dead or alive at that time," says Kinky. "At that time, people weren't calling 911—you think, 'Hell, everybody is going to be arrested.' Bob was working on Tom. He had him in the shower and was trying to revive him. He died on the stage—that was a great loss. It was all Tom's doing, but I blamed myself because I found the tiny envelope of drugs and gave it to him when he asked me for it. You don't know how strong it is when you find it like that or you buy it from somebody and that's what happens. His parents were flying in the next day, and he had tickets for him and them to see the Yankees game. He wasn't planning to kill himself."

Sloman, whose friends Michael Bloomfield and Phil Ochs had also crashed on his couch, understood the danger of potent drugs. "Tom ODed because he didn't realize how pure the heroin was," he says. "The same thing happened to Bloomfield. Michael died of an overdose because nobody told him the heroin was that strong. That was tragic, as was the story with Tom. Tom's passing really affected Kinky—Kinky was very close to Tom, very close to Baker."

Simmons was living in L.A. when he got the call about Baker's death from a mutual friend, who was sobbing. When he talked to Kinky, he got a different reaction.

"I've experienced other people's deaths with him many times—sadly," Simmons says. "When I called up Kinky, he was very stoic. He's usually stoic in those situations. He doesn't show his emotions; he's not an effusively emotional cat. When he talks about his dead friends or loved ones, he always says they 'stepped on a rainbow' or 'were bugled to Jesus.'"

Stoic or not, Kinky was still reeling from the loss eleven years later when he began his 1993 novel *Elvis, Jesus, & Coca-Cola* at Baker's wake. The Elvis in the title refers to a documentary about the influence of Elvis on his fans that Baker had been working on at the time of his death.

"Baker and I were very close," says Kinky. "A very talented man and a very wonderful guy. A troublemaker, moviemaker, Irish brawler, and everything else. When he died, he was the most charming of everybody I knew; he was right at the top. It takes a strong spirit of self-preservation that a lot of the best people don't have. Tom didn't have it; Kacey didn't have it; Michael Bloomfield didn't have it. Tom was a really big talent as an actor; he could have been a movie director. That was a loss, but everybody else keeps on living—except for the person that you care about."

"It was a pretty intense time," remembers Laing. "There was a lot of weird shit around Kinky with Troublemaker Baker and a lot of heavies. They'd say, 'I want to commit suicide today' and then commit suicide—there was no messing around. Baker would come in the Lone Star and say, 'I'm gonna write a screenplay; I'll be back in twenty minutes.' He'd disappear to some junkie's apartment and come back an hour or two later with a screenplay. These were the kind of people who just went and did it.

"I remember staying up all night and going out for Chinese breakfast, where they serve a whole fish," he adds. "Kinky would say, 'Turn the fish around—don't face the head of the fish towards me.' A couple of times they had put the fish pointing at someone and within weeks, that person would be dead. Most weren't my close friends, but one of them was troublemaker Baker."

Two years later, in an odd twist of fate, Kinky made the *New York Post* after going to the aid of a woman being mugged at a Citibank ATM on Christopher Street near Seventh Avenue. When he left his loft to buy cigars and saw a crowd outside the bank watching a woman being attacked, he had no idea it was the woman who had shot the fatal speedball into Belushi's arm.

"You needed a [ATM] card to get in and I had one," Kinky says. "The guy had her down on the floor, and it looked like he was stabbing her. Turned out he wasn't, but he was definitely assaulting her. I got in and grabbed the guy and threw him off. He ran off, but the cops got him. The woman slipped out just before the cops showed up. I thought that was strange. A few days later a guy in a bar said, 'You know who that was you rescued, don't you? That was Cathy Smith, the woman who was with Belushi when he died.'"

Smith, a rock groupie and hanger-on, was later sentenced to three years in state prison for her role in Belushi's fatal overdose. She pleaded no contest to involuntary manslaughter and three counts of furnishing and administering controlled substances to him in the hours before he died.

"That accounts for why she thanked me and then disappeared," adds Kinky. "She was in the country illegally from Canada anyway. Then I went and posed for the picture for the *New York Post* with a guitar and headline 'Country Singer Plucks Victim from Mugger.' Ted Mann wasn't writing for them, but he was a reporter, so he called a friend at the *Post*. He was very impressed with that episode, as was I," Kinky deadpans.

Kinky didn't think about the odds of him saving the woman who had given Belushi his fatal injection until he talked to Tom Waits.

"Tom said, 'Think about that for a minute. Out of twelve million people you could have rescued that night, you rescued the woman that was with your friend John Belushi when he died,'" Kinky says. "'If you don't think that's a message—from God or John Belushi—telling you to stay off drugs . . . It's just too weird that the guy who rescues her happens to be a close friend of John Belushi. And out of all the people who could have been there getting mugged, she's the one. It's New York City, man, not some small town.' Tom was very taken by that, and he might have had a good point," Kinky added.

But Kinky was still too caught up in his own cocaine habit to heed anyone's warning. "I didn't follow the advice for a long time," he says with a laugh. "I still got pretty fucked up. That could have been me, too [dying]. But Belushi was ahead of me in some ways—on a faster track."

Living in New York, Kinky was surrounded by friends who were writers: Mike McGovern, who wrote for the *Daily News*, and Sloman, who wrote for *High Times* and later the *National Lampoon*. There was also *National Lampoon* writer Ted Mann, and *National Lampoon* editor/writers Michael Simmons and Doug Kenney.

When Sloman was writing for *High Times*, the counterculture magazine devoted to marijuana, he convinced Kinky to write an article about his time in the Peace Corps. Other *High Times* contributors included Charles Bukowski, William S. Burroughs, Hunter S. Thompson, and Andy Warhol, so Kinky fit right in. "My Scrotum Flew Tourist—A Personal Odyssey by Kinky Friedman" ran in the September 1981 issue.

A photo of Kinky in only a cowboy hat, cowboy boots, briefs, and a strategically placed gun holster adorned the cover of the August 1982 issue, along with photos of Lucy and Ricky (Lucille Ball and Ricky Ricardo); Lenny Bruce; Bambi, the Acid Queen; the Toughman; and Ganja Man. Kinky's movie reviews, "Nuclear Survival Catalogue: Kinky Picks the Flicks," ran in the "Seeds 'n' Stems" section of the magazine, and another section had several different outfits that readers could cut out and use to dress the Kinky paper doll on the cover.

Kinky and his friends spent many a night at the Lion's Head, a writer's bar on Christopher Street in Greenwich Village, next door to the *Village Voice*. A combination of blue-collar and ethnic, artistic and intellectual, the regulars of the Lion's Head included writers, politicians, musicians, and everything in between.

Journalist and author Pete Hamill immortalized the Lion's Head in his memoir *A Drinking Life* when he wrote, "I don't think many New York bars ever had such a glorious mixture of newspapermen, painters, musicians, seamen, ex-communists, priests and nuns, athletes, stockbrokers, politicians, and folksingers, bound together in the leveling democracy of drink."

"The Lion's Head was great," says Simmons. "It had the highest IQs of any dive bar in New York City. A lot of famous writers hung out there. When a customer had a book come out they would frame the cover—the dust jacket—so the walls were lined with covers of books.

"It was below street level with a grating for the window so you could see people's feet when they walked by. Some bum walks in and he's talking to himself so the bartender comes out from behind the bar and helps him to the door. He goes up to the grating, kneels down and yells, 'You assholes would throw Nathaniel Hawthorne out of here.' Kinky and I bust a gut laughing because it was a few days after a bouncer at a fake country bar called City Limits started screaming, 'Get the fuck out of here!' at closing time and I said, 'You assholes would throw Hank Williams out of here.'"

Kinky's clever wit and way with words, and his love of mystery novels by Arthur Conan Doyle, Agatha Christie, Georges Simenon,

Dorothy L. Sayers, Arthur W. Upfield, Raymond Chandler, John D. Mac-Donald (Kinky has a John D. MacDonald T-shirt), and Rex Stout foretold his future even before he began writing his first detective novel in his Soho loft.

Some of Kinky's friends believe—and it may be just another aspect of his myth—that saving Smith made Kinky see himself as a crime fighter and led to his "Kinky Friedman, amateur detective" series of novels. But Sloman calls it bullshit.

"He did prevent a mugging, but that wasn't the impetus to write the books," Sloman explains. "Kinky was living on Vandam Street, subletting, doing a lot of coke, and basically doing nothing with his life. He was going to Big Wong with me for brunch—three hours later he'd go to Big Wong with McGovern, and then three hours later he went with someone else. He was eating seven meals a day and just hanging out. He was still doing the Sunday nights at the Lone Star and I'm sure he spent all that money on coke or on food because when you go out with Kinky, he always pays."

When Tom Friedman came to New York for a visit, he was troubled by his son's lack of motivation. When Sloman drove him to the airport for his return flight to Texas, Kinky's dad shared his concerns.

"The whole way, Kinky's father kept telling me, 'I don't like what I'm seeing; Kinky's not productive; all he does is sit around and eat, and eat and hang out,'" says Sloman. "He should be writing a memoir of Borneo, touring with Bob Dylan, playing with the Texas Jewboys. Tell Kinky I'll give him an advance to write a book. I told Tom, 'All Kinky reads is mystery novels; maybe he should write a mystery novel.' Tom said, 'That's okay, I'll give him an advance; I'll send him $2,000.'"

When Sloman told Kinky about his father's proposal, Kinky called McGovern to borrow a typewriter. McGovern brought his mother's manual Smith-Corona typewriter to Kinky's Vandam Street loft and he started writing his first detective novel the next day.

"That's how he started writing," says Sloman. "It was his father offering him in advance to give him something to do so he wouldn't waste his life. Tom was an amazing guy. You couldn't think of a better person to run a camp. Most of the kids that went to that camp were Jewish outsiders and had all gone through some dramatic episode in their childhood. Tom was just the perfect ameliorator—the guy who could really help all these kids get over the rough patch in their life. He did that for his own kids, too."

Kinky doesn't remember getting a $2,000 advance from his father but didn't discount the idea.

"Both my parents thought I should write," he says. "My father told me, 'Keep a log, write this stuff down; you're a good writer.' Tom was always very generous with me. He didn't specifically [give me money to write a book], but he thought I should definitely write. Tom wanted me to do something—not just sit around the fucking loft all day and eating Chinese food and God knows what else. I wrote *Greenwich Killing Time* in New York."

With his drug use escalating and his music career winding down, Kinky, and everybody around him, knew it was time for him to return to Texas.

"He was spinning his wheels in New York," says Simmons. "By that time he had been playing every Sunday night and other nights at the Lone Star for years. He was tired and kind of bored with it. He was also burnt out—he was doing too much blow and he needed a break."

It also became obvious to Kinky he had to leave New York to save his life. He knew his drug use was out of control, and didn't want to be another casualty like so many of his friends. So he went home to Texas and quit drugs cold turkey.

"Baker's death certainly got me out of New York," he says. "I left not long after that—came back down here [Texas]. That's what saved me—the Texas Hill Country. Cocaine is a slow, tedious death. It doesn't always kill you per se, but it causes you to make so many bad choices because your main objective is [getting] drugs."

With his music career [temporarily] behind him, Kinky knew he had to channel his creativity and wit into another source of income.

"When Kinky decided to move back to Texas in the early 1980s, he said, 'Emphasize your strengths, boy—emphasize your strengths,'" Simmons says with a put-on Texas drawl. "That was his motto, and he always managed to figure out what he is good at. That's when he came up with the idea of writing mysteries—'cause he loved mysteries. He had Agatha Christie and 'agitato,' and the ranch was always there for him."

9

Back at the Ranch with a Smith-Corona

"A writer's life is hard work, the hours are long,
and the retirement policy is to drink yourself to death.
And that's if you're successful."
—Kinky Friedman

scaping the drug scene by returning to Texas, Kinky couldn't escape the untimely death of another person he loved. The Echo Hill Ranch crew was opening the Friedmans' children's camp for the season, so he moved into his parents' home in Austin. Concerned about her son's health and future plans, his mother stayed up late with him one night for a heart-to-heart talk. Reassured that his self-destructive life-style hadn't affected her love, he vowed to make up for lost time. But he never got the chance. Min collapsed from a massive heart attack in front of Kinky and his dad the next day. An ambulance rushed her to the hospital, but it was too late. The proud and loving mother, who had played her son's records every Sunday afternoon from 1972 until the day she died, was gone forever.

Kinky is still not ready to write or talk about his relationship with his mother. But he's touched by emotion when he shares his memories of the day he packed up her 1983 white Chrysler Le Baron woody convertible to move to the ranch.

"I was leaving Austin to come up here with the three cats—Cuddles, Lady, and Dr. Scat—and my things in her car," he says. "We called it 'Dusty the Talking Car' because it said, 'Door is ajar' and 'Please fasten your seatbelts' in a woman's voice. When I turned on the ignition to leave Austin, someone—and it had to be my mother—had been playing the *Sold American* cassette. The last line is 'Let heaven's golden greyhound roll your soul away.' And that's exactly where it was when I turned that key—'soul away.' Fucking amazing."

"Then we came up here and we did okay," he says to break the spell. Still overcome by thoughts of that fateful day, he bends over to talk to one of his dogs. "Winnie, that was before your time."

Kinky finished *Greenwich Killing Time* in New York and began *A Case of Lone Star* in Texas. With the help of Imus, Kinky signed with literary agent Esther Newberg, who shopped his first book while he worked on the second. She was one of the "Boiler Room Girls," six young women, including Mary Jo Kopechne, who worked on Bobby Kennedy's 1968 presidential campaign. Newberg also attended the 1969 Martha's Vineyard party preceding Ted Kennedy's drive off the bridge at Chappaquiddick that killed Kopechne as well as the presidential aspirations of the last surviving brother of the late president.

Leaving politics for publishing in 1976, Newberg joined ICM (International Creative Management) and is now cohead of the ICM Partners literary department. Considered to be one of the most powerful book agents in the industry, she still holds a grudge against Kinky for firing her in 2002.

Finding a publisher for Kinky's first book was not an easy task. "It took about a year, or a year and a half, and we weren't sure if it was going to happen," says Kinky. The book was turned down by a dozen publishing houses before he signed with Beech Tree Books, a William Morrow imprint.

Kinky pegs his decision to reinvent himself as an author as a move motivated by necessity. His music career had stalled and the lifestyle had almost killed him. "I never wanted to be a writer—I wanted to be a country star like Willie Nelson or Dwight Yoakam," he says. "I have tour bus envy of those guys. But, as Joseph Heller said, 'Nothing succeeds as planned.' So I began searching for a lifestyle that didn't require my presence and provided a payday right up front."

He liked detective novels, and writing an autobiographical series about a self-named former country singer and amateur detective helped him build upon the Kinkster brand. "The Kinky brand was a phenomenon," says Chuck Adams, the Simon & Schuster editor who worked with him on twelve of his novels. "I'm not aware of anybody who has done that—so flagrantly, anyway. He's all about self-promotion. He wanted to get the Kinky brand out there, wanted to get his wisdom out there, and wanted to be a celebrity. To a great extent he got what he wanted."

When asked why he chose to write in the first person, Kinky says, "Sloth," without missing a beat. He pauses for effect before explaining the influence of Belgian mystery writer George Simenon. A prolific author who published hundreds of novels and short stories, Simenon is best known for a French detective named Inspector Jules Maigret, who appears in seventy-five novels and twenty-eight short stories.

"I was reading the Maigret series and was very impressed with Simenon," says Kinky. "He wrote *Inspector Maigret Gets a Blow Job*, *Inspector Maigret Steps on an Ant*—he wrote seventy like that. He wrote ruthlessly with an economy of words and had a lot of color of Paris in that series."

Kinky incorporated the color of New York in his detective series, but only wrote one while living in Manhattan.

"I found it easier to write about New York when I wasn't there," he says. "I don't know why. Maybe it engages the imagery of the mind, like the mind of a child. Arthur Conan Doyle won't tell you the trendiest restaurant of that day in London. You see the fog and the gas lights—like a childhood image of London that never changes. That's what I have."

With his fourth-floor loft on Vandam Street in Soho as the setting, readers learn about the "little Negro puppet head" he attached to a makeshift parachute to toss his key out the window to friends, and the garbage truck staging area that made it impossible to sleep. He included his favorite bars—City Limits, the Monkey's Paw, and the Lone Star Café—and his upstairs neighbor, a ballet dancer reviewed in the *New York Times*. To protect her identity and privacy, he changed her name and the street number of the building and she became Winnie Katz, the lesbian dance instructor.

Thomas Wolfe's classic *You Can't Go Home Again* is an apt description of how Kinky feels when he walks down Vandam Street. "I've been there and been afraid to go in the door because I've seen tourists pointing up to the fourth floor," says Kinky. "The guy who owns a restaurant down the street says lots of European tourists come here and ask, 'Is this the building where Kinky lived?'"

Like Simenon, he developed his storylines around an object or event rather than a defined plot. "I like his style and the fact he had no plot," says Kinky. "That's how I write. If you get a plot in one of my books, you should consider it gravy. He said the hard part was starting. He might start with an address or postcard someone sent him. You go from that and try to do a semi-cohesive thing. I never make an outline—what I do is write for a silent witness. Write for a lover or a lost lover or dead cat or something like that from the past."

Making the protagonist a hard-boiled detective was an easy choice for a man whose lifestyle screams "macho." "With traditional hard-boiled detectives, there is a code, and I felt I was a modern version of that," he says. "I felt I was out of touch and walking alone."

Finding time to write was never a problem. Quickly settling into a routine revolving around his night-owl lifestyle, he began writing a book a year.

"If you don't have a job and you don't have a family you can write at any time of the day or night," he says. "It's a delight for a writer. My old friend Ron Pearlman used to live on a houseboat in Hollywood—he wrote for *Get Smart* and *The Beverly Hillbillies* and died very young. He said when he gets up at 5 a.m. or 4 a.m. and just starts writing, there are fragments of dreams and images in his head that make his writing better.

"When you can use some living architecture—like a fire in the fireplace or a cat or dog—a real smart one like Sophie who's there with you [he says to Sophie, another one his dogs], it's very nice. It's everybody's dream. The idea of not consciously doing what you're doing. Like chopping wood; it's more oblique."

Agatha Christie, who wrote seventy mystery novels and is still considered one of the world's top-selling authors, found writing grueling and said four hours of writing was as exhausting as four hours of working in her garden. As for output, the number of good pages produced can vary from day to day.

"I don't think two or three pages—double-spaced typed pages of 250 words a page—is very long when you get into it," says Kinky. "If you can write four, five, or six pages like that a night . . . When I'm in a fever—*Kill Two Birds and Get Stoned* was written in a real short period of time. So was *Curse of the Missing Puppet Head*. I wrote that in about two and a half weeks."

Kinky adapts the methodology of fictional detectives to help his namesake detective solve his cases. "I solve every crime by being a good student of human nature and thinking, 'What would Miss Marple do,

Kacey Jones, who called Kinky "a marshmallow wrapped in barbed wire," produced *Pearls in the Snow*, a 1998 compilation CD of Kinky's famous friends performing his songs. *(Photo by Leslie Rouffe)*

At the Lone Star Roadhouse in the late 1990s with (L-R) Larry Campbell, Michael Simmons, and Jim Rider. *(Photo by Cleveland M. Storrs)*

With First Lady Laura Bush; Kinky's father, Tom; and his stepmother, Edith, at the Four Seasons in Austin, where Laura Bush hosted the May 2002 Bone-I-Fit fundraiser. *(Photo © Bob Daemmrich)*

With actor Will Smith and Bill Clinton before a Maynard Ferguson concert at the Basement jazz club in Sydney, Australia, in 2002. *(Photo by Little Jewford)*

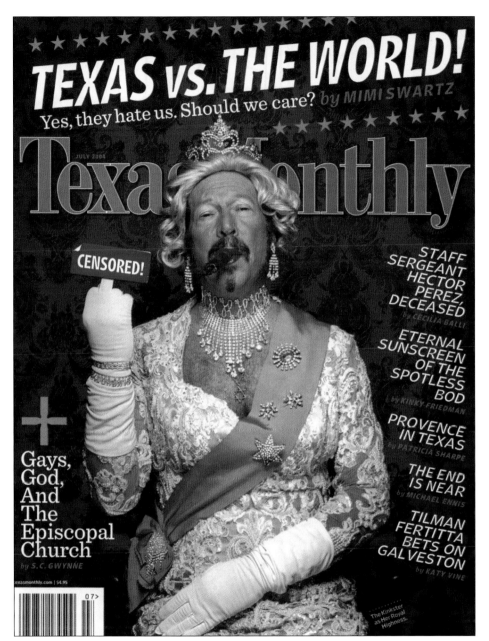

Kinky as a bejeweled queen in a white brocade gown on the cover of the July 2004 *Texas Monthly*. *(Reprinted with permission of* Texas Monthly. *All rights reserved.)*

On the 2006 campaign trail with Little Jewford and Doodles in Alpine, Texas. *(Photo by Melinda Joy Moore)*

Kinky sends a not-so-subtle message to incumbent governor Rick Perry on the cover of the July 2006 *Texas Monthly*.
(Reprinted with permission of Texas Monthly. *All rights reserved.)*

Kinky's writing room at his ranch in Medina, where he still writes books and articles on a Smith-Corona typewriter. *(Photo by Mary Lou Sullivan)*

Hanging out with the Friedmans on Kinky's bucolic ranch in Texas Hill Country. *(Photo by Brian Kanof)*

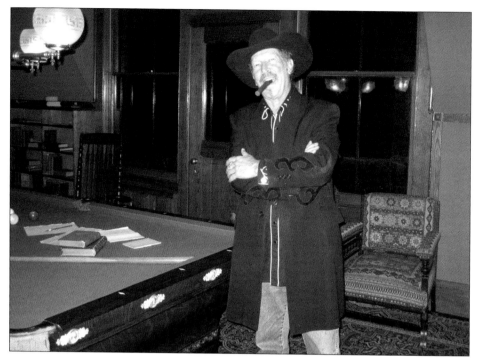

Kinky in the billiard room of the Mark Twain House and Museum after his September 2007 "Pen Warmed Up in Hell" lecture. *(The Mark Twain House & Museum, Hartford, Connecticut. Photo by Augusta Girard.)*

Playing McCabe's Guitar Shop in Santa Monica with his friend Washington Ratso (Jimmie Silman) in 2010. *(Photo by Gary Glade)*

Willie Nelson joins Kinky for a cigar backstage at *Austin City Limits*. *(Photo by Jody Rhoden, Kerrville, Texas)*

Kinky's friendship with Will Hoover, who cowrote "The Loneliest Man I Ever Met," goes back to the early '70s in Nashville. *(Bruce S. Asato, Photographer)*

Kinky rides high in the saddle of a Texas longhorn at the 2014 Utopia Animal Rescue Ranch fundraiser in Kerrville featuring Asleep at the Wheel, Billy Joe Shaver, and Jesse Dayton. *(Photo by Mary Lou Sullivan)*

Discussing politics on *Late Night with David Letterman* during his 2006 run for governor. *(Photo by John Paul Filo/ CBS via Getty Images)*

or Sherlock do, or Nero Wolfe do?'" he says. "Sherlock said what you do in this world is a matter of no consequence; the question is, what can you make people think you've done? Sherlock never reveals his methodology; Nero Wolfe does at the end. Miss Marple may take the most cosmic view of all—she says there is much wickedness in the world and relates everything back to her childhood in England."

For his version of the Baker Street Irregulars, the street urchins who helped Holmes solve his cases, Kinky created the Village Irregulars. There's Sloman as his Watson, as well as Mike McGovern, Chinga Chavin, Cleve Hattersley, Michael Simmons, Steve Rambam, Chet Flippo, Mort Cooperman, Bill Dick, Mick Brennan, and Pete Myers. Kent Perkins, Will Hoover, and Piers Akerman appear in Kinky's books, as do Abbie Hoffman and Tom Baker.

"They were my real friends at the time," says Kinky. "They're all smart, talented in their own way, colorful, and lived in New York."

The Village Irregulars are good-natured pals whose only flaws may be drinking copious amounts of Jameson's, Guinness, or Wild Turkey and getting thrown out of bars for "walking on their knuckles." Stephanie DuPont, Kinky's blonde, leggy neighbor in his novels, is a mean-spirited ball buster. When asked who she's based on, he is uncharacteristically evasive.

"Stephanie DuPont was based on a real person," he says. "She wasn't really a girlfriend—she was just somebody I knew. She was only in two or three books. She got more and more toxic and finally we had to cut her out. But her style made it kind of funny . . . most of the time."

A bit of research uncovered her identity and why Kinky [and scores of other men] still don't want to talk about it. Introduced in 1993 in *Elvis, Jesus & Coca-Cola* as a young, drop-dead gorgeous blonde, the DuPont character was based on Miranda Grosvenor, the fictional name of Whitney Walton, a Baton Rouge social worker who sweet-talked dozens of famous men on the phone. Posing as a 5'11" blonde Tulane University student who moonlighted as a model and took care of her wealthy oil baron father who bankrolled her trips around the globe, she engaged in late-night conversations with an amazing array of famous men. They included Billy Joel, Warren Beatty, Quincy Jones, Richard Gere, Robert De Niro, Eric Clapton, Steve Winwood, Sting, Peter Gabriel, Peter Wolf, Art Garfunkel, Ted Kennedy, Rush Limbaugh, Patrick O'Neal, Buck Henry, and Bono.

According to "The Miranda Obsession," a December 1999 article in *Vanity Fair* that exposed the ruse, "She said she was a beautiful, well-connected blonde named Miranda and she enchanted an astonishing circle of powerful men—Billy Joel, Paul Schrader, Buck Henry, and Quincy Jones among them—with her flirtatious, gossipy phone calls." She never talked about sex or met any of the men in person, but the mystery, fantasy, and gossip she shared about other celebrities kept them enamored. "A lot of nights she was my only friend," Joel told *Vanity Fair*. "As they say, she did give good phone."

Kinky talked to her for seven years, sometimes two or three times a day, says multimillionaire John McCall, a friend of Kinky's who also talked to her and tried to meet with her several times. But Walton never physically met him or any of the men she kept dangling with phone calls. Cutting off contact before the *Vanity Fair* exposé, McCall says he knew she wasn't real and Kinky probably did, too. "Whitney was somebody we all pretended existed and we all probably saw her as a different person," he says.

Kinky, like most of the men she called, cut off contact after the story appeared. Three months later, an ambitious literary agent tracked her down. He negotiated a $1 million book deal with HarperCollins based on the article and a three-page proposal, and a six-figure offer from MGM for screen rights. But De Niro purchased the film rights, the film was never made, and Harper Collins cancelled the book deal. Stephanie DuPont didn't last much longer. She appeared in *The Mile High Club* in 2000 and as a much nastier character in *Steppin' on a Rainbow* in 2001 before disappearing from Kinky's books.

Art imitated life in Kinky's books, which he filled with friends he didn't attempt to disguise. Dylan Ferrero and a number of original Texas Jewboys appear in *Musical Chairs*. Willie Nelson is the intended murder victim in *Roadkill*; Kinky's old buddy Abbie Hoffman is a key character in *Blast from the Past*. Chuck E. Weiss, Kacey Cohen, and Louie Kemp make appearances in *The Mile High Club*.

Cuddles, a cat Kinky found as a kitten on the street in Chinatown, is another constant in his novels. She is simply called the cat. "Honey, I'm home," I said," he writes in *The Love Song of J. Edgar Hoover*. "The cat did not look particularly pleased to see me. Cats rarely do, of course. As young kittens, they were probably never allowed to laugh or cry or to express other intrinsically sensitive feline emotions. This, no doubt, was the main reason why some cats, as well as most people, once they grew up, seemed to turn into assholes."

The hapless recipient of the character's musings and philosophical take on life, the cat was also a vehicle for his outrageous sense of humor. "I was getting damn tired of leaving the cat with the lesbians upstairs," he says in *The Prisoner of Vandam Street*, when he's hospitalized with malaria. "If I kept doing that, the cat was going to turn into a lesbian, and if there's one thing everybody hates it's a lesbian cat."

Cuddles "fought the drug wars" with Kinky, who brought her back to Texas with him, and is probably the silent witness that still inspires him when he writes. When Cuddles had to be put to sleep at the age of fourteen, readers got a rare glimpse of Kinky's heart in a touching epilogue [with a photo] that ran in *Elvis, Jesus & Coca-Cola*. His heartfelt and poetic goodbye brings tears to the eyes of anyone who has ever loved and lost a furry friend.

"She was as close to me as any human being I have ever known . . . . She was always with me, on the table, on the bed, by the fireplace, beside the typewriter, on top of my suitcase when I returned home from a trip. . . I dug Cuddles' grave with a silver spade, in the little garden by the stream, behind the old green trailer where both of us lived in summertime. Her burial shroud was my old New York sweatshirt and in the grave with her is a can of tuna and a cigar. . .

"Now as I write this, on a gray winter day by the fireside, I can almost feel her light tread, moving from my head and my heart down through my fingertips to the keys of the typewriter. Dogs have a depth of loyalty that often we seem unworthy of. But the love of a cat is a blessing, a privilege in this world.

"They say when you die and go to heaven all the dogs and cats you've ever had in your life come running to meet you.

Until that day, rest in peace, Cuddles."

Tender emotion is replaced by Kinky's bizarre sense of humor when the cat's litter box plays a critical role in *The Mile High Club,* his 2000 novel that finds his character holding thirty-five counterfeit passports. Targeted by State Department investigators, abducted by Arab terrorists, and agitated by finding an Israeli "corpse on the crapper," Kinky hides them in his cat's litter box. With his cat taking "theatrically placed dumps" throughout his loft, he makes "brief forays to spirit away the occasional dry cat turds on the tip of the ubiquitous boning knife."

The cat's hatred of Sloman runs throughout the series, as does Ratso's role as Kinky's right-hand man.

"Ratso is the perfect Watson," says Kinky. "He misses the little tiny facial tic—the little thing that is the giveaway. The criminal mind functions very, very differently. You really have to understand the twisted nature. Watson just doesn't get the criminal mind," he adds with a sigh. "He believes in people, believes in human nature, the goodness of man.

"Sherlock, Miss Marple, and Nero Wolfe understood the criminal mind," he explains. "Since those are my guides, my models, sometimes I overlay and begin to think I am them—it's more than just using them as mentors. If I can get into Sherlock's head . . . and I don't mean the little porcelain Sherlock head on my desk that I keep my cigars in. If you can get into the real head of Sherlock Holmes, you can solve a nonfiction crime with fictional direction because fiction is often closer to the truth than nonfiction. Fiction contains great overarching truths, and sometimes little kernels of truth, and can be very revelatory of the person."

One of the threads running through all his novels—and part of their appeal—is the philosophical musings of his character that reveal Kinky's take on life. He considers his books (and songs) a passionate interweaving of his life and his work, similar to that of Allen Ginsberg, Hank Williams, and Willie Nelson. "You'll never know who John Grisham is or Garth Brooks," he says. "They never reveal even the tiniest bit of their souls. My books are a very truthful and melancholy interpretation of my view of life."

Elvis, Jesus & Coca-Cola is extremely revealing. "Historically, I thought, cats and dead people always have been cheap dates," he writes. "Easy to love. Easy to keep in your heart." He describes Elvis impersonators visiting Graceland "as what they truly were—fans. Fans with a curious mixture of love, passion, envy, anger, and beneath that, some arcane form of self-doubt, and what almost seemed to be clinically ill self-loathing . . . just like the rest of us."

One of his best lines in *Road Kill*, where Willie Nelson's life is in danger and the suspects include Willie's exes: "If Willie'd just kept on singing through his nose instead of playing with his hose, none of this shit would have happened." *A Case of Lone Star* captures Kinky's philosophy on traditional lifestyles. "Fortunately, I didn't have to put on a conservative tie and a three-piece suit and drink a little Brim with a mean-spirited, vacuous wife and head for the gray, spirit-grinding office. All I had to do was get dressed and feed the cat. Not a bad life."

After Kinky's first four novels sold 100,000-plus copies, he had the clout to move to a major publisher. How his fifth novel landed at Simon & Schuster depends on who's telling the tale.

"Don Imus loved the book, believed in it, but just didn't understand the ending," Kinky wrote in the acknowledgements of *Elvis, Jesus & Coca-Cola*. "Don approached Simon & Schuster himself about the project, and the book you're reading now vouches for his success."

"Esther didn't like that book and didn't think it was ready to be pitched to anybody," he says. "But Simon & Schuster got ahold of it and their editor Chuck Adams called and said we want the book."

"Esther Newburg was looking to move him and another editor suggested she send his next manuscript to me," says Adams. "I read it and loved it, and bought three books at once—starting with *Elvis, Jesus & Coca-Cola*."

Adams has a vivid memory of his first face-to-face meeting with Kinky.

"He came to New York and met me at a big steakhouse—Smith & Wollensky on Third Avenue," Adams says. "I had never met him before, and it was like I was being interviewed. I wondered if I'd be able to work with him, because he seemed off-putting. I also wondered if he would want to work with me, because Kinky's this exaggerated macho guy and here's this gay editor. Once we got past that evening and I realized he was testing me, it was fine."

The move to Simon & Schuster was advantageous to Kinky and the publishing house.

"He did much better with *Elvis, Jesus & Coca-Cola* than William Morris had done with any of his books," says Adams. "We doubled his sales from his last book. In the first five books—*Elvis, Jesus and Coca-Cola*; *Armadillos and Old Lace*; *God Bless John Wayne*; *The Love Song of J. Edgar Hoover*; and *Roadkill*—we doubled and tripled sales.

"With that boost in sales, bookstores started ordering more copies and taking his book signings more seriously. *Roadkill* came close to being a national bestseller—probably because Willie went on the road with Kinky and signed copies."

When Kinky contacted Willie for his approval of the manuscript, Willie responded on stationery from the Sheraton Desert Inn in Las Vegas. He wrote, "To: Richard Kinky 'Big Dick' Friedman. Dear Big Dick, I've read it. I'm okay with it. You can go with it. I promise not to sue your ass. Cordially, Willie 'Large Scrotum' Nelson." Willie's blurb for the cover, "Kinky is the best whodunit writer to come along since Dashiell what's-his-name," was equally amusing.

But Kinky's sales momentum slowed with the next book.

"After *Roadkill*, sales started to gradually slip again," says Adams. "He never got much past 30,000 or 40,000 copies of hardcover, and was less successful in paperback. His books tended to sell better in hardcover."

Attracting fans throughout the world, Kinky's books have been translated into seventeen languages, including Russian, Hebrew, Japanese, Italian, French, Spanish, Dutch, Swedish, Polish, Finnish, German, and Greek. He's had bestsellers in England, Germany, and Poland, and has a huge market in Australia. "Foreign translations are very rare without a monster book, and we did really well with foreign translations," says Kinky. "The Germans in particular—I have more books translated into German than any other language."

Kinky wrote his novels on a manual Smith-Corona and still refuses to own or work on a computer.

"If you're writing on a computer you have a mindset that if you're not at your best game—if a part is mediocre, you didn't get a character right, or the ending sucks—you can easily fix it on the computer. Whereas I never think that way. I imagine the editor is going to be stabbed to death with a spear and there's nobody to do this but me. If I fuck up on page forty-seven, I'm going to tear it up and throw it into the fire and start that page over again. I'm pretty confident about what I write. Sometimes I copyedit for typos, but you don't need a massive overhaul if it's written well."

Starting a page or two over never hampered his productivity or his ability to meet deadlines. "Kinky was good at deadlines and delivered like clockwork," Adams says. "Every year there'd be a new book. He talked about his typewriter and little green trailer in the hills of Texas, but I never thought any of the pages came out of that typewriter.

"*The New York Times* did an 'At Home With' article about Kinky— where they feature a writer or an artist and interview them in their home. Kinky told me he had to open up the trailer and get it cleaned up so he could do the interview. I knew it was there but I don't think he actually lived or worked in it—it just made for a good story."

However, Kinky insists he lived in the trailer in the summertime for about ten years before it was taken over by a family of raccoons that trashed it. And it certainly added an artsy ambiance to articles about the Kinkster. A 1989 *Dallas Morning News* article described it as "an eyesore of a green trailer on a hardscrabble patch of Texas Hill Country . . . with cat portraits above the sink . . . an aging typewriter beneath photos of Gandhi, Hank Williams, and assorted deceased friends."

The 1995 *New York Times* piece—"AT HOME WITH/Kinky Friedman; Married to the Wind"—described it as "a strange shade of green (a broccoli would recognize it)" with "a watermelon slice painted on the inside of the door. The whole thing looks as if it might topple through the crape myrtle and juniper into nearby Wallace Creek."

The *Times* description included overflowing ashtrays, a "flag-framed Army cot, a little stove with a rickety coffee pot . . . The toilet—perish the thought of a door—sits beneath a century-old one-eyed steer's head. On the bathroom wall, there's a twenty-five-year-old notice he took from a Singapore hotel: 'In order to avoid unpleasant odors, please pull this chain before leaving this lavatory.'"

Promoting his books on what he calls the "corduroy jacket circuit" was a far cry from touring with the Texas Jewboys, with nine people wedged into a station wagon pulling a U-Haul.

"Being an author is better than being an applause junkie, and the hotel rooms are more comfortable on author tours than traveling the country circuit," he says. "There's an oeuvre thing happening on book tour—we use the words genre, milieu, and oeuvre a lot."

When attending a mystery writer's convention in Boulder in the early 1990s, he was amused by the affectations of other writers. "People are wearing their hats at little jaunty angles, fucking corncob pipes, patches on their elbows things like that—it's really very funny," he says. "There were a few real people there, but none of them leap to mind.

"Authors are such stultifying, dull people; I'm positively charismatic compared with most of them," he adds. "And as an author you can be as big an asshole as you want to be; people don't seem to mind an author being really repellent. As an entertainer, you'd die."

But Kinky has always been a natural entertainer and the Kinkster persona continued to serve him well as an author. When the manager of the Barnes and Noble on Fifth Avenue in New York talked to Kinky's publicist about a book signing, the first thing he asked was "Is Kinky going to be wearing his costume?"

"Kinky was good with promotion," says Adams. "He was a trouper, very professional. He would do whatever you needed him to do. When he did an event in New York City, he'd do a little song, a routine, tell jokes, entertain the crowd, read the books and sign copies. Some authors aren't comfortable at book signings. With Kinky, you had a real-life character—a great raconteur that tells great stories—that you could send out on the road."

At a book signing at the Austin Barnes and Noble for *Armadillos and Old Lace*, a man in a dark suit and close-cropped hair waited in line to get a book signed. When asked to "sign one for the president," Kinky had no idea he was talking to a Secret Service agent.

"I didn't really think the book was going to Bill Clinton, so I signed one of my standard inscriptions, "Yours in Christ" or "See you in hell," he says. "Two weeks later the Medina postmaster brought me an express envelope with a letter from President Clinton on White House stationery. At the bottom he had handwritten, "I have now read all your books—more please—I really need the laughs."

In *Kinky Friedman—Proud to be an Asshole from El Paso*, the 2011 Dutch documentary by Simone de Vries, Clinton explains the Kinkster's appeal.

"He certainly is irreverent, and I guess some people would think he's a little too crass and politically incorrect," the former president says with a big smile on his face. "The idea of having a band called Kinky Friedman and the Texas Jewboys whose most famous song is 'They Ain't Makin' Jews like Jesus Anymore.' That's a little tough for some people to take. But if you take it in the spirit he offers it . . . he's a very interesting man and generally funny."

The crew filmed Clinton laughing as he read one of Kinky's books. "Some of it's so dirty, I can't read it, but it's really good," he says. "Some are quite good as mystery novels, but they're all good in the development of his take on life. The dialog is worth [reading] every book."

A later scene shows him laughing as he reads from the 1991 novel

Musical Chairs. "On my way out, I passed Winnie on the stairs. The frosty look she gave me made it seem positively warm by the time I got outside. Too bad she was a lesbian. You couldn't just buy her a new pair of shoes and everything would be alright. I wasn't sure that would work with anyone anymore. We live in a complex world where men are women, women are men, JFK's an airport, RFK's a football stadium, and Martin Luther King is a street running through your town. Life's a magazine, Love's a pain, and death is waiting for you at the end of a needle or a prayer. Waiting like a rat in a gutter to snatch away the last crumbs of somebody's crumbling dream. One new pair of shoes more or less wasn't going to make a hell of a lot of difference anymore." Clinton laughs when he stops reading and adds, "That's sort of the way he talks."

Clinton was still president when he praised Kinky's books in his letter, so his status affected Simon & Schuster's ability to use his blurbs. It was only after he left office in January 2001 that he was able to sing Kinky's praises in the documentary.

"We used Clinton's quote somewhere but couldn't use it as a cover blurb," remembers Adams. "Kinky had good word-of-mouth and he started getting real recognition. Larry McMurtry gave him a blurb and I don't think Kinky asked for it—Larry just liked it. There was a Joe Heller quote, too. I worked with Heller and he genuinely liked Kinky's writing."

His books also earned enthusiastic reviews in prestigious magazines and newspapers.

"Kinky Friedman is to the detective novel what Frank Zappa is to rock and roll. There's just no stopping him. And who wants to?"

—People

"Friedman the author is a taste worth acquiring, too cryptic to be cosmic, too cosmic to be cryptic. Like being in a fortune cookie factory on speed.

—New York Daily News

"The world's funniest, bawdiest, and most politically incorrect country music singer turned mystery writer . . . delightfully potent."

—The New York Times Book Review

"The Kinkster is a catcher, not in the rye, but in the sagebrush, and that's what is truly appealing about him and his work."

—Los Angeles Times

"Friedman can be poetic, hilarious, philosophical, or crude, all within one paragraph, in the spirit of Hunter S. Thompson or Jack Kerouac."

—The Tampa Tribune

"Friedman is a true original whose prose is fresh and razor sharp."

—Publishers Weekly

When *God Bless John Wayne* came out in 1996, Kinky did a book tour in South Africa. When he appeared on a TV talk show in Johannesburg, he made an amazing discovery. "It's such a remarkable story—it sounds like a fantasy but it's true," he says, still marveling about the discovery. "The host of *People of the South* was Dali Tambo, whose father was Oliver Tambo, Nelson Mandela's law partner in the 1950s. The other guest was Tokyo Sexwale. As we were talking it became clear Tokyo was Mandela's right-hand man for most of his political life. He spent thirteen years on Robben Island in a cell next to Mandela.

"Tokyo took me aside at the next commercial break and said, 'Kinky, I think you ought to know Mandela is a big fan of yours.' I said, 'That's wonderful—which book or books has he read?' He says it's not the books, it's the music. Helen Suzman, the only person from the government that visited Mandela in seventeen years, smuggled in a *Sold American* cassette. Tokyo said Mandela liked the song 'Sold American' and played it a lot. But the one he heard him play repeatedly almost every night—for years—was 'Ride 'Em Jewboy.'"

Suzman later confirmed the story when she attended one of Kinky's book signings in San Antonio. He still shakes his head in amazement at the thought of Mandela listening to his music.

"When I made *Sold American* in Nashville in 1973, it was my first record and I was wondering, 'Will the disc jockeys like it, will it be a hit?' You never know who you're going to reach. That's important for any artist or performer to remember—you never know who you're gonna reach. The fact Mandela could be listening to 'Ride 'Em Jewboy' in Robben Island is phenomenal."

Although his publicist had no problem booking him on a highly acclaimed South African TV talk show, booking him on U.S. talk shows was more difficult.

"Publicity tried very hard to get the *Today Show* and *Good Morning America* or a show with Regis Philbin because they really sell a lot of copies," says Adams. "She tried all the shows but she never got him a national break. I think it was because he too quirky, too peculiar; they tend to go with the blander—like Mary Higgins Clark and Sandra Brown. They could get on the shows because they appealed to a mass audience. And they were very accessible as women—attractive, smart, articulate, and not going to embarrass anybody. We were always afraid Kinky would do something to embarrass them."

His publicist couldn't even get him booked on quirky late-night talk shows.

"There was also a resistance to Kinky for shows like David Letterman," says Adams. "We thought Kinky would be a great guest because of his irreverence and Letterman's irreverence—we thought they'd be fun together. But we couldn't get him booked on Letterman because they thought he was too culty [i.e., wouldn't attract a large enough audience]."

Although Simon & Schuster doubled and tripled Kinky's sales, they eventually hit a ceiling they couldn't break beyond. "My stories have always been offbeat—it's not Mary Higgins Clark and whoever the other woman is that writes that crap," says Kinky. "If everybody likes something it can't be very good."

"We talked about cult and wondered if it was because he has a cult following and it's as large as it's going to get," says Adams. "Are we doing something wrong or should we be doing something different with his books? He was sometimes referred to as a cult writer, and he referred to himself as a cult fuck. I don't think he was ever writing for the mass market."

Although Kinky did call himself a cult fuck, he hates the term and felt his writing style, like his music, was just too inaccessible to the average person. "I'm not really a cult person," he says in the documentary. "I'm an established author in the world but I'm not killing enough trees to make the *New York Times* bestseller list here in America. As Charles Bukowski said, 'Being on that list is like swallowing your own vomit.' Those are not the best books, but they still kill a lot of trees."

Kinky's books, like many of his songs, are offbeat, irreverent, and sometimes outrageous. His music never fit into a neat little niche, and neither did his novels.

"Tom Waits says, 'The way you do anything is the way you do everything,'" Kinky explains. "I write very much like I live—it's the curse of being multitalented. When you write a book that's funny and really lyrical, English professors are going to like it, judges like it for some reason, intellectuals like it, and very stupid people like it [he deadpans this line]. But for the mainstream, middle-class stream of person . . . it's very eclectic.

"I like Jimmy Buffett very much and think he's written some really good books. When one of his books goes to #1, the serious literary types are as jealous and horrified as they can be. They don't like seeing someone that is not their precious literary type, *New York Times, New Yorker,* or whatever fucking type of person. You lose a lot of people that way. If we had to just go with the people in New York, God, what would we have? You wouldn't have a Ken Kesey or a Hunter Thompson—or any of the Southern writers, which are most of the great ones."

Kinky's outrageous dialogue, characters, and story lines, teamed with his ability to be "poetic, hilarious, philosophical, or crude, all within one paragraph," attracted great reviews and a dedicated following. Yet he never earned the audience and income of a more mainstream writer.

"Kinky always wanted to have more recognition and more money," says Adams. "He wanted to be really accepted and recognized—just like Kurt Vonnegut. He said, 'I can write like Kurt Vonnegut.' I said, 'Okay, you sit down and write *Slaughterhouse-Five* and we'll talk about you being like Kurt Vonnegut.' But Kinky gave me the same book every time. There would be little changes in the plot, but they were formulaic. He did what he did and was good at it. But he would never take the time or effort to write something that would elevate him. The overriding thing was he was lazy. He just didn't have the drive. He wanted it, but he didn't want it bad enough."

Newberg, like Adams, believed Kinky had the intelligence to write a novel that would reach a wider audience but was too lazy to put in the time and effort. But it was Kinky's ADHD, not laziness, that kept him from having the ability to focus on a complex literary book. "My problem is that people overestimate me," he says in a quiet moment at his ranch.

In 2002, Kinky fired Newberg, who also represented Carl Hiaasen, and signed with David Vigliano. "My best read is after working with somebody for a while; I begin to see what I think you can do, and what I think you can't," he says. "If she starts thinking her client is an offbeat kind of writer and her other writer Carl Hiaasen is going to reach millions, she'll push Hiaasen. I'm not saying Esther slacked off. She believes in anything that sells—any agent does. They will sell *Fifty Shades of Grey* before they sell something that is true greatness. That's just the way it is."

"Esther's a good agent, a great agent," he adds quickly. "She's not the right agent for me—she was the right one to break me in. We're both good people but it just wasn't working."

Newberg disagrees. "It was working, though," she says. "He just wasn't Carl, and I couldn't do anything about that. He thought he should be way bigger, and it aggravated him that many of my clients were. But they worked really hard at their craft. There's an art to writing a mystery or any sort of novel, and he didn't really work at it. He just dashed off what had happened with one or two of his friends and the dance instructor above his head, and there was a novel. He fired me after a book fair he and Carl Hiaasen attended. Carl's line wrapped around the building and Kinky's didn't. It pissed him off and that was the end."

When Kinky appeared at another book event, he noticed a difference between their fans.

"Carl Hiaasen and I did a reading together and both signed books afterwards," he says. "Everybody brought one or two or a pile of old Kinky books to be signed, as well as buying the new ones. Nobody brought any of Carl's old books, and Carl was a much bigger writer than I was commercially. I don't know what that tells you—maybe nothing. But I think they identify with my books stronger than they do with his; that they feel like a part of it."

Kinky's termination of the top agent sent shock waves through the publishing industry, but no one was more shocked than Newburg.

"Esther Newburg was very hurt when he left her," says Adams. "She called me and talked about it. She said, 'He left me for David Vigliano?' Esther had been trying, because she and I had been talking about it. Kinky had the talent to be a bigger writer than he was and needed discipline and direction, and someone to manage his career.

But Kinky wanted the quick buck and David Vigliano promised him the quick buck. I also think Kinky felt Esther was too conservative and David would be much more aggressive."

Working with Vigliano increased both Kinky's productivity and his income. He had written a novel a year with Newberg; after signing with Vigliano, Kinky produced two or three books a year and added nonfiction to his titles. Rather than working with only one publisher, Vigliano sold his books to Simon & Schuster, William Morrow, and St. Martin's Press, and negotiated a deal for a travel book with Crown.

In 2005, author Kinky Friedman killed off amateur detective Kinky Friedman in *Ten Little New Yorkers*, making it his final Kinky Friedman detective novel. He had grown tired of the series and started reusing material, such as essays he had written for *Texas Monthly*, in his last two books, and included a crude scene in *Ten Little New Yorkers* depicting his character during his morning constitutional with four of his dogs crowded around him in "the small, rather dark dumper" at the ranch.

"By that point, Kinky had ceased to shock or amaze anybody at Simon & Schuster," says Adams. "I think he was just kind of wanking off—to be honest about it. He was just finishing up a contract and not putting any effort into it."

However, Kinky put great effort into defending Adams, even at the expense of his own career, when his editor lost his job at Simon & Schuster. In the acknowledgments of *The Prisoner of Vandam Street*, Kinky, who is loyal to his friends, praised Adams and characterized his job loss as "a supposed corporate downsizing move. Corporate thinkers rarely have a notion of who made them what they are or how they got there in the first place," Kinky wrote. "Geniuses like these put Mozart in the gutter, Van Gogh in the cornfield [where the artist fatally shot himself], and Rosa Parks in the back of the bus. Why should anyone be surprised that they fired one of their very best?"

"What Kinky did on my behalf was detrimental to him," Adams says. "Kinky was furious they fired me. The publisher David Rosenthal was also furious and asked Kinky, 'Why would you shit in your own backyard?' Kinky toned his acknowledgments down a bit but left it in."

Although his detective novels provided a steady stream of income, they never generated the royalties of books of well-known authors on the *New York Times* bestseller list.

"People think I'm rich or they see a limo picking me up at the bookstore and rush me back to the airport or rush me to the mental hospital," he says. "They see my books everywhere and think, 'This guy is doing really well.' and that's usually not the case."

With the detective series behind him, he released *The Christmas Pig: A Fable* for the holidays in 2006, along with *Cowboy Logic: The Wit and Wisdom of Kinky Friedman (And Some of His Friends).* He shared the lessons from his gubernatorial race in *You Can Lead a Politician to Water, but You Can't Make Him Think: Ten Commandments for Texas Politics* in 2007, and offered more wisdom in *What Would Kinky Do? How to Unscrew a Screwed-Up World* in 2008. He interviewed friends and included tales of Mark Twain, Joseph Heller, and Winston Churchill for *Kinky's Celebrity Pet Files,* his last solo effort with Vigliano.

Kinky returned to self-publishing with *Heroes of a Texas Childhood,* a heartfelt quick read that offers a glimpse into his soul. "I enjoyed writing it and we published it many, many times," he says. "It's my take on people I liked, read about, or admired when I was a kid."

Throughout his career, critics and reviewers have aptly described Kinky as a contemporary Mark Twain, dispensing wit and wisdom in the tradition of the American writer and humorist. Both satirized the absurdities of politics and social norms with humor, keen observation, and common sense. They also shared a strong social conscience, distrust of politicians and government, and an unjust characterization as racist for using the word "nigger" in a work attacking racism.

When the Mark Twain House & Museum in Hartford, Connecticut, wanted a speaker for its Pen Warmed Up in Hell lecture series—which had featured other contemporary provocateurs including Spike Lee, Henry Rollins, Michael Moore, political writer Charles P. Pierce, and *Rolling Stone* national correspondent Matt Taibbi—Kinky was the perfect choice.

"We started that series to evoke the spirit of Mark Twain, with a sense of his political writing and biting sense of humor," says Jeff Nichols, who was executive director of the Mark Twain House & Museum when Kinky spoke in September 2007. The series name was taken from an 1889 letter written to William Dean Howells, a friend of Twain's and the editor of the *Atlantic.* Referring to *A Connecticut Yankee in King Arthur's Court*, Twain wrote, "Well, my book is written—let it go. But if it were only to write over again there wouldn't be so many things left out. They burn in me; and they keep multiplying; but now they can't ever be said. And besides, they would require a library—and a pen warmed up in hell."

"That quote sums it up," says Nichols. "The series was developed to have the same sort of person come and speak, and obviously Kinky Friedman fits right in there. All the qualities Mark Twain had—as a humorist, comedian, storyteller—are there in Kinky."

Kinky's appearance, which preceded the publication of *You Can Lead a Politician to Water, but You Can't Make Him Think*, sold out the 175-seat auditorium.

"It was a great crowd and there was a lot of laughter," says Nichols. "Kinky had everybody in the palm of his hand all night. His style is similar to Twain—a combination of experience, wit, and timing. Kinky and Twain both used political satire to look at what's going on in the world politically or socially and to transform it into something humorous yet biting."

Kinky's opponents in the 2006 Texas gubernatorial race exploited his satirical use of the N-word in "They Ain't Makin' Jews like Jesus Anymore" to label him a racist. Twain was also deemed a racist for using that word in *The Adventures of Huckleberry Finn*.

"Mark Twain used the word 'nigger' 216 times in *Huckleberry Finn* to make a point," says Nichols. "He used Jim, the African-American character, as a pivotal person, and made Huck Finn and all the people around him to be what they are—racists. Kinky Friedman uses satire the same way . . . to make a point about racial stereotypes."

Twain, like Kinky, developed a brand early in life and enhanced it with a distinctive sense of style. "He was Samuel Clemens, the family man living in Hartford, and Mark Twain, the author, the lecturer, the humorous gadfly," says Nichols. "During the last decade of his life, he began to wear that white suit. With his wild hair and big bushy mustache, that became his brand."

When Twain testified at a U.S. Congressional committee meeting on copyright in 1906, his white flannel summer suit made headlines in the *New York Times*, the *New York Tribune*, and the *New York Herald*. Calling it "my don't care a damn suit," he wore it year-round. "I am considered eccentric because I wear white clothes both winter and summer," he wrote. "I am eccentric, then, because I prefer to be clean in the matter of raiment—clean in a dirty world."

Kinky's trademark attire includes black clothes: a black cowboy hat, black western shirts, a black preacher's coat, black jeans, and custom-made black boots. He dresses in black year-round and had his own brand of Man in Black Tequila. "I've loved Johnny Cash since my early teens, but I don't necessarily dress in black as a tribute to him," he says. "I dress in black so I never have to wash my clothes." Like Twain, he knows his distinctive style of dressing may be considered eccentric, but is quick to beat his critics to the punch. "Anyone stupid enough to wear black in Texas in August is stupid enough to be governor," he quipped during his 2006 gubernatorial campaign.

After Kinky's lecture, Nichols gave him a private tour of Twain's Hartford home, including the billiard room, where Twain wrote five of his most popular books: *The Adventures of Huckleberry Finn, The Adventures of Tom Sawyer, The Prince and the Pauper, Life on the Mississippi*, and *A Connecticut Yankee in King Arthur's Court*. On Friday nights, Twain unwound there with close friends, smoking cigars, telling stories, drinking scotch, and playing billiards till the wee hours. Kinky was so impressed after that visit that he bought a pool table for the living room of his lodge.

"Kinky was very moved by being in the Twain house, especially up in the billiard room where Mark Twain did a great deal of his writing," says Nichols. "Kinky's reaction was like that of so many authors, journalists, and artists that come to the house—a mixture of reverence and joy. Because it's such a personal space—with a big billiards table in the center, and Twain's writing desk in the corner. We let people like Kinky—Kurt Vonnegut was another—walk behind the velvet ropes and interact with more leeway than the average visitor. Because there's a reverence there for Twain from a writer of any type, and Kinky had that same sort of feeling."

He wrote about that visit in "Mark Twain and Bambino Among Others" in *Kinky's Celebrity Pet Files*. Covering up his emotion with humor, he wrote, "Because of an incident some years back when Garrison Keillor hit a cue ball with a stick, practically dissolving it into dust, no one is allowed to play pool on the table. They did, however, allow me to briefly—and reverently, I might add—fondle Twain's balls."

The biting humor and satirical perspective that make Kinky the natural heir to both Mark Twain and popular American satirist Will Rogers were also evident to the editors at *Texas Monthly*.

"There's a similarity to Will Rogers and Mark Twain in the voice, the observations and point of view," says Brian Sweany, who worked with Kinky when he started writing for *Texas Monthly* in the 1990s and is now editor in chief. "If you're reading one of his columns or one of his stories, there's no question who you are reading. His work is individualistic; it stands out. That's something every writer aspires to, but not something every writer achieves."

Kinky's early essays tended to plug his own books or CDs. He wrote "All Politics in Yokel" about his novel *The Love Song of J. Edgar Hoover*; "My Willie" about Willie Nelson, the main character in *Roadkill*; and "A Tribute to Me," to promote *Pearls in the Snow*, a compilation CD of famous artists [and friends] performing songs he had written.

"'All Politics Is Yokel' was hilarious," says Sweany. "The magazine had always struggled to be funny. Kinky is certainly a particular kind of funny, but he always struck a chord with our readers. After running several pieces over the years, Evan Smith [the editor at the time] decided to bring him in full-time."

Kinky's words of wisdom graced that prestigious publication for fifteen years. His "Last Roundup" column ran every month from April 2001 to March 2005, when he took a hiatus to run for governor. His columns ran every other month from March 2008 to May 2009, before dwindling to an occasional column after Smith left *Texas Monthly* in August 2009.

With essays ranging from touching to irreverent to serious to laugh-out-loud funny, Kinky covered topics as disparate as his years with Bob Dylan and the Texas Jewboys, his take on serial killers, his 2004 visit to Vietnam, Jack Ruby, the Dixie Chicks, and—tongue-in-cheek—Texas etiquette. *Texas Monthly* readers learned about his aversion to technology, his belief that the Internet is the work of Satan, and his conviction that real cowboys don't tweet.

He skewered U.S. and Texas politics, but also wrote touching essays about people, causes, and memories he holds close to his heart. They included his father's illustrious military career; hummingbirds at Echo Hill Ranch; his four-legged companions; Lottie Cotton, the "second mother" who helped raise him in Houston; the Utopia Animal Rescue Ranch; and the Austin chapter of a Girl Scout program composed of girls with an incarcerated parent.

Unafraid to take an unpopular stand or offend readers, he questioned Texas's death penalty. He wrote columns praising cigars and trashing cigar haters, and a controversial piece vilifying hunters for "bagging Bambis" and "waging a one-sided war against creation." Titled "Unfair Game," this column generated scathing letters to the editor, with some readers so incensed they canceled their subscriptions.

In his August 2010 article "Gov Hunt," Kinky characterized that gubernatorial campaign as the classic choice between paper and plastic. He called Rick Perry "the incumbent from hell," and recalled Ann Richards telling him, "Bill White reminds me of a talking penis."

Sweany was only twenty-four when he met Kinky. Their breakfast meeting at Katz's Deli in Austin—with Tom Friedman, Little Jewford, and Kinky's entire entourage—was an experience he'll never forget.

"Kinky was in his black preacher's coat and hat putting on a show," he says. "I felt like I was just part of the audience—that I really wasn't there as his editor. I'm fairly laid back, sedate, and grew up in the suburbs in a Christian family that didn't talk about much. So to be with this group of loud guys who were brash and sometimes crude . . . The one thing that stands out: Kinky—God love him—stood up in the middle of the breakfast and announced he had to go to the bathroom to take a Nixon. I was the only person who laughed, because I was the only person who never heard that before. That was the moment I thought to myself, 'What a cool job I have that I'm having breakfast with Kinky and his entourage and they're doing their shtick.'"

Sweany, like anyone who works with Kinky, went through a period of being tested to see if he could hold his own.

"When Evan handed him off to me, he made fun of me for being Church of Christ," says Sweany. "There was a level of 'Can you keep up, and why am I not working with the famous editor Evan Smith?' But I think Kinky enjoyed the ribbing and the show. I liked him and I think he liked me, too. I felt comfortable with him, got his sense of humor, and was very flexible with what would work and what wouldn't work. He knew I went to bat for him—my motto back then was "Let's let Kinky be Kinky.'

Well aware of Kinky's persona, which he describes as "a little bit court jester, a little bit truth with a cold outsider's eye using humor to talk about the hypocrisy and inconsistencies in our culture," Sweany was surprised by Kinky's warmth, professionalism, and commitment to his work. "For as much as a nut that he was and is, he was very thoughtful about every change he made—every word he wrote, every joke he made," he says. "There was a deep thoughtfulness to why he was doing what he was doing and there's no question how smart he is. He knows how to write clearly and directly, how to set the joke up, and how to execute it. He was also fun to work with."

Always a provocateur who loves to skewer sacred cows, Kinky created controversy within the *Texas Monthly* office and with the readers. "I had discussions with other editors who didn't like his work or worried that it wasn't right for our pages," says Sweany. "I thought it was good to have that voice and said, 'You have to let him be Kinky. We hired him to do his thing, so let's not try to make him into something else, or try to print a sanitized version of what he writes.'

"He's also laugh-out-loud funny. I loved his line about people in Fredericksburg—'They still tie their shoes with little Nazis.' It got cut and the pushback was internal. I was as frustrated as he was because it was funny and within the bounds of what Kinky does."

Then there was Kinky's "Psycho Paths" column comparing Sweany to Charles Whitman, who killed fourteen people and wounded thirty-two others in a mass shooting from the University of Texas tower. "He used to laugh that I was so calm and easygoing that I could snap at any moment," says Sweany. "I thought that was the funniest thing; if he's writing about you, then you made the big time. But my mom was mortified."

She wasn't the only one. "A lot of people outside of editorial—advertising, circulation, accounting, and marketing—were talking about it and thought that column was a bridge too far. But in our business the worst thing is not to be talked about. Every one of his columns always elicited letters and they were either 'The funniest thing I ever read—laugh-out-loud, first thing I look at when I get the magazine'—or the opposite end of the spectrum: 'How can you print this, what are you guys thinking, he's a terrible writer.' That's exactly the kind of response you want.

"Kinky would call me every morning at about 9:20," he adds. "Maybe it wasn't every morning, but it sure felt like every morning. He was always calling to check in. I still remember his number after all these years from calling Kinky so many times. Every now and then, we'd get crosswise on a line I thought was a little much for our audience—something he thought was funny but was more crude than anything else. He'd always give me the speech, 'If I was going to let the lawyers and bean counters dictate what was in the column, what use was it anyway?' I heard that more times than I can remember, but it was all part of the process."

Despite their differences in age, upbringing, and political ideology, Kinky and Sweany forged a bond that lasted beyond their working relationship.

"When I left the magazine in 2002, Kinky invited me to a small farewell dinner to thank me for working with him and to wish me well in New York," says Sweany. "For him to take the time to take me to dinner was incredibly thoughtful. That's always meant a lot to me. After I moved to New York and Evan was editing his columns, I missed working with him. Even those 9:20 a.m. phone calls and the calls when he told me if I was going to let the lawyers and bean counters edit his columns, we might as well just call the whole thing off. All of that was pretty endearing."

Evan Smith, who worked directly with Kinky after Sweany left, capitalized on Kinky's popularity and outrageousness by using him in bizarre cover photos. There's the parody of Grant Wood's *American Gothic* painting on the January 2002 cover depicting him as the spinster daughter and Willie Nelson as the farmer. "Willie refused to dress in drag, so I panhandled on the Drag by the UT campus in Austin for a sex change," says Kinky. "That's one of those classic photographs emblazoned upon the scrotum of the public mind."

On the July 2004 cover, Kinky is a bejeweled queen in a white brocade gown with an ornate crown resting on a glamorous wig of loose silver curls. A mustache, soul patch, cigar, and cherry red lipstick heighten the incongruous image of this queen making an obscene hand gesture in long white gloves. The headline? "Texas vs. The World! Yes, they hate us. Should we care?" He also appeared on the July 2006 cover dressed as Uncle Sam in a white top hat and blue jacket.

Throughout the years, Kinky has graced the cover of *High Times*, *Best of Texas Music Magazine*, *Houston PetTalk*, and *Texas Horse Talk*. He appeared on the February 2014 cover of *Dope Magazine* when he ran for Agriculture Commissioner pledging to legalize hemp and marijuana. His most bizarre cover—even for him—was the *Dallas Observer* parody of the Dixie Chicks cover shot on *Entertainment Weekly*.

Under a banner proclaiming "Full Frontal" next to a small image of the Dixie Chicks cover sit three naked images of Kinky, holding a cigarette lighter or a jar of "Kinky Friedman's Politically Correct Salsa and Dip." His hair is long and stringy and his body is emblazoned with "Texas Jewboy," "Big Dick," "War," "Not Airbrushed," "Chicksy Dick," "Hebrew," "Good American," "Buy My Books," "Bush's Rabbi," "Proud to Be from Texas," and "No Apologies." Two copies of *Kill Two Birds and Get Stoned* are propped up in the foreground.

Appearing regularly in *Texas Monthly*, which had a circulation of 300,000 and was read by more than 2.5 million people each month, helped Kinky capitalize on his brand and perpetuate the myth of the Kinkster.

"It was such a popular column, and having it on the back page—which is valuable real estate—was incredibly good for him and for getting his work out there," says Sweany. "We received letters about Kinky every single month. Some people hated him and some loved him, but they were reading his columns. I would imagine a lot of Texas authors would have liked to have a column each month that reminded people, 'Hey, go to Barnes & Noble and buy any one of his nineteen books.' Kinky is a smart businessman. He's a master of self-promotion and it's in large part because he's really good at what he does."

Other magazine editors agree. Throughout the years, Kinky has written for a wide array of publications from *Rolling Stone* to the *New York Times*, the *Daily Beast*, the *New York Post*, *Playboy*, *George*, the *Los Angeles Times*, *High Times*, *American Way*, *Scottish Times*, the *Forward*, and *Tablet Magazine*. "Buddy Holly's Texas," his full-length feature in *Rolling Stone*, takes an insightful look at the Texas music scene in the 1950s, the musicians shaped by it, and what Huey Meaux called "mixed-breeding music."

Like his books and articles, Kinky's larger-than-life persona continues to capture the imagination of people throughout Texas and beyond. What other Texan has had his own line of salsa, cigars, and tequila and has counted Willie Nelson, Dwight Yoakam, Lyle Lovett, Billy Bob Thornton, Tom Waits, Kris Kristofferson, Billy Joe Shaver, Jerry Jeff Walker, Richard Pryor, Ruth Buzzi, Joseph Heller, Molly Ivins, and former Texas Governor Ann Richards among his friends? Not to mention his White House dinner invitations from both Bill Clinton and George W. Bush.

"The truth of whom or what he actually is seems to be irrelevant to most people, especially in Texas," says Roger Wallace, a Knoxville musician who has lived in Austin since 1994. "People love their myths—especially Kinky."

Sweany agrees. "That gets to that larger notion of who is the character and who is the real person, and to what degree that has gotten mixed together so you're not sure where one ends and one begins," he says. "Kinky is known for his hilarious novels and then starts writing a nonfiction column for us. What is exaggerated and what is not? What is for the sake of a joke and what is not? We still love tall tales and outrageousness and there is a willing suspension of disbelief in terms of his stories and the way he presents himself.

"His business card read 'Kinky Friedman is allowed to wander unattended on the grounds—if he's found elsewhere please call . . .'," adds Sweany. "The outgoing message on his voice mail was, 'Howdy! You reached Richard Kinky "Big Dick" Friedman.' Everything was an experience. Texans do like their myths and stories told in a grand outrageous way, and Kinky is the master of that. There's no individual quite like Kinky Friedman and the fact he's been that person for so long and so comfortably is amazing."

10
Friends in High Places

"When the character of a man
is not clear to you, look at his friends."
—*Japanese proverb*

"You can pick your friends and you can pick your nose,
but you can't wipe your friends off on your saddle."
—*Kinky Friedman*

Kinky's charisma and bigger-than-life personality led to many fascinating friendships throughout his life. Bill Clinton, a voracious reader, began sending him witty and philosophical notes after a Secret Service agent picked up *Armadillos and Old Lace* at an Austin book signing. Kinky responded with a letter and some merchandise, and Clinton's follow-up letter on White House stationery displayed his affection for the Kinkster.

"Thanks so much for the books, CDs, and guitar picks," Clinton wrote. "It's always good to hear from you. . . . I deeply appreciate your friendship, your pearls of wisdom, and your continuing support. Please say hello to your father for me."

Thus began a three-year correspondence discussing topics ranging from foreign affairs to metaphysical matters. In a discussion about Israel, Clinton wrote, "I appreciate what he [Kinky's father] said about my friendship to Israel—I have to do it. Jesus was there too, you know!"

When Clinton invited Kinky to a gala White House dinner in January 1997, Kinky brought his dad as his guest. Dressed in a black satin western string bow tie, black suit, and black Stetson, Kinky stood out among the 200 guests. Several made snide remarks about the guest with the audacity to wear a black cowboy hat in the White House. But his detractors grew silent and suddenly found him charming when they saw he had been seated next to the president.

Sherry Lansing, who was then president of Paramount Pictures, was seated on Kinky's other side. Clinton had told her Kinky's books would make great movies, so she asked who he thought should play him in a movie. Rather than take advantage of the opportunity, Kinky answered Lionel Ritchie, which ended the conversation.

When a crowd gathered to chat with the president after dinner, Kinky offered Clinton a Cuban cigar despite the trade embargo that had been in place since the early 1960s.

"We had an arts dinner one night, a black tie affair," explains Clinton in the Dutch documentary. "So Kinky comes in a black suit and a black cowboy hat, which he never took off all during dinner. We're standing in this huge crowd and Kinky pulls out a Cuban cigar, which is still illegal in America. He said, 'I want you to have this, Mr. President.' I said, 'Do you know what you're doin' to me?' There's about fifty or sixty people staring right at me. He says, 'Don't think of it as supporting their economy—think of it as burning their fields.' The whole crowd just cracked up," Clinton adds laughing.

What could have been an international incident didn't put a crimp in their friendship. On a formal notecard imprinted with "THE PRESI-DENT" beside the presidential seal, and sent to Kinky nine months later, Clinton wrote, "Sorry I missed you when you were here—I loved *Roadkill*—Had to read it to make sure it wasn't a biography of me. . . . P.S. Stay after Imus—we all need lost causes."

That fall, Kinky met George W. Bush, who was then governor of Texas, at the Texas Book Festival. "He was just thinking about running for president, and I was thinking about having another Chivas Regal," says Kinky, who was wearing author Larry McMurtry's unclaimed name badge. McMurtry and Diana Ossana opened the 1997 Texas Book Festival with readings in the capitol's House Chamber after Texas first lady Laura Bush made welcoming remarks. So Bush watched in amusement as Kinky played along with the unsuspecting McMurtry fans lining up to have him sign *Comanche Moon*. Watching Bush eye him quizzically, Kinky knew he'd been caught. He tried to wiggle out of it by saying, "Look, Governor. McMurtry's a shy little booger. He'd never do this for himself, so I'm helping the old boy out with a little PR.

"George laughed and whispered something to his aides, and I thought I'd be thrown off the grounds of the capitol," adds Kinky.

"When I wasn't, I asked one of his aides what he'd said. He told me he'd said, 'I want that guy for my campaign manager.'"

Fast-forward to April 2001, after George W. was elected president and Kinky wrote "All Politics Is Yokel," his first monthly column for *Texas Monthly*. The column focused on his disillusionment with politics and his unsuccessful run for Kerrville Justice of the Peace in 1986. His decision to end the column on a high note— "I have hope once again in our political system, thanks to the election of George W. Bush as president" led to a letter from Camp David.

Bush thanked him for mentioning his name in the column "without any curse words" and invited Kinky to dinner and an overnight stay at the White House. Kinky wrote back and said he had four dogs, four women, and four editors and asked if the four women and four dogs could sleep with him in the Lincoln bedroom. Bush responded on a White House note card, "I don't know about the women, but the four dogs, maybe."

Bush hugged him when he arrived, told him to make himself at home, and then rushed to a Marine One helicopter waiting on the White House lawn. On a day that marked the sixtieth anniversary of the attack on Pearl Harbor and less than three months after the terrorist attacks on September 11, 2001, Bush was headed to Naval Station Norfolk in Virginia to make his "We're Fighting to Win" speech.

Kinky stayed in the family compound across the hall from the Solarium, with its floor-to-ceiling windows and a panoramic view of the Washington Monument and the National Mall. "I didn't sleep in the Lincoln bedroom," he says. "But I hung out there long enough to bounce on the bed and soak up what residual ambiance remained after Steven Spielberg, Barbra Streisand, and half of Hollywood had done their best to suck out some of its soul."

Kinky's room had access to the Promenade, so he made his way onto that balcony, found a chair, lit a cigar, and looked over what seemed to be "the foreboding landscape of the nation's capital." When he looked up, he saw two ninja-like figures dressed entirely in black creeping along the roof with automatic weapons.

The time and place were not lost on Kinky. "It was Pearl Harbor Day and the whole country was waiting for the other terrorist shoe to drop, and there I was sitting on the balcony of the White House, which could be the prime target of the enemy," he says.

When the president returned, Kinky joined him, Laura, and a group of forty family members and friends in the State Dining Room for dinner. Seated next to Laura, he sang the praises of the Utopia Animal Rescue Ranch and asked if she'd headline a fundraiser. He admitted he'd already asked Willie Nelson and Lyle Lovett, but neither could make it. She joked about being his third choice, but graciously agreed to do it.

He read several *Texas Monthly* columns, including "The Navigator," a tribute to his dad, "walking around between the tables like a slightly ill mariachi." His most vivid memory of that evening was smoking cigars with George W. on the Truman Balcony, talking about his opening pitch in the first World Series game in New York. Kinky asked how he had pitched a perfect strike despite wearing a bulletproof vest, the excitement of being on the field at Yankee Stadium, and the fears of another terrorist attack.

Bush told Kinky none of that had bothered him—all he could think about was [Yankee shortstop] Derek Jeter's warning that if he pitched in front of the mound or if the ball failed to reach the plate, the crowd would boo him. Later that night, he gave Kinky a private tour of the Oval Office with his two dogs, Spot and Barney.

Despite the warm hospitality of the president and the first lady, Kinky had a lot on his mind. His father had been diagnosed with cancer, and he was about to embark on a February tour of Australia with close friend Billy Joe Shaver, who had had a heart attack in late August. He had misgivings about the tour from the start. His father had just gotten out of the hospital, and he told a reporter, "If I go to Australia he'll die; if I stay at home he'll be fine. . . . I'm sure he'll be fine. There's not much I can do about it at this point."

Little Jewford remembers playing a show with Shaver prior to his August heart attack when "he was popping nitro [nitroglycerin pills to prevent chest pain in people with coronary artery disease] like it was candy," he says. "I knew he had health issues and we should be on top of it. He's a bull anyway, or bullheaded, and when I asked him, he said, 'I'm fine.'"

Shaver says he went on that tour to placate Kinky.

"When I had a heart attack on stage on Gruene Hall, it was like an elephant standing on my chest,' he explains. "They said I didn't have but one artery pumping and it only had ten percent. I blew out all of my valves but one, and my hair turned white overnight. They had to put a stent in the one with the ten percent. I was scared to get operated on in Austin, because the people in Waco told me they could only do one artery. I knew I had to go somewhere else.

"My doctors were upset when I went off with Kinky and was out of touch. I really felt like dying, to tell you the truth. I was feeling rough 'cause I had lost my boy, I lost my wife, I lost my mother, and I felt like going down. [Shaver's wife and mother died of cancer in 1999; his son and longtime guitarist Eddy died of a heroin overdose on New Year's Eve 2000]. That tour had been set up for a long time, before all these things had happened. That's why Kinky told me I was going to ruin his career if I canceled."

Although Shaver tends to blame Kinky for his decision to tour with one artery, five months had passed from the time of his heart attack and the beginning of the tour. Whether it was indeed pressure from Kinky or a natural reluctance to undergo open-heart surgery, he put off his quadruple heart bypass until he returned to Texas in March.

Judging by the photographs of Shaver taken during that tour, he didn't look well. But Kinky may not have realized the severity of his condition.

"I just had a heart attack and Kinky would pick on me 'cause he knew I'd get mad about it," Shaver says. "I finally had to tell him to quit and he did. He's a great guy to play with up and down the road, but he's always insecure. He'd get backstage with me and say, 'You're not nervous?' I'd say, 'No, Kinky, I'm trying not to be nervous—I never was nervous about people; the people should be nervous about me. Grab one of them little girls and see if she ain't trembling.' He couldn't believe I was so calm. Course I was calm because I needed to be calm—I had a heart condition and only one valve pumping."

Kinky and Shaver performed their own songs in a single set— trading back and forth like a vaudeville act—with a lineup including Little Jewford on keyboards and Jesse "Guitar" Taylor and Washington Ratso (Jimmie Silman) on guitar. The gaiety disappeared on February 13, when Shaver got a phone call telling him Waylon Jennings had died at his home.

Jennings had made a major impact on the lives of Kinky and Billy Joe. He taught Kinky about image during his early days in Nashville, and launched Billy Joe's career as a songwriter by recording eleven of Shaver's songs, including the title track, on *Honky Tonk Heroes*, a landmark album considered to be Jennings's finest work and a cornerstone of the outlaw country movement.

"When Waylon died, we had a big ole jug of wine and cried," says Shaver. "Imus called and we all got on the phone and talked to him about it."

Kinky has always had a big following in Australia, and this tour was no different.

"The shows and the audiences were really great," says Shaver. "Kinky pulls in a lot of people; he's a really popular guy. He would get up early in the morning and call up radio stations. I always admired him for that—he always worked hard making himself visible to the public. He's tireless. He goes after it like a ravenous dog. Consequently he's well-known."

There's a great photo of Kinky holding court with Bill Clinton and actor Will Smith at a Maynard Ferguson show at the Basement, a jazz club in Sydney. Although Kinky liked to make an entrance with his entourage, it couldn't compete with Clinton's arrival surrounded by Secret Service agents and Smith's entourage of security guards and friends. Kinky's entourage was missing Shaver that night because he didn't know about the show, even though he says Clinton was trying to reach him.

"Bill called over and asked for me," he says. "I'd known Bill for a long time, because I met him when he was governor of Arkansas. He knew I was there, but when he called, he got Kinky's folks and they kind of circled around me at the hotel. It didn't bother me because I didn't feel up to going anyway—because Bill does a lot of hurrahing. But I didn't know about it because they didn't tell me. I'm used to that—Kinky's that way."

Kinky, however, told Jewford about the call, and they hooked up with Clinton and Smith in the club's VIP room. "They were nice, but there were two funny things that stood out," says Jewford. "When Clinton went to take a piss, there were eight Secret Service guys that went with him. I counted. I'm thinking, really? And you're not even the president anymore. Two had to scout it out, three stood outside, and I think the other ones went in with him.

"When they seated us at a table, I was sitting next to Clinton. We made small talk; then Maynard came out, and he was absolutely wonderful. It was funny because all Clinton did was eyeball the waitresses; his 180-degree head turns watching waitresses were very obvious."

If Kinky had made an end run around Shaver, Jewford wasn't aware of it and said Shaver never mentioned it. Like all of Kinky's friends, Shaver understands that a friendship with the Kinkster, like a relationship with a cat, comes on his own terms and fluctuates with his moods. His friendships won't ever be immortalized on a Hallmark card. They're more in keeping with those of Keith Richards, who says, "It's a true friendship when you can bash somebody over the head and not be told, 'You're not my friend anymore.'" Yet there's a tender and generous side of Kinky that he works hard to keep under cover.

"He's a good, good, good friend of mine," says Shaver. "There's nothing I could ask him for that he wouldn't give me. He bought me a car when I didn't have one. If he had a room in Vegas, I could call him and he'd get me another room or make room for me in his if the place was booked up.

"If you're around important people, he'll bring you over and introduce you to them. He's really such a kindhearted person; he has a heart bigger than Texas. That's why he has that exterior deal—to try to keep people from asking him for things because he's got a big heart. If somebody asks him for something, he'll give it to 'em. But he won't let anybody else know about it. It beats all I've ever seen. For some reason, he hides that. You just have to know him. He's really a fine person. I love him. He's like a brother.

"He has such a résumé of things he's done, and for some reason or other, he's not satisfied. He thinks he hasn't done quite enough and it's always bothering him. I notice that all the time, and I wonder why in the world. To me, he's a big hero of mine, always has been, always will be."

Kinky is a fan as well as a close friend of Shaver's. He has Billy Joe's "Live Forever" bumper sticker on his Silverado pickup and Shaver's "You're as young as the woman you feel" bumper sticker on his refrigerator. He wrote a touching tribute for *Texas Monthly* before Shaver's heart attack. In "Ode to Billy Joe," Kinky called him "an achingly honest storyteller . . . arguably the finest poet and songwriter this state has ever produced."

Kinky's thirty-plus-year friendship with John McCall began on a three-month trip to Australia and almost ended with Kinky's death on a cliff in Mexico. Dubbed the "Shampoo King of Dripping Springs," McCall was the subject of *Shampoo King*, a 2000 documentary by Ellen Spiro, an Emmy Award–winning filmmaker and University of Texas professor. In a parody of *Citizen Kane,* Spiro intercut footage from that classic film with scenes of McCall speeding through Las Vegas in his black limousine and taking Kinky to Hawaii on a private jet.

Calling himself a "recovering lawyer," McCall left the profession to take over the family business when his dad died. The beauty supply distribution company was deep in debt, but he eventually bought out the partners and sold it for $100 million. A savvy entrepreneur involved in a number of businesses, including Farouk Systems, Inc., a hair-care company doing business in ninety-seven countries, the wealthy Texan is now a centimillionaire. "For those of us who can't count that high, it means he's worth a hundred million dollars," says Kinky. "Even with inflation, that's not too bad."

Despite his millions, life hasn't been easy for McCall; he's survived a plane crash in Alaska and four bouts of lymphoma, the cancer that killed his father. He started spending time with Kinky in 1986 when "I was recovering from cancer, and Kinky was recovering from life," he says. Initially meeting Kinky at the Lone Star Café on a night he thought Delbert McClinton was performing, he hired him to play his thirtieth birthday party in 1978. Although Kinky "peed in the swimming pool" and "freaked out" a prim and proper socialite by introducing himself as Richard "Big Dick" Friedman, it didn't impact their relationship.

"Kinky is like my little puppy," he says. "Kinky cannot stand not to be the center of attention. If you have three tables full of people, he's constantly changing places so he can control the conversation. When we went to a Longhorn football game, a lot of people wanted to have a picture taken with him. I've been around stars that say, 'Bullshit, I don't want to do that' and act like they're too good. He actually enjoys people recognizing him and coming up to him. Some people don't have their own personality or ego and Kinky becomes their hero—he's a lot like Peter Pan."

Kinky was staying in McCall's hotel in Allen, Texas, when he invited him on a book and concert tour of Australia. "He did book signings during the day and played shows at hotels at night," says McCall. "I sold T-shirts, collected the money, and schlepped his guitar from the hotel to the train station. We also went to Europe once or twice."

During their travels together McCall saw a side of Kinky very few people see. "Kinky's been to more countries that he doesn't know anything about except the bars," he says. "He doesn't drink much anymore; he goes to the bars because he doesn't want to go sightseeing."

He discovered Kinky's restless nature as well as his unrealistic expectations.

"I always say Kinky loves the woman he's not with," McCall says. "He goes on a trip with Miss Texas and he's talking about another girl. The same thing with location. If we're in Australia, he's talking about being somewhere else. Kinky is never at peace with himself. He expects too much out of life. There is no perfect woman; he's expecting something that doesn't exist."

When they returned to Texas, McCall spent time at Echo Hill Ranch, where he grew close to Kinky's father. But it took a while.

"Because I was a businessman and he was basically a socialist, he didn't think I was worth a damn because I made money," McCall says. "His dad didn't trust me at first; he thought I wanted something from Kinky. Hell, I sold shampoo; he certainly wouldn't be the best advertising for my products. But after many long conversations, Tom became like my father; he was real close to me. He told me, 'There are only two people that don't try to use Kinky—me and you.' I took that as a compliment."

Kinky is rightfully leery of people; his high profile and generosity attracts sycophants and self-serving people trying to make a buck off of his celebrity.

"Kinky probably thinks everybody wants a piece of him, and a lot of people do," McCall adds. "But he doesn't have anything I need. I'm not saying Kinky never asked me for anything, but I don't ever ask him for anything."

In late 1998, McCall invited Kinky and some friends for a getaway at his mansion in Cabo San Lucas, a resort city on the southern tip of Mexico's Baja California peninsula. Kinky went for a solitary walk on the beach one night and didn't come back. When he hadn't returned by the next day, McCall checked Kinky's luggage and found his passport, cash, and cigars. Thinking Kinky had been killed in an avalanche on the beach, he called a friend with the FBI in Mexico City and launched a major search. Using a large blowup of Kinky's passport picture, "which strongly resembled a Latin American drug kingpin," Kinky says, his friends put up posters all over town, offering "recompensa grande."

Both Kinky and McCall admit he almost died that night, but how he ended up stranded on the side of a cliff until late the following afternoon depends on who's telling the story. According to McCall, the tide came up when he was walking on the beach and Kinky climbed up the cliff and couldn't get back down. Kinky's scenario is much more dramatic.

"I had been swept out into the ocean by a freak wave," he wrote in "Cliffhanger," an essay in *Texas Monthly* chronicling the experience. "The undertow, which killed a person that same night, swept me hundreds of yards away from the beach and deposited me at the base of a steep cliff. I tried to scramble up, but I found myself trapped between the tide and the darkness. As the water pounded ever higher along the black, crumbling landscape, intimations of mortality flooded my fevered brain. . . . .

"Late in the afternoon, my hopes were fading. . . . Once again I began stumbling upward, lost in the rocky landscape, trying to find a way to the top of my upscale death trap. Suddenly, while climbing a steep ledge, I was miraculously plucked from my precipice by an intrepid band of Mexicans who were rappelling downward. They had been working on Sly Stallone's house, and McCall had commandeered them. . . . Sly was not home at the time, but McCall was waiting at the top with a warm hug and cold cerveza [beer]."

"Some people you just meet and you like—you don't know why," says McCall. "He's smart, he's quick, he's funny. When I was in the hospital—several times—he's always been there. I know he doesn't like hospitals, so it takes a lot more for him to visit me in the hospital it would take for me to visit someone in a hospital, because I'm used to them. I always appreciated it."

In 2006, when McCall underwent a stem-cell transplant during his third bout with cancer, Kinky went one step further and called on an old friend to help put a smile on McCall's face. He visited Bob Dylan backstage at his Municipal Auditorium show in San Antonio and, for the first and only time, asked him to sign a few items.

"Bob's road guy told me, 'He doesn't sign any autographs or anything; he hasn't signed a fucking thing ever,'" says Kinky. "But Bob signed a guitar and autographed a few things for me for my friend John McCall."

Kinky's friendship with Ruth Buzzi began in the mid-'70s in L.A., where her then boyfriend (now husband) Kent Perkins brought him to her house in the Hollywood Hills.

"I had trimmed Kent's hair and he liked how I did it . . . so he brought Kinky over to my house and asked me to put the shears to

Kinky's bushy Jewish mop," she says with a laugh. "As a child, one of my tasks was to keep our hedges trimmed with shears, so I approached Kinky's pseudo-'fro hairdo like it was a miniature topiary project, and it worked."

A versatile actress and comedienne, Buzzi is best known for a character she created for *Rowan & Martin's Laugh-In*—Gladys Ormphby, the dowdy spinster in a drab brown dress and a bun covered by a hairnet knotted in the middle of her forehead.

She won a Golden Globe for *Laugh-In*, appeared regularly on *The Dean Martin Celebrity Roast*, and earned an Emmy Award nomination for her work on *Sesame Street*. During her forty-year career, she has appeared on TV, in film, and in several music videos, including Kinky's "Get Your Biscuits in the Oven and Your Buns in the Bed," with Richard Moll, who played Bull on the TV show *Night Court*.

"Ruthie, a true American icon, is a dear friend of mine," says Kinky. "And I say without prejudice, she's one of the funniest people alive."

Buzzi, however, had mixed feelings when she first met Kinky.

"I was a little put off by his favorite prop, a lit cigar," she says. "Everywhere he went, he left a distinct smell which apparently drifted in all the way from Cuba by way of smugglers. He wore a fancy cowboy shirt, a black Stetson hat, and a pair of expensive but rather beaten-up cowboy boots with jeans that had been worn at least 500 times between launderings. He was like a caricature of a flamboyant Texan, filling the room with personality. But he was involved with four or five young women simultaneously, and it got tedious hearing about all of them."

Over time she came to like the man beneath the brash persona.

"As I got to know Kinky, I discovered a very thoughtful, deeper side . . . a caring and considerate person, really," she says. "Even though he jokes about being self-absorbed, the truth is, he's more focused on others than himself. Nobody is unimportant to him, and he keeps a wary eye out for how his dinner companions treat waiters. And he's a totally idiotic over-tipper."

She also enjoyed his quick wit and sense of humor.

"As a comedy professional, I recognize writers as the backbone of the industry. . . . And Kinky is a fountain of original humor," she says. "He looks for humor in almost every situation, and finds it . . . and he's fearless. His comedic delivery walks the timing line between Johnny Carson and Lenny Bruce."

Kinky loves to gamble and often invites Buzzi and Perkins to meet him during his frequent trips to Las Vegas. "The most expensive thing in the world is a free hotel in Vegas," he says. "And I'm comped to the eyeballs."

Kinky's free hotel is the Flamingo, the storied casino founded by gangster Bugsy Siegel and the playground of the Rat Pack in the '50s and '60s. With his status as a high roller, the casino pays for his flights; comps suites for him and his friends ("They give me a suite twice the size of the governor's mansion," he says); comps meals and drinks; provides tickets to shows (*The Beatles: LOVE* at the Mirage is a favorite); and provides a generous credit line and $750 in cash.

Like Frank Sinatra, Kinky arrives with his own entourage, which has included New York Ratso, Washington Ratso, Steve Rambam, Chinga Chavin, Mike McGovern, Dylan Ferrero, and Little Jewford. Buzzi and Perkins meet up with him in Vegas twice a year.

"Kinky treats us to a free suite; everything, including all the shows and all our meals, is comped due to his 'Silver Star' status as a big gambler," says Buzzi. "Kinky sits obsessed in front of five-dollar coin slots all day long and smokes his Cubans frenetically like a zombie. . . He really doesn't care too much about money, so he gets a kick out of playing the slots and can lose a lot of money without being upset. He occasionally hits a big jackpot and then has great fun yelling, "I'm one of life's winners!" to the backdrop of flashing lights and bells.

"When he finally tires of playing the Champagne Slots—in the ultimate High Roller area—we have nice conversations over sumptuous meals. We order the seafood tower with lobster claws, shrimp the size of armadillos, and five or six kinds of oysters and clams. These things cost, I don't know . . . hundreds . . . but it's fun eating your way from the top of the tower to the decadent bottom, leaving a lot of crab shells and lobster carcasses along the way. Our friendship started off by mutual appreciation of one another's talent, and has grown to where we really think of one another as family."

By the mid-'90s, Kinky was best known as an author and performer and wanted to be recognized as a songwriter. He has always gravitated towards celebrities and vice versa, and liked the idea of famous artists covering his songs. In 1996, he reconnected with Kacey Jones, whose band Ethel and the Shameless Hussies opened for him in 1988. When she discovered he had a book signing at Tower Books in Nashville, the beautiful redhead sent him a letter and a photo by FedEx, and he called her the next day. They were hanging out in her garden in Nashville when she asked, "Whatever happened to all those beautiful songs you wrote?"

When he "turned around on his boot heel and said nothing," Jones, a singer/songwriter who produced all of her own albums, offered to help. A guitarist and lead vocalist with an irreverent sense of humor reflected in her own CDs—*Never Wear Panties to a Party; Every Man I Love Is Either Married, Gay or Dead*; and *The Sweet Potato Queens' Big-Ass Box of Music*—Jones and the Kinkster were a good match. Kinky thought about her offer to produce his tribute album and said, "If we can get Willie, we can get anyone we want."

Excited about the project, Kinky began toying with names for an album title.

"Every tribute record requires a classic-sounding, moderately pretentious title," he says. His list of titles fit the bill. They included *Night Blooming Cereus* (the Texas cactuses on Kinky's ranch that only bloom at night once a year), *Ridin' 'Cross the Desert on a Horse with No Legs*, *Strummin' Along with Richard Kinky "Big Dick" Friedman*, and *Come Home, Little Kinky*. Don Imus suggested *Hillbilly Has-Beens Sing the Hideous Songs of Kinky Friedman*. But Kinky used a title from his friend Timothy S. Mayer. A playwright and songwriter who had written songs with mutual friend Peter Wolf, Donald Fagen, and James Taylor, Mayer told him his best songs had been lost over the years like *Pearls in the Snow*.

Knowing it would be a tough sell to a major label, Jones decided to create an indie label and license it to a major label. But Kinky, being Kinky, wanted to call it *Big Dick Records*. She didn't like the name and neither did Imus, who said he wouldn't promote it on his nationally syndicated radio show simulcast on MSNBC unless she found another name.

She pulled out her battered copy of *Mrs. Byrne's Dictionary of Unusual, Obscure, and Preposterous Words*, and began looking under "kink" for a word that would work without being offensive. Naming the label Kinkajou Records after the cuddly, long-tailed animals that live in trees in the rainforests was the perfect solution. When Jones's friend designed a logo of a kinkajou smoking a cigar and wearing a ten-gallon hat with a Star of David on it, Kinky and Imus loved it.

Without a major label to provide an advance for production costs, money was an issue. So Kinky contacted his friends. "Johnny Marks in San Antonio coughed up some bucks and officially became our executive producer," he says. "When the bucks ran out after Dwight Yoakam did forty-nine overdubs on 'Rapid City, South Dakota,' John McCall ponied up more bucks and officially became, along with Johnny, coexecutive producer."

With the exception of Bob Dylan, who was hospitalized for ten days with a rare fungal infection and had to cancel a European tour, all of Kinky's musician friends agreed to help.

"Bob Dylan would have done it, but that was when he had this weird inflammation around his heart," says Jones. "He didn't say no; he said, 'I can't right now.' But it was undetermined as to how long he was going to be sick."

Pearls in the Snow: The Songs of Kinky Friedman included performances by Willie Nelson, Delbert McClinton, Lee Roy Parnell, Asleep at the Wheel, the Geezinslaws, Dwight Yoakam, Guy Clark, Marty Stuart, Tompall Glaser, Chuck E. Weiss, Billy Swan, Lyle Lovett, and Tom Waits.

When Jones flew to Austin to record Nelson in his Pedernales studio, it was her first session for the album and the toughest. She said Nelson played the night before at Gruene Hall, an eighty-mile drive from his ranch; had a fight with his wife; and didn't get much sleep. With a flight to Miami at one o'clock that afternoon and a 9:00 a.m. recording session with a producer he didn't know, he was not a happy camper.

"Willie shows up and he's not smiling—you can tell he's not happy to be there at that time in the morning," says Jones. "Kinky told me to make sure Willie uses Trigger, his famous acoustic guitar with a hole in it. But Willie brings in his brand-new guitar—a hollow-body acoustic electric. I'm trying to not irritate Willie any further, but I promised Kinky I would try to get Willie to use Trigger. The engineer's not used to getting sounds and the tone on the new guitar, so it's taking longer and we're trying to play 'beat the clock.'"

Jones gingerly approached Willie, who was sitting in a chair tuning up his new guitar, and got down on her knees in front of him so she wouldn't be towering over him. "I said, 'Willie, we're having a little trouble getting a good tone with this guitar—would you consider using your acoustic guitar?' He looked at me like I had just asked him to cut off his right arm. I started playing country music because of Willie's *Red*

Headed Stranger album; that's how important he was in my life. So when he gave me that look . . . He put the guitar down and he looks at me and says, 'Well, maybe we just won't cut this song today.' And he gets up and walks out of the studio."

Jones panicked and turned to Willie's sister Bobbie for advice. Bobbie, who was there to play piano, told her to give him a minute. But he kept her on pins and needles a lot longer.

"An hour later, Willie walked back in, didn't say a word, and picked up his new guitar," says Jones. "What you hear on the record is his first take. He knew his stuff, he knew the song. He never looked at me again, never thanked me; he just walked out. I knew he'd had a horrible night but I felt so bad because he was one of my heroes."

A month later, when she was producing Asleep at the Wheel's version of "When All Hell Breaks Loose" at Ray Benson's Bismeaux Studio, she discovered where Willie had gone. Benson had been playing golf on Willie's nine-hole course adjacent to the studio. "Willie hopped on Ray's golf cart and they rode around the course and smoked a big old joint," she says.

Despite that rocky session, Willie's rendition of "Ride 'Em Jewboy," which is arguably the best track on the CD, made Kinky realize he'd chosen the right producer. When Jones cranked up that song on a cassette player in a Cadillac convertible at his dad's house in Austin, Kinky grinned and said, "That's the first time I smiled in 200 years."

Once Kinky cleared the way to contact the other artists, Jones sent them a CD of his songs to pick from and gave them their choice of recording studios. Jones produced eleven cuts in Nashville, four in Austin, and one on the West Coast, working with a variety of recording formats and gear. They included twenty-four and forty-eight tracks, a thirty-two track Mitsukoshi board in the Geezinslaw studio, ADAT in Benson's studio, and DAT in Recordio Studio in Van Nuys, California. "The trickiest part of the project was recording with different formats at different studios and making those formats run together like pearls in the snow," she says.

Although he lives in L.A., Dwight Yoakam recorded "Rapid City, South Dakota" in Austin, when he was in Texas to shoot *Painted Hero*, one of his early films. Yoakam has a reputation for being a perfectionist, and although Kinky's comment about forty-nine overdubs was an exaggeration, this session was no different.

"He especially was concerned about the groove—the actual timing," says Jones. "It was a sparse session with a bass player, drummer, Dobro, and Dwight on acoustic, but it took a couple of hours to get the groove he wanted. When we listened to the playback, Dwight said he'd have to come back and do the vocals again. The vocals sounded pretty damn good to me, but he said he had a little congestion and wanted to come back when his throat was clear. Two weeks later, he sang it again and it was better than what we already had. I was surprised he took it up a notch when the vocals had already sounded so good, but he knows his own voice."

Lyle Lovett cancelled Jones's role in "Sold American" the morning of the session.

"It was all arranged," she says. "I flew down to Austin, checked into the Hilton, and we had studio time set up at Ray's studio. Right before I left for the studio I get a call from Ray saying, 'Lyle doesn't want you to be here for the recording.' That felt like a slap in the face. If they knew that before I spent the money to fly down and stay in a hotel, why the hell didn't they tell me when I was still in Nashville? That was the part that pissed me off.

"Maybe he didn't like bossy redheads," she adds with a hearty laugh. "He didn't know I was a bossy redhead, but for whatever reasons he did not want a chick in the studio. So I had to accept it and let it be and I'm grateful to Ray for getting the vocal for me."

Sessions with Delbert McClinton and Lee Roy Parnell were recorded at Soundshop Studio in Nashville on the same day with the same musicians.

"Lee Roy Parnell did an amazing slide guitar solo on 'Autograph,' the song Delbert recorded," says Jones. "It was twice as long as what you hear on the record. I was so stunned by the solo I kept all of it. Imus said, 'Too much Lee Roy, not enough Delbert,' so the slide guitar solo section got cut in half."

Parnell was signed to Arista Records when he recorded "Nashville Casualty and Life" for Kinky's album. Arista wanted to include that cut on one of Parnell's Arista albums, but they weren't prepared for Jones's response when the head of the label called to ask if they could use it.

"I'd had a stressful day, so I said, 'Sure, as long as none of your music row assholes fucks up my mix,'" says Jones. "Music row producers don't let a song breathe. They have a way of plugging every single hole. *Pearls in the Snow* has lots of breathing space on every track, especially with Lee Roy, because he has the most commercial-sounding track on the album. We released it as a single and it did well on the two big stations in Nashville until George Jones came out with a single and bumped it right off."

Jones had fun with Tompall Glaser when he showed up to record "Get Your Biscuits in the Oven and Your Buns in the Bed."

"Because I knew what a proud male chauvinist pig he was, I had a totally female band—all A-Team female musicians," she says. "Tompall walks in the studio, sees all these women, looks at me, and says, 'What's going on?' He was grouchy and the look on his face . . . . But when he heard how great these gals played, he lit up and nailed that song to the wall. The change in him from the moment he walked in till he walked out was radical."

The session with Guy Clark for "Wild Man from Borneo" took a while to get started. "We cut Guy on a Sunday, and in Nashville you can't buy beer on a Sunday until after noon," Jones explains. "The studio time was 10 a.m., but Guy refused to play a note until we had a six-pack of Miller High Life in front of us. I ended up getting a twelve-pack, just for good measure."

The most poignant session was Marty Stuart's recording of "Lady Yesterday." Stuart had been considering several up-tempo songs, including "Silver Eagle Express," but the death of Carl Perkins hit him hard. He had played with the rockabilly star on *Class of '55* along with Johnny Cash, Roy Orbison, and Jerry Lee Lewis. Perkins took a liking to Stuart and gave him his guitar at the end of the sessions. When Stuart arrived at the Soundshop Studio in Nashville, he had just come from speaking at the funeral.

"He was in a melancholy mood after he lost Carl Perkins," says Jones. "That's why he chose a ballad instead of something up-tempo. If you listen to the mandolin playing Marty is doing on 'Lady Yesterday,' it is heartfelt and just so perfect."

Chuck E. Weiss and the G-d Damn Liars cut "Ol' Ben Lucas" in a studio in Van Nuys.

"Kinky asking me to be on the 'pearls before swine' album was pretty cool," says Weiss. "He asked me because he wanted me to ask Tom [Waits] if he'd do it, too. 'Ol' Ben Lucas' wasn't my favorite Kinky song, but he wrote it as a child, and I know what that's like 'cause I wrote songs as a kid too. 'Ain't Makin' Jews like Jesus Anymore' is my all-time favorite, but nobody could do it but him. If somebody else tried it, it would go over like Mother's Day in an orphanage."

In what Kinky calls "a rather triumphant if somewhat tedious reunion of the original Texas Jewboys," the project brought most of the original members to Nashville to record "Silver Eagle Express" and a medley of "They Ain't Makin' Jews like Jesus Anymore," "Western Union Wire," and "Homo Erectus." And nobody was more taken aback than original Jewboy Billy Swan when he learned Kinky wanted him to record "When the Lord Closes a Door (He Opens a Little Window)." "He was so surprised, you'd have thought I said, 'I'm gonna give you a free Cadillac,'" says Jones, who sang harmonies on the song.

Kinky delivered a heartfelt version of "Marilyn and Joe," but only after a couple of false starts and shots of Jameson's Irish Whiskey.

"Kinky wanted his version of 'Marilyn and Joe' to sound like Lee Marvin's 'Wandering Star,'" says Jones. "We started recording around 10 a.m. and he was already in a grumpy mood when he got to the studio. It was not going well. The music track was ready, but the vocal track did not sound like I wanted it to sound or how he wanted it to sound."

Jones knew they needed a break to get the vocals right, so she took him to the Longhorn Steakhouse for "a big old hairy steak." Initially suspicious when she asked to buy him a shot of Jameson's, he ended up having two. "When we went back to the studio, his whole attitude and his voice completely changed," she says. "It softened and got sweeter." It wasn't until Jones had the entire CD mixed that Kinky called from Texas to ask her to add her vocals to the song.

Tom Waits's rendition of "Highway Café" was worked out over the phone.

"The album would have been released six months earlier, but we were literally waiting on Waits," she says. "He sent me a track of just him and the banjo recorded at Prairie Sun Recording Studio in Northern California. I added a keyboard and violin in the studio in Nashville. When I sent it back for his approval, he liked the violin and told me to get rid of the keyboard. I added the sound effects of the truck pulling up."

Pearls in the Snow got great reviews in dozens of newspapers from the *New York Times* to the *Chicago Sun* and *San Francisco Chronicle*. *Billboard* picked it as a spotlight album of the week in December 1998 and it reached #1 on the Americana charts two weeks in a row. But Kinky's refusal to listen to Jones's advice on a distributor killed any chances of it becoming a financial pleasure for any of parties involved.

"The trickiest part of the record business is distribution," she says. "That's when the big rip-off can happen. I had contracts from a number of indie distributors and thought Southwest Wholesale was the most honest and would actually pay us. They were a huge, Texas-based independent music distribution service."

Kinky didn't agree and told her they be "screwed" if they didn't work with a major distributor. Owen Sloane, their attorney in L.A., had a client with an independent label and a distribution deal with BMG. When he suggested that Kinkajou piggyback on that client's label, Jones reluctantly agreed. It wasn't long before Kinky realized he should have listened to her.

"The independent label we piggybacked with ended up going bankrupt and we never got a proper accounting," says Jones. "We sold a certain amount of copies through Imus, thank goodness. He was a big help in selling records through his TV and radio show. But not going with Southwest Wholesale was a huge lost opportunity. Here's a typical Kinky thing—months later, Kinky was pissed at me because of the distribution thing. I said, 'I had the perfect distribution situation with Southwest and you told me not to do it.' And he said, 'You should have talked me out of it,' which really pissed me off because I did try to talk him out of it.

"I didn't make a penny off that album. The distributor ripped off everybody—no one got paid. The artists did it out of love for Kinky. The deal was to pay back the investors before anybody else—including me, Kinky, and the artists—got paid. We managed to pay John McCall and Johnny Marks a substantial amount back, but it still wasn't their full investment."

Like the song "I Hate Your Lousy, Rotten, Stinkin' Guts, But I'm Not Bitter" on her 1997 release *Men Are Some of My Favorite People*, Jones takes it all in stride. "I will say this," she adds with a smile. "It was a great feather in my cap as a record producer, because I got to meet and work with all my favorite artists."

While Jones and Kinky were compiling a list of artists for the record, he was unknowingly about to embark upon his lifelong passion for animal rescue. Anyone who has spent time at Kinky's ranch, which he calls the "world's largest doghouse," knows he has a soft spot for dogs. He treats the Friedmans, a name he affectionately gives his canines—currently Winnie, Sophie, Mr. P., and Louie—like royalty. His ranch is filled with bowls of water and dry food, and with dogs lazing around on his couch, upholstered rocker, dog beds, and pillows. He cooks them steaks and beans (with an occasional hot dog) for dinner; if takeout tacos or Whataburgers (from the fast food chain) are on the menu, Kinky picks up extras for his canine friends. Throughout the day, he lovingly places dog biscuits beside each dog—whether they're on the floor, on a pillow, or curled up on the couch. When they've meandered through the dog door to the front porch, he serves the biscuits alfresco.

All of Kinky's animals are rescues, but the seed for the Utopia Animal Rescue Ranch happened serendipitously. Kinky and his dog Mr. Magoo were driving to Kerrville in his old pickup in the summer of 1996. When he spotted a kitten howling in the middle of the road, he slammed on the brakes, "leaped sideways out of the cab," and discovered it was bleeding profusely from a gaping wound in its right leg. Certain the tiny kitten was dying, Kinky raced him to the Kerrville animal clinic, where he learned it had been shot by what he calls "some great white hunter."

With Kinky's instructions to do whatever it took to save the cat, Dr. Hoegemeyer amputated the leg and gave the kitten two injections during surgery to restart its heart, leaving Kinky with a $1,200 bill and a cat that needed time to heal. But Kinky had a six-week book tour for *Roadkill*, and gigs with Willie Nelson in Mexico. He asked Nancy Parker-Simons, a friend who watched over the Friedmans when he was traveling, to take care of the kitten, too.

In May 1998, Kinky approached Parker-Simons, whom he dubbed Cousin Nancy, and Tony Simons, who is now her husband, about opening a rescue ranch on her land in Utopia, Texas. "Tony and I had nine dogs, I'd been babysitting Kinky's dogs, and he was always rescuing some stray," says Parker-Simons. "I had owned a business with my late husband in Austin, so Kinky said, 'You have the business skills—you can run the ranch. Tony can be the ranch manager and I'll be the Gandhi-like figure that gets the word out and does the PR.' Tony and our friend Mary Beth Couch built sixteen dog pens by the end of summer and we were ready."

True to his word, Kinky sent a letter to 5,000 of his closest friends ("When Kinky was in L.A. in the late '70s, his Rolodex weighed about 200 pounds," quips Buzzi) asking for help. Willie Nelson, former governor Ann Richards, and U.S. Representative Lamar Smith, among others, agreed to be on his advisory board. With the support of friends Billy Joe Shaver, Spike Gillespie, Richard Pryor, Jerry Jeff Walker, Molly Ivins, Dwight Yoakam, John McCall, Robert Earl Keen, Don Imus, Johnny Marks, and Sarah Bird, the Utopia Animal Rescue Ranch achieved nonprofit 501(c)(3) status in December 1998.

That Labor Day weekend, Kinky, his sister Marcie, and Parker-Simons liberated forty-one dogs from three pounds in Kerrville and Hondo. Kinky called it a "Robin Hood-like" rescue for the "death row" dogs scheduled to be euthanized. The trio loaded them into crates in the back of Parker-Simons' fifteen-year-old pickup, and brought them to Hoegemeyer, who agreed to examine each dog and spay or neuter it if needed.

"He had no idea that on Labor Day weekend—when he was already booked with boarding animals—we would show up with that many dogs," Parker-Simons says. "When we finally stopped bringing them, he said he'd do two to four dogs per day, and we could come in every afternoon and pick up another load. He cut us some slack so we could slow pay with whatever money we had. Every day, Tony and I would drive sixty miles to Kerrville, load up the truck, and bring them back to the rescue ranch."

The Utopia Animal Rescue Ranch, which moved to the Friedman ranch in Medina in 2003, costs about $70,000 a year to run, including $10,000 for vet bills. Cousin Nancy and Tony are the only paid employees. On Fridays, senior citizens groom the dogs and walk them down to the creek for a swim. During the week, children from the Medina Children's Home, an orphanage that also serves at-risk children, walk the dogs after school.

It's a labor of love for the three principals, who personally screen every person who wants to adopt a dog. "Kinky and Tony and I have to like the person who is thinking about adopting," says Parker-Simons. "We meet everybody in person and talk to them for thirty minutes about how they feel about animals, pets, or their past pets. If we feel good about it, as long as they've got a fenced yard, we let the dog go."

"This place is like a happy orphanage," says Kinky. "So many dogs came from horrible situations where they were abused or abandoned. Now they have a good life, because Nancy and Tony shower them with love." Publicly, Kinky organizes fundraisers and promotes the ranch; privately, he makes generous personal donations, spends time with the dogs, and stops by to help serve their special holiday dinners.

"On Christmas and Thanksgiving, we give the dogs a human Thanksgiving dinner," says Parker-Simons. "We buy ground turkey; dinner rolls; stuffing with olive oil, cheese, eggs, and garlic; big bags of vegetables; and cook it all up for the dogs. We go out and serve them and Kinky is always here."

Although Parker-Simons, who grew up with dreams of becoming a vet, enjoys her work, there's also the heartache of seeing how some people treat animals.

"People will actually put dogs down for tearing their curtains and things like that," she says. "The number one phone call I get almost every day is from some young woman who is crying and saying, 'Can you please take my eight-year-old Labrador? He's such a great dog and I love him.' When I ask what's going on, it's always a new boyfriend who wants them to euthanize it or take it to the pound because he doesn't like it.

"One day, when I'd had enough and another young woman called with the same story and asked me what to do, I told her, 'Euthanize the boyfriend. If someone loves you, they won't ask you to do something like that. Get out of there and keep your dog, because the dog loves you and the boyfriend doesn't.' And there was a long silence."

Parker-Simons radiates a natural warmth and sweetness. She gives most of the rescues celebrity names, which accompany their photos on the rescue ranch website and grab listeners' attention on Parker-Simons's Pet of the Week radio spots with Gordon Ames on *Big G's Texas Road Show* on KERV 1230 AM and with Harley Belew on KRVL 94.3 FM.

Her website description of a dog she named Willie Nelson: "Willie is a great Labrador mix we rescued from the Kerrville pound. He is approximately two years old and he loves to swim. He is not hyper, not a fence jumper or digger, and our Willie does not smoke pot. He is great with kids and other dogs, too. On Saturday or by appointment, Get On the Road Again and come adopt Willie Nelson."

"I love naming dogs," she says. "If I take someone on the tour I'll say, 'I want you to meet Ruth Buzzi,' and people kinda giggle or chuckle—it relaxes them. The dog realizes they're relaxed, that nothing bad is going to happen. Makes it easier to adopt the dogs because the dogs react to the gentleness and it really helps."

Despite the difficulty of staying afloat financially, Utopia Animal Rescue has been around for more than eighteen years and found forever homes for 2,300 dogs. Parker-Simons credits the longevity and success to Kinky's name and efforts.

"If it'd been Tony and Nancy's Rescue Ranch when we started, we'd have lasted two weeks," she says. "We're very fortunate having Kinky as a celebrity. He always mentions the rescue ranch and asks people to support it when he's being interviewed, and is always trying to find homes for the dogs. Some people would say he pressures people into taking dogs, but he doesn't really," she adds with a laugh. "When people come out to his ranch just to meet him, he always brings them over to see our dogs and asks them to adopt one."

Then there's the friendly pressure Kinky only extends to good friends. "When we were building the pens, Kinky brought John McCall over to our place in Utopia," says Parker-Simons. "Kinky is so funny— he said, 'Do me a favor, John. Give Nancy all the cash you have right now for the rescue ranch.' John started laughing and reached into his pocket. He gave us about $3,000 that day and started regularly sending us generous donations."

Kinky calls upon his musical friends to play at fundraisers called "Bone-I-Fits." The first Bone-I-Fit, which Kinky called "kind of like a Texas Woodstock," attracted a standing-room-only crowd that included Molly Ivins.

Held at La Zona Rosa in Austin in March 1999, that first benefit included performances by Kinky (in a black sequined jacket), Jerry Jeff Walker, the Steve Burton Band, Joe Ely, Ray Benson, the Lounge Lizards, James McMurtry, Lee Roy Parnell, Jimmie Dale Gilmore, Robert Earl Keen, Butch Hancock, and the Geezinslaw Brothers. Greezy Wheels fiddle player Sweet Mary Hattersley, who teaches the Suzuki method to children in Austin, brought the Blazing Bows, a group of six- and eight-year-old fiddle players, to accompany Kinky on "Ol' Ben Lucas." For the silent auction, McCall donated a saddle that had belonged to Jack Kennedy; Willie Nelson donated one of his golf carts; and Don and Fred Imus donated custom field jackets. With all the artists performing for free, the event raised $45,000.

With the help of Don Imus, the fundraising didn't end that night.

He sent one MSNBC camera crew to the Bone-I-Fit and another to the rescue ranch. The nationally aired footage, which included clips of the performers and footage from the ranch, raised even more donations.

Dwight Yoakam, who has sold over twenty-five million records, performed for 3,000 fans at the March 2000 Bone-I-Fit at John T. Floore's Country Store, a legendary Texas honky-tonk in Helotes. Joe Ely, the Geezinslaw Brothers, the Derailers, and the Kinkster opened for Yoakam, whose swivel hips, second-skin jeans, and electrifying performances of "Little Sister" and "Honky Tonk Man" had some women reaching for smelling salts.

First Lady Laura Bush hosted the May 2002 Bone-I-Fit at the Four Seasons in Austin.

When Barney, the Bushes' Scottish terrier, pulled a no-show at the "Lunch with Laura and Barney" fundraiser, Kinky brought one of the Friedmans dressed in a red bow tie. Ever gracious, Laura suggested Hank could be a Norwich terrier mix, but Kinky said he looked more like a flying monkey in *The Wizard of Oz*.

The first lady's slide show of White House dogs kicked off the event, which included music from Delbert McClinton, Sweet Mary Hattersley, and Tish Hinojosa; readings by Sandra Brown and Steve Harrigan; and stories from Liz Carpenter. To celebrate the newly coined slogan "Keep Austin Weird," writer/director/actor Turk Pipkin read *Old Yeller* while escaping from a straitjacket. Four hundred guests, including Texas Representative Lamar Smith and Texas Supreme Court Justice Tom Phillips, paid $125 a plate or $10,000 for a choice table at the upscale luncheon, which raised $125,000 for the rescue ranch.

In between the Bone-I-Fits, Kinky's friends joined him for smaller fundraisers. In 2006, Billy Joe Shaver did four back-to-back fundraisers with Kinky, including one with Jimmie Dale Gilmore in Dallas with a ticket price of forty-four dollars. In 2007, he returned to Dallas with Little Jewford, Washington Ratso, and Sweet Mary Hattersley for a show and a VIP reception to introduce Kinky Friedman Cigars, Kinky and Jewford's latest venture. Handmade by Cubans in Honduras, "Kinky's Select Cigars" sold for $100 a box with all profits going to Utopia.

In 2008, Kinky teamed up with Texas poet laureate Steven Fromholz and Little Jewford for the Puppies and Legends tour. That tour covered eight Texas cities and included a show in Galveston with a fifty-dollar cover and an auction for a guitar autographed by Willie Nelson.

Kinky also opened his home for a fundraiser with Jewford and Washington Ratso that included tours of Utopia Rescue Ranch, dinner with the Kinkster, and an intimate concert. Jerry Jeff Walker and Ramblin' Jack Elliott joined Kinky and Jewford for a private show at his home the following year with a ticket price of $200. "Ramblin' is the real goods," says Kinky. "The fundraiser he did here with Jerry Jeff Walker was one of the best shows I've ever seen."

A group of dog enthusiasts called the NoMads (No Mercy Agility Dudes, Dames, and Dogs) brought Cesar Millan of the National Geographic Channel's *Dog Whisperer* fame to central Texas for a fundraising seminar. The NoMads raised $12,850 from Millan's appearance and donated it to the rescue ranch.

Then there was a 2.57-carat diamond donated by Linda Forse, a woman who babysat Kinky's dogs. John McCall bought the diamond at an auction for $8,000.

Buzzi and Perkins have also been generous supporters. "Kent and I have supported the rescue ranch since its opening day," Buzzi says. "We kicked off the Pen Sponsorship program in 2012—pens are sponsored at $1,000 each per year—and then put the fat arm on friends like Barron Hilton to get more pens sponsored.

"The ranch isn't your typical animal rescue operation," she adds. "Each dog has a pen, a roommate, and at least one real tree of its own. They're talked to, walked, fed well, and live an idyllic life until connecting with 'forever homes' made possible by Kinky's huge heart for animals and his huge ability to persuade people to help."

The couple's online FirstGiving fundraising pages raised more than $26,000 for Utopia in five years. "There are so many philanthropic choices people can make, so it's not easy getting people to give money for dog and animal rescue," she says. "But we put our fundraising page out there for the world to see and push it from time to time on Twitter and Facebook. My Twitter account has more than 55,000 followers . . . I don't hit them too often for money, but when I do, it's referring them to our fundraising pages for the Utopia Rescue Ranch."

In June 2003, Kinky launched Kinky Friedman's Private Stock Politically Correct Salsa and Dip to raise money for the rescue ranch and spread the word in a *Texas Monthly* column. "It tastes great," he wrote, "and the profits go exactly where they should: to Alfred Hitchcock, a rooster that crows at noon; to six pigs, the youngest of whom is named

Babe; to three donkeys named Roy, Gabby, and Little Jewford; to a three-legged cat named Lucky, who single-pawedly killed two rattlesnakes; a dog named Daisy, who was found as a puppy alone in a field of daisies; a dog named Eve who was found shivering on a hilltop on Christmas Eve; to a dog named Cat, who was sent to the pound for the crime of eating a Social Security check, and to fifty-seven other dogs who each have a story, if only they could tell you."

Two years later he penned "My Pet Project," a *Texas Monthly* column about the rescue ranch, calling the never-kill sanctuary "a court of last resort for those at death's door" and imploring his readers to consider adoption. *Texas Monthly* designed a full-color, full-page ad for the rescue ranch and ran it without charge a number of times. H-E-B, a Texas-based grocery chain, also provided free advertising by including that ad in their circulars.

Although Kinky, Parker-Simons, and Simons seem like an unlikely team, their relationship, which is tied into the longevity of the ranch, works well. They're close neighbors who often stop by in a golf cart, and a day doesn't go by without some form of communication.

"We get along beautifully," Parker-Simons says. "It's really odd, because a lot of times partnerships don't work. Kinky and Tony and me—it just works. Kinky is the most generous, kindhearted man. When I met him in 1989, he basically rescued me. I moved to Utopia when my husband died and I was going broke. He bought a lot of my embroidery, hired me to run his fan club, and ended up having me babysit his dog Mr. Magoo."

When Ann Richards helped Kinky get the rescue off the ground in 1998, she said, "I hope this isn't something I'm going to regret for the rest of my life." He promised her it wouldn't be and has kept his promise.

11
The Man in the Arena

"We should limit all elected officials to two terms—
one in office and one in prison."
—Kinky Friedman

Kinky took his first leap into the political arena in 1986, when Hill Country Republicans invited him to run for Kerrville Justice of the Peace in the Republican primary. A small Texas Hill Country town with a population of 16,000, Kerrville lies about sixty miles northwest of San Antonio and eighty-five miles west of Austin. With Kinky's notoriety in hipper circles, the consensus was his name recognition would help him at the polls. But his campaign promises—"If you elect me the first Jewish justice of the peace, I'll reduce the speed limit to $54.95" and "I'll keep us out of war with Fredericksburg [a nearby town]"—kept people from taking him seriously.

Running as a Republican didn't help. Kinky's liberal background and leanings pegged him as a Democrat, and he didn't win any friends in the party by calling his morning constitutional "taking a Nixon." He ran against Pat Knox, an administrative assistant who had been appointed justice of the peace to fill an unexpired term, and Edward A. North, a bail bondsman. Without any Democratic candidates in the race, the winner of the Republican primary would become justice of the peace.

With his first novel months away from publication, Kinky's only claim to fame was as the outrageous leader of the Texas Jewboys. Still, it was enough to attract national coverage. An interview with a Dallas reporter was picked up by the Associated Press and ran in newspapers across the country. The race attracted national TV coverage attention when NBC broadcast a segment about Kinky's campaign on the *Today* program, which included a clip of him singing "Dear Abbie" in an oversized sombrero on *Saturday Night Live*. The Kerrville voters were not impressed.

"The locals reacted negatively to the five-man *Today Show* crew headed by my friend Boyd Matson, who came down from New York to chronicle my campaign," Kinky remembers. "'We're not going to allow anyone to tell us who to vote for' seemed to be the attitude."

Like his gubernatorial campaign twenty years later, it started as a lark and grew serious as the campaign progressed. His red, white, and blue campaign posters depicted a smiling Kinky in a white cowboy hat exhorting voters to "Elect Richard 'Kinky' Friedman Justice of the Peace PCT 1"; matching business cards promised "Justice for All." But Kinky lost the election to Knox, who garnered 2,002 votes to his 917.

His unflagging honesty may have cost him the election. "I got within a few points of the front-runner," he told *George* magazine. "Then a reporter asked me if it was true I'd hid out Abbie [Hoffman, then a fugitive], and I said yes. That was too much for the people of Kerrville, who were already mad that I'd been referring to them as 'Kerrverts.'"

An editorial in the *Kerrville Mountain Sun* concurred with his opinion. "The majority of voters in Kerrville, Texas, are relieved today that Richard Kinky Friedman will remain a country-western crooner instead of a Precinct One justice of the peace."

Kinky hadn't thought about politics until his life flashed before his eyes during his harrowing night on the side of a cliff in Mexico. Facing his own mortality made him want to do more with his life. The die was cast when he later performed in a pub in Northern Ireland. "A guy that looked like a leprechaun told me my patter between songs was better than my music, and I'd make a better politician than a musician."

The idea of running for governor began to solidify during a visit to the White House in 2003, when George W. Bush agreed to be his "one-man focus group" if he entered the race. A few weeks later, he ran the idea by Molly Ivins at the Texas Book Festival. When she asked why, he responded, "Why the hell not?" "Beautiful," she said. "That's your campaign slogan."

With the albeit casual support of Bush and Ivins, Kinky announced his intentions to enter the 2006 governor's race in an interview with the *Kerrville Daily Times* (circulation 8,000). He also told his friend Texas Representative Lamar Smith, and ordered "He's Not Kinky He's My Governor" bumper stickers. With his interview splashed on the front page, and his bumper stickers proclaiming his intentions throughout Hill Country, Kinky was on his way—at least in Texas.

But nothing Kinky does in Texas ever stays in Texas. When the phone rang a few days later, it was *New York Times* reporter Ralph Blumenthal with a request to interview Kinky at his ranch. Blumenthal's in-depth interview—"Guess Who Wants to Be Governor"—ran in the *Times* in late November 2004.

Riding in his "old white Nissan pickup with a Don Quixote statuette on the dashboard and chewed stubs of Cuban cigars in the ashtray," Blumenthal got the full Kinky treatment: truth/facts interspersed with self-deprecating comments and one-liners to keep him guessing. When asked if he was serious, Kinky said, "'Serious' is not a word I would use, because I'm never serious; some things are too important to be taken seriously. The question is whether my candidacy is a joke, or the current crop of politicians is the joke."

Despite Kinky claiming his platform included making the declawing of cats illegal, the *New York Times* story gave his candidacy credibility and national coverage. The response was immediate and chaotic. Kinky's phone rang constantly with congratulatory calls and offers to help from friends in Texas and beyond. Tom Waits, Willie Nelson, Dwight Yoakam, Robert Duvall, Billy Bob Thornton, Jim Nabors, Jerry Jeff Walker, Lily Tomlin, and Johnny Depp called to congratulate him and volunteer to help with his campaign.

Disgusted by politicians without the courage to deviate from the party line and the lack of differences between the two major parties, who "sell themselves to the biggest donors," Kinky ran as an Independent in the 2006 Texas governor's race. "My race for governor was never a political campaign," he says. "It was always a spiritual quest by a group of people from the outside of politics who were searching for the soul of Texas."

He wanted to reclaim the reputation of the Lone Star State tarnished by the fat-cat Texas oilmen and lobbyists that helped Rick Perry get elected. Texas also took a hit when George W. Bush invaded Iraq. Fellow Texan Natalie Maines of the Dixie Chicks created an international controversy during a London show by announcing, "We do not want this war, this violence, and we're ashamed that the president of the United States is from Texas."

Kinky skated around the issue when he wrote a column about the Dixie Chicks for *Texas Monthly*. In a satire about him waking up in "the hostility suite of the mental hospital," he wouldn't publicly attack a man he considered a friend. Yet the subhead "I'm mental about the Dixie Chicks" reflected his mantra: "What's written between the lines is the most important thing." When asked about the Iraq war by the *Times* reporter, he did what he does best—turned his answer into a joke and brought in a friend for the punch line.

"He [Kinky] was originally for the war in Iraq, he said, and argued with Willie Nelson about it," Blumenthal wrote. "'He's a tyrannical bully,' he told Mr. Nelson, 'and we got to take him out.' 'No,' he says Mr. Nelson objected, 'he's our president, and we got to stick by him.'"

"The cowboy ethic has been lost," Kinky lamented to a British journalist covering his campaign. "The cowboy didn't create the Texas people talk about now. The cowboy has never been a bully. Cowboys always stood up for the little fella."

A Texas history buff with a flair for the dramatic, Kinky announced his candidacy at dawn at the Alamo on February 3, 2005. "We're a band of gypsies on a pirate ship and we're setting sail for the governor's mansion," Kinky declared in a live interview on *Imus in the Morning*, which reached 3.25 million radio listeners and 335,000 TV viewers. Despite the frigid predawn temperatures, several hundred friends and fans filled the courtyard as Kinky announced his plans to the world.

"It was at 4:00 a.m. because it was timed to be on Imus, which airs at 5:00 a.m. Eastern time," says Jewford. "It was a crazy scene and pretty exciting. The history of Imus and Kinky goes way back, and Imus announcing it in a live broadcast made it real."

Imus asked tough questions. Still treating the campaign as a lark, Kinky responded with his trademark one-liners. He was running for governor because he needed the closet space; he didn't know how many supporters he had but they all carried guns, and he wasn't concerned about Perry having more money for his campaign because a fool and his money are soon elected.

"Initially it was more of a lark and a bit of PR," admits Jewford, who worked with Kinky from the Alamo announcement until the 2006 election. "It was something to do it and it fit Kinky's persona. He was always good at creating PR."

More than 1,200 miles north of this crack-of-dawn spectacle, Bill Hillsman was intrigued by the broadcast. The Minneapolis media consultant who had helped propel Reform party candidate Jesse Ventura into the governor's mansion in Minnesota in 1998, Hillsman was looking for another candidate who had a chance to win. He contacted Kinky and developed a communications plan within three weeks.

A week later, they hooked up in Minneapolis, on a stop on Kinky's *Kill Two Birds and Get Stoned* book tour. "Give me two million for campaign ads on television and the election will be in God's hands," Hillsman told Kinky. "Give me five million, and I'll take it out of God's hands and you'll be governor of Texas."

When Kinky met with Ventura's former campaign manager, Dean Barkley looked him in the eye and asked why he wanted to be governor. Satisfied with Kinky's response (he loved Texas, didn't like what was happening, and wanted to turn it around), he became the other half of what Kinky called his "Minnesota Mafia."

"I won't sign on with just anybody," Barkley told Kinky. "I turned down Donald Trump when he asked me to run his campaign for president. So I do have some principles." (Trump joined the Reform Party in 1999 with hopes of becoming its presidential candidate in 2000. He left in February, calling the party "a total mess.")

Cleve Hattersley, who had started the campaign, agreed to stay on until Barkley and Hillsman had completed prior projects.

"When Kinky decided he wanted to be governor, there was no team, no ideas, no policy, no programs, no platform," he explains. "It was very general and in terms of 'I'm going to do this and I'm the only one that can do this.' My job was to watch Kinky and to try to get as much infrastructure together as I could before I turned the situation over to Dean and Hillsman."

The first challenge was getting Kinky's name on the ballot as an Independent. According to Texas law, he needed 45,540 signatures—one percent of the votes cast in the previous governor's election. Signatures had to be from people who hadn't voted in a primary, and he had only sixty days from March 7, 2006 (the day of the primaries), to collect them.

Kinky's campaign couldn't reach all the voters in the 268,000-square-mile state in Jewford's Chevy Blazer, so they set up a campaign website and targeted college-age supporters through MySpace and Facebook pages. To get the word out that Texans couldn't sign Kinky's petition if they voted in a primary, his team launched a "Save Yourself for Kinky" campaign.

"We publicized it every time, everywhere, made it a point at every event," says Jewford. "I'd either remind Kinky or announce it, because

I was campaigning with him ninety-nine percent of the time. I did a lot of driving and was averaging two hours of sleep a night for about a year and a half. We drove all through Texas. We did small events, fundraisers, campaigns, everywhere—north, south, young, old, everybody."

Opponents in the race included incumbent Republican Rick Perry, who assumed the governorship in 2000 when George W. Bush resigned to run for president. Chris Bell, the fairly unknown Democratic candidate, was a former congressman from Houston. Carole Keeton Strayhorn, the other independent candidate, had been Austin's first female mayor as a Democrat, and ran as a Republican when she won the 1998 state comptroller race. Calling herself "One Tough Grandma," she had initially planned to run against Perry in the Republican primary.

Kinky joked that most of his volunteers were beauticians or musicians, and told the media, "Musicians can better run this state than politicians. They won't get a helluva lot done in the morning, but we'll work late and we'll be honest." But working with a team of inexperienced volunteers, no matter how inspired and dedicated, comes with its own challenges.

"Independent campaigns are run on a shoestring, so they don't have a lot of experienced people," says Hillsman. "I was a media consultant, but I took on a lot more roles: advising, strategy and tactics, the ground game, and events. Because I knew how to do what they were trying to do."

Using the website, they built a grassroots movement of volunteers throughout the state. Meeting for prearranged roadshows in key metro areas, volunteers went door to door collecting signatures. More than 350 volunteers canvassed neighborhoods in the Fort Worth area and met Kinky later that night at a thank-you party. The same scenario was repeated throughout the state—especially in large metro areas such as Dallas/Fort Worth, Houston, San Antonio, Austin, and El Paso. Within months of launching the website, Kinky had 25,000 emails offering to help with the petition drive, fifteen paid staff members, and a group of thirty volunteers that grew each week. They also spread the word in his Radio Free Kinky campaign, a series of phone calls he took every Thursday from radio stations throughout the state.

Hillsman hired Collection Agency Films to produce three Kinkytoons for the website—short animated spots with Kinky and Jewford cartoon characters.

"The Kinky cartoons were a great idea," says Hattersley. "When you're trying to get the attention of low-information people, nothing is easier than a cartoon."

The "Save Your Vote for Kinky" animated spot focuses on how voters, like the heroes of the Alamo, could listen to their hearts and do what was right for Texas—by electing an independent governor who would fight to change politics as usual. A cartoon Willie Nelson waves from a biodiesel bus as country artists Bruce Robison and Kelly Willis sing "Save Yourself for Kinky." Billy Joe Shaver is truly in character when he sings, "If you want Texas great again, not always being last / Save yourself for Kinky, tomorrow we'll kick ass." Female vocalists end the spot with "Save yourself for Kinky and save our friggin' state."

The "Ten Things Easier to Do than Run for Governor of Texas as an Independent" ad is a whimsical depiction of Texas challenges. "I Looove Texas" won a 2006 Telly Award and opens with Kinky playing poker with six dogs in a smoke-filled room with a pile of bones as the pot.

The Republican and Democratic primaries were held on March 7. Kinky's "ragtag army of patriots and dreamers" arrived en masse at the steps of the state capitol at the stroke of midnight on March 8 to sign his petitions. Thus began a two-month petition drive with volunteers throughout Texas knocking on doors, canvassing shopping centers, and going wherever people congregated to collect signatures.

Three days into the petition drive, Kinky made headlines over "Guinnessgate" when Barkley handed him a cold can of beer during his appearance as grand marshal of the St. Patrick's Day Parade in Dallas. He was waving to the crowd "perched like an aging beauty queen" on the back of a red, white, and blue 1999 Plymouth Prowler convertible when he took the infamous sip. Kinky and the Prowler were decked out for the parade: Kinky in an emerald-green sports jacket, jeans, shades, and a black Stetson; the Prowler with detailed stars and stripes and the proclamation "Governor Kinky." It's difficult to decipher what Barkley was thinking, but the story and a photo ran in the *Dallas Morning News.*

"It takes a lot of balls for a politician to ride in the back of an open convertible in Dallas," says Kinky, referring to JFK's assassination. "I didn't really think about that until I was halfway along the parade route. That's when Barkley gave me the Guinness. That shows you how stupid politics is. I'm riding at one mile an hour and had a sip of Guinness. I wasn't getting drunk. For them to make such a big deal about setting a bad example for young people couldn't have been more incorrect."

Laura Stromberg, Kinky's press secretary, became inundated with calls from irate citizens and Mothers Against Drunk Driving after the photo of Kinky drinking from the can and a story charging him with breaking the state's "open container law" were picked up by newspapers across the state. (Texas law prohibits passengers from consuming alcohol in a moving vehicle.)

After considering the advice of Barkley, who told him, "Never apologize for being yourself," and Clinton, who said, "Stay funny. That's the way you connect with people," Kinky penned his own response. "I am here to admit that I did drink the Guinness. But I did not swallow," he wrote in a press release. That calmed the waters, and an editorial in the *Dallas Morning News* called it "refreshing" to see a candidate that didn't respond like a typical politician by apologizing or talking about rehab.

On the petition deadline, Kinky and his entourage arrived at the Texas Secretary of State's office to a massive, cheering crowd of volunteers and supporters. A ten-foot fuchsia teardrop trailer called the "Guv Bug" carried eleven cardboard boxes of petitions with 170,258 signatures. One signature was from Lucille O'Brien of Breckenridge, who signed the petition on her 100th birthday. A self-proclaimed Yellow Dog Democrat who had run for county tax collector, O'Brien told a volunteer, "I don't really know him, but he's different, and God knows we need something different."

Adorned by a giant cigar protruding from a painted set of lips between a black mustache and soul patch, the "Guv Bug"—or "Hebrew Hummer," as Kinky liked to call it—was designed by Bob "Daddy-O" Wade, who sculpted the Lone Star Café iguana. "We scanned his actual black hat at a place here in Austin that blows things up real big, and made it out of urethane foam," Wade says. "Kinky loved that thing."

"When I contacted Bob and said, 'We need movable kiosks,' it was way off what I was thinking," says Hattersley. "But it was brilliant looking and got press everywhere it went. It became Kinky's best surrogate throughout the campaign."

Pulled by a pickup truck, the trailer served as a mobile store with volunteers selling T-shirts, bumper stickers, posters, and other merchandise across the state. The campaign website called it "Kinky Friedman's conduit to the 'little fellers' in his quest to become the first independent governor of Texas since Sam Houston."

Six weeks later, Texas Secretary of State Roger Williams announced that both Independent candidates would be on the ballot. But grandstanding by Strayhorn's staff, who had turned in 101 boxes of petitions which they claimed held 223,000 signatures, proved to be embarrassing. More than eighty-one percent of Kinky's signatures were certified valid; only forty-nine percent of Strayhorn's signatures survived vetting by the Secretary of State's office.

The early stage of Kinky's campaign had three goals: to keep him in the public eye; to establish him as a serious candidate; and to persuade voters to sign the petition to put him on the ballot. Barkley and Hillsman knew some of Kinky's one-liners might put some people off, but their philosophy was "Let Kinky be Kinky."

"Credibility is a step you need to take at a certain point, but you don't take it until you have gotten enough awareness for the person," Hillsman explains. "We wanted people to know about Kinky, to know he was running for governor and why he was running for governor. Kinky's quotes were great for that. He also had a very robust website with his official position."

Kinky is an entertainer who enjoys making people laugh, on the stage and in his songs, his *Texas Monthly* columns, his novels, and his nonfiction books. Like Mark Twain and Will Rogers, he used humor as a way to get to the truth. But traits that served him well in other endeavors worked against him in politics, where his humor often buried the message.

As a candidate in a state where only twenty-nine percent of registered voters turned out for the 2002 governor's election, he needed new and young voters to win the election, and had the charisma and ability to inspire young people. Calling himself a dealer in hope, he characterized his campaign as a spiritual rather than a political one. Instead of scripted stump speeches, he talked from his heart about Gandhi, Martin Luther King, and Father Damien. "He was the anti-politician to a certain degree," says Jewford.

Jesse Ventura, another candidate who shook up politics and wooed young voters, joined him on visits to college campuses. The former governor of Minnesota challenged students to "throw a monkey wrench into the political machine by voting . . . and sending a message by electing an Independent."

Perry used religion to respond to Ventura's visit, to hurt Kinky's campaign, and to alienate potential voters. His campaign released a statement citing Ventura's remarks in a 1999 *Playboy Magazine* interview calling organized religion "a sham and a crutch for weak-minded people who need strength in numbers." It was a harsh statement to be associated with in a state where fifty-six percent of the population is affiliated with a religion.

"Jesse Ventura was another one of those oddball mistakes," says Hattersley. "His election as an Independent was our marker. But when he came into Texas, his hair was in braids and his beard was in a braid with a bead. It was the last thing Texas wanted to see."

By running as an Independent, Kinky could follow his heart and mind rather than blindly adhering to the party line. He campaigned in favor of prayer in school and gay marriage—the former popular with Republicans, the latter with Democrats. His flip slogan, "They deserve to be as miserable as the rest of us," covered up his feelings about the lack of rights for same-sex partners in a long-term relationship. "Not being able to visit somebody you lived with for thirty years who's in the hospital dying is wrong," he says.

His position on gay marriage, like many of his ideas, was well ahead of his time.

"I have a record of endorsing gay marriage in 2005 and 2006; now everyone endorses it," he says. "It turned on a dime—seven years later. As for prayer in school, what's wrong with a kid believing in something? I don't care if it's a tree or a rock; he should believe in something."

He also wanted to take a closer look at the death penalty. Since the Supreme Court reinstated the death penalty in 1976, Texas has led the nation in executions, accounting for 537 of the 1,436 death row executions. After a 2000 report by the Texas Defender Service detailed racial bias and police and prosecutorial abuse of capital defendants, he wanted to put policies in place to ensure that innocent people weren't put to death. Although he agreed some death row executions were warranted, he asked, "When was the last time we've executed a rich man in Texas?"

He advocated legalizing marijuana to keep nonviolent offenders out of prison and to free up space for violent criminals. He also pledged to work for the release of people already behind bars for small marijuana offenses.

"I personally have known people who got sent away for years because of one joint or a very small amount of dope," Kinky says. "My friend Bob McLane was just back from Vietnam, enrolled in college in Nacogdoches, and got busted with a handful of pot. They were going to give him ten years and his uncle had to put up his little farm to get him out on bail, which was $15,000. When Bob was in jail, he had a cellmate that murdered his wife, had a lower bail, and got out before he did."

Outraged by the state's national status as forty-sixth in education, he advocated cleaning house on the state's education system boards and commissions and appointing people with classroom experience. He advocated increasing teachers' salaries (which were $6,000 below the national average) and getting rid of a curriculum focused on raising scores on the Texas Assessment of Knowledge and Skills test. "Teaching to the test has created a whole generation of supposedly college-bound students who have never heard of Mark Twain and aren't quite sure whether the Civil War took place here or in Europe," he says.

To fund education, he advocated legalizing casinos and a Slots for Tots program to put video poker terminals in bars, dance halls, race-tracks, and convenience stores. "We invented Texas Hold 'Em and we can't even play it here," he said, chronicling the outflow of billions of dollars from Texas into casinos in Louisiana, Oklahoma, New Mexico, Mississippi, and Las Vegas. He also proposed a one percent surcharge on big oil and big gas at the wellhead, and using the funds to raise the salaries of teachers, police, and firefighters.

Kinky called for the "Dewussification of Texas" with the slogan "I'm gonna de-wussify Texas if I got to do it one wuss at a time." That philosophy reflected his his own career, which began by skewering political correctness in 1973, as well as his admiration for political pioneer Barbara Jordan. The first black state senator in Texas, and the first female and first black member of Congress from Texas, Jordan is also the first black woman to deliver a keynote address at the Democratic National Convention. During that historic 1992 speech, she disparaged political correctness as separatism.

Kinky railed against the political correctness that made "left-wing liberals embarrassed to say Merry Christmas," took the Ten Commandments out of public schools, and "practically turned smokers into biblical lepers." Aware that the term "political correctness" had been coined by Joseph Stalin, Kinky believed things had gotten out of control. "Texas is the last line of defense against creeping political correctness," he wrote after the election. "If we lose the battle here, we're all lost for good."

Kinky's immigration platform addressed an issue that still hasn't been resolved: how to stem the tide of illegal immigrants entering the country at the Texas-Mexico border, a 1,254-mile stretch of land running from El Paso to Brownsville. He proposed increasing the number of National Guard troops at the border from 1,500 to 10,000 and reinstating the Bracero Program. Created by an executive order in 1942, the Bracero Program vetted and allowed millions of Mexican men to work in the U.S. on short-term agricultural labor contracts. Kinky also proposed issuing taxpayer ID cards for individuals who pass a criminal background check, and fining employers $25,000 for hiring people without an ID card.

His "five Mexican generals" plan created the most controversy. Kinky proposed dividing the border into five jurisdictions and appointing a Mexican general to oversee each one. Texas would establish an escrow account with $1 or $2 million for each general and withdraw $10,000 each time someone was caught illegally crossing his section of the border. In fact, Kinky got annoyed when his former *Texas Monthly* editor questioned the plan during an interview for *D Magazine*.

"I pressed him on the seriousness of his campaign, and he felt like I was being unfair, not taking him seriously," Brian Sweany says. "We had always been so friendly, but I thought my mode of questioning was fair. His immigration plan was giving the Mexican generals $1 million and deducting money from their account. I thought nobody could possibly take this seriously, and that irked him."

Lack of money was a critical issue during the campaign. Perry had more than $30 million in his war chest; Strayhorn had over $12 million; Bell had the Democratic Party behind him and more than $7 million; and Kinky's campaign had just over $6 million. Independent candidates lack the established fundraising networks available to candidates running as Democrats or Republicans, and potential donors are often reluctant to go public with their support.

"People can't donate to independents because then it becomes public and they're ostracized by their Republican friends," says Hillsman. "It's a combination of not having a network, people who can't do it because it will have a negative impact on them personally, and the notion nobody ever wins when you run as an Independent. And they're right, with the exception of Jesse Ventura."

Following the lead of his political hero Sam Rayburn, Kinky refused to take contributions from special interest groups, lobbyists, or PACs (political action committees) that would expect political favors after he was elected. Rayburn, a Texas Democrat who served in the U.S. House of Representatives for forty-eight years and was speaker of the House for seventeen years, had a reputation for integrity and fairness. "Sam walked his own road," says Kinky. "Whenever banks and railroads and lobbyists offered him gifts or money, he had one response: 'I am not for sale.' Neither am I."

Kinky's biggest contributor was his friend John McCall, who donated $1 million.

"I did it just because," says McCall, who served as campaign treasurer. "I didn't want anything out of it. I did it because he was so excited about running. My business partner Farouk Shami ran in 2010. He was a Palestinian running for governor of Texas. He wasn't going to win, either, but I gave him money. That was his dream and he enjoyed it. Kinky enjoyed running, too. A lot of attention, cameras, interviews."

McCall also provided office space in Austin for Kinky's campaign headquarters. "I didn't give at the office," he quipped. "I gave the office."

Kinky's friends in the music industry also pitched in. Jimmy Buffett, whom Kinky met in Nashville in the early 1970s when they were both struggling songwriters, offered to help.

"Jimmy Buffett is playing stadiums now, but he still has the same spirit," says Kinky. "He called me out of the blue to say he wanted to help my campaign. How sweet is that? And he sold out the Paramount Theater [in Austin], which I can't sell out if I had a year to sell it out. He sells it out in five minutes and gives us the money. And he only asked for one thing—he wanted me to give him Port Aransas if I won the election," Kinky adds, laughing. "That was the deal."

Buffett never did get the coastal town near Corpus Christi for selling out the 1270-seat venue. But his concert raised almost $250,000 for Kinky's campaign.

Willie Nelson opened up his Texas ranch and private golf course for a fundraiser including music by Jerry Jeff Walker and Billy Joe Shaver. Nine contributors, including country artist Bruce Robison and Kinky's pro bono advisor Dick DeGuerin, paid $5,000 for a round of golf with Kinky, Nelson, and Ventura on the nine-hole course. A colorful, high-profile defense attorney in a white Stetson, DeGuerin proved the old adage that politics make strange bedfellows. He had represented Waco cult leader David Koresh, helped a cross-dressing millionaire beat a murder rap, and was representing Tom DeLay, the Texas Republican who had been House majority leader until he was indicted on money laundering and conspiracy charges.

Supporters dined on $1,000 buffet-style lunches of brisket, sausage, barbecued chicken, beans, and rice on picnic tables with red gingham tablecloths. The Texas spread, which included specialty cocktails—Pinky Friedmans and Texas Bloody Marys—was set up near the old western saloon, opera house, hotel, post office, and church built on Nelson's ranch for *Red Headed Stranger*, a western film inspired by his 1975 album. The fundraiser gave Ventura time to share what Kinky called "a virtual gold mine of information," and added $170,000 to Kinky's war chest.

Four months later, at a highly publicized fundraiser that drew TV cameras and Houston's elite to the River Oaks home of socialite/philanthropist Carolyn Farb, DeGuerin told the crowd Kinky could depend on his support. Nearly 150 guests attended the $500-per-head event featuring Little Jewford on piano during the cocktail hour and performances by Shaver and Walker. Kinky gave a rousing speech after taking the podium to the strains of Survivor's "Eye of the Tiger," autographed dozens of talking action figures, and posed for countless photos. But the one thing he didn't do was ask for donations.

"Likability is important in a candidate, and Kinky has good likability," says Hillsman. "He's a curmudgeon, but he's funny and he's actually pretty good with people. He'll tell you the exact opposite, because he used to hate fundraisers. He's one of the worst ever at asking people for money—which is what you're supposed to do at fundraisers."

Kinky is a generous soul who has always been more comfortable giving people money than asking for it. Despite his reluctance to solicit contributions, that fundraiser added $150,000 to his campaign coffers.

A week before the election, Lyle Lovett headlined a $1,000-a-person gala at Farb's mansion. If Kinky felt out of his element surrounded by the River Oaks elite, he handled it with grace. "He can move in any circle with ease, because he treats everyone with the same respect and dignity," Farb observed. The soiree, which included the sale of original artwork and an auction featuring an autographed Jimmy Buffett guitar strap, raised more than $130,000.

The biggest ongoing moneymaker was merchandise: bumper stickers, pins, posters, T-shirts, mugs, pint glasses, a campaign cookbook, and a Kinky Friedman talking action figure. Bumper stickers proclaiming, "My Governor Is a Jewish Cowboy," "How Hard Could It Be?" or "Why the Hell Not?" and sporting a Texas flag with a Star of David appeared on cars and street signs throughout Texas.

An Austin poster artist who was part of the Armadillo Art Squad, Guy Juke is known for his darkly detailed, often shadowy and angular figures inspired by horror films, haunting western landscapes, and loopy cartoon characters. "We wanted somebody that could come up with something distinctive that wasn't red, white, and blue," says Hattersley. "Guy was a natural because he had done so many great portraits of others."

"We raised a lot of money from merchandise because it's a great way to fund-raise and musicians know how to do it," says Hillsman. "We didn't want anyone to walk away from an event without buying something. We knew the Kinky talking action figure would be successful because it was very successful for Jesse Ventura."

To assure that success, the campaign produced a clever thirty-second TV spot timed for the holidays. The commercial shows the figure fielding questions at a press conference on microphones for KJEW and K9TV. When asked if he can get the Democrats and Republicans to work together, he poses pensively and says, "I'm running for governor, not God." The spots aired for a week in the Austin, Dallas, El Paso, Houston, and San Antonio markets and signed off with a slogan from Willie Nelson: "Criticize me all you want, but don't circumcise me anymore."

Packaged in a box adorned with the Texas flag, Guy Juke artwork, and photos of Kinky with Nelson, Shaver, and Little Jewford, the twelve-inch figure sold for $29.95. Clad in a black Stetson, black vest and shirt, blue jeans, and a suede belt with a Texas map buckle, Kinky had bendable arms, hands, and legs; a trademark cigar in his left hand; and the first finger of his right hand poised to make his point.

Kinky's talking action figure (he bristles when it's called a doll) featured twenty-three different sayings in his voice, including "I can't screw things up any worse than they already are." "I'll sign anything but bad legislation," "How hard could it be?" "I'm not pro-life; I'm not pro-choice; I'm pro football," "I don't know how many supporters I have, but they all carry guns," "My heroes are teachers, firefighters, cops, and cowboys," and "Read my lips—I don't know."

The Kinkster also proclaims, "I've got a head of hair better than Rick Perry; it's just not in a place I can show you," "Texas has a capitol that was built by giants, but it's inhabited by midgets," "Why the hell not?" "May the god of your choice bless you," and "If you don't love Jesus, go to hell" (the latter two suggested by Shaver, whom he deemed his spiritual advisor).

Rather than rely on paid advertising, Kinky used his celebrity to generate free media. A reporter from the *New Yorker* joined him on the campaign trail and chronicled his campaign in two feature stories: "Lone Star" in August 2005 and "The End of The Trail" in November 2006. Bill O'Reilly interviewed him on *The O'Reilly Factor* on Fox News, and Kinky appeared regularly on *Imus in the Morning*.

Never missing an opportunity to bask in the media spotlight, Kinky attended a White House Correspondents' Dinner at the Washington Hilton in April 2005. Dinner led to an interview on *CBS News Sunday Morning* in August, when he also discussed politics and his campaign on HBO's *Real Time with Bill Maher*.

In January 2006, he appeared on *The Tonight Show with Jay Leno* and *60 Minutes*. Leno joked with Kinky in a brief interview, but *60 Minutes* journalist Morley Safer conducted an in-depth profile, which included interviews with Barkley and *Texas Monthly* editor Evan Smith. When asked about Kinky's strengths as a candidate, Smith was brutally honest. "His strengths begin with his independence," said Smith. "He's independent of everything and of everybody. And sometimes . . . his mouth is independent of his brain." But Smith, who had worked with Kinky at *Texas Monthly* since he bought his first essay in 1996, knew there was more to him than outrageous comments. His other strengths, said Smith, included "the fact he's willing to take on the establishment—Republicans, Democrats, people in power—and has tapped into a dissatisfaction with the accepted order."

Unlike other candidates, Kinky didn't have the funds to run ads on Texas TV stations the critical week before the election. But he appeared on *The Late Show with David Letterman*. When asked about his White House invitations from both Clinton and George W. Bush, he called

Bush "a good man trapped in a Republican's body." He talked about the traditionally low number of Texans who vote and the need for a high turnout at the polls. "They [the candidates] spent 100 million bucks to drive seventy-one percent of Texans away from the polls last time," he said. "If we can get that number [of people voting] in the forties, I'm going to be the governor of Texas."

"When you have somebody who is very interesting and a threat to the system, it's catnip to the reporters for getting free media," says Hillsman.

Like his rabble-rouser buddy Abbie Hoffman, Kinky understood the value of political theater. He appeared on the July 2006 cover of *Texas Monthly* dressed as Uncle Sam in a white top hat and blue jacket. Like the World War I Army recruiting poster, Kinky is pointing straight ahead. The caption? "I Want You to say 'Adios, mofo!'" alluding to Rick Perry's remark caught on tape after he thought an *ABC News* interview had ended. The reporter said, "Try as I may, Governor, I guess I can't win this one." Perry then smirked and said to his communications director, "Try as I may, I'm not gonna wait that long. Adios, mofo!" A fitting image for "The Weirdest Governor Race of All Time" cover story, but the image and story reinforced the perception that Kinky wasn't a serious candidate.

The "Go Kinky" reality show on CMT (Country Music Television) was even worse. Pitched by David Steinberg, who directed episodes of *Seinfeld, Curb Your Enthusiasm, Friends*, and *Mad About You*, Kinky thought the show would portray him as a "humorist, anti-politician, and man of the people" and demonstrate how difficult it is to run for office as an Independent. But giving the camera crews unlimited and uncensored access to his campaign resulted in the crude footage synonymous with reality shows.

The two pilots included celebrity friends—Willie Nelson, Dwight Yoakam, Bill Clinton, Billy Joe Shaver, and Ray Benson. But they also included scenes of Kinky musing about suicide (one of his shticks); scouting his audiences for potential first ladies; asking, "Who wrote this crap?" while reviewing a speech; stomping out of a strategy meeting so he didn't have to "listen to this shit"; and arguing with Yoakam over whether his friend would let him smoke a cigar in his tour bus when he was governor. On a good day, Kinky doesn't have much of a censor, and adding cameras only adds to the theatrics.

"The reality show wasn't my idea," says Jewford. "I would've never done that. The cameras followed us everywhere. They were in the car, in the truck; they were everywhere. The highlight was at the airport when I put the camera down the urinal as I peed. When I came out they said, 'Nice, Jewford. Nice.'"

"It turned out not to be a good idea at all in the end," admits Hillsman. "It's one thing to do a true documentary, but it was basically a TV reality show, and they edited it the way they edit TV reality shows."

Luckily, it never made it past the two pilots. "I think they wanted to do it on the off chance Kinky won so they'd have something amazing to run," Hillsman says. "But as it looked less and less likely Kinky would win, their interest disappeared quickly."

Kinky's political downfall began at a press conference in Houston when he addressed the rise in crime since 150,000 to 200,000 Katrina evacuees resettled in that city. He called for $100 million and 1,000 to 1,200 additional police officers. "The musicians and writers have mostly moved back to New Orleans now," he added. "The crackheads and the thugs have decided they want to stay in Houston."

Texas media and Kinky's opponents began accusing him of racism for the "crackheads and thugs" remark, even though Kinky had no idea "thug" was code for the N-word in some circles. His comments about the spike in crime hit a raw nerve, too; the harshest attacks appeared in the *Houston Chronicle* and *Houston Press*. National publications were less biased. In February 2006, the *Washington Post* reported evacuees being involved in seventeen percent of the city's homicides and the city's mayor and police chief asking FEMA for $6.5 million to reimburse overtime costs and hire at least seventy new officers.

National and British media, including the *Washington Post*, *NBC News*, *CBS News*, and the *Independent* covered the race more evenhandedly than Texas media. When the *Independent*, a British online newspaper, sent their foreign correspondent Andrew Gumbel to follow the campaign, he had a different take on Kinky's use of humor. No stranger to the dirty tricks employed in American politics, Gumbel was the author of *Steal This Vote: Dirty Elections and the Rotten History of Democracy in America*.

"Unlike Britain, American has little tradition of humor bring woven into the fabric of political discourse," Gumbel wrote in "The Lone Star: How Kinky Shook Up Texas." "That, in turn, explains why a lot of

Friedman's media coverage reads like the review of a comedy show rather than a serious political enterprise."

He also had a different take on the accusations of racism.

"If Friedman represents a threat [to the two-party system] in Texas, then it might explain why the Republicans and the Democrats have been closing ranks and turning on him," he added. "The accusation of racism was flatly contradicted by Friedman's record of student activism against segregation in the 1960s, but didn't make it any less appealing as a line of attack."

Two weeks after Kinky's "thugs and crackheads" remark, the Democratic-oriented website Burnt Orange Report turned up a twenty-six-year-old audio clip of a 1980 nightclub performance. As he had done in "They Ain't Makin' Jews like Jesus Anymore," Kinky used the N-word to hold a mirror up to racism, but the newspapers and his opponents used it to deride him as a racist.

"If you listen to the entire joke it's basically making fun of people who are racist, especially Texans," says Hillsman. "But they took it out of context."

An article in the *Houston Chronicle* stated that the joke, but not the entire routine had been "distributed anonymously to news organizations," but that the press secretary for Democratic State Rep. Garnet Coleman had posted it on the Burnt Orange website. Coleman, a former chairman of the Texas Legislative Black Caucus who endorsed Bell, then indulged in his own brand of doublespeak by saying his office had not been involved in making the audio public.

Although Kinky's opponents denied any involvement, Hillsman knew the posting on the Burnt Orange website had come from from Bell's camp. Timed as an "October Surprise" (when a party creates a news event to influence the outcome of an election), the audio was in the Democrats' possession for a while before they released it—when they thought it would do the most damage.

"Bell was a terrible candidate; one of the loosest cannons I've ever seen in campaigns," says Hillsman. "When you don't have a good candidate or a decent campaign, the best chance of victory is to tear down somebody else."

When Kinky tried to explain his "thugs and crackheads" remark, his honesty hurt his candidacy. Amending his statement to say that many evacuees in Houston were good citizens, not drug addicts or criminals, he admitted he had used cocaine and said he had empathy for crack-heads because he knew how they thought. That too was catnip to the press and his opponents, who focused on his cocaine use.

Exasperated by the attacks, Kinky told a reporter from the *Star Telegram* in Fort Worth that anyone who was offended by his comment should vote for one of the other candidates.

"If I've got to lie to people, sweep the truth under the rug, and worry about offending people, I'm not going to be very effective," he said. "Ann Richards, Barbara Jordan, and Molly Ivins had more balls than all the politicians in Texas put together. You can get a good man and he can't make it in this system. Too open, too honest, too passionate."

Attacks in the media are difficult to overcome because the candidate has only two choices: to explain it or to ignore it. It's a no-win scenario, because either choice keeps the issue in the headlines and gives opponents and detractors more ammunition.

Hillsman knew Kinky had a valid explanation for the leaked joke, but he didn't want Kinky to respond. "I always say that if you're explaining, you're losing, and I didn't think he had a very good sense of that."

Upset and hurt by the false and inflammatory accusations, Kinky ignored Hillsman's advice and explained the twenty-six-year-old joke as lampooning racism and making fun of bigots. "Don't confuse the real man with a satirical stage show," he said. "If you do, you're going back pretty far, and I was always an equal-opportunity offender." He also responded when Perry called his remarks "clearly racist; if not directly racist, obliquely racist."

"When Rick Perry was busy cheerleading in college, I was busy picketing segregated restaurants in Austin, Texas, to integrate them," he said. "That's real life. This is entertainment."

"The racism thing was wrong," adds Jewford. "It's just part of how you're brought down. Trust me, Kinky is absolutely not racist at all. He's a satirist. He's not sitting there like a KKK guy—give me a frigging break. If you know anything about him, which I do from his background to today, I can see how it hurt inside. It's just so wrong. He had to respond, but he didn't want to respond. That's the kind of stuff he didn't really think would happen. They come at you and go for your jugular. They just rip you apart."

With Kinky running as an underdog candidate in a state as big as

Texas, TV advertising was critical. In 2005/2006, TV ads cost about $1 million per week to blanket the state. That was financially unfeasible, so Hillsman determined where the majority of the votes were and focused on those markets. Kinky's "Good Shepherd," "Cowboy Way," and "Clean Energy/Clean Government" ads ran in eighteen large and medium media markets, including Austin, Dallas, Houston, Corpus Christi, El Paso, and San Antonio. When his TV ad campaign launched on September 12, Perry, whose budget was five times larger than Kinky's, and Strayhorn, who had double the amount in Kinky's coffers, had already launched statewide TV advertising campaigns.

Filming Kinky's ads was problematic for Hillman's crew. Kinky had given two other film crews—from CMT and David Hartstein's documentary about the campaign—full access and didn't want to look like he was being controlled in any way.

"Kinky would start posturing for the cameras," Hillsman said. "He didn't want to look like he was being advised by a bunch of what he called 'damn Yankees' telling him what to do. So he'd become really irascible whenever other people were around. If another crew was there when we shot the commercials, he would not work with me or the other director at all."

Although the footage had no resemblance to the script, a film editor in Dallas worked his magic. "It was unbelievable," says Hillsman. "The commercials ended up being very different from what we scripted, and the tone of them was so good. Everybody thought there'd be a lot of wisecracks, but the communications were kinda sweet and worked quite well."

All three spots offered a rare glimpse of Richard Friedman, and a message that came from his heart. Alluding to the biblical parable, "The Good Shepherd" tells the tale of the shepherd who risks his life to protect his sheep "Folks, we don't need a politician as governor anymore," Kinky says. "We need a good shepherd. I want to be your good shepherd . . . and that why I'm running for governor of Texas."

"Clean Energy" depicts a folksy Kinky calling for a change. "For the first time in history, Texas is importing energy," he says, seated in his office at the ranch. "Now, that ain't right. . . ."

"The Cowboy Way" addressed values close to Kinky's heart. "Folks, when a cowboy shakes your hand, it's the law of the land. A cowboy doesn't talk about education; he teaches it. A cowboy doesn't talk about religion; he lives it. The other candidates are spending millions on commercials, going at it like javelinas in heat. Ask any cowboy and he'll tell you, money may buy you a fine dog, but only love will make it wag its tail."

Only Kinky could have written that spot, with its references to the piglike animals in South Texas that served as the football mascot of Texas A&M University-Kingsville, Perry's alma mater.

The *Associated Press* characterized the ads as portraying a "serious, warmer candidate," but the Texas media, even the ones that liked the spot, continued to focus on Kinky's past to disqualify him as a candidate. "It's one of the best political spots I have ever seen," wrote Paul Burka in his *Texas Monthly* blog. "It is completely unexpected. Kinky's voice is perfect. The Hill Country scenes are idyllic. His handling of the animals is loving and gentle. This spot could elect half a dozen people governor. Unfortunately, I don't think Kinky is one of them."

Houston Chronicle reporter R. G. Ratcliffe wrote only one sentence about the "Good Shepherd" spot before reiterating charges of racism from the previous week, using a quote from Rick Perry and a statement from the Texas Legislative Black Caucus.

After Perry's comment that a governor has to be a good role model for children, Ratcliffe asked Kinky if a governor with a past history of illegal drug use would fit the bill.

Kinky was ready with his response—and it wasn't one that would help his cause. "Great answer for that," he said "The only great governor we've had was an opium addict and a drunkard, and that was Sam Houston."

The Texas NAACP invited all the other candidates to speak at its state convention in October. But the organization didn't invite Kinky, because he wouldn't respond to an ultimatum to apologize for the thug comment and the old comedy routine. "I don't apologize to people who try to intimidate," he said. "I don't apologize to people with an agenda. I never apologize for the truth."

Appalled by the NAACP's high-handed decision, Texas African Americans began calling radio stations complaining about his exclusion. One former Texas NAACP officer stopped by campaign headquarters to invite Kinky for breakfast at the convention hotel.

Kinky sensed an agenda, and it wasn't long before the Democratic candidate, who had close ties to the NAACP, asked him to drop out of the race. In a conversation caught on the documentary *Along Came Kinky—Texas Jewboy for Governor*, Kinky told Chris Bell he didn't negotiate with terrorists. Bell responded by saying he didn't understand what Kinky meant.

Debate sponsors offered six opportunities to debate, but Perry only accepted one. The governor's campaign controlled the schedule, so the sole debate was set on a Friday night, when most Texans are watching high school football.

"Debating is incredibly important for independent candidates," says Hillsman. "It's the one time you get to be on the same footing as the incumbent and the other candidates in the race. But because of when it was scheduled, there wasn't a lot of viewership."

Kinky didn't do well in the hour-long debate, which had a game show format with candidates given only fifteen seconds to answer questions. He also became defensive when the questions to him and the other candidates focused on painting him as a racist.

"The debate was bogus," says Jewford. "It wasn't a debate; it was just answering questions. Kinky was slightly out of his element, which was part of the problem. I also thought the questions were skewed against him. A few of them were bogus."

Jewford is referring to "Who is the highest-ranking African American on your campaign?" a question posed to Kinky but none of the other candidates. To drive home the "racist" moniker, the format allowed Perry, Bell, and Strayhorn to weigh in on Kinky's "thugs and crackheads" comment.

One week before the election, Texas Democrats used a joke from one of Kinky's old routines to slander him and his family. Democratic State Senator Royce West sponsored a TV ad with a photo of Kinky accompanied by a voice-over in a thick Texas accent declaring, "You folks know the Friedman family motto now. The Jews own the world. The Catholics run it. The Protestants work it and the [bleep] Mexicans enjoy it." Then Royce, a black politician with a James Earl Jones voice, imparts his message to vote Democratic to "make Texas great again."

The negative ads and the charges of racism took a toll. Despite Kinky's bravado, it hurt him to be portrayed in a way diametrically opposed to who he was and everything he believed in. To smear his family name was unconscionable. He thought about how his father had risked his job as a professor by leading a civil rights march on the University of Texas campus; and how the family's Echo Hill Ranch, run by his parents and his brother Roger, had always hosted camps for inner-city children. His socially conscious sister Marcie, who had headed the Red Cross in Vietnam and was working with the State Department in Liberia, got painted with the same brush.

Nobody listened when he said he had picketed the Plantation restaurant and Rexall Drug on the UT campus for discriminating against black patrons. Or that he was the first performer to bring a black artist onto center stage at Nashville's Grand Ole Gospel Show. Or that he lived with black people, brown people, and pygmies for two years when he in the Peace Corps in Borneo.

"Kinky was really hurt, because he's not a racist," says Jewford.

It was a difficult time, but Kinky kept his sense of humor. Days before the election, he told a reporter, "I'm here to fix Texas. And I guarantee that if Perry wins, I'm retiring in a petulant snit. If Bell wins, I'm moving to France with Barbra Streisand. If Grandma wins, I'll blow my fucking head off."

The charges of racism and the debate hurt Kinky's numbers. He had nineteen percent in the April 26 and July 24 polls, but by October 24 his numbers had dropped to sixteen percent. Although he lost the election to an incumbent Republican in a red state, generating 547,000 votes (12.6 percent of the vote) was a respectable accomplishment for a political newcomer.

He still jokes about winning the election everywhere but Texas, and there's a kernel of truth in that statement. In a Texas for Public Justice Report documenting gubernatorial campaign funds, Strayhorn's out-of-state donations comprised four percent of the total; Bell's were two percent; Perry's were five percent. But nineteen percent of Kinky campaign contributions came from out-of-state donors.

"Kinky would have won if people outside of Texas could vote," agrees Hillsman. "He had incredible support all around the country because he had regular appearances on *Fox News* on *The O'Reilly Factor* and on the *Imus* show. He was very well known nationally, and we milked the press for everything we could get out of them."

McCall knew it wasn't easy for his friend to lose, and is still annoyed when Texas Democrats blame Kinky as a spoiler who helped Perry get reelected.

"He worked hard, and took it hard when he lost," said McCall. "It's hard to put yourself out there and not have people vote for you. The Democrat that lost was an empty suit. He didn't lose because of Kinky. The Democrat that ran against him is a schmuck; he had no chance."

Exit polls showed Kinky earning the vote of eight percent of the Democrats, Strayhorn earning fifteen percent, and Perry earning eight percent. It's highly unlikely that the majority of the people who voted for Kinky would have voted for Bell if Kinky had dropped out of the race.

Kinky, if anything, is resilient. No matter what happens, he quickly moves on to another project. When he told Lamar Smith he was running for governor, the U.S. rep. predicted he'd come out of the race with a book, a wife, or the governorship. Kinky came out with *You Can Lead a Politician to Water, but You Can't Make Him Think*, a book published by Simon & Schuster in 2007.

"I admit to being a little disappointed, but I'm not downhearted," he wrote in the preface. "Remember, the crowd picked Barabbas. . . . I will continue, nonetheless, to endeavor to be a dealer in hope, hope for a brighter future for Texas."

In June 2009, Kinky announced his intention to run in the Democratic primary for the 2010 gubernatorial race. In December, when Bill White, the Democratic mayor of Houston, entered the race with a war chest of $4 million (to Kinky's $30,000), and his friend Farouk Shami joined the race pledging to spend $10 million of his own money, Kinky withdrew his candidacy. Instead, he set his sights on the Democratic nomination for agricultural commissioner. Although he couldn't resist the campaign slogan "No cow left behind," his platform advocated establishing a no-kill animal facility in every county, setting up farmer co-ops and alternative fuel options at truck stops, fighting against toll roads encroaching on farmers' land, and pushing for a statewide public defender to monitor rural issues.

In addition to campaigning at colleges and community events, Kinky continued to perform at concerts and began hosting *Texas Roadhouse Live*, a TV series that broadcast live performances from Texas venues. His opponent, Texas rancher Hank Gilbert, another of the four candidates who had dropped out of the Democratic gubernatorial primary, campaigned by hosting small-town breakfasts and gathering endorsements in West Texas. The rancher beat him in the primary, getting more votes than almost any other Democrat in a Texas race. Allegations that

Gilbert took $100,000 from Shami to drop out of the governor's race were denied by both men.

Always a free thinker who is ahead of the times, Kinky thought about running in the 2014 gubernatorial race with a platform focused on legalizing marijuana and casino gambling. But that was before Texas Senator Wendy Davis staged a thirteen-hour filibuster against a GOP-backed abortion bill to close almost ninety percent of clinics in the state. Standing on the Senate floor in pink sneakers and a back brace, she filibustered her way into the national spotlight via an online live stream watched by 180,000 people. Within two weeks, she had raised nearly $1 million in campaign donations and become the star of the Texas Democratic Party.

Rather than abandon his ideas, Kinky decided to drop the humor and entered the Democratic primary for Texas agriculture commissioner as an "old-fashioned Harry Truman Democrat" with a comprehensive platform. He kept his proposals to legalize marijuana, industrial hemp, and casino gambling and expanded on the agricultural issues. His platform included grants for family farms and public-school gardens, a water conservation plan amending the "rule of capture" law giving landowners the rights to all the water below their land, and creating a state environmental water board to oversee regional water authorities. He also tackled the issue of the five to six million feral hogs in Texas tearing up crops, attacking farm animals and wildlife, and wreaking havoc on the environment.

"What happens to the people that grow the crops affects everybody down the line," he says over a cup of coffee on the porch of his ranch. "We can't just ignore the farmers and ranchers and go to Whole Foods forever."

Advocating the legalization of marijuana and gambling was a risky move in Texas. Most politicians steered clear of the marijuana issue so they wouldn't look soft on crime. Other Texas pols were getting their pockets lined by Native American tribes in Oklahoma to keep gambling out of Texas.

"Legalizing marijuana would create a huge economic engine for Texas and castrate the Mexican drug cartels," says Kinky, who only smokes marijuana on Nelson's bus "as a matter of etiquette," he quips. "All the other politicians talk about education, but I'm talking about how to fund it.

"The politicians are cowards," he adds. "What I'm advocating is political courage—courage, imagination, and common sense. When we have one of the top cancer research centers in the world—M. D. Anderson in Houston—it's a crime we do not have medicinal marijuana.

"Our attitude is, 'We don't want the revenue; leave the gambling money in Oklahoma, Louisiana, and Vegas,'" he says. "'Leave the pot money in Oregon, Colorado, and Washington State—we don't need it.' Well, we do need it. Texans are flooding over the border to Oklahoma so much the Louisiana gambling establishment is complaining that Oklahoma is taking their Texans away. The Choctaw and Chickasaw tribes in Oklahoma have given millions to Texas politicians to keep gambling out of Texas. We're not talking about under the table; we're talking about what's on the record."

The record bears him out. In 2012, Las Vegas Sands chairman Sheldon Adelson, known for aggressively lobbying Congress to abolish Internet gambling, gave $150,000 to the Republican State Leadership Committee in Texas. More than $91,000 went to then Texas Attorney General Greg Abbott. When Abbott ran for Texas governor in 2014, three tribes contributed more than $1.4 million to his campaign to influence the future of gambling in Texas. The Chickasaw Nation donated $670,000, the Choctaw Nation donated $286,000, and the Kickapoo Tribe donated $450,000. Houston billionaire Tilman Feretta, who opened a Golden Nugget Casino in Lake Charles, Louisiana, in December 2014, donated $254,000 to Abbott's campaign.

"We're being played as suckers—we're rubes," says Kinky. "If you put a casino into Galveston or San Antonio or League City, it'll bring in huge revenue and jobs for Texas. The bit about prostitution or drugs or people spending their paychecks comes with the territory. Those guys need a way to piss away their money. If they don't do it here, they'll go to Louisiana or Oklahoma. Why should we build roads and schools in Louisiana and Oklahoma?"

During the 2014 Democratic agriculture commissioner primary, Kinky ran against Hugh Asa Fitzsimons, a buffalo rancher and former teacher near San Antonio, who was endorsed by the Texas Democratic party and newspaper editorial boards across the state; and Joe Hogan, an unknown farmer and insurance agent who didn't campaign. The Democratic Party did everything they could to knock Kinky out of the race. Democratic State Senator Leticia Van de Putte derided him as "a comedian, not a politician" whenever she talked to the press.

A month before the primary, Van de Putte, who was running for lieutenant governor, made a robocall to Democrats asking them to vote for Fitzsimons, "the only real Democrat in this race. It would be no laughing matter to let comedian Kinky Friedman win a spot on the ballot with Wendy Davis and me in the fall," she said. Texas Democratic Party Chairman Gilberto Hinojosa sent state Democratic activists an email with the subject "No Laughing Matter" and the same message from Van de Putte disparaging Kinky and endorsing Fitzsimons.

It was dirty pool, but nobody paid any attention. Kinky received thirty-eight percent of the votes in the primary, Hogan received thirty-nine percent, and Fitzsimons received only twenty-three percent of almost 500,000 votes. When neither candidate received fifty percent (plus one) of the votes, Kinky and Hogan proceeded to a runoff election in late May.

The national press had its eye on Kinky during that election as well. When the *Wall Street Journal* asked him about the unusual protocol of a political party taking sides in a primary race, he pointed to the lack of Democrats elected in Texas since Ann Richards lost to George W. Bush in 1994. "If they had a great track record, then I would say, 'Okay, maybe I'm doing something wrong,'" he said. "But when you look at their comprehensive record of failure over the last twenty years, you realize you have to try something different."

Democrat Chris Bell, Kinky's former gubernatorial race rival, endorsed him in the runoff, as did the *Dallas Morning News*, stating that Kinky "was carrying the flag for marijuana long before Colorado legalized it and Governor Rick Perry softened his stance." The paper also expressed concern that Hogan, in the few interviews he had granted, had been more eager to celebrate his primary win than to focus on a platform. He told the *Texas Observer* that winning the primary "was a miracle and only God could have pulled it off."

In a runoff that attracted 15,000 fewer voters than the primary, Hogan beat Kinky by 5,000 votes. Conservative Christian Texas wasn't ready for a Jewish cowboy who wanted to legalize pot and gambling. But they did like their fried food and soda pop. When Republican candidate Sid Miller won that agriculture commission election, he lifted the decade-old statewide ban on deep fryers and soda machines in public schools.

Kinky's pioneering platform cost him the primary, but it echoed a growing sentiment across the U.S. The *New York Times* editorial board vindicated his ideas on July 26, 2014, in the first of a six-part editorial series calling for the legalization of marijuana.

"Kinky's a contender and always will be," says Shaver. "Sometimes he goes for things he's not suited for, but he's an icon and everybody knows him."

The "Man in the Arena" passage of Theodore Roosevelt's speech at the Sorbonne in Paris, France, on April 23, 1910, sums up the Kinkster.

It is not the critic who counts; not the man who points out how the strong man stumbles, or where the doer of deeds could have done them better. The credit belongs to the man who is actually in the arena, whose face is marred by dust and sweat and blood, who strives valiantly; who errs and comes short again and again; because there is not effort without error and shortcomings; but who does actually strive to do the deed; who knows the great enthusiasm, the great devotion, who spends himself in a worthy cause, who at the best knows in the end the triumph of high achievement and who at the worst, if he fails, at least he fails while daring greatly. So that his place shall never be with those cold and timid souls who know neither victory nor defeat.

12

The Lasting Legacy of Kinky Friedman

*"The thing about Kinky, people know about him from songs
like 'Ride 'Em Jewboy.' But he's such a Renaissance man,
it's impossible to pigeonhole him."*
—*Billy Bob Thornton*

Never one to rest on his laurels or dwell on the past, Kinky is always embarking on new projects. When he left politics behind, he dusted off his Smith-Corona and began writing *Tin Can Telephone*, the long-awaited nineteenth novel in his detective series. By July 2014, he was on the road again, playing his music to enthusiastic audiences throughout the U.S., Canada, Australia, Germany, Switzerland, and Austria. A master of timing, facial gestures, and the comedic pause, he's a consummate performer who never fails to entertain his audiences.

No matter how often you've seen him, he still makes you laugh until your face hurts. A master of engaging his audience, he'll lead a sing-along on "Ol' Ben Lucas" and mention Paladin and the *Have Gun—Will Travel* TV show when he talks about Man in Black Tequila. If the audience remembers that late '50s/early '60s show, he leads them in a sing-along of the theme song. Then he pauses, looks around the club, and says, "This is a gay bar, right?" which brings nervous laughs and abruptly ends the sing-along.

Audiences are a mixture of all ages, from baby boomers to millennials, fans of his music, fans of his books, and fans and followers of his political career and commentary.

"When I played the Jazz Café—one of the hippest places in London—with Jewford and Washington Ratso, there was 500 people, all standing, and I sold it out," he says. "One look at that audience—you had it made before you walked on the stage. Australian cowboys, Orthodox Jews, young people, and crazy punk guys with rings in their noses. It was an amazing audience that knew most of the material.

"This minstrel boy traveling on the road with this high calling of playing songs that have something to say and also having something to say—some is political, some is a little bit of Will Rogers, a little bit of Judy Garland, and a little bit of Mark Twain—seems to be working," he says.

He enjoys performing his own songs as well as putting his own spin on songs that are "spiritually akin" to them. "My 'Pretty Boy Floyd' is pretty close to Woody's but not quite," he adds. "Ramblin' Jack's is a perfect mimicry of Woody, and the Byrds' version is more of a set piece. It's good, but it doesn't have the Woody feel that I give that song. I can deliver that fuckin' song."

But every now and then, that feeling of never being satisfied—of wanting something more—passes through his mind.

"I'll have 150 people in a little theater somewhere, like a show I did in Toronto," he says. "I've sold it out; it's a high-priced ticket. The show killed and I had several standing ovations with people using the words 'great performance' or 'amazing.' I'll make three or four grand, maybe five, and it's fun and it's easy. As I'm doing it, I'm thinking, 'Why this couldn't have been in Vegas for a bigger crowd or more money? Or on HBO—it certainly is that quality.' And it makes me a little sad, but then I think, 'This is meant to be. It's great that I'm able to do this at all, enjoy it, and have an audience that enjoys it, too.'"

Regardless of the venue or the audience, whenever Kinky performs, his only goal is to put on a good show. "I don't pander to an audience," he says. "I do the same show whether I'm playing for 700 Jews in Galveston, like the benefit for the old synagogue, or when I am playing for a bunch of rednecks, like the show outside of Houston last year. That's when a guy came up to me and asked, 'Why did your people kill our Lord?' and I said, 'Because the motherfucker had it coming.'"

When Kinky's on the road, he does three- or four-week tours without a night off. "My shrink Willie gave me the idea of not taking a night off," Kinky says. "He said it would fuck you up the next night; you want to be running on pure adrenaline. Do twenty-three shows, thirty-six shows, whatever, and don't take a night off. There is truth to that, because you're really in the zone. If you take a night or two off, you've lost it."

He turned seventy-two in November 2016 (but he reads at the seventy-four-year-old level) and doesn't let age slow him down. In shows that combine music, irreverent humor delivered in stand-up form, and a professorial reading from his latest book, he performs for fans across the continental U.S. and Hawaii, Canada, Sweden, Scotland, Denmark, Norway, Holland, England, Ireland, Germany, Switzerland, Austria, Australia, New Zealand, and the island state of Tasmania.

Kinky always makes time to meet his fans, pose for photos, and listen to stories about the Jewboys, his books, or why he would have made a great governor. He graciously signs anything he's asked to sign ("I'll sign anything except bad legislation," he says), including piles of books (some fans bring a dozen in backpacks), CDs, albums, and the occasional female breast.

"It does demystify you, but I like to meet these people personally because I love people," he says. "You connect and you can see it. I'm a Wal-Mart greeter, so I meet almost the entire audience," he adds with a straight face. "One of the important things about being on the road is you never know who you're reaching. And I say, blessed is the match that kindles the flame."

The unlikely match that kindled a new flame for Kinky is Brian Molnar, a New Jersey singer/songwriter who began opening for him when he started touring solo in 2012. On one of many visits to Kinky's ranch, Molnar suggested he cut a new CD. Kinky immediately nixed the idea but enlisted Molnar on a project to release his original demo tape and a live show from the Bearsville Theater in Woodstock, New York. Molnar produced *Kinky Friedman's Bi-Polar Tour—Live from Woodstock*, released in 2012, and Kinky's 2013 release, *Lost and Found: The Famous Living Room Tape*.

Molnar still wanted Kinky to record new material, and continued to approach him with different recording ideas. But Kinky wouldn't budge. "I didn't see any point in doing a CD, which is why I stopped making records," Kinky says. "Cultural ADD is so prevalent now. A lot of records go to #1, trend for a week, but instead of getting stronger are number four, or not even on the chart, by the second week. But Brian kept badgering me to let him produce it. I finally said, 'Let's do it. If nothing happens, nothing happens.'"

Molnar's sheer persistence and psychological approach to Kinky finally made the project happen. "From getting to know him and spending a lot of time with him, I started to understand why he hadn't recorded in so long," he says. "I came up with a plan I knew he would like, which was recording in a very relaxed situation and not in a traditional recording studio with the clock ticking. If it didn't go well we could easily bail and not lose any money."

The Loneliest Man I Ever Met, Kinky's first new studio album in almost forty years, hit the stores in October 2015. Prior to its release, *Rolling Stone* ran an interview with a link to an online audio stream of "Bloody Mary Morning," calling the duet with Willie Nelson "one of the standouts." *Rolling Stone* later ran an in-depth interview with Kinky covering his new CD, music in general, Texas, and politics.

The CD generated great reviews in *Newsweek*, the *Wall Street Journal*, the *Guardian* (UK), the *New Yorker*, *Tablet Magazine*, the *Huffington Post*, *Pop Matters*, the *Houston Press*, and other media; airplay on Sirius XM radio; and steady sales. Most reviewers, expecting more of Kinky's in-your-face satire and irreverent humor, were pleasantly surprised.

The Wall Street Journal described the album as "replete with irony and dark humor—more likely to bring tears than raise hackles." *Texas Monthly* wrote, "His sparingly arranged covers of songs by the likes of Dylan, Haggard, and Cash are the last thing you'd expect from the would-be governor: humble and heartfelt."

"Return of the Jewboy: Kinky Friedman at 70" appeared in *Newsweek* more than forty-two years after *Newsweek* journalist Maureen Orth interviewed him for that magazine. "Much like with fellow renegade crooner Johnny Cash before him, there's a renewed appreciation for Friedman's unique brand of political-satire-meets-outlaw-country as he hits his seventies," wrote Dave Wedge in the October 27, 2015, issue. "Now in the twilight of his colorful career, he's winning critical acclaim for his first studio album in three decades—the darkly personal and occasionally haunting *The Loneliest Man I've Ever Met*."

Jewish Journal called it "a deeply soulful and enchantingly melancholy departure from the singer-songwriter-comedian's humorous and satirical works." NPR Music posted a link to "Christmas Card from a Hooker" on its website. "Waits sang, jazzily, in character, as Charley, the recipient of a missive from an incarcerated prostitute," writes Jewly Hight. "Friedman has inserted himself into the story, and changed it into a deliciously wry recitation."

The influence of Dylan and Nelson laid the groundwork for the CD. When Kinky released *From One Good American to Another* in 1995, Dylan told him the songs from the early 1980s *Lights Out* radio show— "Ramblin' Boy," "Old Shep," "Pretty Boy Floyd," "The Ballad of Ira

Hayes," and "Hobo's Lullaby"—were some of the best songs he'd heard Kinky perform.

"It was with that in mind that I eventually successfully approached him with a plan to record," says Molnar. "We wanted that sort of a sound. The songs we picked were not old folk songs, but that's where the concept began."

Kinky detests contemporary Nashville music, which he calls "over-produced pop music that sounds like background music for a bad fraternity party," and has always been passionate about the under-produced and sparse feel of Nelson's *Red Headed Stranger*. But he needed a producer willing to work with him on his vocals.

"I've written and recorded three songs about Nashville, but 'The Loneliest Man I Ever Met' is the one that's recorded right," says Kinky. "The vocals were never quite right on the other ones. The producers were busy getting the bass levels right or the drums and I'm singing in the wrong key. Brian's idea was to emphasize the song and the voice, and he really nailed it."

Using a vintage RCA 77 B carbon ribbon microphone for Kinky's vocals and putting them up front in the mix created an intimate sound perfect for his voice.

"I kept him involved in the arranging process, so we made sure to find and adjust the keys for each song," says Molnar. "I wasn't happy until he was happy, and I don't think the other producers listened to him. He knows better than anybody what he's capable of. He just needs somebody who believes in him and understands his unique process.

"We recorded around the clock for about a week. Whenever Kinky or I felt his voice was in the right spot for each song, we would bring him in and cut a track, maybe adjust the key. The relaxed situation of being able to work when inspired made it doable for him."

Recorded in the annex building on Kinky's ranch, Molnar played guitar on the CD, which included Kinky on vocals; Joe Cirotti on guitar, bass, and mandolin ("Joe Cirotti is a guitar freak and absolutely brilliant," says Kinky); Little Jewford on keyboards; and Mickey Raphael on harmonica. "Bloody Mary Morning," which was coproduced with Nelson and recorded in his Pedernales studio, included Nelson on guitar and vocals, Bobbie Nelson on piano, Kevin Smith on bass, and Raphael on harmonica. Engineers included Michael Stigliano at the Echo Hill Ranch sessions and Steve Chadie at Pedernales studio.

"The beautiful thing about *The Loneliest Man I've Ever Met*—the record is so sparsely produced, you can let your imagination play with it," says Kinky. "As one reviewer said, this is not a record; this is a work of art. Another said, 'This is not a record, this is a mirror.' He might have been closer to the truth. The hooker in Minneapolis has created a beautiful silken web of how beautiful her life is going—when in truth, just the opposite is the case. Many of us do that—you don't have to be a hooker to be a whore.

"Raymond Chandler said scarcely anything in literature is worth a damn except what's written between the lines. There's a lot on the *Loneliest Man* record done between the lines. You hear more in it as you listen more. One reason is the pickers are brilliant—Mickey Raphael and Jewford and Joe Cirotti. Joe's not country, so he can really take a song and make it fly."

Kinky and Will Hoover wrote the title track about Tompall Glaser when they were struggling songwriters in Nashville. "Tompall was an unsung hero of the outlaw movement," says Kinky. "He was the only one of them who was really rich, successful, had his own studio, his own big publishing house. And he shook up Nashville."

In addition to two originals from his early career, Kinky picked songs he had always wanted to record by artists he admired. There's Hoover's "Freedom to Stay," which had been recorded by Waylon Jennings as well as Tina Turner. There's Johnny Cash's "Pickin' Time," Merle Haggard's "Hungry Eyes," Bob Dylan's "Girl from the North Country," Nelson's "Bloody Mary Morning," Lerner and Loewe's "Wand'rin Star" from *Paint Your Wagon*, and "A Nightingale Sang in Berkeley Square," recorded by Glen Miller, Nat King Cole, and Frank Sinatra.

"I had a personal connection with every song on the record," says Kinky. "I interpreted songs by friends like 'Christmas Card from a Hooker' by Tom Waits and 'My Shit's Fucked Up' by Warren Zevon. Mickey Raphael always wanted to play on 'My Shit's Fucked Up,' and he added a whole dimension to the record. He and Joe really took that song to town.

"The best review said 'A Nightingale Sang in Berkeley Square' and 'My Shit's Fucked Up' are done with exactly the same seriousness. It made 'My Shit's Fucked Up' a real treasure. We did something I think Warren would be proud of. Tom Waits is a tough guy to cover—who does things better than Tom Waits? But we delivered that song. I was not really prepared for the critics to love this record as much as they did. I cannot remember a bad word said about it."

When he chose "Wand'rin Star," the theme song from a 1951 Broadway musical, and "A Nightingale Sang in Berkeley Square," a British love song written in 1939, he was following his heart, not the marketplace. "The songs were not chosen so people of today would like them," he says. "'A Nightingale Sang in Berkeley Square' is about as square as you can be if you're a millennial," he continues. "You don't know anything about the war or that era and the song sounds cornball. But that's not what happened. What happened is everybody who listens to it loves it—with just Little Jewford on piano and me singing. Many people think "Nightingale" is the best song on the record.

"'Wand'rin' Star' is a gorgeous song I've always loved. It's a forgotten song. Lee Marvin [who sang it in the 1969 movie version] showed me how to sing it. You get up at three or four o'clock in the morning after you've been sleeping, so it sounds like a cross between Tom Waits and Edith Piaf."

Getting the right sound on "Wand'rin' Star" was a challenge for both Kinky and Molnar.

"The rest of the album took about three days to record; that song took about five days," says Molnar. "We went back to the drawing board many times before we got the take that made the album. It's such a great track and fits him so well we really wanted to get it. But it's so different; it took some adjusting of Kinky's and our state of mind to capture the track."

Buoyed by the success of the CD, Kinky returned to his first love—songwriting—and picked up where he had left off when he wrote his last song in 1982.

"I've only started to write recently," he says. "I've always loved being a songwriter. But my records weren't really going anywhere, so I stopped writing songs and started writing books. Then I got into politics. If I was making vast fortunes with each record, or knew they were actually selling, I might have stayed with it. Now it's a matter of self-expression and knowing—from the success of *The Loneliest Man*—there are people who are listening.

"It's a great feeling of liberation to be songwriting again," he adds. "There's something about songwriting that's very pure. It's not just putting a chord here and a bridge here and building it like the songs written by committees in Nashville, where they say, 'Give us a little bit of a Waylon Jennings feeling or a little Roger Miller rhythm to it.' When I write songs, I feel like Willie Nelson stoned out of his mind, lying in a cheap hotel bed with scraps of lyrics all around—tore up into different little pieces. That's a songwriter. A songwriter is someone who sails as close to the iceberg as he can without sinking the ship and a song should be a vehicle of truth.

"Having to connect the music and the lyrics . . . how that works, nobody knows. Like magic, a little bit of alchemy. This is what drives you to distraction. This is why alcohol helps, drugs, smoking cigarettes, guns, self-pity. Anything that will make you miserable may help. I'm not being entirely facetious here."

Kinky wrote ten new songs for his latest CD, which he plans to release in 2017. "I'm very excited about the new record," says Kinky. "It's got "Jesus in Pajamas," which has a Leonard Cohen/Kristofferson influence; "A Dog Named Freedom"; "Autographs in the Rain"; "Circus of Life"; and a bunch of new songs I'm very happy with. A couple of them I wrote with other people who were drifting through the ranch. Some have a spiritual connection—like Bob McLane, my friend from Shreveport who I hung out with in New York at the Lone Star. Bob adopted a three-legged pit bull ten years ago from the rescue ranch. Bob is a Vietnam vet, very much like the guy in the song. 'Now it's me and a three-legged dog named Freedom and a sign that says "Texas or bust."'

"We plan to bring on Junior Pruneda, a terrific standup bass player who played with Ernest Tubb, and Augie Meyer [Sir Douglas Quintet, Texas Tornados] who plays the accordion and Vox organ. They've both agreed to join us, and of course we want Mickey Raphael on harp. Quite often, when somebody lays off a long time and does a record, he's lost his edge. I haven't. I'm standing on the edge of nothing and have been for a long time."

A true Renaissance man, Kinky is a man of many talents. He's been a chess prodigy, camp counselor, Red Cross–certified swimming instructor, civil rights activist, Peace Corps volunteer, musician, songwriter, entertainer, satirist, and author of thirty books and countless articles. He's been a columnist, politician, entrepreneur (Kinkajou Records, Kinky Fried-man's Private Stock Politically Correct Salsa and Dip, Kinky Friedman

Cigars, Man in Black Tequila), and animal activist who cofounded a no-kill animal shelter in Texas.

When he ran for governor, his friend Mojo Nixon, a psychobilly singer/songwriter ("Don Henley Must Die," "Debbie Gibson Is Pregnant with My Two-Headed Love Child," and "Elvis Is Everywhere") rewrote the latter song for his campaign. "Kinky Is Everywhere" is an apt description of the Kinkster's life.

When the Institute of Texan Cultures at the University of Texas in San Antonio had an exhibit titled "Texans Head to Foot," it featured well-known Texans like Lady Bird Johnson, Mary Kay Ash, Michael Dell, Red McCombs, Henry B. Gonzalez, Dan Rather, and George Strait. Kinky's cowboy hat, boots, and cigar were proudly displayed alongside a hat from Buddy Holly and the boots and a belt from Tejano sensation Selena.

You can find the Kinkster in a handful of movies (he played the governor of Texas in the 2009 film *Palo Pinto Gold* and the president of the United States in the 2010 film *Mars*) and dozens of documentaries. He's appeared in TV shows ranging from *Saturday Night Live* to *Charlie Rose*, *The Joan Rivers Show*, *The John Laroquette Show*, *Austin City Limits*, *Real Time with Bill Maher*, *The Tonight Show with Jay Leno*, *60 Minutes*, *Imus in the Morning*, *The O'Reilly Factor*, and *The Late Show with David Letterman*. There's even a Kinky Friedman talking action figure, made by a company responsible for figures of Abraham Lincoln, John F. Kennedy, Bill Clinton, and George W. Bush.

Capitalizing on his ever-present cigar, he formed Kinky Friedman Cigars with Little Jewford in 2007. Manufactured in the Dominican Republic, his line of cigars included the Governor, the Kinkycristo, the Utopian (with profits going to the Utopia Animal Rescue Ranch), the Lone Star, and the Texas Jewboy. The Kinky Lady had a butt (of the cigar, he says) dipped in honey; the Willie had a little twist on one end; and the Big Richard (which he wanted to name Big Dick) used a blend formulated to enhance the flavor of tequila.

Although Kinky had "no qualms about becoming a Jimmy Dean–style pitchman for my product," some people were offended. "It's sad to see an icon turned into a whore," wrote a disgruntled fan. "I don't care what you call me," was Kinky's response. "Rick Perry calls himself a public servant. Al Sharpton calls himself a civil rights leader. Besides, whores tend to hang around with a better class of people."

A cigar smoker since his twenties, Kinky smokes eight cigars a day and up to twelve a day when he's writing. And he's quick to tell you that his heroes were prodigious cigar smokers. Winston Churchill, who smoked eight to ten cigars a day, primarily Cubans, was almost never seen without a cigar during World War II, he says. And one of his favorite quotes by Mark Twain, who smoked up to forty cigars a day, is, "If smoking is not allowed in heaven, I shall not go."

Kinky Friedman Cigars sold more than 100,000 cigars in an early quarter, with Kinky and Jewford flying around the country for cigar shows and conventions from Vegas to Florida. When Kinky didn't become "the Famous Amos of the cigar world" as Jewford predicted, they left the cigar business. But his namesake brand lives on through a Galveston cigar shop owner who acquired the rights and sells the Kinky Friedman Cigars Signature Series.

Always a man in motion, Kinky introduced Man in Black Tequila when his cigar company started winding down. With his black preacher's coat, black jeans, black Stetson, black boots, and Texas mystique, he was the ideal spokesman for a line of tequila he calls a tribute to men like Paladin, Zorro, and Johnny Cash. "It's not your grandfather's tequila; it's your grandfather's gardener's tequila," he says. His signature line includes Man in Black Plata (Kinky Silver), Man in Black Reposado, Man in Black Anejo, and Man in Black Extra.

Launching the brand with a press conference in San Antonio, Kinky incorporated Man in Black Tequila bottle-signing events into his tours, and shots of tequila into his stage show. Referring to it as "Mexican mouthwash," he'd down a shot in a rocks glass and recommend the cowboy method of "drinking the shot, snorting the salt, and squeezing the lime in your eye." He drank one shot per interview during six live interviews after the press conference, downing his fifth shot during an interview with J.T. Street on "Street's Corner," a regular feature on San Antonio's Fox TV's evening newscast.

"I had heard Kinky's jokes a lot, and I could tell they weren't as crisp this time around," remembers Street. "Kinky's tequila was probably pretty effective. He wasn't sloppy—he held it together, but he was obviously buzzed enough to be part of the story. That all goes back to Kinky's mystique—of a rabble-rousing, tequila-soaked dude in a bar. That's what he was selling that day and it fit into his character."

"If you're talking about a drink that's going to give you the even-mindedness of the Mahatma, tequila is it," Kinky said during the live Fox TV segment. "I was going somewhere with that, but I don't know where the hell I was going. It'll help you connect your thoughts . . . usually."

"It never ceases to amaze me," Street says. "I interviewed Kinky a number of times during my radio and TV career, and it was always something—tequila, cigars, salsa, or running for governor. There was always a hook and it was always entertaining."

Like Will Rogers and Mark Twain, Kinky is a man of intellect and humor whose one-liners and words of wisdom are quoted on dozens of websites and blogs, as well as Twitter and Facebook posts. One of his novels is in a footnote to a legal argument in the *Journal of the Patent and Trademark Office Society*, and he's the only Texan with two quotes on the *Texas Mystique* page on the Texas Gallery of Texas Cultures website.

Joseph Heller, author of *Catch 22*, which is considered to be one of the most significant novels of the twentieth centry, mentioned Kinky in *Good as Gold*, his 1976 novel. A former governor of Texas tells the main character, Bruce Gold: "Gold, I like you. You remind me a lot of this famous country singer from Texas I'm crazy about; a fellow calls himself Kinky Friedman, the Original Texas Jewboy. Kinky's smarter, but I like you more." The governor also favorably compared Kinky to Henry Kissinger, claiming that the latter "Had hair like Kinky, but Kinky is smarter."

The Kinkster is part of the curriculum of an intensive New Testament Greek graduate course at Yale Divinity School in New Haven, Connecticut. Students studying for the ministry are required to read a chapter in *The Misunderstood Jew: The Church and the Scandal of the Jewish Jesus* that references the Kinkster and validates his most well-known song.

"Kinky Friedman—author, Texas politician, provocateur (a tautology with 'Texas politician') and leader of the band 'Kinky Friedman and the Texas Jewboys'—is well known, at least in certain circles, for recording 'They Ain't Making Jews like Jesus Anymore,' wrote Amy-Jill Levine. "The title could serve as an anthem for the Jesus introduced in certain liberal Christian settings. Friedman is correct . . . in that New Testament scholarship is increasingly removing Jesus from Judaism. . . ."

The perennial bachelor can be found in contemporary romance novels. In *Blue-Eyed Devil*, a 2008 novel set in Houston among wealthy River Oaks sophisticates, Lisa Kleypas writes, "When my mother Ava was still alive, she was an annual cochair of the Texas Book Festival and went for smoke breaks with Kinky Friedman."

In *When in Doubt, Add Butter* (2012), by Beth Harbison, the private chef narrator describes the library of a client, who is an attorney. "There were two large dark wooden bookcases full of books. Hemingway, Joseph Conrad, a few Kinky Friedman mystery novels, and a bunch of tomes on economics and investments."

German readers discover Kinky in *The Crazy Never Die: Amerikanische Rebellen in der populären Kultur,* a German-language book of biographical essays on "social outsiders that had a big impact upon the development of popular culture." The Kinkster's fellow rebels include Robert Mitchum, Lenny Bruce, Abbie Hoffman, Hunter S. Thompson, and Lester Bangs.

"They embodied the spirit of resistance, provocation, and dissent, and all on extremely high drug levels," reads the book's description. "Hazardous individuals . . . like Robert Mitchum; eccentrics like Lenny Bruce, who enjoyed going against the rules; enemies of society as Abbie Hoffman, crazy people, who loved to sexual excess and celebrated them; unpatriotics without family; weapons fools like Hunter S. Thompson; deserters from all duties; bohemians, oddballs, and maniacs as Lester Bangs; drug freaks; agitators; cowboys like Kinky Friedman."

When the media wants to make sense of headlines, it often turns to Kinky for his views. His run for governor launched a side career as a political pundit; he appeared regularly on *The O'Reilly Factor* on Fox News for six years. In 2012, Channel News Asia, the Singapore-based English-language TV news channel, sent its U.S. bureau chief to Kinky's ranch in Texas Hill Country to get his take on U.S. politics.

ESPN contacted Kinky when New Jersey governor Chris Christie started a firestorm on Twitter by "hugging, bouncing, and groping" with Dallas Cowboys owner Jerry Jones in his box after the Cowboys defeated the Detroit Lions. When Bob Ley, the host of *Outside the Lines,* asked Kinky what he thought, he didn't mince words. "It's the most important latent homosexual relationship since Sherlock Holmes and Dr. Watson." Ley tried to interrupt with "You don't really mean that," but Kinky was on a roll. "They both desperately want be loved, and I agree that being in the owner's box is not the way," he said. A flustered Ley cut the interview short and ESPN immediately apologized for his comments.

In an even stranger TV appearance, Kinky performed on a "L'Chaim to Life" telethon for Chabad, with an out-of-tune Bob Dylan strumming along like a sideman.

"You'd think you were on acid watching it," says Sloman, who hung out with Kinky that night. "There was Rabbi Cunin, a bear of a guy with a big beard. Jan Murray, the ancient Jewish comedian, was a host; the other host was Angelina Jolie's father, Jon Voight. It was surreal.

"The rabbi would go to the tote board, ask, 'What's the take?' and announce dramatically, 'Now we've raised $1,275,000.82.' Then he would get everybody up and they'd all start dancing around. It was the craziest thing you've ever seen in your life," he adds with a laugh.

"Bob had a yarmulke under his cowboy hat," remembers Kinky with a smile. "Bob wanted to do 'Proud to Be an Asshole from El Paso,' but we did 'Sold American.' We couldn't do 'Ride 'Em Jewboy'—they were religious Orthodox Jews and probably wouldn't have understood it."

Kinky is Everywhere in documentaries about Texas culture, music, politics, animal rescue, and even the Jewish experience in the American South. When the BBC filmed a three-part documentary to showcase the music and history of the Lone Star State, they chose Kinky as the narrator/host. *Texas Saturday Night* covers all styles of music, from country and western to conjunto to blues to western swing, and artists from Willie Nelson, the Texas Tornados, T-Bone Walker, Bob Wills and the Texas Playboys, and Jimmie Rodgers to Buddy Holly. He interviews an array of Texas musicians, as well as Larry Mahan, six-time winner of the World All-Around Rodeo Champion title.

Kinky also took British TV viewers on a narrated tour of Dealey Plaza in Dallas, where JFK was assassinated; the University of Texas tower, where he demonstrated how Whitman took cover behind the ledge and used the carved openings for his rifle; the Alamo in San Antonio; and the Buddy Holly statue in Lubbock.

Kinky shares his love of the Lone Star State in *Too High, Too Wide and Too Long: A Texas-Style Road Trip*, a 1999 documentary; *Barbecue: A Texas Love Story*, a 2004 documentary with Dan Rather and Ann Richards; and *Flight of the Conchords: A Texan Odyssey*, a 2006 New Zealand documentary. Then there's *Rich Hall's You Can Go to Hell, I'm Going to Texas*, a 2013 BBC documentary. He also appears in *Spamarama: The Movie*, a film that parodied the now defunct spoof festival Spamarama, held annually in Austin from 1976 until 2007.

You can't make a film about the Jewish experience in the American South without the Kinkster, who appears in *Shalom Y'all*, a critically acclaimed 2003 documentary airing on *PBS* and the *Sundance Channel*. "A New York Jew does not believe there can be Jews in Texas," he explains, driving his pickup through Medina. "They think Jews in Texas are like leprechauns."

Kinky tells a heartbreaking tale about animal rescue in *Rescue Me*, a 2005 documentary about pet overpopulation. And shares his thoughts about Texas music and musicians in *Townes Van Zandt: Be Here to Love Me*, a 2004 documentary; *You're Gonna Miss Me*, a 2005 documentary about musician Roky Erickson; and *Rocking the Boat: A Musical Conversation and Journey*, a 2008 documentary about Delbert McClinton's musical cruises.

Then there are a number of documentaries focusing on the Kinkster: *Kinky Friedman—Proud to Be an A**Hole from El Paso*, a Dutch documentary with Willie Nelson, Lyle Lovett, Bill Clinton, and others; *Live from Austin, TX*, footage from his banned 1975 Austin City Limits performance; *Profiles Featuring Kinky Friedman*, a thirty-minute celebrity interview show, and *Along Came Kinky: Texas Jewboy for Governor*, a documentary of his 2006 campaign.

The video with Don Imus, Willie Nelson, and Dwight Yoakam that started as an infomercial for *Pearls in the Snow* is a rare find. The roughly edited footage became *How to Lose Friends and Irritate People*, a forty-five-minute video with a number of high points. They include three acoustic duets between Kinky and Willie on an enclosed porch, with Kinky rolling his eyes at Willie as he whistles in "Asshole from El Paso"; Kinky stepping into his fuzzy blue guitar strap in a clever "Biscuits and Buns" music video with Buzzi (as her *Laugh-In* character Gladys Ormsby) and Richard Moll (Bull from *Night Court*); and Kinky getting distracted by a three-year-old wandering around the stage with her violin at a benefit at La Zona Rosa.

There's Imus joining Kinky for the chorus of "Ain't Makin' Jews like Jesus Anymore" live in his TV studio, and Yoakam sighing with his head in his hands, "Yeah, that's the way to end a career—out here hawking Kinky's CD on television." When Nelson is asked why Kinky's songs have remained popular for so long, he attributes their endurance to "torture."

"He keeps torturing material over the years," Nelson explains. "If you put a chicken heart in an agitator, such as a washing machine, it will live for fourteen years . . . if you keep beating it. It's the same thing."

He pauses and then adds with a Zen-like smile, "I believe this is his philosophy."

Nelson shared his own philosophy with Kinky when they began writing *Roll Me Up and Smoke Me When I Die—Musings from the Road,* a 2012 release that was one of several coauthored autobiographical books. The initial deal called for Nelson and Kinky to write every other chapter. Willie wrote "voluminously" and competed with Kinky on word count. If Kinky wrote 20,000 words, Willie wrote 27,000 and asked why Kinky was being so slow. When they submitted their manuscripts to William Morrow, the editor realized two writers translated into two different voices and a confusing book. They kept Willie's manuscript, edited Kinky's 20,000 words down to seven typewritten pages, and used it as the foreword. Kinky didn't mind. His friend still shared royalties on a memoir that reached and lingered on the *New York Times* bestseller list.

He also helped his buddy Billy Bob Thornton on his memoirs. Thornton didn't want a "cheap Hollywood biography where I talk about fighting with an actor on the set, or who had sex with who," so he asked Kinky to work on it with him. Eager to tell his life's story and to share his views on why he believes our culture is crumbling, Thornton signed with Kinky's agent, David Vigliano, who brokered a deal for *The Billy Bob Tapes: A Cave Full of Ghosts.* The Arkansas native wanted to use the Southern tradition of oral storytelling, which includes smaller stories within the main narrative, to tell his tale. J. D. Andrew, cofounder of Thornton's band the Boxmasters, recorded the sessions in the home studio of Billy Bob's Beverly Hills house.

To create a storytelling atmosphere, Kinky invited his friends to be the audience at the sessions in the 11,000-square-foot home. Thornton purchased the sprawling property from Guns N' Roses guitarist Slash, so it was already equipped with a home studio.

Although Kinky told his friends they were all "just furniture," like most celebrities, they had egos too big to keep quiet. Danny Hutton from Three Dog Night talked as much as Thornton; Ted Mann, who wrote for the TV shows *NYPD Blue, Deadwood,* and *Hatfields & McCoys,* aggravated the Kinkster until he told him to "Shut the fuck up." ZZ Top guitarist Billy Gibbons stopped by, as did Louie Kemp, Bob Dylan's childhood friend and the Rolling Thunder Revue tour manager. Kinky also invited Daniel Taub, editor at *Bloomberg News;* John Mankiewicz, TV writer and producer of *House, The Mentalist,* and *House of Cards,* among others; Twink Caplan; Sloman; and Michael Simmons.

Advance publicity for the memoir promised "colorful tales of his modest Southern upbringing, his bizarre phobias, his life, his loves (including his heartbreakingly brief marriage to fellow Oscar winner Angelina Jolie), and his movie career." But Thornton refused to kiss and tell. Jolie wrote an honest and heartfelt foreword, but he never said a word about her, his other five wives, or the two well-known actresses—Téa Leoni and Laura Dern—he had been linked to romantically. Kinky wasn't thrilled about his friend's decision not to talk about his love life or to promote the book, but it didn't affect their friendship.

His latest collaboration is a book with Louie Kemp. Tentatively titled *The Adventures of Bobby and Louie*, the book will be released by Random House in 2018 and filled with anecdotal tales and photos from Kemp's personal collection.

Kinky's own music, writings, and life were immortalized in the musical *Becoming Kinky: The World According to Kinky Friedman*, a stage production written and directed by Ted Swindley, who wrote the musical *Always . . . Patsy Cline*. The seeds for *Becoming Kinky* were planted at a 2009 benefit performance of the Patsy Cline musical at Houston's Stages Repertory Theater.

Carolyn Farb, who had hosted fundraisers for Kinky's gubernatorial campaign, chaired the benefit and seated Kinky and Jewford at her table with Swindley, who founded the theater. Kinky and Swindley hit it off, so when she met the playwright for breakfast the next day, she suggested he write a musical play about Kinky.

The production began with three nights of readings in Nashville in January 2010 and two readings in New York as part of the Midtown International Theatre Festival in June. Famed New York gossip columnist Liz Smith wrote, "One of my favorite people is Kinky Friedman. This Texas phenomenon, who ran for governor and should have been elected if the Lone Star State voters had any sense, has his work back on the boards. I bet this collection of Kinky-isms hasn't seen its last performance. Like the man himself, this show will return."

In August 2010, more than 100 invited guests attended a staged reading at Stages Repertory Theatre. Two months later, Farb also hosted a brunch and reading at Rosewood Mansion in Dallas.

Debuting at McGonigel's Mucky Duck in Houston in March 2011, the *Becoming Kinky* cast included three actors playing Kinky at different stages of his life: Ross Bautsch as Young Peace Corps Kinky; country artist Jesse Dayton as Musician Kinky; and Alan Lee as Politician/Mystery Writer Kinky. The finale featured all four singing "Proud to Be an Asshole from El Paso."

The role of Little Jewford was the last one to be cast. "Kinky called me and said, 'I can't find anyone to play little Jewford—would you take the role?'" says Jewford. "After I agreed to do it, I said, 'There's only one drawback. What if I get a review with a headline "Little Jewford not believable as Little Jewford"?'"

Jewford like the concept and worked with Swindley to change lines that didn't ring true. "Ted took a lot of things, if not everything, from Kinky's books, and it was pretty well written," he says. "My role was a keyboard player, and the pivot person who played off of three different Kinkys. I also played Willie Nelson, Kinky's stepmom Aunt Edith, and Don Imus in little vignettes. For Don, I put on a cowboy hat and 'I talked like this, Kinky,'" he says in a spot-on imitation of the I-Man. "For Edith, I put on a feminine voice. For Willie, I did a little singing behind the piano and had an interchange with the older Kinky. Alan had a number of bits of dialogue, where I'd come out center stage and we'd talk."

In a review of a sold-out performance in Marfa, Texas, *West Texas Weekly* called it a "fast-quipped compendium that covered Friedman's weltanschauung [world view], a fireside flow that sometimes came off like a David Byrne moment, but more like a cutting Lenny Bruce night at the Apollo . . . had the air of America's troubadour age when folksters like Mark Twain and Will Rogers took the stage doing much the same—handing out bits of wisdom and social criticism with astute and compact ploy."

When the Kinkster watched the portrayals of the three Kinkys at the rehearsals in Houston, he found it a bit disconcerting. "It was weird watching it, beyond surreal," he says. But he took an instant liking to Dayton, who had spent days at the ranch studying the man he was about to portray. "To paraphrase Oscar Wilde, I'm glad he's the man I've chosen to mispresent me," Kinky said. "It's gonna kill when it gets to New York and London."

But, as with many projects that never get off the ground, the financial aspects were the issue.

"We were talking about it [going on], but when you get to the next level, everybody wants their points," says Jewford. "Ted was seeing all his points [percentage of the profits] basically being eaten up. He said, 'If you take this to Broadway or even off-Broadway, you're hearing figures like $800,000 and $1 million to get the production going."

Although the production never went further than Texas, Kinky took it philosophically. "Some of these things happen, some of them don't," he says. "They have to happen at the right time." Yet the project had two positive outcomes. It led to Dayton recording *Jesse Sings Kinky*, a ten-song tribute to Kinky's serious and lesser-known songs. With Farb as executive producer, the CD was recorded in ten days and received airplay on XM Satellite Radio with heavy airplay for "Rapid City, South Dakota," and "Lady Yesterday." According to Dayton's website, *Jesse Sings Kinky* opened up a "whole new chapter for him with more radio airplay than ever in his career."

And it led to the discovery of the Kinky connection to Secret Agent 007.

"My friend Carolyn Farb was calling her friend Kristina Tholstup in England," says Kinky. "She's the wife of Sir Roger Moore, who of course played James Bond. Carolyn was telling his wife she was having a party for Kinky Friedman and asked, 'Does Sir Roger know who Kinky is?' And Sir Roger got on the phone and said, 'They ain't making Jews like Jesus anymore.' That was the first time I realize this guy is a cool guy, he's really had his hip card punched. For him to know that is pretty cool . . . And it's not that people who are ignorant of my talents are not cool," he quickly adds.

Nearly sixty years after his first visit to the museum that inspired his love of cowboys and Texas history, Kinky was inducted in the Frontier Times Museum's Texas Heroes Hall of Honor. Although that award "to recognize the contributions of remarkable individuals . . . that keep the pioneer spirit alive and help keep Texas, Texan" proved that little Jewish boy had created the life he had imagined, it didn't mean much to the adult Kinkster.

"I'm like Waylon Jennings in that I think awards are mostly bullshit," he says. "I don't think they mean much. I just have two awards that I remember. One is the Male Chauvinist Pig of the Year award in 1973 from the National Organization of Women. That was an actual plaque I still have—it was for 'Get Your Biscuits in the Oven and Your Buns in the Bed.'

"The other award is not a tangible one; it's the certain knowledge Nelson Mandela played a song off a tape cassette of my first record—

Sold American. Although it sounds like something from a Kurt Vonnegut novel, we have now verified it. He played 'Ride 'Em Jewboy' as a sign-off song the last three years—virtually every night—he was in Robben Island. The knowledge Nelson Mandela was listening to 'Ride 'Em Jewboy' in his prison cell is something you can't put on a mantel but you can certainly keep in your heart. That's the only award I need; it's better than a Grammy and much more significant."

When the odds of that song getting smuggled into Mandela's prison cell in South Africa led to questions about his belief in God and in fate, Kinky did what he always does when he doesn't want to answer a question: he responds with a one-liner or quotes one of his friends. Asked if he believes in fate, Kinky says, "Sure I do, why the hell not?" When asked if he believes in God, he initially hesitates: "Let me think about this, not to be too flip about it." But an honest answer might be too revealing, so he flips back into his default mode.

"As far as God is concerned I would follow one of my inspirations, Joseph Heller," he says. "He told me he had a covenant with God—he leaves God alone and God leaves him alone. I think that would be advisable."

Yet the question keeps haunting him and he eventually answers from the heart.

"After the Mandela situation, it's almost making an evangelical out of me," he says. "Believing in fate, believing that God wanted me to record that song so Mandela would someday get it—at the right time and the right place. Maybe he needed that. I've thought about that a lot. If one song from that record had been about Africa, I could see Mandela playing it repeatedly. But this song is about the Holocaust. It's the mark of the measure of the man that this is the one he related to."

"He belonged to that little fraternity of men—Martin Luther King, Gandhi, Jesus, and Mandela—that had the great ability to inspire long after death, certainly in life, but later, too. He had the kind of inspiration John F. Kennedy had. Bill Clinton would never have been president if he hadn't met JFK and shaken hands with him as a Boy Scout in Washington. There are all kinds of politicians—most of them are dead now—that had that ability to inspire. Churchill is a great example.

"The fat drunk aristocrat somehow wove a bond to the common man and saved the free world. How did he do it? I would argue inspiration. He would say fate is so twisting and fickle that he lost every battle for a year or two in World War II until El Alamein. After that, the Brits never lost again; that was the hinge of fate that turned the war. If Churchill had been voted out before El Alamein—the next guy, whoever he was, would have been regarded as a genius. And Churchill would have been regarded as the loser of everything, even though it was his war."

Kinky is well aware of how fickle fate can be and how quickly it can destroy a reputation or legacy that's been built up over a lifetime.

"I don't remotely care about my legacy. That could be like Mama Cass choking on a ham sandwich, or I might get blown up in Europe in a terrorist attack," he said before departing on a 2016 European tour only weeks after thirty people were killed and more than 200 wounded during terrorist attacks in Brussels. "There are lots of possibilities that would falsely increase or diminish my legacy," he says and cites the fate of the founding father of the Lone Star State.

"Sam Houston was the first president of the Republic of Texas and later elected governor of Texas," he says. "Sam led the troops that defeated Santa Anna's soldiers at the Battle of San Jacinto, and won Texas's independence from Mexico. He was a man who invented Texas, virtually, and years later people are throwing rocks and tomatoes at him because he wanted Texas to stay out of the Civil War," he sighs. "The Texas legislature muscled him out of the way, and there were only twelve people at his funeral.

"Knowing this, all we can do is to do our best. That's all you can do. Never worry about a legacy or what somebody's going to think. Or how much money you have or hammered steel you leave in monuments when you die. None of that's important. Still being able to travel around to bookstores or to music venues—after forty years—without ever having a hit—is a real privilege."

Kinky's legacy is the ability to inspire, to make people laugh, to make them think, to skewer sacred cows and hypocrisy, to continue to move forward, and to be his own man. He inspired 600,000 Texans, including first-time voters, to believe in honesty and integrity, and stuck to his principles and beliefs when a lie and taking campaign donations from lobbyists would have helped him politically.

When he kicked his cocaine addiction cold turkey and never looked back, he proved it could be done. When he reinvented himself as an author after his musical career hit the skids, he proved there is a second act. When he ran for governor of Texas, he made it a three-act play.

He's never let age define him. At seventy, he released his first studio album in thirty-nine years and toured the country in a van with two musicians half his age to promote it. He returned to songwriting the following year after a thirty-three-year hiatus. At seventy-two, he thought nothing of embarking on a thirty-day solo tour in Australia, a country more than 8,500 miles from his Texas ranch. He enjoys performing and meeting people, and having the opportunity to inspire a future generation.

"There are an amazing number of people who would have liked to have my life, and tell me that," he says, somewhat in awe of the fact. "I don't want to sound like an old guy, but when a guy in his twenties comes up and says, 'I like the way you've lived your life'—that's pretty nice. Another guy said, 'It's really nice to see somebody that's enjoying his life.' I see a lot of people out there who certainly don't have the freedom I do. I may be the only free man on this train.

"The best thing when you do live performances, when you write books, and when you make records, is you never know who's going to be listening, whose hands they might fall into," he adds. "Actually seeing an artist perform sometimes makes it happen. There's an old song by Tom T. Hall called 'The Year That Clayton Delaney Died,' about a kid who worships this country singer who has a five-piece band and plays all over the place. He's a big drinker and the kid doesn't know that. As time went by, the kid started singing and playing himself, went to Nashville, and became a big star, quite a bit bigger than Clayton Delaney.

"As a child he idolized Clayton Delaney, and as an adult he understood him. He loved Clayton Delaney, and when he died, the kid went out in the woods and cried. He never realized Clayton Delaney's career was very small-time and was hampered by being a drunk. A child can overlook these things, and that's part of the beauty of childhood. When you grow up, you realize this guy was an over-the-hill, small-time country singer who at least had the distinction of touching this kid who would have never been a star without Clayton Delaney inspiring him."

Although he sometimes toys with the idea of running for office again, writing songs and performing is still his first love.

"As long as Willie keeps playing, I'll keep running, I suppose," he says. "But politics is not as important. Thomas Paine, who wrote *Common Sense*, said it's more important to be able to write a country's songs than it is to make her laws. Politics takes your energy. You meet these people and you say how are you, how's it going etc., etc. Whereas, when you're doing a show, you're expending energy but it's real. And the energy you get back from the audience is a tonic."

With all its twists and turns, his life has finally come full circle.

"Getting up at this age and doing this—in a way it's very comforting; it's very satisfying," he says. "It's not building for anything. When people say, 'You'll get great exposure for doing this radio show, you're really developing an audience you didn't have,' I don't need to do that anymore because I could drop dead at any fucking moment. Most of the people I've loved were bugled to Jesus at much younger ages. They're all gone. So you keep rolling and you hang out with a younger and younger crowd. Even though they're not very inspirational, their hearts are in the right places.

"I have finally come to realize we ride the same horse our whole life—people don't really change. Maybe there's an evil wolf and a good wolf inside you and the one you feed will develop, like the Indians believe—I hope that's true. Some people may develop wisdom in time. If you're the kind of person who is blaming people, blaming your record company, blaming your producer, blaming your parents, blaming the times you lived in, that's what you'll keep doing. If you're the kind of person that believes, 'Give it all you've got, every night till you die,' you can do it. I take great spiritual encouragement from Willie and from Bob that they're able to stay out on the road like they are," he adds. "Willie at eighty-three, Dylan at seventy-five—it's remarkable. Why stop now, for God's sake—what's the point of it?"

Discography

ALBUMS

Sold American, Vanguard Records, 1973

Kinky Friedman, ABC Records, 1974

Lasso from El Paso, Epic Records, 1976

Live from the Lone Star Café, Bruno-Dean, 1982

Under the Double Ego, Sunrise, 1983

Old Testaments & New Revelations, Fruit of the Tune, 1992

From One Good American to Another, Fruit of the Tune, 1995

Live from Down Under (Kinky Friedman and Billy Joe Shaver), Sphincter Records, 2002

Classic Snatches from Europe, Sphincter Records, 2003

Mayhem Aforethought, Sphincter Records, 2005

They Ain't Makin' Jews like Jesus Anymore, Bear Family, 2005

The Last of the Jewish Cowboys: The Best of Kinky Friedman, Shout Factory, 2006

Bipolar Tour: Live from Woodstock, Avenue A Records, 2012

Lost and Found: The Famous Living Room Tape, Avenue A Records, 2013

They Ain't Makin' Jews like Jesus Anymore and Other Humorous Songs, Avenue A Records, 2013

The Loneliest Man I Ever Met, Avenue A Records, 2015

SINGLES

"Sold American" / "Western Union Wire," Vanguard Records, 1973

"Lover Please" / "Autograph," ABC Records, 1974

"Dear Abbie" / "Catfish," Epic, 1976

"Popeye the Sailor Man" / "Popeye the Sailor Man," Epic, 1976

"Boogie Man" / "People who Read *People* Magazine," Sunrise Records, 1983

TRIBUTE CDS BY OTHER ARTISTS

Willie Nelson, Tom Waits, Dwight Yoakam, Lyle Lovett, Delbert McClinton, Marty Stuart, Lee Roy Parnell, Guy Clark, Asleep at the Wheel, Tompall Glaser, Chuck E. Weiss, et al. *Pearls in the Snow: The Songs of Kinky Friedman,* Kinkajou Records, 1998

Kevin Fowler, Bruce Robison and Kelly Willis, Lyle Lovett, Charlie Robison, Dwight Yoakam, Jason Boland and The Stragglers, Todd Snider, Asleep at the Wheel and Reckless Kelly, et.al. *Why the Hell Not? The Songs of Kinky Friedman,* Sustain Records, 2006

Jesse Dayton. *Jesse Sings Kinky,* Stagg Records, 2012

Books

Greenwich Killing Time. New York: Beech Tree Books/William Morrow, 1986.

A Case of Lone Star. New York: Beech Tree Books/William Morrow, 1987.

When the Cat's Away. New York: Beech Tree Books/William Morrow, 1988.

Frequent Flyer. New York: William Morrow, 1989.

Musical Chairs. New York: William Morrow, 1991.

Elvis, Jesus & Coca-Cola. New York: Simon & Schuster, 1993.

Armadillos and Old Lace. New York: Simon & Schuster, 1994.

God Bless John Wayne. New York: Simon & Schuster, 1995.

The Love Song of J. Edgar Hoover. New York: Simon & Schuster, 1996.

Roadkill. New York: Simon & Schuster, 1997.

Blast from the Past. New York: Simon & Schuster, 1998.

Spanking Watson. New York: Simon & Schuster, 1999.

The Mile High Club. New York: Simon & Schuster, 2000.

Steppin' on a Rainbow. New York: Simon & Schuster, 2001.

Meanwhile, Back at the Ranch. New York: Simon & Schuster, 2002.

Kinky Friedman's Guide to Texas Etiquette: Or How to Get to Heaven or Hell Without Going through Dallas-Fort Worth. New York: William Morrow, 2002.

Kill Two Birds and Get Stoned. New York: William Morrow, 2003.

Curse of the Missing Puppet Head. Brooklyn, NY: Vandam Press, 2003.

The Prisoner of Vandam Street. New York: Simon & Schuster, 2004.

'Scuse Me While I Whip This Out: Reflections on Country Singers, Presidents, and Other Troublemakers. New York: William Morrow, 2004.

The Great Psychedelic Armadillo Picnic: A "Walk" in Austin. New York: Crown, 2004.

Ten Little New Yorkers. New York: Simon & Schuster, 2005.

Texas Hold 'Em: How I Was Born in a Manger, Died in the Saddle, and Came Back as a Horny Toad. New York: St. Martin's Press, 2005

The Christmas Pig: A Fable. New York: Simon & Schuster, 2006.

Cowboy Logic: The Wit and Wisdom of Kinky Friedman (And Some of His Friends). New York: St. Martin's Press, 2006.

You Can Lead a Politician to Water, but You Can't Make Him Think: Ten Commandments for Texas Politics. New York: Simon & Schuster, 2007.

What Would Kinky Do? How to Unscrew a Screwed-Up World. New York: St. Martin's Press, 2008.

Kinky's Celebrity Pet Files. New York: Simon & Schuster, 2009.

Heroes of a Texas Childhood. Kerrville, TX: Kismet Press, 2009.

Drinker with a Writing Problem. Brooklyn, NY: Vandam Press, 2011.

With Billy Bob Thornton. *The Billy Bob Tapes: A Cave Full of Ghosts.* New York: William Morrow, 2012.

With Willie Nelson. *Roll Me Up and Smoke Me When I Die: Musings from the Road.* New York: William Morrow, 2012.

Documentaries and Movies

Record City, 1977

Prime Time (American Raspberries), 1977

Loose Shoes, 1980

The Being, 1983

Skating on Thin Ice, Canadian HBO documentary, 1984

Texas Chainsaw Massacre II, 1986

Texas Saturday Night, three-part documentary by Arena, the BBC's multi-award-winning arts strand, 1991

Spamarama: The Movie, 1996

Too High, Too Wide and Too Long: A Texas-Style Road Trip, documentary, 1999

Kinky Friedman—Proud to Be an A**Hole from El Paso, Dutch documentary with Willie Nelson, Lyle Lovett, Bill Clinton, and others, 2003

Shalom Y'all, 2003

Barbecue: A Texas Love Story, documentary with Dan Rather and Ann Richards, 2004

Townes Van Zandt: Be Here to Love Me, documentary, 2004

You're Gonna Miss Me, Roky Erickson documentary, 2005

Rescue Me, documentary on pet overpopulation, 2005

Flight of the Conchords: A Texan Odyssey, New Zealand TV movie, 2006

Live from Austin, TX, 1975 Austin City Limits Performance, New West, 2007

Profiles Featuring Kinky Friedman, Quest Media Entertainment, 2008

Rocking the Boat: A Musical Conversation and Journey, 2008

Along Came Kinky: Texas Jewboy for Governor, 2006 campaign documentary, 2009

Rich Hall's You Can Go to Hell, I'm Going to Texas, BBC documentary, June 2013

Bibliography

Along Came Kinky: Texas Jewboy for Governor. DVD. Directed and produced by David Hartstein. Austin, TX: Blue Suitcase Productions, 2009.

Arrillaga, Pauline. "Kinky Friedman a 'Lone Ranger' on Trail." *The Washington Post*, October 21, 2006.

Bane, Michael. *The Outlaws: Revolution in Country Music.* Nashville: Country Music Magazine Press, 1978.

Balke, Jeff. "Texas Number 14 on List of Most Christian States, Houston Ninth Most Religious Among Cities." *Houston Press*, May 29, 2012.

Batt, Tony. "Gambling, Politics Make Strange Bedfellows in Texas." http//www.gamblingcompliance.com, August 18, 2014.

Bernstein, Jonathan. "Kinky Friedman Talks Music, Texas and a Trump/Sanders Ticket." *Rolling Stone*, September 22, 2015.

Bittermann, Klaus. *The Crazy Never Die: Amerikanische Rebellen in der populären Kultur* (German Edition). Fuego, 2011.

Blumenthal, Ralph. "Guess Who Wants to Be Governor?" *The New York Times*, November 29, 2003.

Blumenthal, Ralph. "Following a Candidate Named Kinky." *The New York Times*, February 17, 2006.

Burrough, Brian. "The Miranda Obsession." *Vanity Fair*, December 1999.

"CMT Goes 'Kinky' with Episodes Chronicling Author's Run for Office." *Associated Press*, November 4, 2005.

Crampton, Liz. "Ag Commissioner Rolls Back Ban on Deep Fryers, Soda Machines." *The Texas Tribune*, June 18, 2015.

Dansby, Andrew. "Every Texan Is a Little Bit Kinky." *Houston Chronicle*, March 28, 2011.

Dougherty, Steve. "Kinky Friedman's Surprising New Album, 'The Loneliest Man I Ever Met.'" *The Wall Street Journal*, September 29, 2015.

Dove, Ian. "Friedman Brings Texans to Town." *New York Times*, May 1973.

Elliott, Jane. "Friedman Feels Sting of Political Attacks." *Houston Chronicle*, October 25, 2006.

Endres, Clifford. *Austin City Limits*. Austin, TX: University of Texas Press, 1987.

Fikac, Peggy. "Friedman Rips Brouhaha over Race-Tinged Remarks." *Houston Chronicle*, September 22, 2006.

Flippo, Chet. "Ride 'Em Jewboy: Kinky Friedman's First Two Premieres." *Rolling Stone*, May 10, 1973.

Flippo, Chet. "Band of Unknowns Fails to Emerge." *Rolling Stone*, December 9, 1971.

Flippo, Chet. "One Week in the Life of Kinky Friedman: Triumph at the Opry. Showdown in Big D." *Rolling Stone*, October 11, 1973.

Friedman, Kinky. "A Tribute to Me." *Texas Monthly*, February 1999.

Friedman, Kinky. "All Politics is Yokel." *Texas Monthly*, April 2001.

Friedman, Kinky. "The Navigator." *Texas Monthly*, June 2001.

Friedman, Kinky. "Hail to the Kinkster." *Texas Monthly*, November 2001.

Friedman, Kinky. "Unfair Game." *Texas Monthly*, March, 2002.

Friedman, Kinky. "Does Not Compute." *Texas Monthly*, April 2002.

Friedman, Kinky. "Psycho Paths." *Texas Monthly*, July 2002.

Friedman, Kinky. "Cliff Hanger." *Texas Monthly*, August 2002.

Friedman, Kinky. "Yesterday Street." *Texas Monthly*, September 2002.

Friedman, Kinky. "The Houseguest." *Texas Monthly*, October 2002.

Friedman, Kinky. "The Hummingbird Man." *Texas Monthly*, January 2003.

Friedman, Kinky. "My Shelf Life." *Texas Monthly*, June 2003.

Friedman, Kinky. "Whistlin' Dixie." *Texas Monthly*, July 2003.

Friedman, Kinky. "Jack Was an Ace." *Texas Monthly*, September 2003.

Friedman, Kinky. "Lottie's Love." *Texas Monthly*, October 2003.

Friedman, Kinky. "My Pet Project." *Texas Monthly*, February 2005.

Friedman, Kinky. "Smoke Gets in Your Eyes." *Texas Monthly*, March 2008.

Friedman, Kinky. "Rhinestone Cowboy." *Texas Monthly*, March 2009.

Friedman, Kinky. "Gov Hunt." *Texas Monthly*, August 2010.

Friedman, Kinky. "Buddy Holly's Texas." *Rolling Stone*, August 19, 1990.

Friedman, Kinky. *Musical Chairs*. New York: William Morrow, 1991.

Friedman, Kinky. *What Would Kinky Do? How to Unscrew a Screwed-Up World*. New York: St. Martin's Press, 2008.

Friedman, Kinky. *Kinky's Celebrity Pet Files*. New York: Simon & Schuster, 2009.

Friedman, Kinky. *Heroes of a Texas Childhood*. Kerrville, TX: Kismet Press, 2009.

Friedman, Kinky. *You Can Lead a Politician to Water, but You Can't Make Him Think: Ten Commandments for Texas Politics*. New York: Simon & Schuster, 2007.

Friedman, Kinky. *The Prisoner of Vandam Street*. New York: Simon & Schuster, 2004.

Friedman, Kinky. *The Mile High Club*. New York: Simon & Schuster, 2000.

Friedman, Kinky. *Elvis, Jesus & Coca-Cola*. New York: Simon & Schuster, 1993.

Friedman, Kinky. *The Love Song of J. Edgar Hoover*. New York: Simon & Schuster, 1996.

Friedman, Kinky. *Roadkill*. New York: Simon & Schuster, 1997.

"*Go Kinky* TV Reality Show Follows Texas Campaign." FoxNews.com, November 9, 2005.

Graczyk, Michael. "Kinky Friedman Falls Short in Texas Governor Bid." *Associated Press*, November 8, 2006.

Gumbel, Andrew. "The Lone Star: How Kinky Friedman Shook Up Texas." *Independent*, October 22, 2006.

Halpern, Dan. "Lone Star." *The New Yorker*, August 22, 2005.

Halpern, Dan. "The End of the Trail." *The New Yorker*, November, 20, 2006.

Hamill, Pete. *A Drinking Life.* New York: Back Bay Books, 1994.

Harbison, Beth. *When in Doubt, Add Butter.* New York: St. Martin's Press, 2011.

Hegarty, Antony. "Antony Hegarty Takeover: Buffy Sainte-Marie." http://www.dazeddigital.com/music/article/14123/1/antony-hegarty-takeover-buffy-sainte-marie, July 30, 2012.

Heller, Erica. *Yossarian Slept Here — When Joseph Heller Was Dad, the Apthorp Was Home, and Life Was a Catch-22.* New York: Simon & Schuster, 2011.

Heller, Joseph. *Good as Gold.* New York: Simon & Schuster, 1976.

Heylin, Clinton. *Bob Dylan: Behind the Scenes.* New York: Viking, 1991.

Holden, Stephen. "Kinky Friedman [album review]." *Rolling Stone*, May 8, 1985.

How to Lose Friends and Irritate People. VHS. Produced by Brent Carpenter and Kacey Jones. Nashville, TN: Kinkajou Records, 1999.

Imus, Don. *God's Other Son.* New York: Simon & Schuster, 1981.

Karp, John. *A Futile and Stupid Gesture: How Doug Kenney and National Lampoon Changed Comedy Forever.* Chicago: Chicago Review Press, 2006.

"Kinky Friedman." *Variety*, May 9, 1973.

Kinky Friedman — Proud to Be an A**Hole from El Paso. Documentary by Simone de Vries. Amsterdam, Netherlands: Lagestee Film BV, 2001.

Kleypas, Lisa. *Blue-Eyed Devil.* New York: St. Martin's Press, 2009.

Koppel, Nathan. "Texas Race Has Democratic Party Squirming." *The Wall Street Journal*, March 21, 2014.

Levine, Amy-Jill. *The Misunderstood Jew: The Church and the Scandal of the Jewish Jesus.* New York: Harper One, 2007.

Live from Austin, TX, Kinky Friedman Austin City Limits Performance. DVD. Los Angeles, CA: New West, 2007.

Maletsky, Kiernan. "Cross Canadian Ragweed, Drowning Pool and Kinky Friedman on Their Worst Gigs Ever." *Dallas Observer*, September 17, 2013.

Milstein, Maggie. "There's a New Kinky Friedman in Town." *Jewish Journal*, November 12, 2015.

Montoya, Melissa. "Friedman Touts No-Kill Animal Shelters, Legal Marijuana." *The Brownsville Herald*, February 24, 2014.

Moody, Sidney. "Citizen McCall." *Austin Chronicle*, November 2, 2001.

Moody, Sidney. "The Real Stephanie DuPont." *Austin Chronicle*, November 2, 2001.

Mulshine, Paul. "The Truth about Rubin 'Hurricane' Carter." *Newark Star-Ledger*, 2000, https://www.martinlutherking.org/hurricane1.html.

Nemy, Enid. "AT HOME WITH/Kinky Friedman: Married to the Wind." *The New York Times*, August 31, 1995.

Northcott, Kay. "Kinky Friedman's First Roundup." *Texas Monthly,* May 1973.

Orth, Maureen. "Star of Texas." *Newsweek,* February 26, 1973.

Patterson, Rob. "Kinky and Grandma Battle for Third." *Salon,* November 4, 2006.

Parton, Chris. "Hear Kinky Friedman and Willie Nelson's Stoned 'Bloody Mary Morning.'" *Rolling Stone,* August 14, 2015.

Patoski, Joe. "What a Disc!" *Texas Monthly,* October, 1992.

Ratcliffe, R. G. "Friedman Has Personal Insight into Drug Problems." *Houston Chronicle,* September 8, 2006.

Ratcliffe, R. G. "Friedman Plays 'Good Shepherd' in His First Ad. But the Fallout from Statements on Katrina Evacuees Hasn't Gone Away." *Houston Chronicle,* September 13, 2006.

Ratcliffe, R. G. "Friedman Says Use of Slur Was Joke." *Houston Chronicle,* September 22, 2006.

Reischel, Diane. "Reinventing Kinky." *Dallas Morning News,* October 1, 1989.

Religious Affiliation in Texas (2010). *Texas Almanac,* http://texasalmanac.com/topics/religion/religious-affiliation-texas, 2010.

Rogovoy, Seth. "A Second Act for Kinky Friedman." *Berkshire Eagle,* April 10, 1997.

Rogovoy, Seth. "Bob Dylan's Bestie to Write Memoir of Their Life and Friendship." http://rogovoyreport.com/2016/04/13/louie-kemp-dylan-memoir/, April 13, 2016.

Rudis, Al. "Look Out, Here Comes Kinky Friedman!" *Chicago Sun-Times,* May 6, 1973.

Shannon, Kelley. "Debate's 'Game Showish' Format Makes for Uninformative, Non-Event." http: lubbockonline.com/stories, October 8, 2006.

Simmons, Michael. "I Was a Texas Jewboy!" *LA Weekly,* July 29, 2010.

Slater, Wayne. "Kinky Friedman Says He May Run for Governor Again." *dallasnews.com,* August 7, 2012.

Sloman, Larry "Ratso." *On the Road with Bob Dylan.* New York: Bantam, 1978.

Sloman, Larry "Ratso." *Thin Ice: A Season in Hell with the New York Rangers.* New York: William Morrow, 1982.

Smith, William Michael. "Q & A Kinky Friedman." *Texas Music,* November 2013.

Smith, William Michael. "Even Though He Doesn't Smoke It Anymore,

Marijuana Is at the Core of Kinky Friedman's Run for Public Office." *Houston Press,* November 20, 2013.

Spong, John. "Friedman's Just Another Word for Nothing Left to Lose." *Texas Monthly,* August 2005.

Swafford, M. Allen. *The Kinky File: Investigating the Mystery of Richard "Kinky" Friedman.* Brooklyn, NY: Vandam Press, 2003.

Swartz, Mimi. "The Year of Living Dangerously: Houston's Katrina Hangover." *Texas Monthly,* October 2006.

Texas Saturday Night. Three-DVD set. Directed by Anthony Wall. London: BBC Arena Presents, August 24, 1991.

Thornton, Billy Bob and Kinky Friedman. *The Billy Bob Tapes: A Cave Full of Ghosts.* New York: William Morrow, 2012.

"Three Tribes Contributed More than $1.4 Million to Politicians in Texas in an Attempt to Influence the Future of the Gaming Industry in the Lone Star State." http://www.indianz.com/, September 8, 2015.

"Vanguard in Country Buy." *Billboard Magazine*, October 14, 1972.

Wedge, Dave. "Return of the Jewboy: Kinky Friedman at 70." *Newsweek*, October 27, 2015.

Weinkrantz, Alan. "Why Kinky Friedman as Agriculture Commissioner Is Good for Texas and Israel." *The Times of Israel*, April 27, 2014.

"Willie Nelson Hosts Fund-Raiser for Texas Gubernatorial Candidate Kinky Friedman." *Associated Press*, October 31, 2005.

Index